ANCIENT ETHICS

To understand ethical theory we need to understand its origins, just as knowledge of ancient philosophy cannot be complete without an understanding of the ethical tradition which formed such a crucial part of it. *Ancient Ethics* is a clear and thorough introduction to the birth of ethics in ancient Greece and Rome for anyone starting out in ethics.

Here, Susan Sauvé Meyer details a history of ethical thought, from its beginnings in the writings of Plato and Aristotle through its development in the Hellenistic period by Epicureans and Stoics, with lucid and accessible explanations of their theories.

Throughout, she critically assesses the arguments on which their thoughts were based, incorporating the responses of their contemporary critics as well as modern-day assessments to show the reader how to think and critique philosophically.

This book will be ideal for anyone beginning an introductory course in ancient ethics or moral theory, anyone interested in learning more about the history of ethical philosophy, or simply those who wish to learn "how to live well".

Susan Suavé Meyer is Associate Professor of Philosophy at the University of Pennsylvania. She specialises in Ancient Greek and Roman philosophy, and has published widely on the natural and ethical philosophy of the period, including *Aristotle and Moral Responsibility* (1993).

ANCIENT ETHICS

A critical introduction

Susan Sauvé Meyer

Routledge
Taylor & Francis Group

LONDON AND NEW YORK

First published 2008
by Routledge
2 Park Square, Milton Park, Abingdon, Oxon, OX14 4RN

Simultaneously published in the USA and Canada
by Routledge
270 Madison Ave, New York NY 10016

*Routledge is an imprint of the Taylor & Francis Group, an
informa business*

Transferred to Digital Printing 2011

© 2008 Susan Sauvé Meyer

Typeset in 10/12pt Sabon by Graphicraft Limited, Hong Kong

British Library Cataloguing in Publication Data
A catalogue record for this book is available from the British
Library

Library of Congress Cataloging in Publication Data
Meyer, Susan Sauvé.
Ancient ethics : a critical introduction / Susan Sauve Meyer.
p. cm.
Includes bibliographical references and index.
1. Ethics, Ancient. I. Title.
BJ161.M49 2007
170.938—dc22
2007023583

ISBN10 0-415-94026-5 (hbk)
ISBN10 0-415-94027-3 (pbk)
ISBN10 0-203-64389-5 (ebk)

ISBN13 978-0-415-94026-9 (hbk)
ISBN13 978-0-415-94027-6 (pbk)
ISBN13 978-0-203-64389-1 (ebk)

CONTENTS

CONTENTS

PREFACE

I would like to thank the many people who have supported, assisted, and encouraged my work on this project. I have learned much about ethics, ancient and modern, from teachers, colleagues, and students, especially Terry Irwin, Gisela Striker, Charles Kahn, Paula Gottlieb, Rahul Kumar, Paul Guyer, Milton Wachsberg Meyer, David Caswell, Autumn Fiester, Doug Paletta, Jason Rheins, and Anna Cremaldi. I am grateful for helpful written comments on the manuscript from Charles Kahn and Jason Rheins and for stimulating discussion of parts of the work in progress at colloquia at the University of Toronto, the University of Pennsylvania, and the University of São Paolo. I remember especially helpful comments on these occasions from Ulrike Heuer and Gary Hatfield. Jason Rheins did yeoman's work on the bibliography, and both he and Anna Cremaldi were assiduous in checking the citations. Thanks to Matt Bateman, Marcy Latta, and Daniel Muñoz-Hutchinson for checking the proofs, to Elizabeth and Alice Vienneau for their work on the *index locorum*, and to Kate Mertes for the general index. Michael Weisberg shared generously of his time and technical expertise and Scott Weinstein has been unstinting in his support and encouragement. An early stage of my research was supported by a Fellowship for University Teachers from the National Endowment for the Humanities in 1995, and in its final stages a grant from the Philosophy Department at the University of Pennsylvania helped me bring the project to completion. My family has endured much over the course of my work on this project and I am grateful beyond what words can express for the support of my husband, Milton, partner and philosopher extraordinaire.

Philadelphia, Pennsylvania
April 2007

ACKNOWLEDGEMENTS

We are fortunate to have today a variety of excellent translations into English of most of the central texts in the Ancient philosophical tradition. When quoting the Ancient texts in this volume, my policy has been to quote from published translations that are easily available to the reader, with preference for translations that render whole works rather than short excerpts. I am grateful for permission to quote extensively from Raphael Woolf's translation of Cicero's *De Finibus* in Julia Annas (ed.) *Cicero: On Moral Ends* (copyright © Cambridge University Press, 2001; reprinted by permission of Cambridge University Press; all rights reserved) and from the translations in Brad Inwood and Lloyd Gerson, *Hellenistic Philosophy: Introductory Readings*, 2nd edition (Copyright © 1997 Brad Inwood and L. P. Gerson; reprinted by permission of Hackett Publishing Company, Inc.; all rights reserved).

To my mother
Lois Sauvé

And to the memory of my father
Robert Sauvé (1934–2005)

ABBREVIATIONS

Ac.	Cicero, *Academica* (ed. Plasberg 1922)
Aetius	Aetius, *Placita Philosophorum* ('Views of the Philosophers') reconstructed in Diels (ed.) 1879
Ap.	Plato, *Apology*
Att.	Cicero, *Letters to Atticus* (ed. Shackleton Bailey 1987)
Catg.	Aristotle, *Categories*
Charm.	Plato, *Charmides*
Comm. Not.	Plutarch, *De Communis notitiis contra Stoicos* ('On common conceptions against the Stoics') (ed. Cherniss 1976)
Cr.	Plato, *Crito*
DA	Aristotle, *De Anima* ('On the soul')
Deip.	Athenaeus, *Deipnosophistai* (Wise sayings for Dinner) (ed. Kaibel 1887)
Diss.	Epictetus, *Discourses* (ed. Schenkl 1916)
DL	Diogenes Laertius, *Lives of the Philosophers* (ed. H. S. Long 1964)
EE	Aristotle, *Eudemian Ethics* (ed. Walzer and Mingay 1991)
EN	Aristotle, *Nicomachean Ethics* (ed. Bywater 1894).
Ench.	Epictetus, *Encheiridion* (Handbook) (ed. Schenkl 1916)
Ep.	Seneca, *Epistulae morales* (Moral Letters) (ed. Reynolds 1965)
Eu.	Plato, *Euthyphro*
Euthd.	Plato, *Euthydemus*
Fin.	Cicero, *De Finibus Bonorum et Malorum* (On Moral Ends) (ed. Reynolds 1998)
Gellius	Aulus Gellius, *Noctes Atticae* (ed. Marshall 1968)
Gorg.	Plato, *Gorgias*
H. Maj.	Plato, *Greater Hippias*
IG	B. Inwood and L. Gerson (eds) (1997) *Hellenistic Philosophy: Introductory Readings*, Second edition. Indianapolis: Hackett
Ir.	Seneca, *De Ira* (On Anger) (Reynolds 1977)
KD	Epicurus, *Kuriai Doxai* (Principal Doctrines), DL 10.139–54

La.	Plato, *Laches*
LS	A. A. Long and D. N. Sedley, *The Hellenistic Philosophers*, 2 vols, Cambridge: Cambridge University Press, 1987
Lucr.	Lucretius, *De Rerum Natura* (On the nature of things) (ed. Bailey 1947)
Lys.	Plato, *Lysis*
M	Sextus Empiricus, *Adversus Mathematicos* (Against the Professors) (ed. Mutschmann 1912–54, Vols II, III)
Men.	Epicurus, *Letter to Menoeceus* (DL 10.121–35; Usener 1887)
ND	Cicero, *De Natura Deorum* (On the Nature of the Gods) (ed. Ax 1933)
Off.	Cicero, *De Officiis* (On Duties) (ed. Winterbottom 1994)
PH	Sextus Empiricus, *Pyrrhoneae Hypotyposes* (Outlines of Pyrrhonism) (ed. Mutschmann 1912–54, Vol. I)
Phd.	Plato, *Phaedo*
Phdr.	Plato, *Phaedrus*
Phlb.	Plato, *Philebus*
Phys.	Aristotle, *Physics*
Plac.	Galen, *De Placitis Hippocratis et Platonis* (On Hippocrates' and Plato's Doctrines) (ed. P. De Lacy, 1978–84)
Pol.	Aristotle, *Politics*
Pr.	Plato, *Protagoras*
PS	Cicero, *Paradoxa Stoicorum* (ed. Molager 1971)
Rep.	Plato, *Republic*
Soph.	Plato, *Sophist*
St. Rep.	Plutarch, *De Stoicorum Repugnatiis* (On Stoic self-refutations) (ed. Cherniss 1976)
Stob.	Stobaeus, *Eclogae* ('Selections') (Wachsmuth 1884)
Strom.	Clement of Alexandria, *Stromateis* ('Miscellany') (ed. Stählin 1960)
Stsm.	Plato, *Statesman*
SVF	J. Von Arnim, *Stoicorum Veterum Fragmenta* (Fragments of the Older Stoics) 4 Vols. (Leipzig: Teubner, 1923–38)
Symp.	Plato, *Symposium*
TD	Cicero, *Tusculanae disputationes* (Tusculan Disputations) (ed. Dougan and Henry, 1905–34)
Tht.	Plato, *Theaetetus*
Tim.	Plato, *Timaeus*
Vir. Mor.	Plutarch, *De Virtute Moral* (On Moral virtue) (ed. Patton *et al.* 1929)
VS	Epicurus, *Sententiae Vaticanae* (Vatican Sayings) (ed. Usener 1887)

1

WHAT IS ANCIENT ETHICS?

This study offers a critical introduction to the tradition of ethical thought first articulated in the writings of the Athenian philosopher Plato (c.430–347 BCE) and developed over the next several centuries by subsequent Greek philosophers – especially Aristotle (384–322), Epicurus (341–270), the Stoic philosophers Zeno (333–264) and Chrysippus (280–207) – and by their intellectual heirs in the Roman empire – most notably Seneca (4 BCE–65 CE) and Epictetus (50–130 CE).

'Ethics' in this context does not simply mean the particular codes of conduct or systems of values adhered to or espoused by Greeks and Romans.[1] Rather, it is a type of reflective and systematic *inquiry* into questions of conduct and value that Plato presents as a distinctively philosophical enterprise. Just what makes the inquiry philosophical will emerge over the succeeding chapters. What makes it ethical is its focus on the ultimate practical question, 'How should we live?', as well as on the closely related but no less practical question, 'How do we become good?'. At the hands of Plato and his intellectual successors, inquiry into these very practical questions requires, in addition, investigation of theoretical issues such as the nature of the good, the route to and limits of our knowledge of it, as well as the structure and nature of the human psyche.

Anyone who has struggled with the problem of how to live a good and worthwhile human life will be familiar with the concerns that motivate the ancient ethical tradition. The manner in which that tradition addresses these concerns, however, may be unfamiliar or off-putting to readers today. Even though philosophical ethics today has roots in the ancient world, it is also shaped by an additional two thousand years of religious, philosophical, and historical development. We think about ethical questions from a vantage point quite removed from that of the ancients. My goal in this study is to provide the reader with an understanding of the ancient ethical tradition in its own terms, and in consequence, an appreciation of the extent to which its projects and presuppositions overlap with or differ from those of present-day ethical thinking.

1

My intended audience is students and scholars of ethics or classical philosophy who seek an entry point into the field of ancient ethics, as well as the general reader who is not averse to sustained argumentation. The introduction I offer here is, like its subject matter, philosophical. My aim is not simply to describe the ethical philosophies of the ancient world, but to consider the arguments with which they were supported by their proponents as well as the criticisms that they encountered from their contemporaries. I consider also some questions and objections raised by later readers, including those of the present day; however, my focus is on the issues in the ancient debate. A proper understanding of the project of ethical inquiry as the ancients themselves conceived it should resolve at least some of the perplexity modern readers encounter when studying their texts. It may also show, at least in some cases, that the questions we bring to the ancient ethical texts are not ones we are likely to find answered there.

The ancient ethical tradition, we will see, is far from homogeneous and undergoes considerable development over many centuries. The present study therefore faces the challenge of providing sufficiently detailed coverage to meet its goals while still keeping to the moderate length that best serves the interests of its intended audience. Accordingly I have restricted my focus to the four major philosophies and schools that arose during the Classical and Hellenistic periods: those of Plato, Aristotle, Epicurus, and the Stoics. I omit the ethics of the Pyrrhonist school, whose main development (even if not its inspiration) is post-Hellenistic.[2] Within the targeted time period I also omit systematic treatment of some of the smaller schools – in particular, the Cynics and Cyrenaics – discussing these only in relation to the Stoics (heirs of Cynicism) and the Epicureans (rivals to the Cyrenaics). Nor do I discuss the Hellenistic development of Plato's and Aristotle's schools, except insofar as they engaged in disputes with their Epicurean and Stoic contemporaries.

Recent decades have seen a surge of scholarly interest in the ancient ethical tradition. A huge body of valuable scholarship in many languages has deepened and broadened our understanding of virtually every aspect of the ancient ethical tradition; yet, we still lack a comprehensive account of that tradition as a whole.[3] The present volume is a modest contribution towards filling that gap. Since there is still considerable disagreement among scholars about many important issues, this volume is not a textbook of received scholarly opinion, but a contribution to the ongoing interpretive project. In presenting a connected account of the development of ethical philosophy over the five centuries of this study, I have had to take a stand on many disputed issues, and have been led by my assessment of the 'lie of the land' to adopt unorthodox positions on others. In the interests of readers who are looking for an entry point into the vast literature on the subject, rather than a detailed foray into the complexities of the disputed terrain, I have not defended my individual interpretive decisions in detail against rival alternatives. Instead, my strategy has been to cite as fully as possible the primary ancient texts bearing on the question at issue, and to use the footnotes and bibliography to point the reader towards the range of scholarly opinion (with an emphasis on publications that are relatively recent and in English). I also hope that my various interpretive stands derive at least indirect support from the coherence and plausibility of the connected picture of the ancient ethical tradition to which they contribute.

An ethics of virtue?

The two central notions invoked in ancient ethical theory are those of *aretê* (excellence, or virtue) and *eudaimonia* (happiness, or the good life). It is common these days to refer to the ancient ethical tradition as an 'ethics of virtue'. The succeeding chapters, however, will reveal less homogeneity within the tradition than this categorization would seem to imply, and indeed a closer connection between the notions of *aretê* and *eudaimonia* than is usually recognized in contemporary philosophical scholarship.

We shall see that the 'virtue' pursued by the ambitious young Greeks portrayed in Plato's dialogues is not the excellent moral psychology (or state of character) that goes by that name in contemporary virtue ethics. It amounts, roughly, to success in life, where such success is measured largely if not entirely in external terms – in the extent to which one has acquired the typically recognized good things in life: wealth, power, friends and the like. On this pre-philosophical understanding of *aretê*, there is little difference between excellence (*aretê*) and happiness (*eudaimonia*). To quest for one is to quest for the other.

It is largely as a result of the philosophical theorizing of Plato and Aristotle that *aretê* is internalized and redefined as a state of character. This theoretical reorientation of the notion of *aretê* opens up conceptual space between 'virtue' (the goodness of a person) and the success in life that is captured by the label '*eudaimonia*' (happiness). However, I shall argue, this 'space' is not recognized or at any rate explored by either Plato or Aristotle. So great is the pull of the pre-philosophical considerations that identify the life of excellence with the happy life that it is not until the Hellenistic period that philosophers clearly formulate and debate the question of whether a person living a virtuous life might still fail to be happy.[4] Even then the affirmative answer is the minority opinion, held by Aristotle's Hellenistic successors. Both the Stoics and Epicureans conceive of the virtuous life as necessarily happy. If their reasons for doing so are unconvincing to modern readers this is at least partly due to the fact that we moderns lack access to the considerations that make such conclusions attractive.

While the internalized conception of virtue as a state of character is adopted by all the philosophers in our study, it is still misleading to

3

characterize their ethical philosophies generically as an 'ethics of virtue' – at least to the extent that this designation attributes a central explanatory role in their theories to the notion of a virtuous state of character. At best, this characterization is true of Plato and, to a certain extent, Aristotle. But even Aristotle subordinates the virtues of character to the virtues of intellect – hence his notorious claim that the best life is the life of reflection (*theoria*) disengaged from all practical concerns.

'Virtue ethics' is even less apt as a characterization of Epicurean ethical philosophy. As a critic quips, one is hard pressed to find an Epicurean talking about virtue – except in fighting a rearguard action against critics.[5] On the Epicurean view, the virtues are only instrumentally valuable – hardly an ethical theory that takes virtue of character to be a fundamental notion. The Stoics, by contrast, do take virtuous activity to be valuable for its own sake. Even so, the central notion of their ethics is not virtue as a state of character, but rather virtuous activity – where such activity is conceived not as an expression of human psychology, but as an assimilation to cosmic nature. For both Stoics and Epicureans the fundamental explanatory notion in ethics is that of *eudaimonia*, which they understand according to Aristotle's clarification as the 'goal of life'. The Stoics and Epicureans are 'eudaimonists' rather than virtue theorists.

A morality of happiness?

The common feature of ancient ethical theory (to the extent that there is one) is its assumption that happiness (*eudaimonia*) is our goal in life, and its organization around the question, what is happiness (*eudaimonia*)? Ancient ethics is an ethic of *eudaimonia* – or, as Julia Annas has aptly characterized it, a 'morality of happiness' (Annas 1993). The term 'morality' comes to us via the Latin translation of the Greek term from which we get the English term 'ethics'; yet, there are those today who balk at identifying the project of ancient Greek ethics with that of morality.[6] Morality, on such a view, is intrinsically bound up with conditions of autonomy and motivation that are either inconsistent with or absent from the conception of human agency delivered by the eudaimonist tradition. The assumption, within that tradition, that every action is 'for the sake of happiness' is taken to imply a self-interested motivation inconsistent with genuinely moral motivation, and the emphasis (at least in Plato and Aristotle) on the social conditions necessary for forming a virtuous character is taken to preclude the autonomy that in the modern tradition is the hallmark of moral agency. We shall see, however, that autonomy is a very important feature of the ethics in the ancient tradition (especially for the Stoics, but with roots going back as far as Plato), and that the motive of the virtuous agent is no more self-interested than the modern conception of properly 'moral' motivation.

Such a promissory note can only be fulfilled by a detailed examination of the ancient tradition itself. So let us now turn to that task.

Notes

1 Greek 'ethics' in this sense is well described in Dover 1974, den Boer 1979, Bryant 1996, and Carter 1986: chapter 1. On Roman ethical attitudes, see Kaster 2005 and Earl 1967. The *Memorable Doings and Sayings* by the Roman Valerius Maximus (translated into English in Shackleton Bailey 2000) is a compendium of examples illustrative of Roman ethical standards. On the Roman genre of *exempla*, see Roller 2004. Thanks to James Ker for assistance on this point.

2 The figurehead of Pyrrhonism is Pyrrho of Ellis, a shadowy figure of the fourth or third centuries BCE about whom little is known. Early in the first century BCE 'Pyrrhonism' was reportedly revived by the skeptical philosopher Aenesidemus of Cnossus; however, the philosophical school seems to have had little impact during the Hellenistic period. Only in the writings of Sextus Empiricus, two centuries later, do we have any extended discussion of Pyrrhonism as an ethical philosophy. On Pyrrhonist ethics, see Bett 1997.

3 Julia Annas's magisterial study *The Morality of Happiness* (Annas 1993), which is organized thematically rather than historically and omits a discussion of Plato, is not intended to present such a history. Prior 1991 is highly selective, giving only a cursory treatment of philosophers later than Aristotle, and discussing only one text of Plato.

4 While Aristotle is clearly familiar with and takes a stand on the issue of whether a person who lacks the external goods can live a happy life, we shall see that this a different issue from whether a virtuous life might fail to be a happy one.

5 Cicero, *Fin.* 2.51.

6 For statements of the distinction between ethics and morality, see Williams 1985 and MacIntyre 1984. For further discussion of the relation between ancient and modern ethics or morality, see Striker 1988, Annas 1995, Broadie 2006, and Kraut 2006a.

2

PLATO AND THE PURSUIT
OF EXCELLENCE

Plato and his predecessors

We begin our study with Plato, but this is not because Plato's predecessors failed to address ethical questions. Indeed, Plato and his contemporaries inherited a rich literary tradition in which poets such as Homer and Hesiod (eighth and ninth centuries BCE), Archilochos and Solon in the seventh century, Simonides in the sixth and Pindar in the fifth, as well as tragedians such as Aeschylus, Sophocles, and Euripides in the fifth century, articulate ethical ideals and attitudes.[1] An educated person would learn many such poems by heart, thereby internalizing the ethical attitudes they expressed.[2] As a character in Plato's *Republic* says, it is from the poets that one gathers 'an impression of what sort of person he should be and of how best to travel the road of life' (*Rep.* 365a–b). That is, the poets offer answers to the central questions in Greek ethical inquiry. Ethical inquiry of the sort that this study concerns, however, consists not just in consulting traditional authorities for ethical advice, but in subjecting those answers to critical scrutiny by considering and evaluating the reasons that can be offered in their support.

Greek city states during the fifth century BCE saw a great rise of interest in the use of reason as a critical tool and an instrument of argumentation and persuasion, especially as applied to ethical questions. Relish for the give and take of argument, either as a participant or a spectator, was a feature of popular culture.[3] Itinerant intellectuals (known as 'sophists', *sophistai*) such as Protagoras, Hippias and Prodicus – as well as teachers of rhetoric such as Gorgias – wrote and lectured on ethical subjects. They attracted large followings among ambitious young men who wished to become persuasive speakers.[4] The Athenian Socrates (470–399 BCE) was among those who had a reputation for being a clever speaker (*Ap.* 17a–b), and he too attracted a significant following among Athenian youth (*Ap.* 23c, 33d–34a; *Phd.* 59a–c). These included Plato and a number of others who like him later wrote dialogues in which Socrates is the main speaker.

The 'sophists' were viewed with considerable suspicion and hostility by more conservative members of society, who feared that the verbal techniques and logical pyrotechnics they taught undermined traditional ethical values, and thus 'corrupted' the youth.[5] Among his contemporaries, Socrates was generally perceived to be just another sophist. In fact, he was eventually charged with corrupting the youth, tried and convicted by an Athenian jury, then executed. Plato goes to great lengths in his dialogues to defend Socrates against the charge of corruption, and to distinguish Socrates' brand of inquiry and argumentation, which he labels 'philosophy', from those of the other so-called sophists.[6] Indeed it is largely due to Plato's success in this endeavour that the term 'sophist' came to have pejorative connotations, reflected in the English word, 'sophistical'.[7]

The sophists, Socrates, and the poetic tradition thus provide the background and context for Plato's ethical writings. However, even if we begin our study of ancient ethics with Plato, we will not be neglecting that context, because the context is itself preserved and set up for examination in Plato's dialogues. The poets are regularly quoted and discussed, the major sophists and teachers of rhetoric, along with their devotees, appear as characters, and Socrates is the dominant speaker in all but a few of the dialogues. Plato portrays his teacher as interrogating sophists and orators, along with well-known Athenian public figures from the fifth century.[8]

These dialogues are not accurate reports of conversations between Socrates and the characters depicted. Rather, they are dramatic creations in which Plato uses the figure of Socrates to work through the ethical issues of the day. Indeed, in certain cases it is historically impossible or highly improbable for such conversations to have taken place.[9] The extent to which the views articulated by Plato's Socrates are faithful to the philosophy of the historical Socrates is another matter, and a disputed one.[10] There is little in the way of corroborating evidence, since Socrates himself wrote nothing, and what little remains of the 'Socratic dialogues' written by others shows considerable variation in the doctrines and personality attributed to Socrates.[11] The Socratic dialogues of Plato, Aeschines, and Antisthenes and the teachings of the Socratic Aristippus inspired such different ethical traditions that, in later Greek philosophy, Socrates is revered as a figurehead by schools that espouse rival doctrines.[12] Regardless of their historical accuracy, however, Plato's dialogues were influential in shaping much of that later conception of Socrates, so we have good reason and no better alternative than to begin our study with Plato.

The fact that Plato writes dialogues rather than treatises makes identifying his own views a rather delicate matter – delicate, but not impossible. One cannot assume, of course, that the message intended by Plato in a given dialogue corresponds simply to whatever is said by Socrates (or by the dominant speaker) in that dialogue.[13] Nonetheless, this is often a large part of Plato's message – especially in less dramatic dialogues, such as books II–X of the *Republic*, for example, and much of the *Laws*. In these works, Socrates or the dominant speaker holds forth at length, while other characters have barely more than walk-on parts. The dialogue form, however, allows Plato many additional means of making a point. For example, even if the character Socrates is stumped by a puzzle and gives up the inquiry in bewilderment, the course of the dialogue may point the way to a solution to which Plato is directing his readers. In addition, Plato's choice and characterization of interlocutors, the relation between them, sometimes even their order of appearance, along with the historical setting and dramatic structure, can each communicate significant messages to his intended audience, and Plato is a master at controlling these variables.

The quest for excellence

Regardless of the interpretive difficulties posed by Plato's choice of genre, his masterful use of the dialogue form has its corresponding benefits. Highly dramatic dialogues such as *Laches*, *Meno*, *Protagoras*, and *Gorgias* bring brilliantly to life the urgent practical enterprise that sets the context for Plato's ethical philosophy. We may call this 'the quest for excellence (*aretê*)'. These works abound with characters who seek excellence for themselves or for their children, volunteer advice as to how it is to be acquired, or offer to teach it for a fee.

The dialogue *Protagoras* opens in the hours before dawn. Socrates, asleep in his bed, is awakened by Hippocrates. The excited youth begs to be taken to the house where Protagoras, the sophist, has just arrived for a visit. He wants Socrates to convince the famous sophist to take him on as a pupil. Hippocrates is so eager to study with Protagoras that he is willing to bankrupt his family and friends in order to pay the sophist's fees (*Pr.* 310e). What will he learn from Protagoras? Excellence, Protagoras promises (318a–319a). Another ambitious seeker after excellence is Meno, the title character in another dialogue. The young Thessalian has elected to apprentice himself to the orator Gorgias in order to achieve this goal (*Meno* 71c–d, 76c, 91a, 92d). Callicles in the dialogue *Gorgias* is likeminded. The dialogue *Laches* opens as two elderly fathers, Lysimachus and Melesias, ashamed about not having lived up to the reputations of their illustrious fathers, seek advice about how to educate their sons to achieve their grandfathers' excellence (*La.* 179c–180a).[14] In the *Euthydemus*, Crito is preoccupied with the question of whom he should hire to educate (*paideuein*) his son Critoboulus (*Euthd.* 306d–307a).[15]

These dialogues are thickly populated as well with a cast of characters who offer to teach excellence, for a fee, to those who seek it.[16] These self-styled educators include historical figures such as Protagoras, Prodicus, Hippias and the lesser known Euvenus of Paros (*Ap.* 19e–20a, *Pr.* 314e–316a, *H. Maj.* 283c–284b; cf. *Gorg.* 519e) along with Euthydemus and

Dionysodorus in the dialogue *Euthydemus* (306e). The sophists' claim to be teachers of excellence is considered effrontery by conservatives like Anytus, who champion the traditional view that one learns excellence by associating with worthy fellow citizens.[17] The famous orator Gorgias seeks to avoid the hostility directed at the sophists by insisting that he teaches his pupils only rhetorical skill (*Gorg.* 456a–457c). But he too is popularly seen as a sophist,[18] and in any case, the seekers after excellence flock to him in the expectation that they will acquire what even Gorgias advertises as the greatest power known to men (*Gorg.* 451d; cf. 466b).

In sum, these dialogues portray a cultural and intellectual climate in which people agree that it is extremely important to acquire excellence, but disagree about how it is to be acquired: hence the debating question that opens the *Meno*:[19]

> Can you tell me, Socrates, can virtue be taught? Or is it not teachable but the results of practice, or is it neither of these, but men possess it by nature or in some other way?
>
> (*Meno* 70a)[20]

In seeking excellence for themselves or their loved ones, these characters in Plato's dialogues are pursuing a thoroughly traditional goal – with a pedigree at least as old as the Homeric poems. Plato's dominant speaker in *Laws* refers to the ambitious seekers of excellence as 'those who seek to become the best (*aristous*) as quickly as possible' (*Laws* IV 718d7–e1)[21] – a clear echo of the Homeric ideal articulated in the *Iliad* by the aged Peleus, who urges his son Achilles to 'always be the best (*aristeuein*) and prevail over others' (Homer, *Iliad* 11.783; cf. 6.206–10).

This is not to say that the conception of excellence has remained static in the centuries between the time of Homer and that of Plato. The excellence glorified in Homer is that of the warrior chieftain whose greatness consists in his fame (*kleos*) and prowess in battle, is proportional to the number of people he rules, and is measured by the property he has accumulated as a result of his dominance (*Iliad* 1.225–284). The social context in which Socrates' interlocutors seek excellence is, however, not the Bronze Age battlefield where warriors clash, but the fifth-century *polis* (city state). The excellence sought in the latter context is 'the human and political (*politikê*) kind' (*Ap.* 20b4–5).[22] Accordingly, Protagoras claims that he instructs his students in 'the political craft' (*politikê technê*, *Pr.* 319a4; cf. *Euthd.* 291b–c).

The 'political craft' encompasses both the art of the citizen (*politês*, *Pr.* 319a5), as well as that of the political leader or statesman (*politikos*). The art of the citizen consists in doing one's share in the cooperative project of the *polis*, and taking no more than one's share of the benefits; thus good citizenship requires justice and self-restraint (*Pr.* 322b–323a; *Rep.* 352c).[23]

9

Good citizenship, however, is hardly all that the ambitious seekers after *aretê* hope to achieve. The political excellence that the elderly fathers in the *Laches* wish to inculcate in their sons is displayed, they think, by eminent statesmen like their own fathers, Aristides and Thucydides. They want their sons not merely to be just and temperate, but to emulate the accomplishments of their grandfathers, who achieved 'a great many fine things . . . both in war and in peace in their management of the affairs both of their allies and of the city' (*La.* 179c). The fathers' worry is not that their sons will turn out to be anti-social pariahs, but that they will be undistinguished (*akleeis*, 179d4) in the management of public affairs. So too the excellence of interest to the ambitious Meno concerns 'taking care of public business' or 'managing a city' (*Meno* 71e; cf. 91a), and this too Protagoras promises to teach the young Hippocrates:

> What I teach is sound deliberation, both in domestic matters –
> how best to manage one's household, and in public affairs – how
> to realize one's maximum potential for success in political debate
> and action.
>
> (*Protagoras* 318e5–319a2)

The Homeric ideal of excellence, which glorifies competition and dominance, sits rather uncomfortably with the ideal of political excellence – in particular with the ideal of the good citizen, whose justice and self-restraint are in sharp contrast to the aggressive self-aggrandizement of the Homeric hero (G. 483d–e).[24] The Homeric picture, however, still exerts a strong pull on the imaginations of the ambitious seekers after excellence depicted by Plato. These tend to find attractive the preeminence and dominance that come with political leadership. They are eager to exercise power over others and less interested, if at all, in living up to the demands of justice and self-restraint. Hence temperance and justice are deliberately omitted from Callicles' list of the qualities of the 'superior person' (G. 491b–d), and Socrates makes a point of adding them to Meno's conception of excellence (*Meno* 73a), and then has to remind him to add them again at 78c–e.

One of Plato's projects in his dialogues is to address the tensions between the Homeric and the political conception of excellence, and to defend an account of political excellence that applies to private citizen and ruler alike. As the Athenian says in the *Laws*, the 'complete citizen . . . knows how to rule and be ruled with justice' (643e6), and one must first learn how to be ruled before one takes on rule (762e). This larger project of Plato is one of the reasons why Socrates typically responds, to those who ask how they might acquire excellence, that they must first think carefully about what excellence is. Thus in the *Meno*, the opening question, Can excellence be taught?, is quickly succeeded by the more fundamental question insisted upon by Socrates: What is excellence?

This question informs all of Plato's ethical writing – so let us be sure we understand what it means.

Excellence, virtue, and happiness

The word that I have been translating as 'excellence' (*aretê*) is often, and quite properly, translated as 'virtue'.[25] This rendering can, however, give a misleading impression of the question to which Plato's Socrates urges his interlocutors' attention. First of all, as it is used in English today, 'virtue' tends to refer to a character trait – a feature of a person's psychology. That this is so, however, is partly the intellectual legacy of Plato and Aristotle, at whose hands *aretê* comes to be defined as just such an internal phenomenon: 'the condition of one's soul (*Rep.* 444d13–e2; cf. *Ap.* 29e).[26] This definition, however, is a theoretical refinement of the notion of *aretê* understood by Socrates' interlocutors.

Aretê, as Plato's and Socrates' contemporaries understand it, can certainly apply to such recognizable virtues as courage, wisdom, self-restraint (*sôphrosunê*), and justice (although the last two are controversial for those attracted to the Homeric ideal). We regularly find these four virtues listed as the four 'kinds of *aretê*' in Plato (e.g. *Meno* 74a, *Pr.* 329d–330a, *La.* 198a, *Rep.* 428a, *Laws* 963a–964b). Socrates' interlocutors, however, are more likely to understand courage, self-restraint and justice as patterns of behaviour than they are to conceive of them as psychological conditions.[27] Indeed it takes some coaching (*La.* 191e–192b) for Socrates to get Laches to agree that virtue is a 'power' (*dunamis* 192b6) of the soul. In any case, these interlocutors clearly understand *aretê* to encompass many things other than the cardinal virtues. Such things as noble birth, bodily strength, good looks, social status, wealth, and success in competition are generally considered by Greeks of Plato's day to be very important aspects of *aretê*.[28] These can in no way be understood as psychological traits. Thus Meno answers Socrates' question, 'What is *aretê*?', with the proposal that *aretê* is 'ruling others' (*Meno* 73d) or 'acquiring gold and silver' (78c6–7). However unimpressive these proposals may be as ideals of human excellence, it is clear that Meno does not take *aretê* to be a state of character. Similarly, the disappointed sons of Aristides and Thucydides who want their own sons to achieve the *aretê* of their illustrious grandfathers have in mind not the characters of these famous statesmen, but their great accomplishments.

Those whom Plato depicts as questing for excellence are primarily interested in improving not their characters but their lives. As a result, the natural way for them to understand Socrates' question, 'What is excellence?' is as a normative issue about how one should live, rather than a psychological issue about states of character. This normative question is a central motif in dialogues such as the *Gorgias* and the *Republic*, which attempt to resolve the competing claims of the life that looks good by

Homeric standards, and the life that meets the norms of a functioning polis. The issue is typically articulated as a choice between lives: the life of the self-aggrandizing strong man unshackled by the political norm of equality (*isonomia*) among citizens, as opposed to the life of the person who restrains his pursuit of worldly advantage in the light of the norms of justice.[29]

The dispute is explicitly articulated by Callicles in the *Gorgias* as a question about which sort of life is excellence (*aretê*, 492c5), although it is more regularly presented in the dialogue as a question about what life is happy (472c–e, 493d, 507a–508b; cf. 492c). Alternatively put, the question concerns 'how one should live' (492d5, 500c) or the correct way to live (491e, 487a; cf. 461c, 481c), or 'the best way to live' (*hôs arista bioiê*, 512e5; cf. *Rep.* 344e). Thus Socrates' question, 'What is excellence?,' inquires into the best way to live.[30]

Modern readers of Plato are prone to ask, best in what way? Does Plato have in mind the life of the best sort of person (a good person), or the life that is *best for* the person who leads it (a good life)? The answer is that he has both in mind. The two value terms associated with excellence in Plato's discussion are the '*kalon*' (fine, admirable) and the '*agathon*' (good, beneficial). It is tempting for readers today to assume that *kalon* (the fine or admirable) applies to the life of the good person, while the notion of good (*agathon*) applies to the life that is good *for* a person.[31] Polus in fact attempts to make such a distinction, in the dialogue *Gorgias*, in support of his claim that the life of injustice can be superior to that of the just person. While the unjust life, he admits, may be more shameful (*aischron*, the opposite of *kalon*), it is still a better life (more *agathon*) (*Gorg.* 474c–d). However, Polus makes no headway with this improvisation, which gets him involved in a muddle (474d–475c; cf. 477b–479c).[32] Moreover, he receives no support for this argumentative strategy from any other character in the dialogue, including the most strident defender of the glories of 'injustice'. Callicles, who takes up the debate with Socrates after Polus has proved inept, explicitly rejects the latter's attempt to drive a wedge between the *kalon* and the *agathon*: 'whatever is worse is also more shameful' (*Gorg.* 483a; cf. *H. Maj.* 296e).

In this respect, it is Callicles, not Polus, who is more faithful to the original notion of excellence. While the ambitious young people (and their parents) portrayed by Plato understand excellence to be admirable and fine (*kalon*), something they would be ashamed to lack,[33] they also consider the excellent life to be flourishing, successful, and prosperous – that is, good for the person who lives it. The Greek term for such success in life is '*eudaimonia*' ('happiness' or well-being), synonymous with 'doing well' (*eu prattein*, *Euthd.* 280b6). This is what parents wish for their children (*Lys.* 207e), and it is what we all want for ourselves (*Euthd.* 278e, 282a; *Meno* 78a).[34]

In dialogues whose central motif is the quest for excellence, this quest is not distinguished from the pursuit of happiness. Thus Callicles sums up the choice between lives in the *Gorgias* as a question about which life is 'excellence and happiness' (*aretê te kai eudaimonia* – *Gorg.* 492c5–6; cf. 507c). After spending many pages in the *Euthydemus* determining what a person needs in order to be happy (278e–282d), Socrates refers to this as what will make a person 'a happy man and a good one' (282e). Indeed, the very thing that Meno identifies as excellence – the power to acquire good things such as wealth and influence (*Meno* 77b–78b) – appears in the *Euthydemus* as a popular conception of happiness (278e–279b). Socrates' interlocutors readily agree or assume that to harm someone is to make him less excellent (*Rep.* 335b; *Meno* 91c).[35] In general, any proposal in Plato's dialogues about what excellence is must pass the test that it be good for a person, as Socrates regularly reminds his interlocutors.[36] Indeed the dispute in the *Republic*, whether justice is a virtue (*Rep.* 348e, 350d, 351a), turns on whether justice is good for the just person.

This is not to say that the notion of *aretê* at play simply collapses into the notion of self-interest, as we understand it. Granted, Plato's intended readership and Socrates' interlocutors are disinclined to judge a course of action admirable (*kalon*) unless they think it is beneficial to the person who performs it (*La.* 192d; cf. *H. Maj.* 296e). Indeed, they are likely to think it admirable precisely because it is beneficial (*Rep.* 364a) and shameful to the extent that it harms the agent (*Ap.* 28b, *Gorg.* 486a–b; cf. 509c). On the other hand, they are also disinclined to think something is good unless they also think it is admirable. Hence a popular song about the greatest goods does not count wealth as a good unless it is honestly acquired (*Gorg* 451e; cf. Solon I, 3–8). Most people, Socrates reports, even if they are inclined to think pleasure is good, do not consider shameful pleasures to be good (*Pr.* 351c). Callicles is a case in point (*Gorg.* 494e–495a, 499b).

It is important not to confuse this background assumption about the relation between excellence and happiness, which is shared by Socrates and all of his interlocutors other than Polus, with the disputed normative thesis about justice debated in the *Gorgias* and the *Republic*. In these dialogues, Socrates addresses the scepticism of those who doubt that justice (not *aretê* in general) is good for a person – that is, whether it is a genuine excellence (*Rep.* 348d, 351a). This controversial thesis concerns the choice between lives: is the life of justice better than the life of successful injustice? The uncontroversial background assumption, by contrast, has no normative implications. It implies nothing about which lives are admirable and good, but functions instead as a constraint on how one is to form and integrate judgments about what is admirable and who is happy: if something is admirable, it has to be good, and if good, admirable.[37] If it seems to you (as it does to Polus) that justice is admirable but that it may not be good for a person, the background assumption constrains you to reject either the judgment that justice is admirable, or the standards of well-being according to which it is not beneficial. In the normative dispute that pervades the Socratic dialogues, Plato portrays Socrates' opponents as taking the first option while Socrates takes the second.

The modern response to the impression that justice is admirable but not necessarily beneficial has been to endorse both conjuncts of the impression. But this is implicitly to reject the background constraint that operates in the Platonic dialogues. The modern ethical tradition has concluded that the goodness of persons is of a different kind than the goodness of lives. This is the route to the modern distinction between morality and self-interest, but it is not the route that Plato takes. Plato shows no interest in investigating ethical matters outside the scope of the assumption that what is admirable and what is beneficial in human life converge – hence the short shrift given to Polus's proposal to the contrary (*Gorg.* 483a–b; cf. *Rep.* 348e–349a).

To see why this assumption about the good life and the good person seems natural and plausible to Plato's contemporaries, consider the parallel case of health. Socrates identifies it as both the excellence (*aretê*) of the body, and its well-being (*eudaimonia*) (*Gorg.* 479a–c, 478b–c). Even to modern philosophical sensibilities, this equivalence should seem quite straightforward. Plato and his contemporaries assume that the excellence and happiness of a human being are related in just the same way. What is admirable in a human being is expected to coincide with what is good for that person. In the dialogues of Plato, we find the inquiry into the good life conducted in the optimism (to modern views, perhaps naïve optimism) that these two types of value converge.

Excellence and knowledge

The eager questers after excellence in Plato's dialogues are not pledging themselves to a life of selfless and altruistic 'virtue'. On the contrary, they are seeking to live well in every sense of the term. One might be puzzled then at Socrates' claim in the *Apology* that he has devoted his life to exhorting his fellow Athenians to 'care about *aretê*' (*Ap.* 31b; cf. 29d–30b, 36c; *Euthd.* 275a, 278d). If *aretê*, as his contemporaries understand it, requires no recommendation, what is Socrates doing in exhorting his fellow citizens to care about it?

First of all, Socrates' exhortation is not that people should seek excellence – for they are busy enough doing that without his urging. He exhorts them rather to 'take care' or 'be careful' (*epimeleisthai*) in this pursuit. Socrates thinks his ambitious contemporaries are not being properly careful or discriminating about what they seek to acquire under the name of excellence. They are obsessed with the question – how to acquire excellence – to the neglect of the prior question insisted upon by Socrates: what excellence really is. The eager young Hippocrates in the *Protagoras* is an example of this lack of due deliberation. In his ambition to become great, he is eager to jump on the latest bandwagon, thinking that whatever Protagoras can teach him will be just what he needs. Or, even worse, he mistakenly believes that all he needs to learn in order to live well is how to be a clever speaker (*Pr.* 312d).

Second, Socrates is urging on the Athenians a particular conception of excellence:

> Are you not ashamed of your eagerness to possess as much wealth, reputation and honours as possible, while you do not care for nor give thought to wisdom and truth, or the best possible state of your soul?
>
> (*Apology* 29d–e; cf. 30a–b, 36c)

According to Socrates, care of one's soul or psyche (Greek *psuchê*) is more important in the quest for excellence than the accumulation of such external objects of ambition as wealth, reputation, and political power. One cares for one's soul, in his view, by seeking 'wisdom and truth' – that is, by engaging in philosophy, the practice of examining the ethical beliefs of oneself and others (*Ap.* 28e–29a). Thus Socrates' exhortation to 'care about excellence' is an exhortation to engage in philosophy, as he indicates explicitly in the *Euthydemus* (275a, 278d; cf. 288d, 307b–c).

Socrates supports this exhortation at *Euthydemus* 278e–282a by arguing that knowledge provides everything one needs for living well. He offers this set of arguments to the two self-styled teachers of excellence, Euthydemus and his brother Dionysodorus, as an example of how to exhort someone to care (*epimeleisthai*) about '*aretê* and wisdom' (278d–e). The argument begins from the uncontroversial premise that we all want to 'do well' (*eu prattein*) (278e) – that is, be happy (*eudaimon*, 282a; cf. 280b–e). This much all the seekers after excellence agree. But what does happiness consist in? (278e). Socrates begins by considering the view that doing well is simply a matter of possessing good things (278e; cf. *Meno* 77b–78b). He offers a fairly long list of popularly recognized goods, beginning with wealth, health, good looks, satisfaction of bodily needs, noble birth, living in a powerful country and honour (*Euthd.* 279a–b; cf. *Gorg.* 467e, *Laws* 661a–d). To these he adds self-control, justice, bravery and wisdom (*Euthd.* 279b–c) – even though, he recognizes, the first two may be controversial to those enamoured of the Homeric ideal. Finally, he finishes off the list by adding good fortune (*eutuchia*, 279c).

Socrates then sets out to show that all the other items on the list depend on 'wisdom'. He argues first that wisdom is responsible for good fortune (279d–280b). He supports this improbable assertion by citing examples of disciplines (music, navigation, medicine, military science) in which those with the relevant knowledge have 'better luck' than those without it: for example, the skilled sailor has better luck at sea than the unskilled (279e). One might object that although Socrates is right to conclude that having knowledge considerably reduces the scope of luck (good and bad) in our lives (this is why one goes to the doctor when ill, or sails with an experienced navigator, rather than simply 'trusting one's luck'), he is wrong to infer the stronger claim that 'wisdom makes men fortunate in every case' (280a). This is to claim, quite improbably, that knowledge or skill is sufficient to eliminate the effects of good and bad luck in our lives. Even the best doctor, for example, cannot eliminate the risk that you will come down with a deadly and untreatable disease.

Plato, however, does not introduce any such objection into the dialogue. Instead, having eliminated good luck as an independent source of happiness, Socrates proceeds to consider the relation between wisdom and the other goods on the list. He argues that none of these 'goods' is in fact good for you unless you possess wisdom, and that wisdom is what makes them good (*Euthd.* 280c–281e; cf. *Meno* 88a–89a). This is because, first of all, it is not the possession but the use of such things that benefits a person (*Euthd.* 280c–d). Second, one must not only use them, but use them properly (280e–281a). Money and power, for example, are of no benefit to someone who does not know how to use them well (cf. *Gorg.* 469d–e). Even courage and temperance can bring about great harm if controlled by ignorance rather than knowledge (*Euthd.* 281c).[38] Thus, in order to be happy, one needs knowledge of how to use properly the conventionally recognized 'goods' (280d–e). The other putative 'goods' on the list (wealth etc.) are not good in themselves; only if they are used wisely is a person better off having rather than lacking them (281d–e; cf. *Ap.* 30b).[39]

The conclusion so stated amounts to the thesis that wisdom is necessary for living well, and does not depend on the more questionable argument, at *Euthd.* 279d–280b, that wisdom is responsible for good fortune. However, Socrates also draws the stronger conclusion, that wisdom is sufficient for happiness: '[wisdom] is the *only* thing that makes a man happy and fortunate' (282d), and this stronger thesis does depend on that dubious argument. Socrates' main interest, however, is in the further conclusion that he derives, quite legitimately, from either thesis: that a person who wants to live well must strive to become as wise as possible (282a, 282d). To pursue such wisdom is to 'engage in philosophy' (*philosophein*, 282d1).

The subject matter of this wisdom is politics, Socrates goes on to argue (*Euthd.* 291b–c). The nature of political wisdom is further explored in dialogues such as *Laches* and *Charmides*, where Socrates elaborates upon the implication of the *Euthydemus* (279a–281d) that, respectively, courage and temperance (*sôphrosunê*), must be 'used properly' in order to be genuine goods. Fearless resolution on the one hand, and self-restraint on the other, can be bad for a person unless they are informed by wisdom.

In the *Laches*, the subject of inquiry is courage, whose scope Socrates expands beyond the traditional military context (where one's life, health, and safety are at stake), to apply to all contexts where one of the bodily or external goods on the *Euthydemus* list is at risk. Thus he claims, for example, that one can be courageous in illness and poverty (*La.* 191d–e).[40] It is quickly established that simply enduring such risk or loss is not courageous (for it can be foolish or shameful to do so). Only enduring when it is wise to do so is courageous (192d). The rest of the conversation with Laches raises puzzles about what sort of wisdom this could be. It cannot be knowledge or skill that insures you against the risk (as knowledge of diving makes it relatively safe for an experienced person to dive into wells, and knowledge of business makes it safe for a skilled investor to invest money in an enterprise – 192e–193c). Rather, it is knowledge of when it is good to undergo a genuine risk to one's life, or health, or property, and when it is not.[41] This is knowledge of good and bad (199b–d). Here we have impressed upon us that knowing how to 'use' such advantages as wealth and health includes knowing when to forgo their pursuit or risk losing them (cf. *Meno* 78d–e).

The *Charmides* concurs in this conception of the knowledge required for living well. Here temperance (*sôphrosunê*) is the topic of discussion. While a popular conception of temperance identifies it with modesty[42] (*aidôs*, 160e4), a policy of modesty is not always a good one to follow. For example, the naked and shipwrecked Odysseus's need for food and shelter would not have been well served had he modestly refrained from enlisting the help of the young Nausikaa (161a).[43] Thus living well requires knowing when to be modest and when to be bold. This is a version of the 'using science' of the *Euthydemus*, here dubbed 'knowledge about knowledge' (*Charm.* 166e ff). The dialogue ends with a series of puzzles about this knowledge, which can be solved by invoking the conception of knowledge that ends the *Laches*: that it is knowledge of good and evil, specifically of when it is good to pursue the things that other human skills can secure for us.[44]

Knowledge vs. rhetoric

That you need knowledge of good and bad in order to live well is also a major argument of the *Gorgias*. In contrast to dialogues such as *Euthydemus*, *Charmides*, and *Laches*, Socrates here argues for this conclusion against opponents who explicitly reject it. The famous orator Gorgias and his Athenian admirers, Polus and Callicles, think that rhetoric (skill at persuasion) is the only knowledge one needs to acquire in order to live well. Rhetoric, according to Gorgias and his devotees, is the finest type of knowledge (*Gorg.* 448c, e; cf. 466b) and deals with 'the greatest human concerns' (451d).

This is to accord to rhetoric the same honorific status that Socrates attributes to the knowledge that he urges his compatriots to seek.[45] In *Euthydemus*, where he identifies this wisdom as political knowledge (288d–290d; 291b–d),[46] he explicitly rejects the pretensions of rhetoric to this status (289d–290a; cf. 305c–e). Here in the *Gorgias* he offers a similar repudiation of rhetoric's claim to be the key to living well. Rhetoric of the kind celebrated by Gorgias and Polus is only an ingratiating imitation of the genuine political craft (*Gorg.* 463a–d; cf. 481d–e; *Euthd.* 289e–290a).

While Plato recognizes that persuasion is an important tool to be used by the true statesman (*politikos*), his dominant speakers consistently maintain that its use must be subordinated to the statesman's goal of caring for the *polis* and its citizens (*Stsm.* 303e–304d; cf. 305d; *Euthd.* 289c–d). The practice of rhetoric, on this view, must be governed by the norms of justice. Gorgias and his followers, by contrast, have a very different conception of the uses of rhetoric. With the power to persuade the other citizens in a public forum, the skilled orator can convince them of the justice of whatever endeavour he proposes, even if it advances his interest at their expense. In general, Gorgias boasts, rhetoric is the 'source of rule over others in one's own city' (*Gorg.* 452d). It enables you to bend others to your own will, making them in effect your slaves (452d–e).

In a democracy such as Plato's Athens, political power depends on being persuasive. Rhetoric, the art of persuasion, is accordingly prized very highly by those with political ambitions. This is why so many of the ambitious, like Meno and Callicles, seek out teachers of rhetoric rather than sophists. In Plato's dialogues, it is primarily the unscrupulous (like Meno) or the cynical (like Callicles and Polus) who take this route. Plato thereby emphasizes that the ability to persuade others, and thereby 'rule them', as Gorgias promises, is attractive independently of its connection to justice. Hence Plato depicts the famous master of rhetoric as denying that he teaches justice (*Meno* 95b–c; *Gorg.* 456c–457c),[47] while the orator's acolytes extol the benefits of wielding power over others without being constrained by the norms of justice (*Gorg.* 471a–d; 483b–484c).

Rhetorical skill has the added benefit, in their eyes, of enabling you to defend yourself successfully against prosecution. With this knowledge, you will never be vulnerable to malicious prosecution, as Socrates was (*Gorg.* 486a–c: *H. Maj.* 304b). And if you should be prosecuted for crimes of which you are guilty, skillful use of rhetoric will ensure that you evade legal sanctions or punishment (*Rep.* 365d; cf. *Gorg.* 478e–479c). Rhetoric therefore gives you the power to do what you want with impunity.[48] It is the wisdom you need in order to live well, according to its disciples, because if practised successfully (which they concede not everyone will be able to do) it enables you to do whatever you want.[49]

Callicles is the ultimate defender, in the dialogue, of the thesis that living well is being able to do whatever you want. Indeed, he claims, the more you are able to do what you want, without being subject to any constraints – internal or external – the better your life is:

> The man who'll live correctly ought to allow his own appetites to get as large as possible and not restrain them. And when they are as large as possible, he ought to be competent to devote himself to them by virtue of his bravery and wisdom, and to fill them with whatever he may have an appetite for at the time.
>
> (*Gorgias*, 491e8–492a3)

The 'wisdom' (*phronesis*) that Callicles here attributes to the person who is living well is quite different from the 'using craft' conceived of by Socrates (cf. *Gorg.* 521b). The great person, in Callicles' eyes, is wise about how best to fulfill his desires, not about whether it is good or bad to get what he wants.

Callicles defends this picture of the good life by invoking hedonism – the thesis that pleasure is the good (*Gorg.* 495a). Such a life is better, he claims, than the restrained alternative proposed by Socrates at 492e because it contains more pleasure (494a–495a). Socrates responds by showing that Callicles does not really believe that all pleasures are good. Some pleasures are shameful, even Callicles concedes (497e–499b). Thus Callicles cannot consistently invoke hedonism, since he does not accept its central tenet, that pleasure, in and of itself, is good. Although Callicles attempts to save face by denying that he ever really meant to endorse hedonism (499b), Socrates succeeds in establishing that, even by Callicles' own standards, living well requires the ability to discriminate between good and bad. Thus, Callicles must agree with Socrates that in order to live well one needs knowledge of good and bad.

One might object that Callicles goes overboard in rejecting all forms of self-control at 491e–492a. In his initial description of the best life, which has clear Homeric origins, the excellent person is entitled to rule over and exploit his inferiors (483a–484c). Realistically, however, such a life must surely involve some kinds of self-control, and Socrates is able to exploit this fact in his refutation of Callicles.[50] Why then does Plato choose to depict Callicles as rejecting temperance and espousing hedonism?

Presumably it is because one of Plato's main goals in the dialogue is to refute the view that being able to do whatever you want is what makes for the best life. This is the view that motivates the admiration for rhetoric expressed by Polus and other characters, and it is this view that receives its ultimate expression in hedonism and the rejection of self-restraint. In the *Gorgias*, Plato shows that this view, however appealing it may seem on first glance, is, on reflection, unacceptable even to its proponents. While

Callicles clearly disagrees with Socrates about the characteristics of the good life, he must agree with Socrates' contention that living well requires knowledge of good and bad.

The dearth of knowledge

A striking counterpart to Socrates' insistence that we need knowledge of good and bad in order to live well is his equally emphatic contention that no one has this knowledge. At the opening of the dialogue *Meno*, Socrates shocks the title character by denying that he has ever met anyone who knows what excellence is (71b–c). This claim is one of the themes of his defence speech in the *Apology*, where he claims that he has spent his life interrogating Athenians who have a reputation for wisdom. While he concedes that many of them are knowledgeable about various technical matters (22d–e), he claims to have determined that none of them has knowledge about 'the most important things' (21b–22e; 22d–e). He has arrived at this conclusion by interrogating those with a reputation for or a conceit of goodness or excellence (29d–e), challenging them to 'give an account of [their] lives' (*Ap.* 39c; cf. *La.* 187e10–188a2). Thus that 'most important' issue (*Ap.* 22d–e; cf. *Gorg.* 487b, *La.* 200a) about which Socrates interrogates his fellow Athenians, and claims that no one is wise, is how one should live.

The three 'dialogues of definition', *Laches*, *Charmides*, and *Euthyphro*, as well as the first part of the *Meno* (70a–79e), illustrate the type of interrogation that licenses Socrates' conclusion that the Athenians do not have knowledge of excellence. The interrogations proceed on the assumption, explicitly stated in the *Charmides*, that the excellent person should be able to state what excellence is (*Charm.* 159a). This assumption makes perfect sense in the light of the arguments in the *Euthydemus* (278e–282a), considered above, that doing well depends on having knowledge of how to live, and the background assumption that 'excellence' is naturally understood to be a kind of life rather than a state of the soul or other psychological condition. If knowledge of temperance is knowledge of some thesis in moral psychology, Socrates would seem to be operating on a dubious assumption. However, if knowledge of temperance is knowledge of how to act temperately (and hence of how to act well), then it is not unreasonable to assume that someone who claims to be living well should be able to explain why he is right to act as he does. Unless his success is entirely a matter of luck, it must be due to knowledge.

The interrogations that expose the interlocutor's lack of knowledge follow a common pattern. In the *Laches*, Socrates asks two respected Athenian generals, Laches and Nicias, about one type of excellence, courage. Laches proposes first that courage is standing one's ground in battle (190e). However, this obviously won't do, Socrates points out, since sometimes standing one's ground is foolish, and retreating is not always cowardly (190e–192c). He then suggests that what Laches really means is that courage is wise endurance (192d). Laches readily accepts this proposal, but he shows no understanding in the aftermath (192e–199e) of the sort of wisdom that would be required – being unable to distinguish the wisdom that allows one to escape unharmed from dangerous situations (which a skilled well-diver might have – 193a–c), from the wisdom that tells one when it is right to risk harm (cf. 195c–e; *Gorg.* 511c–512e; *Laws* 707d, 727d).[51]

Nicias does better than Laches, and indicates (*La.* 195b–d) that the requisite knowledge is the 'using kind' identified in the *Euthydemus* – which amounts (as Socrates readily points out) to knowledge of good and evil (*La.* 196d–199e). But even this proposal does not amount to knowledge of what courage, or excellence, is – unless we understand the inquiry into excellence as a psychological inquiry into the nature of the good person's soul. As an answer to the practical question, 'How should we live?', it is worthless. It will not enable one to discriminate between those cases of endurance that are courageous, and those that are foolish, or the cases where one should stand one's ground, and those where one should not. Nor will it allow Nicias or anyone else to answer the practical question immediately put to them by the elderly fathers whose quest frames the dialogue: whether training in a newfangled variety of combat will in fact make their sons courageous.

A similar pattern is exhibited in the *Charmides*, which investigates the nature of temperance (*sôphrosunê*). There Socrates interrogates the young Charmides, along with his uncle and mentor, Critias. Charmides is widely admired for being temperate (*Charm.* 157d). When questioned by Socrates about what temperance is, the youth begins, in the manner of Laches, by proposing that temperance is keeping quiet (159b), or being modest (160e). He then quickly concedes, when pressed by Socrates, that neither kind of behaviour is always temperate (159b–161a). Charmides at this point defers to his uncle Critias, who supplies in sequence a number of proposals: that temperance is minding one's own business (161b);[52] that it is doing good things (163e); and that it is doing good things as a result of knowledge (164a–d). As in the *Laches*, the dialogue concludes with a series of puzzles about the nature of this knowledge – all of which point towards the solution that temperance is knowledge of good and evil.[53] Although Critias is unable to solve the puzzles, Plato clearly portrays him, like Nicias, as partial to the view that living well requires knowledge of good and evil (e.g. 174b). Nonetheless, even if Critias were able to solve the puzzles, this would not show that he has the knowledge of how to act temperately.

Socrates includes himself in the sweeping denial that no one has knowledge. His disclaimers of the knowledge he seeks are a persistent theme in Plato's dialogues (*Ap.* 21b–22e, 23a; *Meno* 70b–71a; *La.* 200e–201a). Many readers are puzzled by or sceptical of this disavowal,[54] which is puzzling if we take inquiry into excellence to be distinct from inquiry into the good life. Doesn't Socrates at least think he knows that virtue is a kind of knowledge? We have seen, however, that he does not credit Nicias and Critias with the requisite knowledge on the basis of such claims. This tells us that his question, 'What is excellence?' investigates a person's claim to have knowledge of good and bad. If all a person can say to substantiate his claim to have this knowledge is that one needs knowledge of good and bad in order to live well, this is no evidence that he has such knowledge. So Socrates has no reason to attribute such knowledge to himself if this is all he can say.[55]

A modern reader of Plato might be unconvinced that these interrogations succeed in establishing that the refuted interlocutors lack knowledge of how to live well. Might not a person know how to live well, and exhibit such knowledge in his or her life, but be unable to articulate it in a general formula?[56] Thus, the objection might go, Nicias' or Laches' failure to articulate what the courageous person knows does not show that they lack this knowledge, and similarly Charmides and Critias' failure to articulate what the temperate person knows does not show that they lack the requisite knowledge.

Plato's intended readership, however, would never make such an objection. That audience, which is at least a generation later than the dramatic date of these dialogues, knows very well that Charmides and his mentor turned out to be rapacious scoundrels who committed great crimes against the Athenian democracy at the end of the Peloponnesian war (twenty-eight years after the dramatic date of the dialogue). Critias was the leader and Charmides a member of the oligarchic junta installed as rulers of Athens in 404 BCE by the victorious Spartans. Known as 'The Thirty', they ruled with great violence and intemperance – expelling, murdering, and confiscating property (in the manner fantasized by Polus – *Gorg.* 468b) until they were overthrown and the democracy restored less than a year later.[57] These historical facts would have been vividly in the minds of Plato's original readers.

Nor does Plato expect his audience to have a high opinion of Nicias and Laches, who were military leaders during the Peloponnesian war. The dialogue *Laches* is set in the early years of the thirty-year conflict, when Athenian power still prevails and the Athenians are optimistic of victory. Nicias and Laches enjoy high public repute at the time, which is why the elderly fathers consult them about how their sons might achieve excellence. The dialogue is written, however, after the bitter and humiliating defeat of Athens, and after Nicias, in particular, has been disgraced by foolish decisions that led to the defeat of the Athenian expedition against Syracuse in 413. Indeed, Plato deliberately draws the readers' attention to this fact.[58]

Another failed pretender to knowledge of excellence, Meno, is known to Plato's audience as a rapacious and opportunistic political and military adventurer.[59] And finally, consider Euthyphro, of the eponymous dialogue investigating the nature of piety. While we have no independent information about the historical Euthyphro,[60] Plato goes to great pains in the dialogue itself to paint him as a fool – engaged in a prosecution that all of his contemporaries and Plato's readership would have regarded as highly impious. He is prosecuting his father for murder (*phonos*) – not as a public prosecutor, but as a private citizen bringing the charge on behalf of the deceased. This scandalizes his contemporaries because it violates the norms of filial piety. Regardless of the merits of the case against his father (which Plato presents as doubtful), a charge of murder would be expected to be prosecuted by a relative of the victim. Euthyphro defends his action by claiming to have specialized knowledge of piety and justice (4e–5a; cf. 3b–c, 4b). However, upon examination, Euthyphro shows no more evidence of his professed knowledge than the other refuted interlocutors we have considered.

Far from displaying their professed ethical knowledge in their lives, those whom Socratic examination shows to be lacking in knowledge also failed to display such knowledge in their lives.[61] Euthyphro prosecuted when it was impious to do so; Nicias foolishly held his ground when he should have retreated; and Critias and Charmides' conduct while in power gave no one reason to believe they had knowledge of temperance.

Plato's indictment of the Golden Age

Plato's intended audience live in the fractious 4th century BCE in a weakened Athens that looks back with nostalgia to the 'Golden Age' of the early fifth century, the time of Pericles (495–429), Themistocles (582–462), and Cimon (d. 450), under whose leadership Athens became a wealthy imperial power. This audience tends to be harsh in its judgment of later leaders like Nicias (470–413) and Laches (d. 418), who failed to preserve Athens' former glory and prosperity, or like Critias and Charmides, who subverted its most revered institutions. On the other hand, they tend to agree, with interlocutors in Plato's dialogues, that Pericles, Themistocles and Cimon were clear exemplars of political excellence. Plato's indictment for ignorance, however, extends even to these revered leaders of the 'Golden Age'.

In the dialogues we have been considering, Socrates regularly observes that none of these legendary statesmen succeeded in passing on his supposed excellence to his children. The sons of Pericles, he points out more than once, did not amount to anything. Nor did those of Themistocles, Aristides the Just, or Thucydides the general (*Meno* 93a–94e; *Pr.* 319e–320b; cf. *La.* 179c–d). Plato's dialogues propose two different explanations of this. One, offered in the *Meno*, is that these politicians had divinely inspired correct belief, not knowledge, and this is why they were unable to pass on their competence to anyone else (*Meno* 99b–100b).[62] This is hardly a complimentary portrait of the eminent Athenians, as Anytus comments explicitly in the *Meno* (99e).

Even more devastating is the explanation advanced forcefully by Socrates in the *Gorgias*, where he alleges that Pericles, Themistocles, and Cimon were charlatans rather than true statesmen. Their conduct of the city's affairs manifested not divinely inspired correct judgment, but the greatest ignorance. The only revered figures who are omitted from this indictment are the grandfathers from the *Laches*: Thucydides, who opposed Pericles' policy of imperial expansion, and Aristides, who was a hero of the Persian wars which liberated Athens from Persian aggression.[63] By contrast, he claims, those who led Athens in the pursuit of wealth and empire were adept not at protecting and benefiting the city, but at flattering the population and catering to its appetites (*Gorg.* 515c–517c). These so-called 'statesman' were adept at the flattering persuasion taught by Gorgias (463a–465e), rather than the political knowledge sought by Socrates.[64] Thus, Plato tells his readers, virtually none of the revered political figures of Athens' 'Golden Age' who serve as exemplars and role models for the ambitious youth portrayed in Plato's dialogues, exemplified political excellence. They did not know what excellence is.

Politics and justice in the Republic

In dialogues that abound with seekers after political excellence, we find a variety of competing models of that excellence. On the one hand, there is the model, inspired by the Homeric ideal, of the leader who dominates his subjects and enriches himself at their expense. In the context of the *polis*, as opposed to the Homeric battlefield, such domination may be secured by the power of persuasion, rather than by military force. Thus those who are inspired by this conception of political success take rhetoric to be the primary qualification for public office. In addition to Polus and Callicles in the *Gorgias*, Plato presents us with Thrasymachus in Book I of the *Republic* as an outspoken proponent of this conception of politics.[65] Like Callicles, Thrasymachus thinks that the truly great ruler is entitled to rule over and exploit his inferiors. The true politician, in his view, cares for the citizens in the way that a shepherd tends his sheep – that is, with a view to fleecing, slaughtering, and selling them (*Rep.* 343a–b). In opposition to Thrasymachus, Socrates insists that the true politician rules for the benefit of the citizens and that his primary qualification for office is knowledge of good and bad.

Thrasymachus, like Callicles, thinks that what goes by the name of 'justice' in a *polis* is whatever laws the majority have set up for their own benefit (*Rep.* 338e–339a; *Gorg.* 483b–c; cf. *Rep.* 359a–b). If a political leader abides by those laws and refrains from taking advantage of his public office to enrich himself at the public expense, then he is benefiting the other citizens rather than himself (*Rep.* 343c–344b). Indeed by justly refusing to use his political influence to advance his own interests, he is worse off than he would be if he had acted unjustly (343e; cf. 358e–359b). Thus injustice, if one can get away with it (whether by force or by guile), is more to a ruler's advantage than justice (344b–c).

At stake in the *Republic* is the issue of whether justice is a genuine excellence (348d, 350d, 351a). Given the background constraint that excellence must be good for a person, Socrates cannot defend his contention that justice is part of the excellence of a political leader unless he can establish that it is more to one's advantage to act justly than unjustly. This he sets out to do in the rest of Book I, delivering a battery of arguments that, while they effectively silence Thrasymachus, are unconvincing even to Glaucon and Adeimantus, who agree with Socrates' conclusion (*Rep.* 357a–b, 358b; cf. 347e–348a, 361d–e).[66]

These sympathetic interlocutors reopen the question in Book II and demand that Socrates offer a more convincing argument to show that acting justly is always in one's interest. Not only are they unconvinced by Socrates' arguments against Thrasymachus in Book I, they also find inadequate the popular rationale for justice. This is roughly that, in addition to divine favour (364b–365a), justice will earn you a good reputation in the *polis*, thereby enhancing your opportunity to enter into contracts and alliances, and to gain public office (358a, 362b–c, 362e–363a). These promised rewards are merely contingent rather than inevitable consequences of justice, Glaucon and his brother complain, for even an unjust person might secure a reputation for justice (361a–362c), and the gods, it is said, can be bought off by sacrifices (364b–365a). Thus the brothers demand that Socrates demonstrate the intrinsic benefits of acting justly, 'whether or not one escapes the notice of gods and men' (427d6–7; cf. 445a2–3, 580c6–7).

This Socrates sets out to do, in Books II to IV, by invoking an analogy between a *polis* (city) and the human psyche or soul (*psuchê*). If we first identify what justice is in a city, that will make it easier for us to identify in an individual person (368d–369a).[67] Socrates begins by identifying the goal of a *polis*: people come together to form a city in order to make life better for themselves than it would be if they lived in isolation (369b–c). They expect to be better off, first of all, in meeting their most basic needs – for food, clothing, shelter, etc. Thus the rudimentary city will consist of farmers, builders, shoemakers, and the like – who, if each can specialize in his own profession, and trade the results with the others, will make everyone better off than if each tried, in isolation, to provide all these goods for himself (369d–e).

Of course people want not just the bare necessities of life, but also luxuries, as Glaucon is quick to point out (372c). Socrates responds by enlarging the range of occupations to be pursued in the city to include barbers, beauticians, swineherds, actors, hunters and more (373a–c). However, he points out, pursuing goals beyond necessity will involve the city in conflicts over scarce resources with other cities who are doing the same. Thus a military force will be required to defend the *polis* against attack, and presumably also to attack other cities (373d–374e). If the soldiers are to be good at these military functions, they must be fierce and aggressive (375a–b). But this introduces the risk that they will use their power to take advantage of the population and exploit it for their own benefit – as on Thrasymachus' view of the true ruler (343b–c). In order to guard against this and ensure that the soldiers function as proper guardians of the city, they must be properly selected and trained (375d–412b; cf. 440d), forbidden to own property (416c–417b), and led by rulers who are wise about what is best for the city (412b–414a). Under such an arrangement, the rulers are the true guardians, and the military their auxiliaries (414b). Hence we have the three main political classes in the city: the producers (*demiourgoi*), the auxiliaries, and the rulers.

Under the leadership of the rulers, the auxiliaries will guard the city not only against external dangers but internal ones as well. For example, the leaders will take care that the city does not get so large or wealthy as to be susceptible to faction (*Rep.* 421d–423c; cf. *Laws* 742d). Thus the guardian classes do not function simply as an instrument for the pursuit of luxuries that generated the need for guardians in the first place. A well-governed city will in fact be purged of many of the occupations first mentioned as the list of goods to be produced expanded beyond the limits of necessity (cf. *Rep.* 399e). It will not be restricted to the meagre subsistence level of the original 'city of pigs', where there are no delicacies (*opson*) or even any furniture 372d.[68] Nonetheless some significant, though unspecified, limits are in place on the goals it will pursue. The rulers will use their wisdom to determine those limits. Thus the well-functioning city is itself an entity that exercises self-restraint in light of what is good for itself. This good does not consist simply in satisfying whatever desires the population has (as Socrates complains of Pericles and his cohort – *Gorg.* 515c–517c), but in maintaining the stability and integrity of the city as a whole.

The self-restraint of the well-functioning city will not, however, be like that of a police state, where the rulers determine what the producers are allowed to do, and the auxiliaries enforce this against an unwilling population of producers (*Rep.* 414b). Rather, all three classes in the city will be of one mind about who should rule. This 'agreement about who should rule' is the city's temperance (*sôphrosunê*) (431b–432a). The good judgment of the rulers about what is best is the city's wisdom (428a–429a), and the auxiliaries' willingness to carry out that judgment whatever the dangers or risks to themselves, is the city's courage (429a–430b). The justice of the city consists in the fact that each of the rulers, auxiliaries, and producers 'does his own work' (433a–434c) – that is, membership in these classes is determined by proper qualifications.[69] Disaster will strike the city if it is ruled by those who lack the ruler's understanding of what is good for the city, and are fit instead only to be auxiliary guardians, or are unfit for political participation at all and hence properly relegated to the producing class.

Having thus identified justice in a city, Socrates proceeds to argue that justice in a person is structurally analogous. Each of us has in our psyche, he claims, three parts corresponding to the three parts of the city.[70] Our ability to form desires for natural goals such as food, drink, shelter, and sex as well as for objectives that go beyond the limits of necessity, corresponds to the producing class of the city. Socrates labels this part of the psyche 'appetitive' (*epithumetikon* – 439d; cf. 436a). Corresponding to the fierce class of auxiliaries, ready to go forth aggressively against the city's enemies, is what Socrates labels our 'spiritedness' (*thumos*) – the part of us that gets angry at injustice, and that is able to endure hardship and opposition in pursuit of what we value (439e–440d). And finally, the part of our psyche that functions like the ruler exercising forethought on behalf of the whole city is our reason or calculating (*logistikon*) part (439c–d, 440e–441a, c; cf. 435e–436a).[71]

It is possible for these three parts of the soul to be in conflict with each other. For example, you may feel a desire to eat what you know full well is bad for you (439b–c), struggle against an angry impulse that you know will lead to no good (390d; cf. 441b), or feel disgust at your own desires (439e–440a). Indeed the fact of potential conflict is Socrates' ground for distinguishing the three parts from each other (436b–437a). However, such conflict is not inevitable; in a well-functioning psyche, he claims, there is concord and agreement between the parts. The reasoning part of the psyche is in charge, while spiritedness and appetite are willingly obedient to it. This condition of rational self-control within a person is analogous to justice in the city (442c–d), since reason, unlike spiritedness and appetite, is fit to rule, while spiritedness is fit to be its ally, and appetite needs to be ruled by both (441e–442a). Thus a just person is one in whose psyche, reason, spirit, and appetite rule or are ruled according to their fitness. Socrates identifies justice with this condition of inner harmony under reason's rule:

> One who is just does not allow any part of himself to do the
> work of another part or allow the various classes within him to
> meddle with each other. He regulates well what is really his own
> and rules himself. He puts himself in order, is his own friend, and
> harmonizes the three parts of himself like three limiting notes in a
> musical scale – high, low, and middle. He binds together those

27

parts . . . and from having been many things he becomes entirely one, moderate and harmonious.

(*Rep.* 443d–e)

The unjust person, by contrast, lacks such rational self-control. According to Socrates' account, his reason is overpowered by or engaged in 'civil war' against his appetite or his spiritedness (444b). Injustice, so conceived, is like a serious mental illness. So even if being just leaves you with less wealth and power than you might gain by injustice, the unjust person secures these 'external' advantages at an extremely high cost to his psyche. This trade-off, Socrates maintains, is an extremely bad bargain. No gain in wealth, power, or other worldly advantages is worthwhile if it comes at the cost of engendering such 'civil strife' in one's soul:

> Even if one has every kind of food and drink, lots of money, and every sort of power to rule, life is thought to be not worth living when the body's nature is ruined. So even if someone can do whatever he wishes, except what will free him from vice and injustice . . . how can life be worth living when his soul – the very thing by which he lives – is ruined and in turmoil?
>
> (*Rep.* 445a–b)

Thus Socrates answers Glaucon and Adeimantus' challenge to show that justice is in itself beneficial to the person who possesses it, rather than simply 'a benefit to the other guy' (*allotrion agathon*, 343c), as in the popular conception. But is his answer satisfactory? While it is clear that the condition of psychological harmony and rational self-control that he calls 'justice' is a great benefit to a person, and that 'injustice' as he describes it is an extraordinary liability, is it clear that these conditions are the same as the justice and injustice about which Glaucon and Adeimantus (and Thrasymachus) raise their original challenge?

One obvious difference is that justice and injustice, as Socrates' interlocutors understand it when they raise their challenges, are types of behaviour. On Socrates' definition, by contrast, they are internal psychological conditions, which we might call 'states of character'. This difference on its own, however, is not problematic for Socrates' argument, as long as the psychological condition that he identifies as justice issues in the type of just behaviour that his interlocutors have in mind (and similarly for injustice). Socrates explicitly claims that it does. The person with psychological justice will never embezzle, rob, steal, betray friends or country, violate an oath, commit treason or adultery, or fail to pay due respect to his parents and the gods (442e–443a), and 'the cause of all this is that every part within him does its own work, whether it's ruling or being ruled' (443b1–2).

It is this claim that has seemed the weak link in the argument, according to many modern interpreters. Why does Socrates take it as obvious that one cannot commit injustice coolly, with forethought and deliberation, and with the same kind of rational self-control that he attributes to the 'just' psychology? Indeed, one might object, the sort of injustice that Glaucon and Adeimantus are concerned about is not that of the axe-murderer running amok (who might well have a psyche that is 'unjust' by Socrates' standards). Rather, the 'completely unjust person' as Glaucon describes him knows his own limits and does not undertake any illicit activity unless he is sure of succeeding without detection (360e–361a) – a disposition that surely involves considerable foresight and self-control. Why does Socrates not allow that rational self-control can issue in unjust as well as just behaviour?[72]

One answer is given in Books VII–IX, where Socrates elaborates upon the different types of unjust constitutions of both cities and psyches. He identifies two different ways in which a person's psyche might be organized around a conception of 'what is good for the whole soul' that allows for overreaching, but still have a semblance of discipline and control – even very tight control. One of these is the 'timocratic' soul, which values victory and dominance over others but harbours secret unfulfilled desires for wealth (548e–549b; cf. 548a–c). The other is the 'oligarchic' soul, which is wholly devoted to the miserly accumulation of wealth, even if this involves embezzlement or other dishonesty (553b–554d). Each of these types of psychology is unstable, Socrates claims, and liable to degenerate, either directly or indirectly, into the riotous abandon of the 'democratic' psyche, in which all desires compete on an equal footing (558c–561b).[73]

The 'democratic' person may eventually succeed in repressing his most evil and lawless desires (561b, 571b–d), but in the end these will break out and come to dominate the psyche, which thereby becomes 'tyrannical' – driven by mad desires and hopelessly out of control (572d–575a). The tyrannical soul perfectly fits Socrates' account of the unjust soul in Book IV, and the tyrannical person engages (574a–d) in the sorts of activities he identifies as unjust in Book IV (442e–443a). According to Socrates, it is this frenzied and tormented person, rather than Glaucon's coolly calculating selective lawbreaker (360e–361a), who exemplifies 'complete injustice'. However cool and calculating the selective lawbreaker may be, his self-discipline will eventually degenerate into the tormented psychological conflict that Socrates has identified as injustice.

One problem with this explanation is that the psychological degeneration that Socrates describes occurs across generations, rather than in the life of a single person. It is the son of the timocratic father who develops the oligarchic psyche, and the latter's son who develops the democratic psyche, and so on (549c–d; 558c–d, 572b–e). The 'psychology of decline' establishes at most that psychological constitutions that allow for overreaching cannot be stably transmitted across generations. This is an important point for the political project of the *Republic* (as we will see later), but it does not show that an individual person whose psychology allows some disciplined over-reaching will himself or herself inevitably develop the strife-laden 'unjust' psyche.

The norms of the *polis*

Let us now consider a different explanation of Socrates' confidence that the psychological state he identifies as justice will never issue in unjust behaviour. Socrates raises this issue in Book IV by asking whether 'someone similar in nature and training to our city' (442e4–6) would embezzle, rob, betray friends, and so forth – to which Glaucon readily responds in the negative. In framing his question thus, Socrates indicates that the just psyche is not only analogous to the just city ('similar in nature'), but also arises from the same kind of training.

The training that makes the city just is the education of the guardians detailed in Books II and III. Recall that the problem to be solved by their education is that of reconciling the ferocity and aggressiveness that qualify them as effective soldiers with the gentleness and restraint that qualify them as proper rulers (375a–376c). These are the opposing tendencies that underlie the Homeric and political conceptions of excellence: on the one hand, the tendency to use force and aggression, on the other, to use persuasion (399a–c). Each tendency is valuable and important in a city, and similarly in a human life, and the task of education (*paideia*), Plato tells us in the *Republic*, *Statesman* and *Laws*, is to harmonize these tendencies with each other under the guidance of wisdom.[74] So harmonized (*Rep.* 441d–442a), they yield the psychological condition that Socrates calls 'justice' (*Rep.* 442a–d; cf. *Laws* 631c–d).

The two traditional components of *paideia* are cultural education (*mousikê*) and physical training (*gumnastikê*) (*Rep.* 376e, 441e; *Laws* 795d, 672e; cf. 764c). Physical training includes athletic and military exercises, which rouses and strengthens our spiritedness, while cultural education (mainly poetry, literature, and music) tempers spiritedness and inculcates the norms in the light of which the two tendencies are to be regulated (*Rep.* 410b–412b).[75] Socrates complains at length and in detail in Books II and III of the *Republic* (e.g. 377c–378e) that the poetry that dominates the traditional curriculum provides unsuitable norms for this task. The only poems and stories to be allowed in the properly functioning city will be ones that encourage the listener to be pious, respectful of elders, and serious about having friendly relations with fellow citizens (*Rep.* 386a). Permissible poems must encourage the young guardians and auxiliaries to be courageous, by showing fortitude in the face of death or other misfortune (386a–389d), as well as temperate – not money-lovers, bribe-takers, or otherwise inclined to wickedness (389d–392a).[76]

It is not at all surprising that people educated in this way should be averse to all the types of unjust activity listed by Socrates in his list of 'ordinary cases': embezzlement, temple robbery (the ancient equivalent of bank robbery), theft, betrayal of friends or city and the like (442e–443a). The norms in the light of which the three parts of the soul have been harmonized under reason's leadership are, in effect, precisely those about which Glaucon and Adeimantus have raised their question.[77] Now, this isn't entirely to beg the question against the brothers, for Socrates has been asked to show the benefits of following such norms, and he does demonstrate the benefit a person gets from internalizing such norms in rational self-control. One might still object, however, that one could get the same benefit from internalizing a different set of norms. Couldn't one have just as much self-control and psychological harmony if the norms around which one's psyche was organized allowed a little temple robbery, a little judicious betrayal, and so on?

This objection, in effect, is to ask about a set of norms that violate the goals of the *polis*. It is no accident that Plato has Socrates address the challenge to justice in the context of an account of a well-functioning city – and in particular of the programme of education intended for the citizens thereof. The norms to be inculcated in such education are those that allow fellow-citizens to engage successfully in the long-term project of living together in cooperation rather than conflict. And if the city is to survive, the norms must be ones that can be perpetuated from one generation to another. Recall that the psychological degeneration outlined in Books VIII–IX takes place across generations, not within a single person. Since the excellence of a citizen (and of a ruler) must be capable of being perpetuated stably across generations, it cannot accommodate anti-social norms of the sort that this objection posits.

The kind of excellence that all the ambitious seekers we encounter in Plato claim to desire is *political* excellence: excellence in the context of a city.[78] Their pursuit of excellence is public, and its success understood to be admirable. Any ideal of such excellence that violates the norms of the city by allowing cheating, backstabbing, or treachery against fellow citizens is one that cannot be publicly affirmed without incurring shame – hence the repeated motif of embarrassment in the *Gorgias*, on the part of those who, like Gorgias and Polus, are 'too ashamed to say what they really think' (*Gorg.* 482c–d, 488e–489b, 508b–c). Thus the orator Gorgias allows under pressure of Socrates' cross-examination that he will, after all, teach his pupils to be just (460a) and Polus concedes that it is at any rate shameful to commit injustice (474c). In Protagoras' Great Speech, justice goes hand and hand with a sense of shame (*Pr.* 322c–d).

The challenge to justice in Plato's dialogues is raised from the perspective of an individual seeker after excellence – someone who wants to live a great life, but doubts whether justice is a help rather than a hindrance in this pursuit. Plato's answer to that challenge, by contrast, takes the perspective of the statesman (*politikos*) who is concerned with the welfare of the citizens and with the success and longevity of the *polis* itself. From this perspective, the question is not 'how do I become good?', but 'how to make the citizens good?'[79] – hence Plato's preoccupation with education (*paideia*) in the *Republic* and *Laws*.[80] His goal is to articulate and defend a conception of excellence that is civic and political – one that can be inculcated in the citizens of a *polis* collectively, and that can be perpetuated stably across generations. On such a conception of political excellence, a person's competence to take on a leadership role in politics is to be judged by how firmly and unwaveringly he is loyal to the common project of the *polis* (412d–e). The alternative norms we have considered ('the norms of injustice') can be neither employed in the *polis* by the population in general, nor stably perpetuated across generations. Thus they cannot qualify as the norms for political excellence.[81]

Paideia: learning to be good

On the conception of political excellence defended in Plato's dialogues, the task of the true *politikos* is not to enrich himself but to benefit the citizens or 'make them good'.[82] In the *Euthydemus*, we saw, Socrates argues that knowledge is the only truly beneficial thing (281e). This knowledge of good and bad, or what we might call 'the using craft', is what one needs, according to dialogues such as *Laches* and *Charmides*, in order to be excellent. One might then expect that the ruler's job is to impart this knowledge to the citizens (cf. *Euthd.* 292c–d). But do the rulers in the city described in the *Republic* inculcate such knowledge in the citizens whom they are supposed to be benefiting? No clear answer is given in Books I–IV of the *Republic*, which we have been considering so far. However, in Books V–VII, which introduce and develop the provocative thesis that the well-functioning *polis* must be governed by philosophers, Socrates makes it clear that it is only the philosopher-rulers, not all those who receive the education outlined in Books II–III, who have the requisite knowledge (521d–522a). The education (*paideia*) that harmonizes the aggressiveness and gentleness of the would-be guardians only 'prepares the way' for such knowledge (*Rep.* 402a, *Laws* 653a–c, cf. *Rep.* 429d–e), whose acquisition requires many additional years of study in a demanding intellectual curriculum (*Rep.* 539d–540b).

Before turning to examine this curriculum and the kind of knowledge that it is supposed to yield, let us look more closely at the education (*paideia*) that prepares the way for it. The programme of musical instruction detailed at length in *Republic* Books II–III (376d–412b) is for all citizens who have the natural aptitude to become members of the ruling or auxiliary classes.[83] The two traditional components of *paideia* in Plato's time are, as we saw above, *mousikê* and *gymnastikê*. The latter is physical training, on which Socrates spends relatively little time in the discussion (*Rep.* 403c–410a, *Laws* 795d–796d).[84] The former, which Socrates takes to be the more important (*Rep.* 401d) includes a wide range of cultural education, not just what we would call 'music' proper. But music in the strict sense (melody, harmony, and rhythm) is inextricable from the poetry that typically dominates the traditional curriculum; thus, for simplicity, I shall refer to this part of *paideia* as 'music' or 'musical'.

'Musical' training aims at cultivating a person's feelings of pleasure and pain (*Laws* 653a–c; cf. *Rep.* 403c, *Laws* 636d–e, 643d–645b).[85] It begins in earliest childhood, with the stories about gods and heroes that children are told and sung (*Rep.* 377a–378b, 395c; *Laws* 664b–c), even the games they play (*Laws* 643a–d). Plato's dominant speakers (Socrates in the *Republic* and the Athenian in the *Laws*) insist that it is of the utmost importance that the content of these stories, as well as their harmonies and rhythms, be strictly controlled.[86] As they grow older, children and youths memorize and recite stories and poems (*Laws* 654a–c, 811a). Such public performance, rather than silent reading, was the standard way of experiencing literature in Plato's time. Since reciting a speech (as opposed to narrating events in the third person) amounts to 'imitating' the character of the speaker, the effect, especially after repetition, is to mould the performer's psyche to be like what he imitates (*Rep.* 395c–d; *Laws* 655d–656a; cf. 668b). Thus Socrates in the *Republic* further restricts the content of allowable literature to allow the first person to be used only for the words of good characters. The words of inferior persons must be presented in reported rather than direct speech (*Rep.* 394d–398b).

As the Athenian stresses in the *Laws*, performing such poetry uses not only the voice, but the whole body (*Laws* 654b), since the words are sung and accompanied by dance.[87] The melody and rhythm must be suitable to the content of the words (*Rep.* 398d; *Laws* 655a–b, 660a). Given the power of melody and rhythm to insinuate themselves into a person's psyche (*Rep.* 401d), the regular performance of suitable poetry will have the effect that the character imitated becomes pleasant to the performer. The performer finds the words and deeds of such a character to be congenial when he encounters them in real life, whereas he experiences the opposing character as unpleasant and alien (*Rep.* 396d–e; *Laws* 655e–656a).

Thus trained, a citizen will come to love and perceive as *kalon* people of good character, and to feel disgust at those with the opposite character (*Laws* 654d). Such a person will take pleasure in the prospect of being 'a complete citizen, ruling and being ruled with justice' (643e5–6). As a result, he will feel disgusted at the prospect of committing injustice – the very thing that Adeimantus implies is needed in order to resist the apparent attractions of committing injustice (*Rep.* 366c). This is what Socrates means when he says that the goal of *paideia* is to inculcate in us a love (*erôs*) for the *kalon* (403c; cf. 401d–402a).

The term *kalon* and its opposite *aischron* are also properly translated 'beautiful', and 'ugly', respectively. They apply not only to narrowly ethical categories of evaluation, but to the aesthetic dimension as well. Hence Socrates in the *Republic* insists that art and architecture must be as tightly controlled as stories and music (401b–d). Beauty, Plato's dominant speakers insist, is not in the eye of the beholder. What is beautiful in character, words, and action is akin to what is beautiful in architecture because the excellence of a soul that *paideia* aims to inculcate is a kind of order (*taxis*) or harmony (*harmonia*) (*Gorg.* 503e–504e, 506d–507a; *Rep.* 410e, 522a), which mirrors the order or the cosmos (*Gorg.* 507e–508a; cf. *Tim.* 30a, 47b–c, *Laws* 966e, 967b).[88] While we are naturally constituted so as to enjoy order – and especially, from an early age, the order manifested in rhythm (*Laws* 653d–654a), this capacity must be trained by exposure to and practice in the right sorts of rhythms and orders (659d–660a). Since one can be mistaken in one's judgments about what is *kalon* and *aischron* no less than in one's judgments about what is large and small,[89] it is important to be surrounded not only by truly beautiful stories, melodies, and rhythms, but also by beautiful artefacts and architecture, so that from all sides one's soul will be nurtured in its appreciation for and ability to take pleasure in what is truly *kalon* (*Rep.* 401d–e, 403c).[90]

Our ethical and aesthetic sensibilities, thus cultivated, prepare the way for the later development of knowledge (*Rep.* 401d–402a, *Laws* 653a–c; cf. *Rep.* 429d–e)[91] because what *paideia* inculcates is not a vague Pollyanna-like desire to do good, but rather a developed discriminatory capacity for recognizing what is good and bad. The properly cultivated person is able to identify instances of what is fine and the opposite, not only in material objects, but also in actions and characters (*Rep.* 402c). To these he reacts both with feelings of pleasure (or displeasure) and with the judgment that this is *kalon* (or *aischron*). These desires and feelings, on the one hand, and judgments, on the other, are not fully separable from each other. As the Athenian says in the *Laws*, 'We are pleased when we think we are doing well (*eu prattein*), and when we are pleased we think we are doing well' (*Laws* 657c5–6; my translation). On the view that emerges across Plato's dialogues, knowing (or even believing) that something is good requires that one desire or take pleasure in it. Hence learning to take pleasure in something is part of learning that it is good.[92]

There is no such thing, on this view, as knowingly doing wrong. We all want the good (*Rep.* 505e, *Meno* 78b). That is, whenever we do something, we do it for the sake of the good (*Gorg.* 467c–468b). Thus, if we do something bad, our action must be explained by ignorance (*Laws* 860d–861a; cf. 731c, 863c–d). Cases in which it appears that someone knows his action is wrong, but is led to do it anyway because of his emotions or desires, are really cases of ignorance, Socrates argues in the *Protagoras* (353a–357e; cf. *Tim.* 86b–c, *Soph.* 228b–230d). Such a person doesn't even really believe that his action is wrong (*Pr.* 358c–d).[93] Even in the *Republic*, where the division of the psyche in Book IV explicitly allows that a person's rational impulses can conflict with her emotions and desires (439b–440a), Socrates insists that those who are properly qualified to become rulers, and thus to undertake the course of higher education that leads to knowledge, will have proved to be best at retaining the lessons of the 'musical' training that has cultivated their ethical sensibilities (*Rep.* 412d–414a).

Knowledge: understanding the good

Knowledge, for Plato and his successors, is not simply a matter of having correct beliefs. Plato's Socrates readily allows that the programme of *paideia* outlined in the *Republic* will instil in the citizens true beliefs about right and wrong (*Rep.* 430b3) and the ability to discriminate between right and wrong, and good and bad (*Rep.* 401d–402c). Nonetheless, he claims, it does not yield knowledge (521d–522a). In the *Meno* he has explained that one has knowledge when one's correct beliefs have been 'tied down' or made secure by reasoning (*logismos*) about the explanation (or cause, *aitia* – *Meno* 97e–98a; cf. *Rep.* 534b).[94] In the *Phaedo* he tells us that the ultimate explanations (or causes) of things are super-sensible realities – sometimes called 'forms' (*eidê*) or 'ideas' (*ideai*) (*Phd.* 66e, 100b–e). In Books V–VI of the *Republic*, Socrates indicates that knowledge involves the grasp, by the intellect, of these forms (*Rep.* 476c–d, 479a–480a, 504e–506a, 511a–e; cf. *Phdr.* 247c–e).[95]

Book VII of the *Republic* outlines the further course of studies that leads to the grasp of forms. At the age of twenty, those who are most accomplished in *paideia* are enrolled in a sequence of studies designed to train the intellect to detach from the body and from the sensible world in general (*Rep.* 521c–d, 523a–525a, 526a–b, 527b). It begins with arithmetic (522c–526c) and geometry (526c–528d) – preliminary versions of which were learned through childhood games (536e) – continues with astronomy (528e–530c) and harmonics (530d–531c), and culminates with the study of 'dialectic' (532a–535a). This is the discipline by which the successful philosopher will ascend to grasp the first principles of all things – the fine itself, the just itself, and the good on which all these things depend (533e–534c, 508d–509a).[96]

To engage in 'dialectic' is to inquire into the principles or reasons that explain and justify the beliefs one has so far taken for granted in one's inquiries. One's intellectual studies up to this point have investigated what follows *from* the basic hypotheses (*axiômata*) of arithmetic, geometry, and so on (510b, 533b–d). To engage in dialectic is to try to go above these hypotheses, and uncover their bases, 'the unhypothetical first principles' (510b–511d) on which all of arithmetic, geometry, astronomy, etc. depend. These 'first principles' are the forms. Having grasped them, one then understands and has knowledge of arithmetic, geometry, and all the other sciences that one previously understood only 'on a hypothesis'. The same goes for ethical truths. Dialectic aims at grasping the bases of the norms that *paideia* has inculcated into one's ethical sensibility (538c). On Plato's world view, it is the fine (*kalon*) and the good (*agathon*) that underlie all truths, be they truths of mathematics or truths of morality.[97]

Inquiry into the grounds of ethical claims, Socrates says in the *Republic*, is dangerous if engaged in at too young an age (*Rep.* 539a–c; cf. *Laws* 634e). Without a firm and stable commitment to the ethical truths under examination, and without proficiency at dialectic (as practised in geometry, astronomy, and the other intellectual disciplines of the philosophical curriculum), frustration at the difficulty of finding the rationale behind such common precepts of justice as 'return what you've borrowed' or 'keep your promises' can lead to doubt of the precepts themselves. It might open one up to persuasion by the arguments of those who criticize justice as 'another's good', thus leading to the amoralism and scepticism that were popularly feared to be the results of the kinds of inquiry inaugurated by intellectuals in the 5th century, and that led to the charges against Socrates.

Properly conducted, however, and by persons of a suitable maturity and training, dialectic is capable of taking the inquirer beyond his original ethical commitments without undermining them to grasp the ultimate first principle of morality and of reality: the form of the good (*Rep.* 539c–540a). In contrast to the objects of perception, the forms are eternal, unchanging realities (*Phd.* 65d–66a, 78c–79a; *Rep.* 479d–480a). As such, they are divine and godlike. The philosopher, who engages in dialectic in order to gain knowledge by grasping the forms seeks to become as much like them as possible (*Phd.* 79d–80b; cf. 84a–b). Indeed, the pursuit of wisdom is regularly described in Plato as seeking to 'assimilate oneself to the divine' or 'become like god.'[98]

The philosopher who has succeeded in assimilating himself to the divine occupies what Socrates describes as the 'pure realm' (*Rep.* 520d8). One who achieves such divine assimilation enjoys the most perfect happiness of which anyone is capable (*Rep.* 516d, 519c, 540b–c; cf. 581d–e). This condition is a far cry from that achieved by the properly 'cultivated' citizen, whose *paideia* has incorporated into his dispositions the norms of civil life and who interacts on amicable and reciprocal terms with his fellow citizens. The philosophical life of pure and uninterrupted intellectual activity is superior to the public life of a political leader (519c–520a) to such an extent that philosophers will be disinclined to engage in the mundane concerns of life in the city (517c, 519c), and it is only for reasons of justice that they will agree to come down from their ivory tower and rule the city (519d–520d, 540b). As rulers of the city, philosophers must concern themselves not with the divine forms of justice and goodness, but with changeable, pale imitations of these in the sensible world (*Rep.* 520c, 540b).

The competing pulls of the philosophical life and the political life as standards of human excellence will reappear again in Aristotle's account of human happiness.[99] For our present purposes we may note that the experience of the philosophical life in all its splendour supplies the philosopher with the two main qualifications for holding public office. First of all, he is not eager to rule; he sees holding public office as a cost and a burden that takes him away from a better life he could be living (500b–c, 520e–521a). This distinguishes him from most of the seekers of excellence we encounter in Plato, who are eager to exercise power in the city. Those who are eager to rule are most likely to rule badly and ruin the city, Socrates claims (426b–d, 520c–d, 521a–b; cf. 345d–347d), since what attracts these would-be statesmen to the prospect of ruling is not the benefits they can bring to the city and its citizens, but the advantage they hope to gain for themselves. The philosopher's unwillingness to rule is a safeguard against such improper and dangerous motivation.

The philosophers' second and decisive qualification to rule is the fact that they possess knowledge of the good, the *kalon*, and justice (*Rep.* 517b–c, 520c–d), and can apply this knowledge to the circumstances of life in the *polis*. Philosophers' grasp of these unchanging realities makes them the best qualified to make laws for the city, to identify threats internal and external to the city's well-being, and to design and maintain the city's institutions. In particular, their knowledge qualifies them to determine what norms will be inculcated into the citizens in *paideia* (500d–501b).

With such norms inculcated in their psyches, the citizens get the benefit of the ruler's knowledge of the good and the fine, even if their own grasp falls short of the conditions for knowledge. Proper *paideia* passes on to the citizens a version of the philosopher's 'divine reason' (*Rep.* 590d4):

> We don't allow [children] to be free until we establish a constitution (*politeia*) in them, just as in a city, and – by fostering their best parts with our own – equip them with a guardian and ruler similar to our own to take our place. Then, and only then, we set them free.
>
> (*Rep.* 590e2–591a3)

The institutions of the city thus provide for what we may call the 'social diffusion' of the philosophers' knowledge. The firm dispositions inculcated in the citizens by the knowledgeable rulers enable them to recognize and respond appropriately to what is fine and shameful and thus to use properly such external goods as health, wealth, and power, and to pursue them appropriately – at least within the constraints set for them by the legislators.[100]

Virtue and external goods

While Plato argues that it is impossible to derive any benefit from the external goods unless one has knowledge, and hence virtue, later philosophers raise a further question: whether, if one has this knowledge, one still needs the external goods? That is, if a person possesses virtue and acts virtuously but fails to secure such things as health, financial stability and material comfort, is he nonetheless happy? Stoic philosophers, a century and more after Plato, answered this question with a vigorous affirmative, while their Peripatetic contemporaries (heirs of Aristotle) insist on the negative (Cicero, *Fin.* 3.41–44).

However astounding the Stoic answer may be (and we will examine their reasons for it in Chapter 5), the question itself deserves comment. To be in a position to ask it, one must have travelled a significant philosophical distance from the context in which Plato begins his ethical theorizing. Recall that Socrates' arguments are addressed to those who take it for granted that such things as health and wealth are what make one happy (*Euthd.* 279a–c), and that 'virtue' (*aretê*) is the life in which one makes use of and enjoys such advantages (*Meno* 77b–78b). On such assumptions about *aretê* and happiness, excellence involves success in the pursuit of external goods, and it makes no sense to wonder whether one can be happy (or even excellent) without such external success. It takes Plato's philosophical development of the notions of excellence and happiness to open the way to raising the question.

Through the figure of Socrates, Plato develops an alternative conception of excellence. Rather than external success in life, it is the internal perfection of a person, a 'state of one's soul'.[101] With *aretê* thus internalized (which naturally suits the translation 'virtue'), it is possible to distinguish it from the external success with which it was originally associated, and conceptualize the possibility of a life that has the former but lacks the latter: that of the good person who is wise, courageous, temperate and just, but extremely unfortunate in his pursuit of the external advantages. The most extreme version of such a case is described by Glaucon: the good person who nonetheless has a reputation for great injustice (*Rep.* 361c), and as a result is 'whipped, stretched on a rack, chained, blinded with fire, and at the end, when he has suffered every kind of evil . . . impaled' (*Rep.* 361e4–362a2; cf. *Gorg.* 473c). Such a person has virtue in the internal sense identified by Plato, but lacks all the sought after 'external goods' – including even the minimal condition of freedom from pain.

The figure of 'the good person on the rack' becomes a chestnut among later philosophers, and the question about virtue and external goods tends to be formulated as whether the good person on the rack is happy.[102] However, even though the figure originates in Plato it is far from clear what Plato's answer would be to the question, which is never raised explicitly in his dialogues. The Stoics, who claim that the good person is happy even in such circumstances, take their inspiration from Plato – in particular from Socrates' famous dictum that 'the good person can't be harmed' (*Ap.* 41d; cf. *Gorg.* 527d).[103] Later Platonists also interpret Plato as subscribing to the Stoic view that virtue alone is sufficient for happiness.[104]

How plausible is this as an interpretation of Plato?[105] To be sure, many things said by the dominant characters in his dialogues are quite suggestive of such a position. If the good man can't be harmed, doesn't this show that the sorts of losses that can be visited upon him by others (the loss of property, family, reputation, and bodily integrity, or the experience of excruciating and unremitting pain) make no difference to his well-being? Perhaps not, for we have seen that in the *Euthydemus*, which provides arguments in support of this inspirational proclamation from the *Apology*, Socrates' exhortation to 'love wisdom (*philosophein*) and care for virtue' (*Euthd.* 275a; cf. 278d) is based in part on the argument that wisdom secures one against ill fortune (279d–80a). That is, wisdom assures us against the loss of the external goods that happiness is ordinarily taken to involve.[106] Given this assumption (however dubious it may be), virtuous activity would indeed suffice for happiness; however, it would secure the external goods as well. Thus Socrates in the *Euthydemus* does not endorse the position that virtue makes one happy even without the external goods.

The *Republic* gives mixed signals about whether a person can be happy without external goods. Socrates requires that the education of the guardians inculcates in them the disposition to withstand with equanimity misfortunes such as impoverishment, the loss of loved ones, and so on (*Rep.* 387d–388d; cf. *Laws* 632a–b). This is the appropriate attitude to take if virtue is the only thing that makes a life good.[107] However, the thesis about the goodness of justice that Glaucon and Adeimantus challenge Socrates to prove is a comparative thesis, not a sufficiency thesis.[108] Socrates devotes the argument of books II–X to answering the question of whether one is *better off* being just, thereby forgoing the external advantages that one might gain from successful injustice, than one would be as a result of committing successful injustice. Even if the former life is better than the latter one, it does not follow that all versions of the former (including the just person on the rack) are themselves happy – unless we assume that any unhappy life is just as bad as any other. Absent this assumption, the just person on the rack can still be better off than the successful unjust person (in virtue of the latter's inner psychological turmoil), even if his own physical torments prevent him from being happy.[109]

In the *Gorgias*, Socrates indicates that it is possible to rank unhappy lives as better and worse (*Gorg.* 469b; cf. 473d–e). There, as in the *Republic*, his main argument is for a comparative thesis about virtue – in this case, that one is better off being unjustly treated (and thereby losing external goods) than in committing such injustice (*Gorg.* 474c–475c, 508c–509c). Still, in at least two places, he says explicitly that the virtuous person is happy (470e, 507b–c). These are not, however, in contexts that raise the possibility that the virtuous person might be lacking in external goods. Indeed, the assertion at 470e concerns the Great King of Persia – renowned for his wealth and power. At 507b–c, Socrates' claim concerns the scenario in which one might increase one's external goods by acting intemperately. It is not a situation in which one risks falling below even a minimal level of such goods.

The evidence in the *Laws* is similarly inconclusive. Here there is no spectre of the good person on the rack, just a sober discussion among would-be legislators about the best laws to institute for a real, soon-to-be founded city, in contrast to the ideal city of the *Republic*.[110] A number of passages in *Laws* 660e–663d would seem to support the sufficiency thesis.[111] Furthermore, we are told, the main goal of the legislators is to instil virtue in the citizens (631a), and in particular to cultivate their attitudes towards the external goods of health, wealth, and so on – here called 'human goods', in contrast with the 'divine goods' of wisdom, temperance, courage and justice (631b–d).[112] Nonetheless, the message that the legislator is supposed to teach the citizens is *not* that the divine goods are all one needs in order to be happy. It is rather that the human goods depend on the divine ones: health and wealth and the like are not good unless guided by the wisdom that informs the virtues (661c). This amounts at most to the necessity thesis, not the sufficiency thesis.

As city planners, the legislators in the *Laws* are quite naturally concerned with ensuring that the citizens will be adequately supplied with the human goods. The 'great benefits' they supply to the citizens include the human goods (631b). These include an adequate food supply, sufficient private property, and honour (as reflected, for example, in funeral rites and interactions between generations).[113] Even though they aim to protect the citizens against the corrupting effects of excessive quantities of such goods,[114] the legislators can hardly use as a guiding principle for their legislation the maxim that human beings can achieve happiness even without the 'human goods'. To the extent that such a principle is true, it applies to individual persons, not to a *polis* or other community.

Plato's Socrates in the *Republic* and the Athenian in *Laws* adopt a political rather than individual approach to raising ethical questions. Instead of focusing on an individual person's question, 'How do I become good?' or 'How do I become happy?', they take the perspective of the statesman or legislator concerned with how to make the citizens good and happy. Given this perspective, it is unlikely that either work is conceived by Plato as addressing the question: can a virtuous person be happy even if he lacks the external goods? Without good reason to suppose that Plato is addressing this question, we should be wary of trying to divine his answer to it. For similar reasons, we should be wary of finding an answer to this question in the *Euthydemus*, where Socrates' goal is to exhort us to care about philosophy and virtue, or in the *Gorgias*, where Plato's project is to establish the importance of cultivating knowledge and self-control. Given these purposes, either the necessity thesis or the sufficiency thesis will do.

We may conclude that although Plato's ethical philosophy paves the way to raising the question of whether the external goods are necessary for happiness, he himself fails to articulate the question or to address it in any of his works. It remains for his philosophical successors to engage in that debate.

Notes

1 For a discussion of these ethical attitudes, see Kahn 1998; Irwin 1977: 13–30, and 1992. The fifth-century philosopher Democritus also addressed ethical questions, and his writings, now largely lost to us, influenced later Epicurean ethics. On Democritean ethics, see Warren 2002.

2 On the importance of poetry in education, see *Pr.* 339a. Xenophon tells us that the general Nicias (who appears in Plato's dialogue *Laches*) had his son Niceratus memorize all of Homer (Xenophon, *Symposium* III 5). Characters in Plato often quote from Homer and other poets from memory (*Rep.* 331a, 362b, 379d–380a and passim; *Gorg.* 484b; *Pr.* 339b–c).

3 Relish for argument as a spectator sport is dramatized in dialogues such as *Euthd.* 271a, 274d, 304d–e, *Gorg.* 447a–448a, 458c–d, 506b; *Pr.* 335d, *Rep.* 338a; *Ap.* 23c; *H. Maj.* 282c, 286a–e.

4 The few remaining fragments of the sophists' writing are collected in Diels and Kranz 1952 and translated into English in Freeman 1948, Sprague 1972, and Waterfield 2000. On Sophists in the fifth century, see Guthrie 1971, Kerferd 1981, and Adkins 1973. On Plato's portrait of the sophists see Sidgwick 1905 and Nehamas 1990.

5 On the expression of hostility to the sophists, see *Meno* (91a–92b; cf. 96a–b) as well as *Pr.* 316c–317d; *Gorg.* 519e–520b; *Eu.* 3c–d; *Euthd.* 306e–307a.

6 On the struggle to appropriate the term 'philosophy' (*philosophia*) see Nightingale 1995.

7 Aristophanes' comedy *Clouds*, which was written during Socrates' lifetime, portrays Socrates as a sophist who corrupts the youth by teaching them to 'make the weaker argument the stronger'. On this portrait, and the stock charges against the sophists, see Plato, *Ap.* 18a–19d. On the original, non-pejorative meaning of 'sophist', see Guthrie 1971: 27–34.

8 On the historical status of the characters in Plato's dialogues, see Nails 2002: 288–90.

9 For example, the *Gorgias* contains many conflicting indications of the dramatic date, from 429 (shortly after the death of Pericles) to no earlier than 411 (the date of Euripides' *Antiope*). See Dodds 1959: 17–18. In *Menexenus*, Socrates delivers a funeral oration for Athenians fallen in battle, including those who died during the Corinthian war of 395–87 BCE, which took place after the historical Socrates' death in 399.

10 For differing views on the historical accuracy of Plato's depiction of Socrates, see Irwin 1977, 1995 and Vlastos 1991 (who take some of the dialogues to present an accurate account of Socrates' own views, if not of his actual words), and Kahn 1992 and 1996 (who argues against this position). For scepticism about the extent to which Plato's dialogues can be dated relative to each other, see Kahn 1996: 42–8 and Keyser 1991 and 1992.

11 On the Socratic dialogues written by others than Plato, see the essays in Vander Waerdt 1994 and Chapter 1 of Kahn 1996. The fragmentary textual remains of the non-Platonic tradition are collected in Giannantoni 1990.

12 The hedonist Cyrenaics trace their Socratic pedigree through Aristippus, while the Cynics, who are followers of the Socratic Antisthenes, influenced the early development of Stoicism. Zeno, the founder of Stoicism, is a pupil of the Cynic Crates (DL 7.2). Thus the anti-hedonist Stoics and the hedonist Cyrenaics both claim a 'Socratic' pedigree. The main philosophical rivals of the Stoics, the Academics, also take Socrates as their model (Cicero, Ac 1.44–5). On the Socratic roots of the various Hellenistic philosophical schools, see Long 1988. More detailed discussion of Cynicism may be found in Dudley 1937, Billerbeck 1991, Branham and Goulet-Cazé (eds) 1996, and Price 2006. On the Cyrenaics, see Irwin 1991a: 57–62, Long 1992, 1999, Annas 1993: 227–36, and Fine 2003. On the Socratic roots of both schools, see McKirahan 1994.

13 For example, in the dialogue *Euthydemus*, when Socrates professes his admiration for the verbal wrangling (*eristic*, 272b10) of Euthydemus and Dionysodorus and announces his intention to become their pupil (271c–272d, 304c), Plato is clearly not intending to endorse their pseudo-intellectual practice. The dialogue as a whole has set up their practice for ridicule.

14 The famous grandfathers are Aristides, nicknamed 'the Just' (d. 467), hero of the Persian wars and opponent of Themistocles, and Thucydides, son of Melesias (b. 500), general and political opponent of Pericles in the mid-fifth century (not to be confused with the historian Thucydides). In *Meno* and *Protagoras*, Socrates adds Pericles (495–429 BCE) and the statesman Themistocles (582–462 BCE) to the list of those who failed to pass their excellence along to their sons (*Meno* 93a–94d; cf. *Pr.* 319e–320b).

15 On *paideuein* (educating) as the profession of the sophists, see *Gorg.* 519e7–8; *Euthd.* 306e4; *Pr.* 317b4.

16 On fee-charging sophists, see: *Ap.* 20b; *H. Maj.* 281b, *Meno* 91b–92b, 95e; *Pr.* 311b, 328b–c; *Gorg.* 520c–e; *Rep.* 493a, *Euthd.* 304c; cf. *La.* 201a. Socrates insists he never charged a fee: *Ap.* 19d; on the stigma of charging a fee, see *Gorg.* 520e, Guthrie 1971: 35–37.

17 Learning excellence by associating with worthy fellow citizens: *Meno* 92e; *Pr.* 316c–d; cf. *Ap.* 19e; 24e–25a. Socrates is invited to be such a mentor by the fathers in *Laches* (180e–181c; 200c–d). At *Theatetus* 150e–151a, we are told that the young Aristides became a companion of Socrates, but left his company too early.

18 Socrates refers to Gorgias as a sophist at *H. Maj.* 282b. On the alleged distinction between sophists and orators, see *Gorg.* 520a–b.

19 Aristotle (*EN* 1099b9–12) indicates that Meno's question is still alive more than a generation later, although he phrases it as a question about *eudaimonia* rather than *aretê*. Socrates expresses scepticism that excellence can be taught at *Pr.* 319a–320b, 361a–b; cf. *Euthd.* 282c–d; cf. 274e.

20 Translation by Grube in Cooper (ed.) 1997. Unless otherwise indicated, all translations from Plato will be from Cooper (ed.) 1997, with occasional adaptations to fit my own choice of terminology.

21 On the concern to acquire excellence quickly: Euthydemus and Dionysodorus advertise that they can teach excellence more quickly than anyone else (*Euthd.* 273d; cf. 304c).

22 Even the charge of corrupting the youth that was leveled against Socrates is construed as the charge that he made them 'bad citizens' (*politais ponêrais, Ap.* 25c6).

23 Political wisdom is knowledge of justice (*Charm.* 170b). Political expertise concerns what is 'just and lawful' (*Pr.* 327b3–4).

24 On the tension between the 'competitive virtues' extolled in the Homeric ideal, and the 'cooperative virtues' in the political, see Adkins 1960.

25 The English term 'virtue' comes from the Latin '*virtus*', which Cicero uses to translate the Greek '*aretê*', even though the Latin term in non-philosophical contexts connotes only a particular kind of excellence, namely, 'manliness' (from the noun '*vir*' man).

26 On the development of an internalized conception of excellence in authors before Plato, see Kahn 1998: 32–7.

27 Glaucon and Adeimantus conceive of justice as a pattern of behaviour in *Republic* II. Most of the proffered definitions of the 'virtues' offered by Socrates' interlocutors in Plato's dialogues cite types of behaviour, although the interlocutors agree readily enough to Socrates' usual suggestion that a virtue is a power (*dunamis*) of the psyche (*Charm.* 159b–160d, *La.* 191d–e). It seems that the generic notion *aretê* is more likely to be considered an activity or life, while the particular kinds of *aretê* (courage, temperance, etc.) are more easily used for or taken as powers of the soul (internal psychology) – although Heraclitus (sixth–fifth century BCE) uses *aretê* for temperate activity (Diels and Kranz 1952, B 112).

28 On the importance of birth and social status, see Homer, *Odyssey* 17.322–3; Plato, *Euthd.* 306d–e; *Rep.* 618b–619b; cf. *Pr.* 316c. On wealth as a criterion for a good reputation, see *Meno* 70a.

29 The choice of lives: *Gorg.* 472e–473d, 483b–484c, 488b, 491e–494a; *Rep.* 360d–362a, 617d–620d. On equality (*isonomia*), see *Gorg.* 483c, 489a.

30 In choice of lives in the Myth of Er in *Republic* X, Socrates characterizes a life (*bios*) as 'worthy' (*chrêstos*) or 'vile' (*ponêros*) (*Rep.* 618c4–5), using terms which more usually apply to persons. But the popular criteria surveyed here for making this choice (618c8–d4; cf. 618a7–b1) are the standard measures of the happy life: wealth, power, etc.

31 But when Meno proposes that excellence consists in acquiring 'fine things' (*kala, Meno* 77b), the things he has in mind as 'fine' (*kala*) come from the standard popular list of goods (*agatha*): wealth, etc. (78c).

32 At *Rep.* 348e–349a, Socrates indicates that it is easy to refute someone who (like Polus) claims that injustice is more advantageous, but still more shameful, than justice. In *Laws*, the Dorian interlocutors (Megillus and Cleinias) espouse a version of Polus' claim (662a), which the Athenian takes to be evidence of their faulty education (*paideia*).

33 Excellence is fine and admirable (*kalon, Pr.* 349e; *Charm.* 159c, 160e; *La.* 192c, 193d). Lysimachus and Melesias are ashamed to lack excellence (*La.* 179c6). Thus the fact that being a sophist is considered shameful (*Pr.* 312a) casts doubt on the sophists as suitable teachers of excellence.

34 cf. *Gorg.* 467c–468c and *Meno* 77c–78a.

35 Conversely, to benefit people, which is what the true ruler does to the citizens (*Rep.* 342e), is to make them better or more excellent (*Gorg.* 502e–503a; 515a–517c, 519b–520e; cf. *La.* 186c–d).

36 Excellence must be good for its possessor: *Euthd.* 279a–b, *Meno* 87e, *Charm.*
   160e–161a, 175d–176a; *La.* 192c–d; cf. *Rep.* 336d; *Pr.* 360b. On this guiding
   assumption, see Irwin 1977: 39, 1995: 48–9.
37 We might say that the shared assumption is part of the formal conception of
   excellence, while the view that justice is an excellence is a substantive concep
   tion of excellence. A parallel point is often made about the two sorts of claims
   Aristotle makes about happiness in *EN* I.
38 In this context (*Euthd.* 279a–281e), temperance (*sôphrosunê*) and courage
   (*andreia*) are not the virtues defined by Socrates in the *Republic* (442b–d; cf.
   429b–433b), but more like the so-called 'natural virtues' Aristotle mentions
   in *EN* 1144b4–14. Here in *Euthydemus*, Socrates uses the notions of courage
   and temperance as they are popularly understood, and as the Eleatic Stranger
   uses the terms in *Stsm.* 306a–308a: that is, as tendencies towards restraint and
   towards aggression respectively. These dispositions are only 'part of virtue'
   (*Stsm.* 306a–b), in the sense that they need to be tempered with a correct
   opinion about what is fine, good, and just (309c) in order to be fully-fledged
   courage and temperance (*Stsm.* 309b–e; cf. *Rep.* 410e–412a). On courage and
   temperance in the *Statesman*, see Rowe 1995: 242–5; Lane 1998; and Hobbs
   2000: 262–7.
39 On the argument at *Euthd.* 278e–282a, see also Irwin 1995: 55–8 and
   McPherran 2005.
40 In contrast, Aristotle explicitly rejects this expansion of courage, which he
   insists is a purely military virtue (*EN* 1115a17–31).
41 In the *Laches*, Nicias introduces the proposal that courage is a kind of wisdom (194d). He attributes the proposal to Socrates and explains that the
   wisdom in question concerns when it is good to pursue such goods as life and
   health and when it is not (195b–d, cf. *Charm.* 164b–c).
42 On the connection between temperance and modesty see *Pr.* 322c–323a.
43 Homer, *Odyssey* xvii.347, quoted by Socrates at *Charm.* 161a, and again
   at *La.* 201b.
44 Critias' proposal that temperance is a 'science of science' (*Charm.* 166e)
   recalls the 'using science' of the *Laches* and *Euthydemus*. But Socrates first
   interprets it as 'knowledge of what one knows and does not know' (*Charm.*
   167b). After raising problems about the subject matter of such knowledge
   (169d–171c), he asks how it could be beneficial (as temperance must be). He
   considers two proposals. On the first, such knowledge would benefit us
   because everyone would stick to doing what he is skilled at doing. Thus all
   the first-order crafts would be practised excellently; we would have excellent
   food, clothes, shelter, armies, etc. (171d–172d; cf. 167a). The second proposal
   (173a–175a) calls into question the assumptions about benefit in the first:
   without the additional science of good and evil, one will not be in a position
   to benefit from these other craft products. Socrates then complains that the
   benefit would come, not from temperance, but from the science of good and
   evil (174d–175a). So temperance, construed as a 'science of science', turns out
   to be of no discernible benefit. An obvious response to this difficulty is to
   identify temperance with the science of good and evil (i.e. with the 'using
   craft' of the *Laches* and *Euthydemus*).
45 Socrates seeks wisdom concerning the greatest human concerns (*ta megista*): *Ap.*
   22d–e; cf. *Gorg.* 487b; *La.* 200a; *Rep.* 504a–505a. In the *Statesman*, the Eleatic
   Stranger characterizes the statesman's craft as the 'finest and greatest' knowledge
   concerned with human beings (*Stsm.* 281d; here the weaver's knowledge is
   invoked as the analogue of the statesman's; cf. 289c–d, 291a–c, 303d–304a).

46 Socrates explicitly identifies politics as the requisite knowledge only at *Euthd.* 291b–d, where he resumes the conclusions of the argument at 288b–290d, but this makes it clear that he takes it to have been established in that prior argument.

47 Socrates embarrasses Gorgias into claiming that he does after all teach his students to be just (*Gorg.* 460a), but this involves him in a contradiction at 461a. Callicles comments on Gorgias' embarrassment at 482c–d.

48 Socrates turns on its head the notion that rhetoric is to be valued because it allows the guilty person to escape legal sanctions (*Gorg.* 480a–d).

49 See *Lys.* 207d–210c for criticism of the ideal of doing what you want.

50 See Irwin 1995: 107.

51 Thus the knowledge of how to live well is not the knowledge of how to preserve one's life (as in the parallel with the skilled diver at *La.* 193a–c). At *Gorg.* 512d–513a, Socrates distinguishes the pilot's life-saving knowledge from the competence characteristic of the excellent person (cf. *Charm.* 174b).

52 That temperance is 'minding one's own business' (*to ta heautou prattein*) is first articulated by Charmides at 161b, but Socrates, not unreasonably, attributes the proposal to Critias (*Charm.* 161c and 162a–d). 'Minding one's own business' reappears in the *Republic* – this time as the definition of justice (*Rep.* 433c–434c, 443c–d).

53 On the end of the *Charmides*, see note 44 above.

54 Socrates' disavowal of knowledge has generated an enormous literature. See e.g. Vlastos 1985, Benson 2000, Brickhouse and Smith 1994, and Matthews 2006.

55 See *Republic* 505b for ridicule of the claim that the good is knowledge of the good.

56 The Eleatic Stranger (the dominant speaker in Plato's *Statesman*) explicitly denies that the statesman's knowledge can be formulated into exceptionless general principles (294b–295b). Aristotle follows Plato in this (*EN* 1094b14–22; cf. 1139a6–8).

57 Among those put to death by the Thirty were Polemarchus, son of Cephalus, who appears in *Republic* I (Lysias, 12.7), and Niceratus, son of Nicias (Xenophon *Hellenica* II 3,39; Lysias 19.47).

58 According to Thucydides, *History of the Peloponnesian War* 7.50, Nicias delayed the retreat from Epipolai by the badly beleaguered Athenian navy for 'thrice nine days' because of warnings from soothsayers. As a result of the delay the fleet was destroyed and Nicias himself was captured and executed (7.84–6). Plato's ironic mention at *La.* 195e of the wisdom of soothsayers is a deliberate reminder to his readers of Nicias' ignominious end. Nor is Plato's portrait of Laches in the dialogue *Laches* particularly flattering; he deliberately pokes fun at him in the *Symposium*, implying that he was not courageous at all (*Symp.* 221a–b, retelling the events described by Laches himself at *La.* 181b). Aristophanes pokes fun at both Nicias and Laches. He coins the verb 'to Nicianize' - (*mellonikian*, meaning to delay indecisively – *Birds* 640 and portrays Laches as a litigious dog in the comedy *Wasps*.

59 Meno's career is described in Xenophon, *Anabasis* 2.6.21–9. On the question of whether Meno's reputation among Plato's readers would be as black as the portrait Xenophon paints, see Klein 1965: 35, Bluck 1961: 124, and Sharples 1985: 18.

60 Euthyphro also appears in Plato's *Cratylus* (396d, 399e, 428c).

61 A modern reader might still object that one can have knowledge even if one's actions do not display it – for example, in cases of weakness of will. But

Plato's dominant speakers famously deny that there is any such thing as knowingly doing wrong (*Pr.* 354e–357e; *Laws* 860c–e; cf. 731c).

62 For more on divinely inspired true belief: *Ap.* 22b–c, *Ion* 533d–535a.

63 Aristides is an explicit exception to Socrates' condemnation of fifth-century leaders at *Gorg.* 526b. On his reputation for justice, see Herodotus, *Historiae* 8.79.1.

64 Although they were less successful in the end at even this enterprise, when the population turned against them (*Gorg.* 516d–516e) – hence Socrates' claim at 517a that they failed at even the flattering kind of politics.

65 On the historical Thrasymachus, see Guthrie, 1971: 294–8, Nails 2002.

66 On Socrates' arguments against Thrasymachus, see Joseph 1935: 15–40.

67 A preliminary version of the city-soul analogy is given in *Republic* I, 351c–352c.

68 The account of 'necessary desires' at *Rep.* 558d–559d indicates that 'delicacies' (*opson* – 559b1) are among the natural and appropriate objects of desire.

69 On the extent to which these qualifications are natural, as opposed to the results of social conditions, see Meyer 2005.

70 On the division of the soul in *Republic* IV, see Woods 1987; Lovibond 1991: 45–53; and Lorenz 2004. On the different parts of the soul, see Cooper 1984, Irwin 1995: chapter 15, Reeve 1988: chapters 2–3, Bobonich 2002: chapter 3; and Moss 2005.

71 The three parts of the soul are described again in at *Rep.* 580d–e; cf. *Tim.* 42a–b, 69c–72d, 90a–d.

72 A forceful statement of this objection is given by Sachs 1963, and goes back at least as far as Grote 1885, vol. 4. On Grote's formulation of the objection, see Irwin 1995: 385n10. For further discussion, see Vlastos 1971, Kraut 1973, 1992, Annas 1981: chapter 6, and Irwin 1995: chapter 15.

73 On the 'democratic soul', see Scott 2000. On the degeneration from the timocratic to the tyrannical soul, see Annas 1981: 294–305 and Irwin 1995: chapter 17, Jones 1997.

74 Education is to harmonize the aggressive and gentle (or 'philosophical') tendencies: *Rep.* 399a–c, 410c–e, 522a; *Stsm.* 306a–309c; *Laws* 681b, 649b–c. According to the Athenian in *Laws*, Dorian constitutions (such as those of Sparta) promote the aggressive tendencies (*Laws* 625c–626c, 633a–c) while Athenian institutions promote the restrained (635e–642a, cf. 666e–667a). For further discussion of these opposing tendencies, see Jones 1997; Rowe 1995: 242–5; Lane 1998; Hobbs 2000: 262–7; and Meyer 2006: 384.

75 *Rep.* 441e8–442a2 makes it explicit that the program of music and gymnastic training that harmonizes these two tendencies is what brings it about that reason rules and that spiritedness is its obedient ally.

76 The dominant speakers in the *Statesman* and the *Laws* concur that instilling these virtues in the citizens are the goals of education (*Stsm.* 306a; 308e–310a; *Laws* 630d–632d).

77 In the *Republic*, Socrates explicitly stops short of requiring that the poets teach that justice is better than injustice (392a–c), since this is the question at issue. But in the *Laws*, this teaching is part of the mandated curriculum (*Laws* 660e–663a).

78 Thus Meno and the other seekers after *arête* are labelled '*politikoi*' (*Meno* 95c), and Callicles is presented in *Gorgias* as an eager seeker of political office (*Gorg.* 515a).

79 The task of the statesman (*politikos*) is to make the citizens good: *Gorg.* 513e, 515c–e, 521a; *Rep.* 500d, *Euthd.* 292c–d, *Stsm.* 297b, *Laws* 643e; cf. *Meno*

94a; *Gorg.* 503a, 517b–c, 519b–d, *Laws* 770d–e. Thus the failure of eminent politicians to teach their alleged excellence to their sons (*Meno* 93c–94e; cf. 100a) is grounds to doubt that they were practitioners of the true political craft. And Socrates, who exhorts the Athenians to care about virtue, turns out to be the practitioner of the 'true politics' (*Gorg.* 521d).

80 Although *paideia* (education) is not emphasized in the *Statesman*, there too the true statesman is said to be responsible for educational institutions (*Stsm.* 308d–309a).

81 On this interpretation of Socrates' answer to Glaucon and Adeimantus, he does not address the so-called problem of the 'free rider' made famous by Hobbes (*Leviathan* chapter XV). He does not rule out that a single person might, with deliberation, forethought and discipline, manage to violate the norms of a city undetected, thereby reaping the benefits of injustice without incurring the ordinary judicial penalties, or the psychological penalties described by Socrates. For alternative assessments of the goals and success of Socrates' argument, see Nettleship 1901, Joseph 1935, Murphy 1962, Cross and Woozley 1964, Vlastos 1971, Kraut 1973 and 1992, Irwin 1977 and 1995, Annas 1981, Reeve 1988, White 1988, Dahl 1991, Keyt 2006.

82 On making the citizens good, see note 76.

83 Or so the 'myth of the metals' promises the citizens (*Rep.* 415a–c). For scepticism about whether the institutions of the city developed in the Republic make good on this promise to the children of the producers, see Meyer 2005.

84 In the *Laws*, the Athenian (the dominant speaker) criticizes at length political constitutions, like those of the Spartans, that over-emphasize this part of education (*Laws* 634a–b, 635b–e, 666e–667a, 673b).

85 Plato discusses 'musical training' at length in both the *Republic* and *Laws*. The accounts in the two works are consistent, complementary and overlapping; hence I supply citations from both.

86 Censorship of games: *Rep.* 424e–425a, *Laws* 643b–d. Restrictions on the content of stories: *Rep.* 377b–392c, 424b–d; *Laws* 659d–664a, 670d–671a, 801a–802e, 810e–812a, 829c–e, 886b–e; on style: *Rep.* 392c–398b; Modes and rhythms: *Rep.* 397e–399c, 400a–e; *Laws* 656a–657c, 669b–670a, 700a–701b, 814d–816d.

87 Hence the Athenian's claim that dancing counts as *gymnastikê* (physical training) as well (*Laws* 672e–673a, 795e–796a); more traditional *gymnastikê* (sports and military training) is not discussed until 796a.

88 On the cosmological dimensions to Plato's ethical thought, see Betegh 2003 and Carone 2005: chapters 3 and 10.

89 According to the Athenian in *Laws*, the proper standard for judging what is *kalon* are the pleasures of the properly educated person (*Laws* 658e–659c; cf. 654e–655d). Aristotle develops this idea in *EN* 1113a22–b1. For discussion see Gottlieb 1993.

90 On cultivating citizens' love for what is *kalon*, see Hobbs 2000: 227–30, and Richardson Lear 2006a.

91 The message of Socrates' speech in the *Symposium* is that love of the *kalon* (which the *Republic* tells us is the product of *paideia* – 403c), when itself properly cultivated, leads to knowledge (*Symp.* 210a–e).

92 Burnyeat 1980 discusses the role of pleasure in Aristotle's account of moral education. The picture applies equally well to the account of moral training in *Rep.* II–III, from which Aristotle's own account is derived.

93 For further discussion of these 'Socratic Paradoxes', see Santas 1964, Saunders 1968, Vlastos 1969, Roberts 1987, and Segvic 2006. On the relation between thought and desire in Plato, see Penner 1971.

94 The ethical beliefs of those who have had a proper *paideia* are certainly stable and firmly entrenched (*Rep.* 412e, 413c–414a), indeed 'dyed in the wool' (429d–430b). Yet their stability is not due to a grasp of the underlying reasons behind their firm moral convictions, so they do not amount to knowledge.

95 On the theory of forms, see Nehamas 1975, White 1976, Fine 1993: chapter 4; Dancy 2004, and Rowe 2005.

96 On the ascent to knowledge in Plato's Republic, see Gentzler 2005.

97 On the relation between the good (*agathon*) and the admirable (*kalon*): in the *Republic*, the good is the ultimate object of knowledge (505a, 517c) – but philosophers must know both the good and the *kalon* (506a; cf. 484d), and the good is *kalon* (508e; cf. Symp. 201c). In the *Symposium*, the *kalon* is the ultimate objective of the seeker of knowledge (*Symp.* 210d–e), but one can substitute 'good' for *kalon* (204e).

98 Reason is 'akin to the divine': *Rep.* 490a–b, 518e. Assimilation to the divine: *Phd.* 84a–b; *Rep.* 611e, 613a; cf. *Phd.* 80a–81a, 82b–c, 83e; *Rep.* 383c, 500b–d, *Tht.* 176a8–b3, *Laws* 716a, *Tim.* 90b–d. See Sedley 1997 and 1999; Annas 1999: chap. III; and Russell 2004.

99 See Aristotle, EN X 7–8, to be discussed in the next chapter.

100 In the *Republic* and *Laws* the citizens' scope of activity is tightly regulated by the state. This fits with the Eleatic Stranger's explanation in the *Statesman* that true knowledge, of the sort the statesman must have, cannot be perfectly expressed in the sorts of principles that will apply to all circumstances (*Stsm.* 294b–295a). The city designers make up for the citizens' lack of such knowledge by limiting the conditions in which they are called on to rely on their own judgment.

101 For parallel developments of the internalized conception of *aretê* in the fifth and fourth centuries, see Kahn 1998: 32–4.

102 The good person on the rack: Aristotle, *EN* 1153b18–21; Epicurus: DL 10.118); Cicero, *TD* 2.17–19, 5.31; *Fin* 2.88, 3.42; Epictetus, *Diss.* 4.1.90, 172.

103 The Stoic Antipater attributes to Plato the thesis that 'only the admirable (kalon) is good (*agathon*) (Clement, *Stromata* v 97.6 /SVF III Antipater 56, cited by Irwin 1995: 199). Irwin also cites Plutarch *St. Rep.* 1040d as evidence that the Chrysippus did not accept this interpretation.

104 The so-called 'middle Platonists' include Alcinoous, Plutarch, Apuleius and Albinus (all from the 1st and 2nd centuries CE). On their interpretations of Plato, see Annas 1999: 1–2, 43–51. On later, 'Neo Platonic', interpretations of Plato, see Gerson 2004.

105 For a fuller discussion of competing answers to this question, see Irwin 1995: 199–200, and Annas 1999: chapters 2 and 4.

106 *Apology* 30b2–4 may also make the claim that excellence secures the external goods. It is however, also possible to translate the passage as making a different claim: that excellence 'makes wealth and everything else good for men' (Grube in Cooper (ed.) 1997). On the translation of the passage, see Irwin 1995: 58–9, 363n22.

107 Hence the Stoic doctrine that the wise person will be free from all 'passions' such as grief (Cicero, *Fin.* 3.35, DL 7.116). For further discussion of the Stoic view on the passions, see Chapter 5.

108 So Irwin stresses (1995a: 191–2).

109 One might complain that the argument in *Republic* II–IV is insufficient to establish that the just person is better off than the unjust person, even if the former is on the rack. However, this objection, even if successful, would not help the case for attributing the sufficiency thesis to Plato.

110 The city of the *Republic* as an ideal: 592a–b. The non-ideal status of the city in the *Laws*: 739a–e; cf. 817b. The geographical particulars and historical circumstances leading to the founding of the city (*Laws* 702b–e, 704a–705d, 747d–e). See Morrow 1960 for a detailed discussion of the empirical and historical grounding of the legislative project in the *Laws*.

111 For different interpretations of *Laws* 660e–663d, see Annas 1999: 46–9 and Irwin 1995: 343–7.

112 The distinction between divine and human goods is discussed again at *Laws* 697b–c, 726e–728e.

113 The legislators provide for the citizens' needs (*Laws* 806d), property (729a–b, 744b–745b; cf. 847e–848b, 737a–738a), and honour (632b–c, 717a–718a).

114 The corrupting effects of excessive wealth: *Laws* 704d–705b, 729a, 743a–c, 918a–919c.

3

ARISTOTLE AND THE
PURSUIT OF HAPPINESS

Aristotle (384–323 BCE) was a member of Plato's Academy for twenty years and later founded his own school in Athens, the Lyceum. He was a prolific writer, admired in antiquity for his prose style.[1] Unfortunately, virtually all of the works he prepared for publication have been lost to us. Nonetheless a very large body of his writing remains, larger than the Platonic corpus. This includes two ethical treatises, known to us as *Nicomachean Ethics* and *Eudemian Ethics*. The former is generally considered to be the later work, and will be the main reference point of the discussion below.[2]

Aristotle's ethical treatises, which were not intended for publication in their present form, tend to be rather dry and technical. Despite their marked stylistic difference from Plato's vivid dramatic dialogues, however, they centre around the same set of practical questions. Aristotle writes for an audience who, like the ambitious seekers after *arête* whom we encounter in Plato, desire to become good (*EN* 1103b27–9).[3] They assume without question, like Plato's Socrates and his interlocutors, that we all want to 'do well' (*eu prattein*) or 'live well' (*eu zên*) – that is, to be *eudaimôn* ('happy' – 1095a17–20; cf. *Euthd.* 278e). Like Plato, Aristotle recognizes that his contemporaries disagree about what sort of life is the best one to live (1095a20–2). While Plato typically construes this issue as a question of which life (*bios*) is best, and addresses it by raising the question, 'What is *arete*?', Aristotle construes it as a dispute about what *eudaimonia* (happiness) is.

Aristotle's project in the EN is threefold. First of all, he aims to clarify the notion of *eudaimonia*. What is it that people are asking when they raise the question, what is *eudaimonia*? Second, he intends to settle the dispute about the answer to this question. The difference between the first issue and the second is analogous to the difference between clarifying the criteria for holding a particular office (e.g. President of the United States), and settling a dispute over who meets those criteria.[4] Third, and most importantly, Aristotle aims to offer practical advice about how to achieve *eudaimonia*.

Happiness as the goal of life

Eudaimonia, or happiness, as Aristotle famously explicates the notion, is our ultimate goal (*telos*) in life. It is that for the sake of which we do everything we do (1102a2–3, 1094a18–19, 1097a15–b21). In order to understand what this definition means, it is important to avoid a very common misunderstanding. Aristotle is *not* saying that we do everything for the sake of pleasure. While 'happiness' in contemporary English does often refer to pleasure or contentment, this is not what the Greek term '*eudaimonia*' means. It simply means, Plato and Aristotle tell us, 'doing well' (*eu prattein*) or 'living well' (*eu zên*) (EN 1095a19–20, 1098b21; *Euthd.* 278e, 282a, 280b–e). In using the term 'happiness', Aristotle is referring to the goodness of a life. He is not prejudging the disputed issue of whether it is pleasure, as opposed to something else, that makes a life good.[5] In calling happiness the goal (*telos*) of life, he is clarifying rather than answering the question, 'What is happiness'?

In order to understand this conception of happiness, which informs all of subsequent Greek and Roman philosophy (Cicero, *Fin.* 1.11), we must understand what Aristotle means by a goal (*telos*). A *telos*, as Aristotle employs the notion, is something aimed at. In the case of human activity, a *telos* is the point or reason for doing something. A ubiquitous feature of human activity, Aristotle stresses in the opening lines of the *Nicomachean Ethics*, is that it is goal-directed:

> Every sort of expert knowledge (*technê*) and every inquiry and similarly every action and undertaking seems to aim at some good.
> (1094a1–2; cf. 1095a14–15)[6]

For example, I am boiling water. Why? To make some coffee. Making the coffee is my goal in boiling the water. Now this goal is most likely for the sake of some further goal, which in turn may be for the sake of another. Why make coffee? In order to drink it. What's the point of drinking coffee? Here I might answer: I enjoy it. I like the taste and the way it makes me feel.

Two different sorts of reasons or goals (*telê*) occur in this chain of motivation. On the one hand, there are things I do or pursue only because of some further goal, for example: boiling water and brewing coffee. There is nothing about these activities themselves that inclines me to engage in them. I do them simply because I want to do something else, that is, drink coffee. On the other hand, there are things I pursue because of themselves, or 'for their own sake'. Drinking coffee, in the example above, is a goal of this sort. In pointing out that I enjoy drinking coffee, I have given a reason that makes sense of the whole sequence of boiling, brewing and so forth.

Without a goal of the second sort, one desired for its own sake, the sequence of activity is pointless. To see this, suppose instead that I don't enjoy drinking coffee. I drink the coffee, not because I like it (in fact, I don't), but in order to be alert. I don't particularly want to be alert, either (I'd rather be asleep), but I need to be alert in order to drive to the store (I hate driving by the way). Why do I want to go to the store? To buy paper. What do I want to do with the paper? And so on. If the reason I give at each point in the chain of questions always points to a further objective, and not to something I want or value in the goal at hand, then there really is no point to my boiling the water (or doing anything else in the chain). This is what Aristotle means when he says that unless there is something we desire for its own sake, our desire will be empty and vain (*EN* 1094a20–21).

The ubiquitous human phenomenon of doing things for reasons, therefore, depends on there being at least one thing we pursue for its own sake. Happiness, according to Aristotle, is a goal of this sort (1097a34–b1). Of course, it is not the only such goal. We desire many things for their own sakes: pleasure, honour, prosperity, health, friends and family are just a few of the things people desire in this way. According to Aristotle, happiness differs from these other objects of pursuit in that we pursue everything else (including the items on this list) for the sake of *it* (1097b2–5). This makes happiness not simply *a* goal of our actions, but *the* goal.

Understanding exactly what is involved in doing everything for the sake of a single goal is one of the most difficult and disputed questions about Aristotle's ethics. One helpful thing to keep in mind however, is that Aristotle is not simply recommending that we pursue such a goal. He thinks this is something that people actually and typically do – not just philosophers and monomaniacs, but ordinary people:

> To judge from their lives... most people, the vulgar, seem...
> to suppose [happiness] to be pleasure; that is why they favour the
> life of consumption.... People of quality, for their part, go for
> honour.
> (*EN* 1095b14–17, 22–23; cf. 1095a22–3)

An adequate interpretation of 'doing everything for the sake of happiness' must therefore be consistent with Aristotle's confident assertion that such activity is ubiquitous among ordinary agents.

We would also do well to keep in mind Aristotle's remark, in the *Eudemian Ethics*, that it would be a mark of 'great folly' not to have a single goal at which one aims in life (*EE* I 2, 1214b7–10). He offers no explanation there – presumably because he thinks his audience does not require one. One explanation with which his audience would be familiar is sketched in Plato's *Republic*, where Socrates claims that having a single *skopos* (target) for one's life gives unity to the life and integrity to the person who leads it (*Rep.* 519c2–4).[7]

Although Aristotle does not make the point explicitly, it is clear from the examples of goal-directed activity that he offers in EN I 1 that pursuit of a goal typically unifies a person's activities. This is because goals naturally and typically introduce hierarchies, as Aristotle points out in his opening remarks:

> Just as bridle-making falls under horsemanship, along with all the others that produce the equipment for horsemanship, and horsemanship along with every action that has to do with expertise in warfare falls under generalship – so in the same way others fall under a separate one.
>
> (*EN* 1094a10–14)

In such hierarchies, the subordinate enterprises are pursued 'for the sake of' (*charin*)[8] the higher ones (1094a15–16). For example, bridle-making has a goal (making bridles), which is itself 'for the sake of' the equestrian craft (specifically that of the cavalry rider), which is in turn for the sake of the general's craft, whose goal (victory, 1094a9) is itself for the sake of the political craft (1094a10–14, b4). A similar chain of teleological subordination can be sketched for the blacksmith who shoes the cavalry's horses, as well as for the other disciplines that are subordinate to the general (e.g. those of the hoplite and the infantryman), or subordinate to the political craft (for example rhetoric – 1094b3). In the grand image that Aristotle takes over from Plato's *Statesman* (303e–305e) he envisages the activities of all the various enterprises in the city being unified under a single goal – that of the statesman exercising the political craft (*EN* 1094a26–b11).

Goals also naturally introduce unity within a single person's life. Most goals we pursue give the point not just to one or two individual actions, but to a whole range of behaviour. To return to the previous example: my goal of drinking coffee gives a point not only to my boiling water – but also to a significant number of other activities as well: grinding beans, filtering water, purchasing and maintaining brewing equipment, and so on. In another example, everything I did this morning can be subsumed under two goals: revising this chapter and doing the laundry – even though there were dozens of different things I did – trips up and downstairs and between keyboard and desk, fiddling with the printer, looking for this note or that folder, finding a hair band to keep the hair out of my eyes.

Nor is the unifying effect of goals restricted to the time span of a morning, a day, or any other relatively short stretch of time. It can, and for some types of goals typically does, extend across a whole lifetime or a significant portion of one.[9] Growing a garden, being a parent, or engaging in a profession are all goals of this type. To engage in these enterprises is to perform a wide range of very different activities that are scattered over many different locations and times of life and interspersed with activities that fall under different goals. For example, the range of activities involved in parenting spans at different times of life midnight feeding and diapering, games of hide and seek in the woods, visits to the emergency room, late-night long-distance phone calls, and emergency financial assistance. These may be interspersed quite regularly with activities that are not instances of parenting at all (for example, going to work, or weeding the garden), but are quite consistent with the goals of parenting. Similarly with the other two goals: gardening and having a profession. Each of these three goals unifies a large swathe of different activities in a life, and together they provide unity and focus to a whole life. Thus as goal-pursuing creatures there is not only a point to particular things we do; there is coherence and structure across the many different things we do. To the extent that we pursue goals, our lives are coherent and intelligible rather than random collections of actions.

Considerations such as these lend credence to the view that it is foolish not to have goals that we desire for their own sake, and that it is wise to have a small rather than a large number of such goals. However, the explanation falls short of establishing what Aristotle claims: that one should pursue a single ultimate goal in life. While unity and coherence are important, we might object, it is possible to have too much of a good thing. There are many worthwhile things to pursue, and a life is impoverished to the extent that it fails to incorporate enough of them. A life that has parenting and gardening as goals along with working in a profession is undoubtedly less unified than one oriented solely around professional goals, but it is far from obvious that it is an inferior life. Indeed, to the extent that it includes more of the 'good things' in life, it is arguably a better one.

So, at any rate, goes a very common set of misgivings about the Aristotelian vision of doing everything for the sake of a single goal. Is this not the life of a monomaniac?[10] Here, however, it is important to recognize that Aristotle is not claiming that, in pursuing happiness, one's ultimate goal in life is the *only* thing one pursues or desires for its own sake. He explicitly recognizes that we desire some things for their own sake, as well as for the sake of happiness (1097b2–5). Thus, on his view, it is possible for me to 'do everything for the sake of happiness', while still pursuing a variety of different ends in life – ends that I value for their own sakes (e.g., parenting, gardening, and a profession) – as long as I *also* pursue these ends for the sake of happiness. So the key to understanding the pursuit of happiness, as Aristotle conceives it, is to grasp what is involved in pursuing something for its own sake *as well as* 'for the sake of' a further goal.[11]

As it turns out, Aristotle gives us a concrete illustration of such a life in his portrait of the person living what Plato would call 'the political life'.

Once we understand how such a life involves the pursuit of a single goal, we will be able to appreciate why Aristotle thinks the pursuit of happiness is a commonplace and widespread human phenomenon.

The choice of lives: *EN* I.5 and X.7–8

In *Nicomachean Ethics* I 5, Aristotle identifies three main contenders for the happy life: the life of pleasure, the political life, and the 'reflective' (*theoretikos*) life,[12] to which he briefly adds a fourth: the life of money-making (1095b17–1096a7; cf. 1095a22–3). Aristotle here gives short shrift to the life of pleasure,[13] which he dismisses as no different from that of a 'grazing beast' (1095b19–20), and he is equally dismissive of the life devoted to making money, on the ground that money is for something, and thus cannot be the ultimate end of a life (1096a5–7). He raises some problems about how to understand the goal of the 'political' life (1095b 22–1096a2), but does not reject it outright as a candidate, and indicates that the 'reflective' (*theoretikos*) life will be the subject of the ensuing discussion (1096a4–5).[14]

In fact, the reflective life does not appear again in the *Nicomachean Ethics* until almost the end of the work (*EN* X 7–8), where Aristotle indicates that it is a life consisting exclusively of reflection (*theoria*) upon eternal truths (1177a12–21, b24–6) – his version of Plato's portrait of the philosopher in the *Republic* (540a; cf. 511b–d). In contrast with the political life, and like its Platonic counterpart, the reflective life is very narrowly focused, we might even say monomaniacal (cf. *Rep.* 485d). It is the pure life of the intellect, in which one grasps what is truly real and divine, and eschews, as far as possible, social, bodily, and emotional concerns. Like Socrates in the *Phaedo*, Aristotle takes the goal of such a life to be 'to become like the divine'.[15] This life is without question, he claims, superior to the political life (*EN* 1178a7–10).[16] Unfortunately, however, it is not a life of which a human being is capable (1177b24–1178a2, a10; 1178b33–35). Unlike the gods, who have no bodies, desires, or emotions, and thus can engage in continuous and uninterrupted *theoria* for the whole of their existence (1178b8–22), human beings are physical, emotional, and social creatures who must devote time and attention to meeting their needs as such (1178b5–7). As a result, they can engage in *theoria* at best episodically.

For human beings, the happy life is what in *EN* II 5 he calls 'the political life' (1095b18). This is the life of a person active in the affairs of a *polis* who displays the excellences of justice, courage, temperance and the like (1178a9–25; cf. 1177a28–32). We will consider later Aristotle's reasons for concluding that both the theoretical and the political lives are happy. For our present purposes, let us examine the political life in order to identify the way in which it is organized around a single goal.[17]

The political life

The excellences that inform the life that Aristotle dubs 'second best' in *EN* X. 8 (1178a9) include not only those familiar from Plato – justice, temperance, and courage – but a whole host of excellences, relating to virtually every aspect of public and private life, which Aristotle identifies and describes in detail in Books II–V of the *Nicomachean Ethics*. The general term Aristotle uses to characterize these admirable features is 'ethical excellence' (*êthikê aretê* – 1103a4–8; often translated as 'virtue of character'). Since Aristotle recognizes additional excellences besides the ethical,[18] it is misleading to refer to the person who possesses the ethical excellences as simply 'virtuous' or 'excellent'. For want of a better term I shall use 'ethical' to characterize this person and the life he leads.

Aristotle's detailed enumeration of the particular ethical excellences in Books III–V make it clear that the ethical person organizes his activity around a single goal, 'the admirable' (or 'fine' – *kalon*) (*EN* 1111b12–13; *EE* 1230a25–35).[19] The brave person withstands life-threatening dangers only when it is *kalon* to do so or *aischron* (shameful) not to (*EN* 1115b13). The temperate person differs from the intemperate in that he declines to pursue opportunities for shameful bodily gratification (1119a2). The 'liberal' person will not seek or accept income from sources that are shameful (1121b1). The friendly person shares the pleasures of others as long as they are fine (1126b32). The 'witty' (*eutrapelos*) person, unlike someone who will 'stop at nothing' to get a laugh (1128a6), has a standard of decency and avoids shameful jokes (or jokes that would be shameful to tell in the circumstances – 1128a20).[20]

If we understand Aristotle's ethical excellences in this light – as dispositions to regulate the pursuit of activities such as joking, truth-telling and so on in the light of normative ideals such as the *kalon* and *aischron* – it is easy to avoid the common objection that Aristotle's ethical excellences are not moral virtues. Wit, one might object, is not a moral virtue. It is not incumbent on us, if we want to be good persons, to be witty. But this objection mistakes the goal of the virtue Aristotle calls 'wit' (*eutrapelia*) as telling jokes or amusing others. The goal is to regulate such pursuits by the norms of the *kalon* and *aischron*.

The domain of the ethical excellences, on Aristotle's picture, encompasses the whole of a person's private, social, and political life: pursuit of bodily pleasures, maintenance of one's health and safety, performance of military service, receiving honour (and dishonour), looking after the economic interests of oneself and one's family, assistance to those in need, displays of wealth, expenditures for the common good, financial transactions with others, cooperating with, associating with, supporting, being amusing to and amused by others. In all of these pursuits, the ethical person aims at doing what is *kalon* and avoiding its opposite: the *aischron*.

It is in this respect that the ethical life, as Aristotle conceives it, is organized around a single goal.

Notwithstanding this central focus, however, it is a life that involves the pursuit of a wide range of objectives that are valued for their own sakes. These range from the large and important (bodily pleasure, life and health, family security, personal honour, being agreeable to others) to the relatively less significant (making people laugh or entertaining them richly). Although there is considerable variation from person to person and across cultures, these are the sorts of things a person wants to do, likes to do, or values: not instrumentally, but for their own sakes. In also pursuing them 'for the sake of the *kalon*', the ethical person is simply regulating his pursuit of them in the light of his unwavering commitment to doing what is *kalon* and avoiding what is *aischron*.

If it seems odd in English to say that every choice I make – down to the decision of whether to play the piano or read this afternoon – is 'for the sake of' what is admirable, this is simply because 'for the sake of' does not perfectly precisely translate the expressions Aristotle uses: '*heneka* + genitive' or '*charin*' + genitive. Plato for example, when describing the restrictions on the physical intimacy allowed between lovers in the ideal state, gives a very nice example of '*tou kalou charin*' ('for the sake of the fine') used to describe a regulative ideal. The lover may be with, kiss, and touch his beloved 'for the sake of what is fine': that is, he will not engage in any intimacies that are shameful. (*Rep.* 403b–c).[21] That an activity can be 'for the sake of' a goal in virtue of being regulated by pursuit of that goal is furthermore evident in Aristotle's opening hierarchical example in *EN* I 2 (1094a26–b7). Military strategy, the general's enterprise, is 'for the sake of' politics – not that it is a means to politics, but that (in a well-run polis) it is regulated by the knowledgeable statesman (*politicos*).[22]

It is important to notice that the ethical person's commitment to the *kalon* as a final goal does not serve as a 'comprehensive guide to conduct'.[23] It is not sufficient to determine or explain all of his actions, or even all of his subordinate goals.[24] To be sure, there are some situations in which his commitment to the *kalon* makes it clear what he must do (or not do). This is the case, for example, when standing his ground in battle and risking his life is called for, and fleeing his post would be shameful; or when being agreeable to a tyrant, laughing at a particular joke, or failing to take offence, would be shameful. However, many more, perhaps even most of the situations in which one acts are ones in which nothing admirable or shameful is at stake. Shall I go to the movies or stay home and read a book? Shall I become a doctor or a dentist? Should I marry George? Shall I have tea or coffee with my breakfast? Should I accept the job in Toronto or in New York?

While it is easy to dream up circumstances in which something ethically significant is at stake in these choices, this is not invariably the case in these as well as myriad other choices we make in the course of our lives. What we do in such situations, even though it is regulated by the norms of the *kalon*, does not promote the *kalon*, and is not a means to achieving it. Thus the pursuit of the *kalon* as an ultimate goal leaves open a very wide range of options in life, both large-scale and small. A life devoted to the pursuit of the *kalon* can involve the pursuit of a wide variety of other goals that are valued and pursued for their own sakes, as long as a person's pursuit of them is regulated or limited by her pursuit of the ultimate goal. Indeed, it must contain other such goals, or else she will be unable to make most of the choices she faces in life.

Aristotle's portrait of the ethical agent shows that the pursuit of an ultimate goal in life has much in common with the way commitment to religious ideals functions in many people's lives today. Although the degree to which a person's daily activities and other pursuits are constrained by her commitment to a religion varies considerably among religious traditions (and even among different strands within the same tradition), a person whose ultimate value is to live up to the ideals and commandments of, for example, Christianity or Judaism will make many choices and pursue many options in which that goal is simply not at stake. Commitment to that ultimate goal simply involves the readiness to refrain from acting on subordinate pursuits in circumstances in which this would conflict with the ultimate goal. This is not to say that one will inevitably have to sacrifice those subordinate goals for the sake of the higher one. In tragic cases, one might, but most of the things we desire for their own sakes are 'determinable' rather than 'determinate' ends. My desire to grow a garden does not require me to pull the weeds right now, when decency requires I attend the funeral of a loved one, just as my desire to be a good parent does not require me to turn down all opportunities for out-of-town engagements.

Aristotle's account of the ethical life shows how a person can be doing everything 'for the sake of' a single goal without being monomaniacal or leading an impoverished life. Like Plato's Socrates in the *Apology*, Aristotle's ethical person will always take into account in his actions 'whether what [he] does is right or wrong, whether [he] is acting like a good or a bad person' (*Ap.* 28b–c). This is an ordinary and familiar pattern of human motivation, even if it is one that is hard to execute with perfect fidelity. It is also recognizable as the pattern of motivation characteristic of Plato's 'using craft' – as Aristotle acknowledges at *EN* 1120a4–6. The knowledge that enables one to live well, we are told in the *Euthydemus* (280c–281e), tells us when it is good to pursue such goals as health, wealth, personal safety, or honour. The person living according to Plato's 'using craft' will be regulating his pursuit of the usually recognized good things in life in terms of his understanding of the good. So too the Aristotelian agent, in acting for the sake of an ultimate end, regulates his actions by his grasp of what is admirable or good.[25] The person living according to Plato's 'using craft' is (in Aristotle's idiom) 'doing everything for the sake of happiness'.

Philosophy in the political life

So far we have seen that Aristotle's portrait of the ethical life illustrates how one can have a single unifying goal in life without being monomaniacal. Our discussion of that life is, however, incomplete, for Aristotle's view of the ethical person's motivation is more complicated than we have been considering so far.

Although Aristotle thinks human beings must live political rather than reflective lives, he does not recommend that the ethical life should be devoid of reflective activity. The activity of reflection is still in Aristotle's view an important part of a human life, indeed the best part. Even if we, being human, are unable to engage in this activity continuously throughout our lives, we should make every effort to 'become like the immortals' (athanatizein, 1177b33) by engaging in it. Indeed, he indicates that such purely intellectual activity is a further, and more ultimate, goal of the practical activity of the ethical person. Reflective activity is the most complete and 'self-sufficient' activity (1177a27–b1, 1178b33–1179a5) which is the mark of the ultimate telos (1097b6–15). In fact, he tells us at the end of EN VI, the practical thinking of the person living an ethical life is 'for the sake of' reflective activity (ekeinês heneka, 1145a9), a point repeated at the end of the Eudemian Ethics (1249b12–15). Practical reasoning, he tells us, stands to reflective activity as medical knowledge stands to health; its goal is to bring it about (1145a6–11; responding to the puzzle raised at 1143b33–35).[26]

In spite of Aristotle's clear statement on the matter, it is controversial among interpreters whether he really thinks that reflective activity is the goal of the ethical life.[27] No doubt this is largely because the claim raises a formidable puzzle that we are now well positioned to appreciate. We have just seen that the ethical life has its own telos: abiding by the kalon. How can it also be for the sake of reflection? As a first step to understanding how this could be so, it is helpful to recognize that, once again, this is a case of pursuing an objective for its own sake (ethical activity) and also pursuing it 'for the sake of' a further goal (reflective activity, theoria). We may therefore appeal to the model that applied to the previous case, where the pursuit of the subordinate goal was regulated by the pursuit of the higher end. In the present case, this means that one's pursuit of reflection is supposed to regulate one's pursuit of practical activity. When and whether one engages in practical activity (as opposed to reflective activity) is regulated by one's prior and more ultimate commitment to engaging in reflection.

So far so good, but now the most pressing worry can be articulated. Does this not imply that one's commitment to ethical ideals is only provisional? For example, if I can finance a year's sabbatical by embezzling some money (let us assume that this will allow me to engage in uninterrupted *theoria*), why should I not do it? Yes, it would be shameful and unjust, but if it goes undetected, is it not an excellent means to my highest and most important goal of engaging in reflection? The worry in its general form is that the goal of the ethical life, abiding by the *kalon*, may be impeded or compromised by being subordinated to the pursuit of opportunities for reflection.

To defuse this worry, it is helpful to look to the hierarchical structure of pursuits that Aristotle invokes at the beginning of the *Nicomachean Ethics*. Bridle-making is for the sake of horsemanship. Horsemanship (the expertise of the cavalry) is for the sake of waging war, in which the general is expert (1094a10–13). Similarly, warfare is subordinate to, and 'for the sake of' politics, in which the statesman (*politikos*) is expert (1094a27–b3). Aristotle's remarks here are normative rather than descriptive. He is no less familiar than we are with states in which the activities of the generals are not so regulated. His point is that in a properly functioning polity the political rulers regulate the activities of the generals in the same way that the generals regulate those of the cavalry. This sort of regulation is what is involved in the subordinate pursuit being 'for the sake of' the higher.

In none of these cases, however, is the subordinate activity impeded or compromised by the subordination. That bridle-making is 'for the sake of' horsemanship does not impede the ability of the bridle-maker to produce good bridles. Similarly, that waging war is subordinate to the political craft does not imply that the general's conduct of the war will be interfered with or compromised by the political rulers. Rather, in a properly functioning polity, the political rulers regulate the conduct of war in two ways. They determine, first of all, the norms regulating the conduct of warfare, and, second, when and whether to wage war at all. Once the decision has been made to wage war, the general's ability to pursue victory within the determined norms is not further constrained or compromised by the political rulers.

These examples show that in cases where one pursuit is regulated by another, we can distinguish two very different questions. The first is whether to engage in the regulated pursuit at all. Thus the statesman deliberates about when and whether to go to war, and the general deliberates about when and whether to employ the cavalry. The second question is whether to interfere with the regulated pursuit once it is engaged in. Regulation that addresses questions of the second sort involves the real danger of impediment and compromise to the regulated pursuit. Such would be the case if the generals, in addition to telling the bridle-makers what kind of bridles to make and how many, override the bridle-maker's expert judgment about what kind of leather to use and how to cut it.

Regulation that concerns the first question, however, does not impede the regulated pursuit. This is the sort of regulation performed by the higher pursuits in the hierarchical example in *EN* 1094a10–13. That bridle-making is 'for the sake of' the general's craft does not imply that the general will interfere with the bridle-maker's functioning; it means simply that the general determines what kind of bridle and how many the bridle-maker will make. Given Aristotle's emphasis on the ethical person's uncompromising commitment to the *kalon*, we must also suppose that this is how the ethical person's higher commitment to reflection regulates his pursuit of the practical life. His higher commitment to reflection determines when and whether he will engage in practical activity as opposed to reflective activity, but it will not compromise his ability, when engaged in practical pursuits, to abide by the standards of the *kalon*.

Since reflection is a higher goal than practical activity, the ethical person will opt for the former when she has the opportunity to choose between engaging in it, on the one hand, and engaging in practical activity on the other. This is not to say, however, that she will choose reflection even in circumstances in which it is shameful to do so – for example if her children will go hungry as a result or an ailing parent will be unattended.[28] In circumstances where opting for reflection would be shameful, the agent does not have a genuine choice between practical and theoretical activity, for the domain of practical activity encompasses all choices in which the *kalon* and the *aischron* are at stake. When one has the opportunity to engage in reflection only at the price of doing something shameful, one has the opportunity to withdraw from the *ethical* life, but not from the *practical* life. If the *kalon* and the *aischron* are at stake in one's decision, one is thereby already enmeshed in the practical life. Only in situations in which nothing fine or shameful is at stake – hence, only in cases in which one can engage in *theoria* without violating the standards of the *kalon* – is one mandated, on Aristotle's view, to opt for reflection. To the extent that such circumstances are rare, or relatively rare in life, the ethical person's ultimate commitment to reflection as his highest goal will have relatively few practical implications for the choices he makes. But since *theoria* is the best activity in life, not simply another goal to be regulated by the pursuit of the *kalon*, a person whose highest goal is to engage in reflection is mandated (not just permitted) to engage in reflection when it is a genuine alternative to practical activity.[29]

To continue the analogy with religious commitment above: while the ethical person's commitment to the *kalon* is analogous to a religious person's commitment to live up to the ideals and constraints of her religion's practical teachings, her higher commitment to *theoria* is like the religious person's commitment to certain spiritual practices. One can recognize that it would be wrong to engage in such practices at the price of violating one's obligations to others, but still think such practice is the most important thing in life, without which the rest of life would have no meaning.

In Aristotle's view, living an ethical life and engaging in reflective intellectual activity are the two greatest things of which a human being is capable. A happy life will contain both. The greatest bulk of that life will consist of practical activity, which exercises the virtues of character. Much smaller in bulk will be the episodes of reflective activity, but these are far more important, and one cannot lead an excellent human life without engaging in reflection. 'Even though it is small in bulk, the degree to which it surpasses everything in power and dignity is far greater' (*EN* 1177b34–1178a2).

The human function

It is now time to examine why Aristotle thinks that both the ethical and the philosophical life count as happy (*eudaimôn*). As we have seen, the three main contenders that he recognizes for the happy life are the life of pleasure, the political life, and the life of reflection (*EN* 1095b17–19; cf. 1095a22–3). Aristotle dismisses the life devoted to pleasure as unfit for a human being (1095b19–20). By contrast, the political and the reflective lives are in his view properly human, since each involves the exercise of the capacity, reason, that distinguishes human beings from other animals (1097b34–1098a5).

The exercise of reason, being the distinctive (*idion*) activity of a human being, is the human function (*ergon*), Aristotle says (1097b24–1098a7). Once we recognize this as our function he thinks it is but a short step to having a correct answer (albeit a sketchy one) to the question, 'What is happiness?' (*EN* 1097b24–5). The reasoning that spells out this famous inference – known to many as the 'function argument', is set forth in *Nicomachean Ethics* I 7 (1097b22–1098a22; cf. 1106a15–24).[30] Two aspects of this argument are worth commenting on here. First of all, why does Aristotle think a human being has a function in the first place, and why does he think that this function is to use reason? Second, even if using reason is the human function, how can this help us answer the question about happiness?

For something to have an *ergon*, as Aristotle employs the notion, it is not necessary that it have a designer, creator, or user. All it needs is a characteristic activity. Its *ergon* is simply that activity. Thus a dancer's function is to dance, a carpenter's function is to build, and a carburettor's function is to mix gasoline and air in the proper proportions for combustion. More precisely, the function of X is whatever X does *insofar as it is X*. Thus the function of a human being is whatever a human being does, insofar as s/he is human. Now a particular human being is many things in addition to being human. He may also be a dancer or a carpenter, and as such his function is to dance or to build. He is without doubt a living thing ('ensouled' (*empsuchon*) in Aristotle's terminology), and as such his function, distinctive (*idion*) to living things, is to grow, maintain, and reproduce himself. He is also an animal, and as such his function, which distinguishes animals from plants, is to perceive, desire, and engage in locomotion. As a human being, his function is to perform the activity that distinguishes human beings from the other animals, and this, Aristotle claims, is to use reason (1097b33–1098a3; *DA* 414a32–b19).[31] We are functioning as human beings, not merely as animals or vegetables, when we use reason.

It is natural to worry that in calling reason the human function, Aristotle is overlooking some important aspects of humanity. Are not our emotional and aesthetic sensibilities, as well as our capacities for social interaction and interpersonal relationships, also characteristically human? But before addressing this worry (which in the end Aristotle is able to accommodate), let us turn to consider why Aristotle thinks that identifying the human function will help to answer the question about what happiness is.

Aristotle's thinking is, in essence, quite simple. It begins from the uncontroversial platitude of EN I 4 that happiness is 'doing well' or 'living well' (*EN* 1095a18–20). Aristotle assumes that happiness is performance of the human function because 'doing well' for a human being will be doing well *whatever it is that a human being does, as a human being*. Since a human being, as such, uses reason (1098a3–5), it follows that doing well for a human being amounts to using reason well. In other words, happiness is excellent activity of reason or, as Aristotle puts it 'the exercise of excellence (*aretê*) [sc. of reason]' (1098a16–17).[32]

The function argument

1. Happiness is 'doing well'. (1095a18–20; unstated in EN I 7)
2. 'Doing well' for a human being is performing the human function well. (1098a8–11, 14–16)
3. The human function is to exercise reason. (1098a7)
4. Therefore, happiness for a human being consists in using reason well. (unstated, from 1, 2, 3)
5. Therefore, happiness for a human being is activity of excellence of reason. (1098a16–17; from 4)

Aristotle does not draw conclusion (4) explicitly, inferring (5) instead, which is simply a restatement of (4) in different vocabulary. In invoking the notion of excellence (*aretê*) in conclusion (5), Aristotle is simply restating, using the abstract noun, 'excellence', (*aretê*), the conclusion articulated in

(4) using the adverb 'well', (*eu*). If (4) doing well for a human being consists in using reason well, then (5) the good for a human being is activity according to excellence of reason. The 'good for a human being', in these contexts, is perfectly analogous to 'the good for a carpenter' or 'the good for a hammer'. The 'for' in these cases renders the dative article, which is well translated as 'the good *in the case of* a human being'. The good in the case of X, where X has a function, is the 'doing well' of X. Like Socrates' interlocutors in Plato's dialogues, Aristotle assumes that *eudaimonia*, or something's doing well, is the activity of its proper excellence.

Thus it is a mistake to suppose that Aristotle's 'function argument' attempts to answer the question, 'What is happiness?', by making a substantive (and controversial) claim that what is *good for* a human being (self-interest) is what a good human being does (the activity of ethical excellence). Beyond identifying reason as the capacity that must be exercised in the happy life (and thus ruling out the life of pleasure), Aristotle does not here make any further headway in answering the question, What is happiness? His claim that the happy life is the exercise of excellence counts rather as a further clarification of the notion of happiness.[33] By introducing the notion of excellence, and articulating his conclusion about human happiness in the light of it, Aristotle furthers instead his practical project of addressing those who seek to achieve happiness, or become good. One must cultivate excellence, he tells them. This recommendation will not come as a surprise to Aristotle's readers, but it sets the stage for his third main project in the *Nicomachean Ethics*: to give an account of human excellence, and advice about how to acquire it.

Ethical excellence

Human excellence, according to Aristotle in *Nicomachean Ethics* I 7, is excellence of reason (1098a12–18). In *EN* I 13, Aristotle recognizes two main types of rational excellence (1103a3–10; cf. 1138b35–1139a1), corresponding to two different rational capacities of the human soul (1098a4–5, 1102b13–1103a3). There is a part (or capacity) of the soul that 'has reason' in the sense that it is itself capable of thinking and judging. This is reason in the 'strict' sense (*kuriôs* – 1103a2). The excellence of this kind of reason is what Aristotle calls 'intellectual excellence' (*dianoetikê arête*). He devotes Book VI to an enumeration and discussion of these excellences, which include knowledge (*epistêmê*), wisdom (*sophia*) and practical wisdom (*phronêsis*). We will consider these excellences later.

Purely intellectual excellences do not, however, exhaust the scope of human rationality, on Aristotle's view. He notes that a set of capacities that humans share with non-rational animals is also capable of being rational in a way. This is the part of the soul that issues in desires and feelings (1102b30; cf. 1105b19–25). In human beings, this part shares in reason because it is 'capable of following reason', and hence its excellence (or good disposition) will count as an excellence of reason (1102b13–31, 1098a4–5). This is the excellence Aristotle calls 'ethical excellence' (*êthikê aretê*, 1103a4–7). Thus one of the two main types of human excellence, in Aristotle's view, involves not just the purely ratiocinative powers of a human being, but the full range of emotions, desires and feelings that make up the rich array of human experience. As it turns out, the only capacities Aristotle leaves out of human excellence are those of the nutritive soul: growing, digesting, breathing, and reproducing. These are incapable of following reason and hence are not part of human excellence (1102b12).

Aristotle devotes Books II through V of the *Nicomachean Ethics* to a detailed discussion of the ethical excellences. These include the virtues familiar from Plato's discussion – courage, temperance, and justice[34] – as well as a wide array of lesser-known virtues, some of them without names in ordinary language.[35] These include gentleness, liberality, magnanimity, truthfulness, and even 'wit'. Each of these virtues concerns a particular range of emotion and action. For example, courage concerns feelings and actions regarding danger in the battlefield: fear, confidence, standing one's ground, fleeing. Temperance (*sôphrosunê*) concerns appetites for bodily pleasures, as well as the activities of indulging in or refraining from satisfying them. Liberality (*eleutheriotês*, sometimes translated as 'generosity') concerns one's desires and feelings about money, as well as the actions involved in acquiring it, spending it, and giving it away. Magnanimity (*megalopsuchia*) concerns one's desires for and feelings about honour, as well one's pursuit of it and reactions to failure to receive it.

Virtue of character, Aristotle explains, is a disposition (*hexis*)[36] of our capacities for those feelings, desires, and actions. Of course not every disposition of these capacities is a virtue. Irascibility, for example, is a bad disposition concerning feelings of anger and responses to perceived insults and injustice. The irascible person tends to get upset at relatively minor provocation, and overreacts to slights, insults, and injuries (1126a13–30). Slavishness[37] and prodigality are bad dispositions concerning money: the slavish person will stoop to anything to make money (1121b1–3, 31–4; 1122a11–13; cf. 1120a31–2), while the prodigal person will spend too much of it and on the wrong things (1120b20–5; cf. 1107b11–14). The coward and the rash person are both badly disposed regarding fear, confidence, and the related actions: the former is disposed to feel too much fear, and on the wrong occasions, and to stand his ground less than he should, while the latter is disposed to feel overly confident, to stand his ground unnecessarily and to take foolish risks (1107b1–4; 1115b28–1116a3). As this list shows, dispositions (*hexeis*) are stable and enduring traits of character (1105a33; cf. 1114a13–18).[38] Aristotle says that it is in virtue of our *hexeis* that 'we are well or badly disposed' concerning feelings and actions (1105b26) because it is one's *hexis* that determines how (and whether) one's capacities for feelings, desire, and action, will be exercised in different circumstances.

A disposition of these capacities is an excellence if it disposes the person to have the proper feelings and desires, and to engage in the appropriate actions in that particular domain. A vice of character, by contrast, is a bad disposition of these capacities. This is not to say that a vice disposes one *always* to have inappropriate feelings, or *always* to do the wrong action. For instance, even the coward will sometimes feel fear when he should, and stand up to the enemy when he should. Similarly, some of the prodigal person's expenditures may be appropriate – for example, any that take care of his family's needs. Others, however, will be inappropriate. For example, he may have a weakness for luxuries, and will spend on them resources he really cannot spare. Similarly, there will be certain kinds of situations in which the coward is properly fearless and stands his ground. These may be different situations for different cowards (just as different spendthrifts have different spending patterns). But what every coward (or spendthrift) has in common is that his disposition regarding the particular range of feeling and action does not reliably get things right across the full range of situations in which he may find himself.

The doctrine of the mean

Aristotle expresses this point in what has come to be known as the 'doctrine of the mean'.[39] Given the domain of any virtue of character, one can be disposed to engage in its feelings and actions either too much or too little (that is, more often or less often than one should). Furthermore, where there is a range of intensity for the exercise of a feeling or action, one can express it either too strongly or too feebly. For instance one can be angry more vehemently than one should on a particular occasion, or one can strike someone harder than one should. Similarly, one can fail to be angry enough at a particular insult, or return a blow too weakly, or (to use a modern example) one's handshake can be too feeble (1126a4–11). One can err, in feelings and actions, either in the direction of excess (indulging in the emotion or engaging in the action too vigorously, or on more occasions than is appropriate) or in the direction of deficiency (indulging in the action or feeling less often or less strongly than one should). A disposition that errs in either of these two ways is a vice of character, while the disposition that avoids both excess and defect is a virtue of character. This is why Aristotle claims that for every ethical excellence there are two opposing vices: one of excess, and one of deficiency. To courage there correspond the opposing vices of cowardice and brashness. To liberality there correspond the vices of prodigality and stinginess. To self-control (temperance – *sôphrosunê*) there correspond the diametrically opposite vicious dispositions: self-indulgence and 'insensibility'.[40]

In contrast with the vices, which dispose a person to be either excessive or deficient in feeling and action, Aristotle says that the virtuous disposition is 'intermediate' and that the virtuous person 'hits the mean' in both feeling and action. By this he does not mean that a virtuous person is always 'moderate' in his feelings and actions.[41] In some circumstances, even a moderate amount of fear is inappropriate; and sometimes what is called for is a vigorous response rather than a measured one. Rather, 'the mean' – whether it is vigorous, mild, or moderate – is what is appropriate given all the particulars of the situation. Aristotle illustrates this by analogy to the case of nutrition. How much food should the doctor advise a person to eat? It depends on the person's size, health, and occupation. The best diet to prescribe for the heavyweight wrestler Milo will be excessive for an ordinary person, while the proper diet for the latter will be insufficient for Milo (1106a36–b7).[42]

Similarly, there is no simple algorithm to identify the feelings and actions that are appropriate for a person on a particular occasion. Simply averaging the strongest and weakest of the available options is to determine what Aristotle calls 'the mean in the object' or the 'arithmetical mean'. The mean observed in ethical excellence, by contrast, is 'relative to us' (*pros hêmas* – 1106a26–b7). By this he does *not* mean that different ethical standards apply to different people. To be sure, he thinks that facts about a person can make a difference to what actions are appropriate for her to perform. For example, whether or not you are the owner of a wallet makes a difference to whether it is appropriate for you to put it in your pocket and walk away with it. Your relation to other people involved may also be relevant (1126b36–1127a2). The fact that Oedipus is the son of the insolent old man who abused him at the crossroads makes it wrong for him to respond with lethal force.[43] However, the agent's status is only one among the many particular facts that are relevant to whether his action 'hits the mean'. Other factors include, but are not limited to, facts about other people and the circumstances in which one acts.

For example, are you at a wedding, a funeral, or another occasion where it is inappropriate to pursue a quarrel? Is the person who spoke rudely to you experiencing great grief or distress? If so, it is proper to overlook the remark rather than take offence at it. Does the person asking you for money need it? Has she been a benefactor to you in the past? This makes a difference to whether you should grant her request. Are there people present who will be insulted or pained by the joke you are considering telling? This makes a difference to whether you should tell it, or should join in the laughter if someone else has told it. In Aristotle's oft-repeated formula, the ethical person acts and feels 'as one should, when one should, to whom one should, to the extent one should, and for the reasons one should'.[44] All of these factors are relevant, in Aristotle's view, to the mean relative to us:

> To be affected when one should, at the things one should, in relation to the people one should, for the reasons one should, and in the way one should is both intermediate and best, which is what belongs to excellence. In the same way with acting too, there is excess, deficiency, and the intermediate.
>
> (*EN* 1106b21–4; cf. 1109a24–30, b12–16)

Here it is useful to take a historical perspective. Although Aristotle's ethical writing has made the doctrine of the mean famous, the idea does not originate with him. It appears in Plato's *Statesman* (283d–284e), and seems to have been a prominent motif in the fifth- and fourth-century understanding of the technical crafts.[45] The notion of the 'mean' or 'intermediate' (*meson*) as deployed in these contexts is closely related to the notion of the '*kairos*' (the right moment, or appropriate time), as well as the 'appropriate' (*prepon*).[46]

Across these different applications of the notion, there is no such thing as 'the mean' *tout court*. The mean is always 'relative to' (*pros*) a goal. The notion applies when a certain range of activity (be it emotion, desire, or action) is regulated with reference to a further goal. For example, one hour may be too long to bake the bread while ten minutes is too short. The right length of time is determined by the goal of the baker's enterprise: the production of a loaf of bread. The right baking time is whatever is necessary, in the circumstances, to yield this result.[47] Similarly, the general who determines when and where it is best for the cavalry to attack (neither too early nor too late, neither too far from the enemy's position of strength nor too close to it) is regulating his troops' activity in the light of his overall goal of winning the battle.

The mean observed in ethical excellence concerns a very broad range of activity (feelings and actions) and its reference point, Aristotle says, is, 'us'. That is, the mean in ethical excellence is relative to (*pros*) our goal as human beings. This goal, of course, is to live well. Thus in saying that the ethical mean is 'relative to us', Aristotle indicates that the mean is relative to our project, as human beings, of living well. As his portrait of ethical excellence makes clear, to live well is to regulate our activities in the light of the *kalon*. Thus the 'mean' in feelings and actions is whatever observes the constraints imposed by the pursuit of the *kalon*.

Prohairesis

In addition to 'hitting the mean' in feelings and actions, a good ethical disposition also involves having the right sort of motivation. For example, both the generous (*eleutheros*) person and someone with an imperfect disposition may perform a generous action. What each person does is the same, but their motivation for doing it is different. For example, Sam might give money to Oscar in order to gain a reputation for largesse, while Sarah might do so in order to make sure that Oscar does not go hungry. Janice might perform a just action because she wants to please her parents, while Jim might do so because he thinks it is the right thing to do (1144a13–20). While Sam and Janice hit the mean and do '*what* the generous (or just) person does', neither does so '*as* the generous (or just) person does it'. By contrast, Sarah and Jim do both what the generous (or just) person does and *as* such a person would do it.

It is not simply *what* one does but also one's reasons for doing it that issue from one's character. Aristotle puts this point by saying that an ethical disposition is a '*hexis prohairetike*' (EN 1106b36, 1139a22–3; EE 1227b8; cf. EN 1106a2–4) – roughly, a disposition of one's motivation – and that it is one's *prohairesis* (or motivation) rather than one's action that best reveals one's character (EN 1111b5–6; 1178a34–5; cf. 1105a28–32; 1144a20, a31–b1; 1145a4–5).

Prohairesis, which I will leave untranslated,[48] captures the general phenomenon of doing something for a reason. Aristotle sketches the notion in *Nicomachean Ethics* III 2–3 and VI 2, as well as in *Eudemian Ethics* II 10. According to this account, *prohairesis* has two crucial features. First of all, it is a decision to do something that is in the decider's power to do then and there (1111b25–30), and that actually moves him to act (1139a31–2; cf. 1113a5–7, 9–12). Thus *prohairesis* contrasts with vague and general desires that Aristotle labels cases of 'wish' (*boulêsis* – 1111b22–29). One can have a wish to be healthy, or for an end to world hunger, but a *prohairesis* is a determinate decision to take specific steps towards realizing the wished-for goal (1111b22–9).

Second, and most importantly, *prohairesis* is informed by deliberation (EN 1113a9–14, 1139a23; cf. 1112a15, EE 1226b5–20), and deliberation (*bouleusis*), Aristotle insists, is always in the light of a goal:

> [People] deliberate not about ends (*telôn*) but about what forwards those ends (*ta pros ta telê*). . . . They take the end for granted and examine how and by what means it will come about; and if it appears as coming about by more than one means, they look to see through which of them it will happen most easily and best, whereas if it is brought to completion by one means only, they look to see how it will come about through this, and through what means that will come about, until they arrive at the first cause, which comes last in the process of discovery.
> (EN 1112b11–20; cf. 1113a13–14, 1140b16–20,
> 1144a31–3; EE 1226b9–13)

Although Aristotle's remarks in *EN* III 2–3 leave the impression that action performed on *prohairesis* is always preceded immediately by a bout of deliberating, this does not seem to be his considered view. In other contexts, he recognizes that one can act even when there is no time to deliberate (1117a17–22). At other times there is no need to deliberate, for Aristotle tells us himself that we deliberate when it is unclear what to do (1112b8–9). Thus in the obvious and easy cases, where it is clear what one's goal requires and this is easy to do, one need not go through an explicit process of figuring out what to do. For example, the honest person does not need to figure out whether to pocket the proceeds of the charity fundraiser. It is obvious that he should not and the thought of doing so probably does not even cross his mind.[49] In such cases, the deliberative reasoning would be explicit, if at all, only after the fact, if the agent was concerned to scrutinize or explain why she acted as she did.

Acting on *prohairesis* therefore conforms to the general teleological schema that Aristotle sketches at the opening of the *EN* (1094a1–3). The same action, we have seen, can result from very different *prohaireseis* (plural) (1144a13–20). Therefore, when Aristotle says that it is *prohairesis* rather than action that best reveals one's character, he is referring not to what one has decided to do, but rather to the goal (*telos*) or reason for the sake of which one does it. For it is this goal, rather than the action decided upon, that reveals the giver's character. In such contexts, one's *prohairesis* is the reason for which one acts.[50]

Voluntary action

Aristotle gives his account of *prohairesis* in the context of a general discussion of voluntariness (*to hekousion*, *EN* III 1–5) which is the last topic he takes up in his general discussion of the ethical excellences. Actions expressive of character (those done from *prohairesis*, deliberation, and wish) have the common feature that they are voluntary, Aristotle explains (1113b3–6). He is concerned to discuss voluntariness because it is for voluntary actions that people are praised and blamed (1109b30–1). He is interested in praise and blame because virtue is a 'praiseworthy disposition' and vice a blameworthy one (1103a9–10, 1146a1–4) – by which he means that the former disposition hits and the latter misses the mean:

> In everything, intermediacy (*to meson*) is an object for praise, whereas the extremes are neither to be praised, nor correct, but to be censured.
> (EN 1108a14–16; cf. EE 1222a6–12, 1222b12–14)

Unlike many modern readers who take praiseworthiness and blameworthiness of states of character to depend on whether we are responsible for them, Aristotle consistently indicates that the praiseworthiness of the ethical excellences (and the blameworthiness of the ethical vices) depends on the goodness (or badness) of the actions, feelings, and motivations to which they give rise.[51] His goal in articulating and defending an account of voluntariness is to capture the conditions in which a person's action shows whether her disposition hits or misses the mean.[52]

Voluntariness rather than *prohairesis* is the central notion here even though, as Aristotle insists, *prohairesis* reveals character better than action does (1111b5–6). This is because the action too is revealing. For example the acratic person acts against his *prohairesis*, but his action still reveals a significant weakness in his character (EN 1145b10–12; EE 1223a36–b3). In general, a good person never does something bad voluntarily (1128b 28–9, 1146a6–7).

Aristotle explains and defends two explicit criteria for voluntariness: one concerning the agent's causal role in the action, and the other concerning the agent's knowledge. In each case, he is concerned to resist alternative criteria that would classify as involuntary actions that *do* express the agent's ethical character.

First of all, a voluntary action must 'originate' in the agent (EN 1111a23; cf. 1110a15–17). By this Aristotle means nothing more mysterious than that it is the agent, rather than someone or something else, who moves his own bodily parts. (Being kidnapped or being blown away by the wind are cases where this condition is not satisfied 1110a1–4). This understanding of what it takes to be the 'origin of action' entails that cases of unwilling or reluctant behaviour (for example, handing over one's money at gunpoint) are nonetheless voluntary (1110a4–b5). Aristotle endorses and emphasizes this result, which constitutes a revision of ordinary uses of the terms 'hekousion' and 'akousion'[53] – noting that people are still praiseworthy and blameworthy for what they do in such situations. For example, Euripides' Alcmaeon is blameworthy for committing matricide simply in order to avoid being cursed (1110a27–9). One can also be praised for doing the right thing in such situations when the decision is difficult, or hard to abide by – for example, putting up with torture to avoid divulging an important secret (1110a19–23).

Aristotle is happy to call such actions voluntary because what a person decides to do in such cases reflects his character – unless of course the person is ignorant of some crucial fact about what he is doing or the circumstances in which he is acting. For example, the man who stabs his sparring partner with a spear that he mistakenly thinks is a practice weapon with a blunted end does not kill voluntarily. Likewise Oedipus, who does not know that the hostile stranger he kills is his father, does not commit patricide voluntarily. Thus the second criterion for voluntary action is that the agent know what Aristotle calls 'the particulars' of the action (1110b33–1111a1, 23–4).

The 'particulars' that the voluntary agent must know are those relevant to the doctrine of the mean:

> There is the matter of who is acting, what he is doing, in rela
> tion to what or affecting what, sometimes also with what (as for
> example with a tool), what the action is for (e.g. saving someone),
> and how it is done (e.g. gently or vigorously).
>
> (EN 1111a3–6)

Recall that doing what one ought, when one ought, to whom one ought, as one ought (and so on) is to 'hit the mean' (1109a24–30, b12–16). Aristotle goes to great lengths to distinguish the voluntary agent's knowledge of the particulars from the ethical person's knowledge of what he may and may not do, given those particulars. Ignorance of the latter sort, which he calls 'ignorance in the *prohairesis*', 'ignorance of the good', or 'ignorance of the universal' does not make an action involuntary, Aristotle insists (1110b30–1111a1).

In so doing he is registering emphatic disagreement with a notorious claim in Plato's dialogues: that no one does wrong voluntarily (*Laws* 860d–e). The rationale behind the Platonic assertion starts from the premise that all wrongdoing results from ignorance of the good (*Meno* 78a–b, *Gorg.* 468b–c, *Pr.* 357c–e; cf. EN 1145b25–7). But if wrongdoing results from ignorance, the argument continues, it must be involuntary. Aristotle agrees whole-heartedly with the premise of this reasoning, since he thinks any wrongdoing is a result of ethical ignorance (as we will see in more detail when we discuss the intellectual excellences). But he rejects the inference to the Platonic conclusion precisely because wrongdoing is a premier instance of blameworthy activity. An unacceptable consequence of the Platonic view is that only our good actions, and never our bad ones, are voluntary. This is the thesis that Aristotle singles out for refutation in EN III 5 (1113b14–17, 1114b12–13, 19–20).

Aristotle insists that ignorance of the good, when displayed in action, reveals the character of the agent (1110b32). By contrast, ignorance of the particular facts severs the connection between the agent's character and what she does. An action performed in such ignorance fails to be regulated by the agent's views about what is *kalon* and *aischron*. Thus, he concludes, only ignorance of the latter sort is a basis for calling an action involuntary.[54]

The role of reason in ethical excellence

The account of voluntariness and related notions concludes Aristotle's general account of ethical excellence, which he summarizes as follows:

> We have now given a general account of the [ethical] excellences:
> that they are means (*mesotêtes*) and dispositions (*hexeis*), that
> they give rise to the same sorts of actions from which they arise,
> that they are up to us and voluntary,[55] and are as right reason
> (*orthos logos*) dictates.
>
> (*EN* 1114b26–30; cf. 1106b36–1107a2, 1138b18–25)

The 'right reason' (*orthos logos*) that appears in the definition (1114b29) has not in fact been discussed in the preceding discussion of ethical excellence, although it appears regularly in Aristotle's accounts of the particular ethical excellences (1103b32, 1115b12; cf. 1115b19, 1125b35). It is a crucial element of the account because human excellence is for Aristotle rational excellence (1098a3–17, 1102a14–b3). The desires and feelings involved in ethical excellence are rational, not in themselves, but only insofar as they are capable of following reason (1102b13–31). The 'right reason' that determines the mean of these desires and feelings (1106b36–1107a2, 1114b26–30, 1138b28–9, cf. 1147b31–2) is one of the purely intellectual excellences, which Aristotle distinguishes from the ethical excellences in *EN* I 13 (1103a3–10, 1138b35–1139a1). It is the intellectual excellence that he calls '*phronêsis*' (practical wisdom) – 1107a1–2, 1144b23–4, 26–8). In order to understand the kind of rationality that Aristotle thinks is exhibited by the ethical person, we must therefore turn to Book VI, where he discusses the intellectual excellences.

Intellectual activities and excellences

When he turns to discuss the excellences of reason strictly conceived, Aristotle makes a distinction between what he sees as two fundamentally different activities of reason (1139a6–15). On the one hand there is the kind of cognition involved in grasping eternal, unchanging, immutable truths (1139b19–24). This is the activity that he calls *theoria* and identifies with the ultimate human good in Book X (1177a12–18). Let us call this 'theoretical reason'. Aristotle contrasts it with what he calls practical (*praktikê*) reason (1139a36), which deliberates about what to do (1139a11–13; cf. 1142b31–3). Excellence of such reasoning, according to Aristotle, falls into two types: *technê* (skill or craft, defined in VI 4) and *phronêsis* (practical wisdom, defined in VI 5).[56] Practical wisdom (*phronêsis*) is the excellence of reason involved in the ethical excellences (1144b21–8). It is the 'right reason' (*orthos logos*) that identifies the mean (1107a1–2).

As deliberative excellences, both craft and practical wisdom are types of knowledge about how to realize goals. In the case of the crafts (e.g. medicine, navigation, carpentry, flute playing), the goal is an easily specifiable product, result, or activity. That of practical wisdom, by contrast, is 'doing well' (*eupraxia* 1140b7) or 'living well' (*eu zên* 1140a28). Aristotle intends to capture this difference with the general claim that the crafts concern production (*poiêsis*), while practical wisdom is concerned not with production, but with action (*praxis*) (1140a2–6; cf. 1139b1–4, 1140b6–7). Practical wisdom is knowledge of what to do – not in order to bring about this or that result (e.g. what must be done not in order to cure the patient, or fix the roof) – but in order, quite simply, to 'do well' – not as a carpenter, or a doctor, or a navigator, but as a human being.

The deliberation at which the person of practical wisdom excels is not simply instrumental reasoning. Mere proficiency at figuring out how to realize or execute one's goals is mere cleverness (*deinotês*), rather than the sort of 'good deliberation' (*euboulia*) characteristic of practical wisdom, Aristotle says, since both the ethical and the unethical person can be clever (1144a23–9). He insists that the end(s) achieved by practical wisdom must be good (1142b18–22). For example, one person might have calculated proficiently that a rendezvous out of town is the best way to commit adultery without being detected. Another might have calculated that refusing money to a panhandler and donating instead to a food service for the homeless is the best way to make sure the panhandler does not go hungry. Let us suppose that in each case the agent's deliberation is instrumentally proficient. Nonetheless, the adulterer's deliberations do not count as an exercise of practical wisdom, since the goal in the light of which he deliberates is not good and fine (1142b20–1, 1144a26).

Nor is it clear that the deliberations of the donor to charity count as an exercise of practical wisdom. Granted, the donor's goal (alleviating hunger) is good, and her reasoning about how to realize that goal is proficient. Nonetheless, reasoning about the best way to alleviate hunger does not fall within the distinctive expertise of practical wisdom. It falls rather within the expertise of a 'productive' craft – e.g. economics. While the practically wise person should defer to expertise about how best to alleviate hunger and poverty, (for example, it would be a fool who decided to set about alleviating world hunger by relying on astrology), practical wisdom of the sort Aristotle is interested in is not itself exercised where there is a specific expertise (*technê*) for realizing the goal in question, Aristotle insists (1140a28–30).

Rather, the end in the light of which the person of practical wisdom deliberates is the most general and ultimate end that a human being pursues: living well (1140a28). Practical wisdom is the correct grasp of this goal (1142b33). It is knowledge of what is just and fine and good (1143b21–3) and of 'what one must do and refrain from' (1143a8–9). It tells us not *how* to execute some determinate goal (such as committing adultery or alleviating poverty), but rather *whether* it is good or fine or just to do so – in general, or in particular circumstances.

Aristotle illustrates this important point in the last chapter of EN VI, where he explains why genuine ethical excellence must involve practical wisdom. A person might possess one of the ethical excellences 'by nature,' he allows, but without *phronêsis*, such a disposition puts her at risk for serious ethical error:

> Everyone thinks that each of the various sorts of character traits belongs to us in some sense by nature – because we are just, restrained (*sôphronikoi*), courageous, and the rest from the moment we are born. . . . But without intelligence (*nous*)[57] to accompany them, they are evidently harmful. Still, this much appears to be a matter of observation, that just as a powerful body when moving without sight to guide it will fall with a powerful impact because of its sightlessness, so in this case too.
>
> (1144b4–6, 8–12; Rowe's translation, slightly altered)

The naturally virtuous persons whom Aristotle has in mind are presumably the naturally 'temperate' and 'courageous' types that occupy Plato's attention in the *Statesman* (306a–309e). The naturally 'temperate' person is by temperament gentle and conciliatory, and seeks to avoid conflict wherever possible. The opposing natural tendency is that of the 'naturally courageous', or 'spirited' person who is by temperament vigorous, assertive, and inclined to respond aggressively to provocation. Each type of person is liable to a ruinous kind of error, Plato tells us. The 'temperate' type is likely to back down from conflict when resolution and resistance is called for, while the 'courageous' type is too ready to engage in conflict – each with potentially ruinous results (*Stsm.* 307e–308b). Only those in whom the rulers have inculcated a correct grasp of the just, the fine and the good (309c) will be restrained when the occasion calls for it and aggressive when the occasion calls for it (309d–e).[58]

This Platonic point is presumably what Aristotle has in mind when he says, in EN VI 13, that only when informed by practical wisdom will the naturally 'restrained' or the naturally courageous person avoid the risk of serious ethical error:

> But if a person acquires intelligence (*nous*), it makes a difference to his actions, and the disposition (*hexis*) which was merely similar to excellence in the proper sense (*kuriôs*) will then be that excellence.
>
> (*EN* 1144b12–14)

The naturally temperate person desires and takes pleasure in things (peace, avoiding conflict) that are good in the right circumstances. So too does the naturally courageous person, who values standing up to aggression. Asserting oneself is an important and good thing to do, but only in the appropriate circumstances. Thus a person will have a genuine ethical excellence – one that 'hits the mean' – only when such goals as these are tempered by an understanding of when it is proper or fine to pursue them, knowledge of when it is shameful to back down from conflict, and when it is shameful to fight.

In deliberating whether to pursue peace in the given circumstances, the ethical person considers whether it would be *kalon* or *aischron* to do so. That is, he regulates his pursuit of something he values (avoiding conflict) in the light of his higher commitment to the *kalon*.[59] The person with practical wisdom deliberates excellently about 'living well' precisely because he knows when and whether it is good and fine, rather than harmful or shameful, to seek peace, pursue a quarrel, tell a joke – or, in general, to engage in any of the activities in the domain of the various ethical excellences. We might say that he exercises 'good judgment' in what he sets about to do. And in fact 'good judgment' is in many contexts a very apt translation of '*phronêsis*'.

Universals and particulars

In striking contrast with Plato, who portrays the knowledge one needs for living well as the philosopher's grasp of other-worldly eternal truths (*Phd.* 65d–66a; *Rep.* 479e), Aristotle insists that the knowledge expressed in the ethical excellences is practical rather than theoretical. One of his main projects in *EN* VI is to demarcate the difference between deliberative reason and its excellences, on the one hand, and theoretical reason and its excellences, on the other (cf. 1143b14–17). We have already discussed one of the differences he sees between them: that practical reasoning is deliberative (1139a12–13) and therefore goal-directed (1144a31–3). Another fundamental difference, emphasized by Aristotle at the opening of *EN* VI, concerns the sorts of truths each type of reason is suited to grasp.

On the one hand, he says, there are eternal, immutable, necessary truths, which are expressed in perfectly universal generalizations (1139a6–8, b19–24). The kind of reason that aims to know such truths is called 'scientific' (*epistêmonikon*, 1139a12). Its excellence, which is the condition of actually knowing these truths, is called 'science' (*epistêmê*) (1139b19–36). Such knowledge is not simply a grasp of isolated facts, but a systematic grasp of an integrated body of knowledge that is deduced from a set of ultimate first principles.[60] Aristotle gives a detailed account of what it is to have such knowledge in the *Posterior Analytics*.[61] It is his version of the condition that Plato attributes to the philosopher who grasps the forms and is thereby assimilated to the ultimate, divine, realities (*Rep.* 490a–b, 611e; cf. *EN* 1177b30–1178a2). According to Aristotle in *EN* X 6–8, excellent activity of this kind of reason is what constitutes the best life (1177a12–18).

On the other hand, there is the domain of truths about variable things – those that 'admit of being otherwise' (1139a8, 12–14, 1140a33–b4, b25–8, 1141b9–12). These can be expressed in generalizations that are true only 'for the most part' (*hos epi to polu*, 1137b14–16 cf. 1094b19–21). Human affairs are of this sort, as are the productive enterprises that are grouped under the label '*technê*' (craft). By 'craft' Aristotle means such disciplines as carpentry, pottery, medicine, and navigation. Thus, according to Aristotle, it is a general feature of deliberative reasoning that it concerns matters about which there are no true universal generalizations.[62]

Aristotle's denial that there are universal truths in ethics – that what is just and fine admit of much variation from circumstance to circumstance and resist formulation in exceptionless practical principles (1094b14–22; 1104a3–5; 1137b13–19; cf. 1107a29–32) – is well known and often misunderstood.[63] It does *not* imply, in particular, that there is no fact of the matter about whether the particular action someone performs is just, or fine, or shameful. While returning what you've borrowed at the appointed time is not always just (as the example in *Republic* I 331b–d shows), it is in fact just in many different circumstances. Nor does the denial imply that there can be no knowledge of practical truths – of the *kalon*, of justice, etc. – for practical wisdom is precisely knowledge of these things. In order to appreciate just what the denial of universal principles does tell us about Aristotle's conception of ethical reasoning, it is useful to keep in mind that he thinks it applies to the crafts, no less than to practical wisdom.[64] So let us make sure that we understand why Aristotle thinks it applies to the crafts.

It is important to keep in mind the difference between the technical crafts as practised in Aristotle's day and the technology (from the same root, *technê*) employed in modern mass production. In the latter, a perfectly general formula adhered to religiously in a highly controlled environment is capable of producing a uniform product, time after time. By contrast, a genuine craft, which we often contrast with the former sort of enterprise using the phrase 'it is an art rather than a science', is exercised in relatively uncontrolled environments, where there are no simple algorithms that, if adhered to exactly, will guarantee the desired result.

For example, the activity of the artisan baker differs in this respect from the production line in a Wonder Bread factory. To be sure, the baker has a recipe that specifies the relative quantities of flour and liquid as well as the kneading and rising times, along with the baking time and temperature. However, adhering religiously to this recipe will not always produce the same results. Variations in the ambient temperature and air pressure, the humidity, and the freshness of the flour, for example, call for adjustments to the basic recipe. Depending on these uncontrolled variables, one might need to mix in more flour or less liquid, or knead for a longer time. The skilled baker knows how to adapt to these different circumstances. He kneads not just for the length of time specified in the recipe, but until the dough is ready to rise, and similarly lets it rise until ready to bake and bakes it until it is done. In order to observe the mean[65] for each of these variables, he departs from the standard recipe as the situation requires, and his ability to do so reliably is a mark of his expertise.

Of course it is perfectly consistent with the observations just advanced that there are perfectly general principles (which take into account all the variables, controlled and uncontrolled) that can explain the artisan baker's success. Thus one might object that the difference between an art and a science is not in the generality of the principles that apply, but the extent to which the relevant variables are controlled. This objection must, I think, be conceded. Nonetheless, even if Aristotle is wrong that there is no perfectly general theory that applies to baking, navigation, or any other practical enterprise, he is still right to deny that expertise in such a craft involves the grasp or use of such a theory. The principles of physics, chemistry, and microbiology that could at least in principle explain why *this* is exactly the right amount of this flour to add to the dough in *these* atmospheric conditions are far too long and complicated to be actually used in the baker's deliberations. The cognitive condition characteristic of the expert baker does not involve the grasp of such a theory.

Similarly in the case of ethical expertise: even if Aristotle is wrong to deny that there are general principles that can explain why *this* is the right thing to do in *these* circumstances, or why *that* would be shameful in *those* circumstances, it is still reasonable of him to deny that the person of practical wisdom employs such principles in deliberating about how to act. Aristotle's main interest in discussing practical wisdom is to illuminate the sort of cognitive disposition it is, and the sort of reasoning it involves, since these are relevant to his practical project of how to acquire practical wisdom. Let us therefore concentrate on this aspect of his claims.

The ethical person, Aristotle tells us, is more like someone exercising a craft skill (where general rules are at best fallible guides to correct action) than a worker on a modern assembly line.

Knowing how to live well isn't as easy as having a set of rules to follow mechanically. Rather, it involves having good judgment about how to realize our goals (or 'hit the mean') in the concrete situations in which we find ourselves. Thus the ethical disposition informed by this knowledge is far from the rigid, habitual, routine-following disposition so familiar from caricatures of Aristotle's ethics.[66] Instead, it is highly responsive and adaptive, enabling a person to react appropriately in all the different circumstances that come her way. The steadfastness and reliability that belong to character in Aristotle's account (1105a33) have to do with proficiency at realizing its goal (the *kalon*) – rather than in the principles and routines involved in its judgment and deliberations.

Aristotle regularly characterizes the distinctive cognitive competence of the *phronimos* as a grasp of particulars (1142a21–3, 1143a28–31; cf. 1147a25–34, b4–6).[67] The 'universals' with which he contrasts these particulars are general practical principles about what is *kalon* and *aischron* (e.g. principles about returning what you've borrowed, or not telling lies) in the light of which she regulates her pursuit of the other things she values in life. These are the sorts of general principles that Aristotle says are true only for the most part. What distinguishes the *phronimos*' competence is not his grasp of such general principles. Knowing that injustice is shameful is relatively easy, as is knowing that, in general, it is just to return what you have borrowed. However, knowing whether returning what you've borrowed in this particular situation would be shameful is more difficult (EN V 9 1137a9–17). It is good judgment about the latter sort of question – about whether a particular situation falls under a general principle – that is the distinctive expertise of the *phronimos*. Hence Aristotle's description of it as a grasp of the 'particulars'.

It is perception rather than deliberation that grasps the particulars, Aristotle says (1112b33–1113a2, 1126b1–4, 1142a25–30, 1147a25–6). Practical wisdom, he says in uncharacteristically metaphorical language, is 'the eye of the soul', by which the good person 'sees aright' (1144a29–31; cf. 1143b13–14). In another context, he likens this grasp of particulars to *nous* (sometimes translated as 'intuition') – a grasp of facts unmediated by reasoning (1143a35–b5).[68] Taken outside the context of Aristotle's other claims about practical wisdom, these remarks can yield the misleading impression that Aristotle thinks *phronêsis* issues in inarticulate or unreasoned 'gut' feelings: that the practically wise person 'just sees' what is the right thing to do. But this cannot be Aristotle's view. For the cognitive mastery of such a person, we have seen, is structurally similar to the diagnostic capacity of an experienced physician, whose clinical experience enables her to apply properly the diagnostic criteria that can be learned from.[69] Hence the 'good eye' of the *phronimos* will be like that of the diagnostician who can 'see' that this is a case of mumps or that the child's ear is infected but is perfectly capable of explaining and giving reasons in support of her judgment.

Reason, desire, and knowledge

As a deliberative expertise characterized by a correct grasp of 'particulars', practical wisdom is no different from technical deliberative expertise. What distinguishes it from the crafts is a combination of two features. One difference, which we have already discussed, concerns its characteristic goal, 'living well' (1140a28, b7). The other difference is that practical wisdom, unlike technical know-how, requires having desires of a certain sort (cf. 1105a30–3).

Reason without desire moves nothing, Aristotle explains – whereas thought that is 'for the sake of something' brings about movement and action (1139a35–6). In the case of the technical crafts, the craft knowledge on its own is insufficient to generate activity. The knowledge of how to build a boat, for example, does not move the shipwright to action unless he decides to build a boat. Still, the desire to build a boat is not a necessary condition for the knowledge of how to build it. In the case of practical wisdom, by contrast, Aristotle insists, correct desire and feeling are necessary for knowledge. This is partly because practical deliberations have as their starting point a *telos* that is itself the object of a desire (1139a31–5, b3–4; cf. 1140b11–20; 1144a7–9, 20–2, a31–b1; 1145a4–6) but also because the outcome of the deliberation (a decision of what to do in the circumstances) must be desired by the agent (1139a25–6). For the same reason that one cannot have *prohairesis* without an ethical disposition (*êthikê hexis*, 1139a33–4), one cannot have practical wisdom without having ethical excellence (1144a36–b1, 1178a16–21) – that is, without desiring and feeling pleasures and pains about the right things.

The function of reason is to grasp truths, Aristotle says (1139b12). In contrast with the sort of truth aimed at by theoretical and technical reason, the truth aimed at by practical reason is 'truth in agreement with right desire' (1139a29–31). This is not to say that the truth of a practical claim itself depends on my desiring it. If in the circumstances the right thing to do is to hold my tongue, then that is the truth regardless of whether I feel like, or am capable of, holding my tongue. Aristotle's position is rather that I do not grasp securely and understand that truth (which is what practical wisdom involves) unless I desire to do it. I do not truly know that holding my tongue is *kalon* unless I desire to do so.

These considerations provide the context for appreciating Aristotle's famous claim that excellent activity is pleasant to the ethical person:

> The pleasure and pain that supervenes (*epigignomenê*) on what people do should be treated as a sign of their dispositions; for someone who holds back from bodily pleasure and does so cheerfully is a moderate person, while someone who is upset at doing so is self-indulgent, and someone who withstands frightening things and does so cheerfully, or anyway without distress, is a courageous person, while someone who is distressed at them is cowardly.
> (*EN* 1104b3–8; cf. 1099a17–21, 1120a26–31, 1121a1–4)

Feelings of pleasure and pain are signs of our desires. Thus, for example, a person who performs a temperate action (the action prescribed by *orthos logos*) but is pained at doing so has a conflicting desire. She exercises not the virtue of temperance (*sôphrosunê*) but rather self-control (*enkrateia*). Hence she lacks practical wisdom, and thus does not truly *know* that her action is the right thing to do. By contrast, the person who not only does the temperate thing but enjoys it has a temperate, rather than merely self-controlled, *hexis*. Her disposition expresses 'truth in agreement with right desire' (1139a29–31), and thus she, rather than her self-controlled counterpart, really knows that this is what she should do in the circumstances.

This picture of the relation between practical reason and desire may be counterintuitive to readers today, who are inclined to suppose that it is one thing to know or think you should do something, and quite another to desire doing it. But Aristotle is self-consciously writing in the tradition of Plato's Socrates in the *Protagoras*, who resists the view that one can know the right thing to do, but desire or feel like doing something else (*Pr.* 352b–357e; cf. *EN* 1145b21–7). Aristotle agrees with Plato's Socrates that knowing what one should do is impossible without properly cultivated desires and sensibilities. To think or know that something is good involves desiring and taking pleasure in it. This is why Aristotle, in his own discussion of *acrasia* (weakness of will) in *EN* VII 1–3 agrees with the Socrates of Plato's *Protagoras* that people with conflicting motivations – the weak-willed (acratic) person who fails to do what he thinks he should (and thus is pained at what he does), and the self-controlled (encratic) person who overcomes his disinclination to do what he thinks is right (and thus still acts with pain) – do not fully 'know' this is the right thing to do.[70] While their desires may conflict with an impulse that issues from reason, the rational faculty lacks knowledge.

Learning to be good

Since acquiring practical wisdom involves acquiring the appropriate affective and emotional sensibilities, learning how to live well requires training of those sensibilities. Aristotle's general term for these feelings and desires is *'pathê'* (plural; singular *'pathos'*).[71] These include 'appetite, anger, fear, confidence, jealousy, delight, liking, and hate' (1105b21–3). The feature that all these *pathê* have in common is that they 'involve pleasure and pain' (b23). Since pleasure and pain play such an important role in ethical excellence, Aristotle concludes:

> This is why we must have been brought up in a certain way from childhood onwards, as Plato says, so as to delight in and be distressed by the things we should; this is what the correct education (*paideia*) is.
>
> (*EN* 1104b11–13; cf. 1103b23–25)

Aristotle here explicitly defers to Plato's account of *paideia*, the musical (cultural) and physical education that trains one's feelings of pleasure and pain to accord with reason. The media of this training, we saw in the last chapter, are cultural activities: stories, hymns, songs and dances, even the material culture in the surroundings, and the sorts of games children play

– all carefully selected so as to have the effect of moulding souls to delight in the *kalon* and be pained at the prospect of doing what is *aischron*.

Such cultivation of a person's aesthetic and ethical sensibilities shapes not just his feelings, but also his beliefs about what is *kalon* and the *aischron*. Proper *paideia* gives him the ability to discriminate between them in concrete situations (*Rep.* 402c). One learns, for example, that Achilles was brave although overly prone to anger, and that Odysseus was wise. The tales in which these characters and other exemplary figures appear provide plenty of data about the sorts of actions that are *kalon* and *aischron*. This 'musical' training supplies the starting points, Aristotle claims, from which eventually one can develop the understanding characteristic of practical wisdom (*EN* 1095b4–8, cf. 1098b2–4).[72]

Aristotle has very little to say about the process that transforms such initial correct belief into *phronêsis*, although his remark at 1095a30–b4 is reminiscent of Plato's account of the philosopher's ascent to the first principles of dialectic in *Republic* VI (511a–e). Nor is there consensus among interpreters about the form such knowledge takes.[73] But one thing Aristotle clearly insists upon is that, unlike the knowledge characteristic of the philosophical life, which can be acquired by teaching (*EN* 1103a15–16, 1139b25–6), practical wisdom must be acquired through experience (1095a2–4, cf. 1143b5–9). Teenagers can become expert in mathematics – or other 'theoretical' disciplines that involve grasping universal principles (1142a11–16) – but only a more experienced person can develop expertise in a practical discipline, and only such a person is in a position to profit from intellectual discussion of such matters (1095a2–4).

The relevant experience, Aristotle insists, is that of actually engaging in the activities of the practical discipline. In the case of the physician, this means engaging in clinical practice. In the case of the navigator it means spending a time at sea. In the case of the person who wants to live well, this involves much practice in engaging in the business of life: dealing with other people, with one's appetites, and with one's fears, to name just a few. It is from this sort of experience that one acquires the intellectual expertise that enables one to grasp and respond appropriately to the particulars of the situations that life brings along.

Aristotelian ethical excellence has, nonetheless, acquired an unfortunate reputation of being a 'habit' – a mindless, unreflective pattern of behaviour devoid of understanding and discrimination. No doubt this is because Aristotle opens his general account of virtue of character in Book II of the *EN* by focusing on the practical question, how does one acquire such virtue? The question he raises has a standard menu of answers in antiquity, reflecting the range of opinion on the question: from nature, from practice or habituation, from teaching, or from divine dispensation (1179b20–1; cf. 1099b9–11, *Meno* 70a). Aristotle's concern in *EN* II is to respond to those who think that it is from teaching (e.g. listening to lectures and engaging in purely intellectual activity) that one becomes good (1105b12–18). Such a position reflects or implies the view that ethical knowledge is an intellectual excellence like scientific knowledge (*epistêmê*), rather than the sort of practical knowledge that arises from experience and practice. Thus Aristotle famously says that we become just by doing just actions, temperate by doing temperate actions, and so on (1103a31–b2, b14–21; cf. 1105a17–19, b9–12; 1114b27–8; 1180a1–4).

Such repeated practice is a kind of habituation for which the term in Greek is '*ethismos*' which is cognate with the term for character (*êthos*, 1103a17–23). The sort of habituation Aristotle has in mind in these contexts is repetition of action, and the simple behavioural processes he describes do not seem to have any systematic relation to training of desires and emotions, or appreciation of reasons, let alone appreciation for the *kalon*. If we focus on these remarks outside their proper context, and assume that they constitute the whole of the process by which one develops the virtues and vices of character, then it is easy to arrive at the conclusion that virtue of character is, for Aristotle, a kind of habit: an unreflective behavioural disposition.[74]

However, this is not the whole of Aristotle's account of ethical development. When Aristotle makes these remarks, he is presupposing the Platonic picture of *paideia* – of training the emotional sensibilities through inspirational literature, rhythm and song. He is addressing an audience that has already been 'raised in good habits' (1095b4–6) and thus already loves the *kalon* and is averse to what is *aischron* (1179b24–31). It is from such an audience of seekers after *aretê* that he entertains the question, 'How do we become good?'. That is, 'Where do we go from here?'. To this audience, he answers: practise. Do not 'take refuge in arguments and discussion' (1105b13) in an attempt to acquire practical wisdom by a purely intellectual route. Rather, take care that you practise what you have learned so far. Be assiduous at performing the actions that you have learned are *kalon*, and eschewing the activities that you know are *aischron* (1105b 9–18).

Aristotle recognizes that these actions are not always easy to perform, even for the well-raised young person. However much someone who has received a proper Platonic *paideia* revels in the prospect of being as brave as Achilles or as self–controlled as Odysseus, he will not find it easy to stand his ground when the enemy approaches, or to exercise restraint in the face of outrageous provocation. Such actions are difficult, even painful, but become easier, even pleasant to do, once one has become used to doing them (*sunêthê genomena* 1179b35–1180a1). But if one gets used to doing the wrong actions in these situations, even a good *paideia* will become undone, Aristotle insists (1179b31–1180a5). Thus even if a proper Platonic *paideia* is necessary for becoming good, no one has a chance of becoming good without practice – that is, without acting appropriately in the relevant situations. Someone who regularly acts badly in those situations will become vicious rather than good.

We can recognize three distinct stages of moral development and learning on Aristotle's view. The first stage is the one on which Plato focuses — the cultivation of sensibilities and shaping of aspirations from the earliest age. Aristotle calls this stage that of 'nurture and care' (1179b34–5), and he explicitly claims that this training is not enough to ensure that one will have a good character. Once one has grown up, one must take care to practise the right activities (1179b35–1180a4). Practising the right sorts of actions is necessary to complete the good disposition inculcated in childhood, while practising the wrong sorts of actions will undo even a good early education. Ethical excellence requires restraint on the sorts of desires or emotions that people naturally have, and one's early education (*paideia*) is insufficient to produce this – not least because their domains include activities and emotions beyond the scope of a child's experience. However much a well-raised young person wishes to be courageous and knows that it is *kalon*, it is still difficult, and an acquired disposition, to be able to stand one's ground in the face of the enemy's advance. Similarly, it is difficult to resist the temptations of various bodily pleasures and the prospects for illicit gain that come with adulthood experience.

One learns to do this, Aristotle claims, not by pursuing the route advocated in Plato's *Phaedo* and *Republic* of withdrawing from the sensible and social world and from all bodily concerns, but by immersing oneself in that world and training oneself by acting properly there. One also acquires thereby the ability to make finer and more difficult discriminations than one's early education will have prepared one for. Thus an important second stage in the acquisition of virtue that Aristotle insists on as a necessary supplement to Plato's emphasis on early education is the stage of habituation by adult activities – the stage at which 'practice makes perfect' (in the best case), but at any rate 'practice makes permanent.'[75]

The third stage, about which Aristotle says the least, is the stage of further intellectual inquiry that results in *phronêsis* (practical wisdom). Whatever the merits of those who advocate intellectual inquiry as the route to ethical knowledge, Aristotle insists that one cannot acquire such knowledge without immersing oneself in the full domain of human social life, thereby acquiring the relevant experience to engender not only the right feelings and desires, but also the right convictions and capacity for discernment.

If we view in this wider context Aristotle's remarks about habituation by repeated action we will lose the temptation to see excellence of character, on his picture, as a mindless, behaviourally conditioned habit. Rather, we will be able to see these remarks as describing one necessary and important stage in the process whereby one develops the fine-grained discriminatory and motivational sensibility that he attributes to the person of practical wisdom.

Responsibility for character

Recognizing the three stages of ethical development assumed by Aristotle also gives us the proper context to understand his claim, famously argued in EN III 5, that we are responsible for our states of character (1114a4–31). Aristotle's argument for this conclusion is very simple. He first appeals to the general account of character formation that he outlines in EN II. We become just by performing just actions, temperate by performing temperate actions, and so on (1114a4–6). His second point is that we know this when we are performing the character-forming actions. We know that we are doing what will make us just (or unjust), temperate or intemperate (1114a7–10). Thus, he concludes, we voluntarily become the sorts of people we are: 'If someone knowingly does the sorts of things that make him unjust, then he is unjust voluntarily' (1114a12–13).

A frequent objection to this argument from modern readers is to say: But what if someone has been raised in deprived conditions, and does not know, for example, that stealing is wrong? We are not responsible for knowing what is just and unjust, since – as Aristotle himself accepts and emphasizes – this is a product of our upbringing and social context. Thus, the objection concludes, Aristotle is wrong to conclude that people are responsible for their states of character.

The objection, however, makes the mistake of supposing that Aristotle's argument depends on the assumption that we are *responsible* for knowing what sorts of actions are unjust, intemperate, and so on. Aristotle, however, starts from a much weaker assumption: that we do in fact know this. This assumption should not surprise us, since all along he has made it clear that he is addressing an audience who have received a good ethical education, and that he is addressing the practical question of such an audience: What must we do to become good? The fortunate young people in that audience are, in Aristotle's view, no more responsible for having a correct general outlook on right and wrong than the person raised in a den of thieves is responsible for having a mistaken one.

Aristotle is keenly aware, as Plato was before him, that only someone who has been raised in optimal conditions will have the correct views about what is fine and shameful. With the correct starting points, he says, one has already 'half of the whole' (1098b7). That is why, he insists, one needs to have been raised under correct laws, which dictate not only the adult activities people may engage in, but also the earliest stages of *paideia* they will receive (1179b31–1180a5; cf. 1103b1–6). Someone who has not received such a correct *paideia* has virtually no chance of becoming good. Even at the stage of habituation by adult activities, Aristotle notes, it is necessary to have good teachers (1103b8–13). A person can no more learn on her own and in unfavourable circumstances to be a navigator than she can learn to be good. Thus it is a mistake to suppose that Aristotle is attempting to argue in *EN* III 5 that, no matter what the circumstances in which a person is raised, he is still responsible for becoming virtuous or vicious. Rather, Aristotle is addressing the practical concerns of the audience who have in fact been blessed with a correct upbringing, good laws, and competent teachers. He is telling this audience that now it is up to them to complete the process that will make them the sort of people they aspire to be.

It is important to recognize that Aristotle's discussion of voluntariness and related notions (*EN* III 1–5) is not concerned exclusively, or even primarily, with the voluntariness of character. It is only very late in the discussion, halfway through chapter 5, that he introduces the claim about character (1114a4–14).[76] Voluntariness interests Aristotle primarily as an expression, rather than a source, of character. Modern readers tend to assume that unless our states of character are up to us, we are not morally responsible for our actions. Aristotle, by contrast, is quite innocent of this assumption. He explicitly acknowledges that the sort of responsibility for character he argues for is at best partial: 'we are co-causes in a way (*sunaitioi pôs*) of our characters' (1114b23; cf. 1114b2). Such partial responsibility, however far it is from what modern readers seek as a basis for moral agency, is perfectly sufficient for the practical project with which Aristotle and his intended audience are concerned.[77]

External goods

Aristotle's portrait of the person living the life of ethical excellence has much in common with Plato's. Indeed, we can recognize his *phronêsis* as an Aristotelian version of Plato's 'using craft'.[78] The latter, we saw in the last chapter, is knowledge about when and whether it is fine and good to pursue the usually recognized 'good things' in life: wealth, health, security, family, and so on. These are the things that Aristotle classifies as desirable for their own sakes (1097b2–3) but whose proper use is regulated by the ethical excellences:

> Each thing is used best by the person possessing the excellence relating to that thing.
>
> (*EN* 1120a5–6)

The person of ethical excellence, on this portrait, regulates her pursuit of such objectives in the light of her higher commitment to the *kalon*. Aristotelian practical wisdom (*phronêsis*) is the knowledge that allows her to do so successfully.

Of course, pursuing these external advantages only when it is *kalon* to do so (or *aischron* not to) is not thereby to succeed in securing them. Thus living an ethical life, so conceived, does not guarantee that one will achieve the external prosperity that most people identify with (or take to be necessary for) happiness. Aristotle seems explicitly to recognize this:

> Those who claim that the man being broken on the wheel and engulfed by great misfortunes is happy, provided he is a good character, are talking nonsense.
>
> (EN 1153b19–21; cf.1095b32–1096a2)

The figure of the excellent person on the rack is the most extreme version of a case in which a person possesses ethical excellence yet lacks the external advantages. We saw in the last chapter that although this figure originates in Plato's *Republic* (361d–362a), Plato himself does not explicitly raise the question of whether such a person can be happy. Aristotle's remarks here (EN 1153b18–21) indicate that the question has become a popular subject of debate, with some parties already defending the affirmative answer that the Stoics will later make famous.

Aristotle makes it clear in many contexts that he thinks happiness requires a certain level of success at securing the natural objects of pursuit: wealth, power, friends, family, and so on (EN 1099a31–b8, 1101a14–16, 1178a28–33, Pol. 1323a24–7; cf. EN 1177a30–b1, 1178b33–1179a9). However, he is still some philosophical distance from raising and engaging with the question on which, a century or more later, his Peripatetic successors disagreed with the Stoics.[79] The Hellenistic debate concerns whether a person who exercises the ethical excellences (and does not merely possess them) can be happy even if he lacks the 'external goods'. Aristotle, by contrast, explains that happiness requires the 'external goods' because they are necessary for the unimpeded exercise of the ethical excellences:

> [Happiness] clearly also requires external goods in addition . . . for it is impossible, or not easy, to perform fine actions if one is without resources. For in the first place, many things are done by means of friends, or wealth, or political power, as if by means of tools; and then again, there are some things the lack of which is like a stain on happiness, things like good birth, being blessed in one's children, beauty: for the person who is extremely ugly, or of low birth, or on his own without children is someone we would be not altogether inclined to call happy, and even less inclined, presumably, if someone had totally depraved children or friends, or ones who were good but dead. As we have said, then, one seems to need this sort of well-being too.
>
> (EN 1099a31–b7; cf. 1100b28–30; 1153b17–19)

One might find it hard to believe that all the external advantages that Aristotle here identifies as necessary for happiness are required for the exercise of the ethical excellences. For example, what ethical excellence requires good looks to be exercised?[80] More importantly for our present purposes, Aristotle's explanation of why external goods are necessary for happiness falls short of claiming, and indeed does not even allow the possibility, that a person might successfully exercise virtue of character and still lack health, wealth, and the other natural objects of pursuit. These remarks here commit Aristotle to the position that the good person on the rack is not happy because he is unable to exercise the ethical excellences.[81]

Aristotle's explanation of the necessity of 'external goods' for happiness makes sense only in the light of a very narrow construal of the notion that virtue is a 'using craft'. If virtue is the knowledge of how to use well the usually recognized 'good things in life' – health, wealth, power, and so on – then it follows trivially that there is no such thing as exercising virtue while lacking the external goods. One cannot use what one does not have. This narrow understanding of the using craft is, however, seriously defective as a model for virtue, and fails to do justice to Aristotle's detailed understanding of it. Aristotle's own accounts of the various ethical excellences show that he thinks human excellence can be manifested not only in a person's use of the external goods that she possesses, but also in her decisions about whether to pursue them – as in the case of the courageous person and the liberal person, who decline to promote their own bodily or economic security in circumstances when this would be shameful. Indeed, he claims, excellence can in fact be displayed in circumstances in which external disaster strikes:

> Even in these circumstances the quality of fineness (*to kalon*) shines through, when someone bears repeated and great misfortunes calmly, not because he is insensitive to them but because he is a person of nobility and greatness of soul (*megalopsuchos*). . . . For we consider that the truly good and sensible person bears what fortune brings him with good grace, and acts on each occasion in the finest way possible, given the resources at the time, just as we think that a good general uses the army he has to the best strategic advantage, and a shoemaker makes a shoe as finely as it can be made out of the hides he has been given.
>
> (*EN* 1100b30–33, 1100b35–1101a5)

Aristotle makes these remarks as part of his argument in *EN* I 10 (reminiscent of Socrates' protreptic argument at *Euthd.* 278e–282c) that it is ethical excellence, not the possession of external goods, that is responsible for happiness. Excellence is to be cultivated above all else, he claims, because it is what makes us happy and makes our happiness stable and impervious to most vicissitudes of fortune (*EN* 1100b2–22; cf. 1099b20–8).[82] The resulting invulnerability to fortune, however, is not complete. Just as the shoemaker can't make shoes without any hides whatsoever and the general can't achieve victory without any troops or weapons, the excellent person is unable to live well if sufficiently grave disaster befalls him (1100b28–30, 1101a9–11).[83]

Even in such cases, however, Aristotle does not allow that the lost external advantages are independently necessary for happiness; their loss, he says, 'obstructs many sorts of activities' (1100b29–30).[84] Here, as before, he claims that external goods are necessary for the activities of excellence (1099a31–3). Since, according to the function argument, these activities constitute the happy life (1098a16–17) Aristotle is not in a position to raise, let alone address, the question of whether a person living a life of ethical excellence can be happy even if he suffers significant loss in external goods. It remains for Aristotle's successors to address that issue in the Hellenistic period.

Notes

1 Cicero mentions the stylistic flourish of Plato and Aristotle in the same breath (*Fin.* 1.14) and commends the eloquence of Aristotle (*TD* 1.7).

2 A third treatise, known as the *Magna Moralia*, is also attributed to Aristotle. It is doubtful that Aristotle is the author, although it seems to bear a very close relationship to Aristotle's own writing. On the Aristotelian ethical treatises, see Rowe 1971, Kenny 1978, Cooper 1975 (with reply by Rowe 1975) and Bobonich 2006.

3 On the explicitly practical orientation of Aristotle's ethical writing, see *EN* 1095a1–6, 1105b11–18, and 1179a35–b2.

4 For example, underlying the dispute over whether Gore or Bush won the US Presidential election in 2000 was a shared agreement that the duly elected president is the candidate who wins the majority of votes in the electoral college. The disagreement was over which candidate satisfied that criterion. The disputed question Aristotle addresses about happiness is like the dispute over which candidate won the election. The definitional question with which he begins, by contrast, is like an attempt to spell out the criteria for holding the office.

5 We will see in the next chapter that Epicurus advocates such a hedonist view; but even he takes this to be a controversial answer to Aristotle's question, 'What is happiness?', rather than a straightforward interpretation of the question itself.

6 All translations for the *Nicomachean Ethics* will be those of Christopher Rowe (Rowe and Broadie 2002), occasionally adapted to fit my own terminology.

7 The unity, purpose and value of a life results from following the principle of specialization: one person, one task (Plato, *Rep.* 406c–407b; 423d).

8 'For the sake of' renders the Greek expression '*charin* + genitive' at *EN* 1094a15 (cf. 1097a18, 1097b4, 6, 1102a2–3). Aristotle also uses the equivalent expression: *heneka* + genitive (e.g. 1097a21), which is more frequent in his teleological remarks about natural philosophy (e.g. *Phys.* 194b33, 198b10). Both these locutions can be paraphrased using *dia* + accusative:, to say that A is pursued 'for the sake of B', is equivalent to saying that one pursues A 'because of B', as at *EN* 1094a19 (cf. 1097a26, 1097a31–b3).

9 This is particularly so in the case of goals that are not products, but activities, a distinction emphasized in the opening lines of the *EN* (1094a3–6). On the significance of the distinction, see Ackrill 1974: 18–19.

10 Interpreters of Aristotle are divided on the question of whether Aristotle thinks the happy life requires pursuit of a monolithic ultimate end. Those who reject such an interpretation include Ackrill 1974, Devereux 1981, Keyt 1983, Cooper 1987, Irwin 1991, Crisp 1994. Defenders of the 'monolithic' interpretation include Kraut 1989, Richardson Lear 2004, Heinaman 2003, and Cleemput 2006. For a taxonomy and criticism of the dispute, see Natali 2001: 111–17.

11 Thus Ackrill (1974: 18–20) identifies the crux of the matter.

12 I follow Rowe in rendering *theoria* as 'reflection'. Other translations include 'contemplation' (Ross 1925, Crisp 2000) and 'study' (Irwin 1999).

13 Elsewhere in the *EN* Aristotle offers more careful assessment of pleasure's claim to be the highest good: 1152b1–1154b31 and 1172b9–1174a12.

14 The choice of lives appears again in *Pol.* VII 1–3.

15 Becoming like the divine: *EN* 1177b26–27; cf. 1177b34, 1178b21–23.

16 His reasons for claiming that the 'reflective' life is superior (outlined in detail in *EN* X 7) appeal to an array of additional 'formal' criteria for happiness outlined in EN I 7, and originating in Plato's *Philebus* (20d–21a): that it is complete (*teleion* 1097a28–b6, 1177b1–18) and 'self-sufficient' (*autarkes*, 1097b6–16, 1177a27–b1). The latter criterion becomes especially prominent in Hellenistic ethics. On the criterion of self-sufficiency, see Heinaman 1988, Broadie 1991: 32–3, Kenny 1992, S. White 1992, Cooper 2003a, Richardson Lear 2004: chapter 3.

17 On the two lives in EN X, see Cooper 1975: chapter 3, Nannery 1983, Keyt 1989, Kraut 1989: chapter 1, Broadie 1991: chapter 7, Lawrence 1993, Charles 1999, Scott 1999, Natali 2001: chapter 4, and Richardson Lear 2004: chapter 8.

18 Aristotle distinguishes the ethical excellences from 'intellectual excellences' or 'excellences of thought' (1103a4–10).

19 On Aristotle's conception of the *kalon*, see Owens 1981, Rogers 1993, Irwin 1985b and 2004, Cooper 1996, and Richardson Lear 2006, 2004: chapter 6. On acting for the sake of the *kalon*, see also Whiting 2002 and Lännström 2006.

20 On wit as a virtue, see Lippitt 2005.

21 At *EN* 1102a23–4, Aristotle too uses the locution '*charin* + genitive' to indicate a regulative goal. The politician who aims at making the citizens excellent must study the human soul up the point that this interest requires – e.g. not in the depth that Aristotle himself pursues the inquiry in his work *De Anima* ('On the Soul').

22 For alternative accounts of the 'for the sake of' relation in Aristotle, see Ackrill 1974, Hardie 1980: chapter 2, Kraut 1989: chapter 4, and Richardson Lear 2004: chapter 4.

23 The phrase is from Wolf 1982: 434. Wolf is primarily interested in criticizing the Kantian and utilitarian versions of the life committed to morality as an ultimate goal, but the interpretation offered here of the Aristotelian life organized around the pursuit of the *kalon* is not vulnerable to many of the objections that Wolf levels against such an ideal.

24 If the ethical person's pursuit of the *kalon* counts as pursuit of happiness, does this mean that happiness *is* 'the *kalon*'? No – the ultimate goal of any person pursuing happiness is to 'live well'. The *kalon* is the regulative ideal in such a life.

25 Aristotle makes it clear that happiness in not only *kalon* but also *agathon* (good): *EN* 1099a27–28.

26 On *phronesis* prescribing 'for the sake of' *theôria* see Woods 1982: 193–8, Kraut 1989: 263, Irwin 1999: 255, Broadie 1991: 207, 260n7, 375–6, 386, Natali 2001: 163–4, Richardson Lear 2004: 108.

27 The difficulties are articulated forcefully by Ackrill 1974. Kraut 1989 and Richardson Lear 2004 offer very different versions of the 'monistic' interpretation of the final goal.

28 To paraphrase an example in Kraut 1989.

29 This sketch of the place of reflection in the life of the ethical person has some similarity with the picture of the 'reflective life' in Natali 2001: 174–5; but unlike Natali, I take this to show how ethical activity is 'for the sake of' reflection. For a different account of how ethical virtue is 'for the sake of' reflection, see Richardson Lear 2004: 196–207.

30 Plato articulates a version of a 'function argument' at *Rep.* 352e–354a.

31 I use the more cumbersome locution 'to use reason' rather than the simple verb 'to reason' because 'reasoning' in English tends to refer to the activity of figuring out an answer, whereas the activity of reason, as Aristotle understands it, includes the activity of grasping the answer itself. Indeed the latter is more properly the function of reason on his view.

32 Oddly enough, Aristotle does not state the 'of reason' explicitly here; but he takes it to be implied by the conclusions above, at 1098a7.

33 His introduction to the function argument promises to achieve no more that this (*enargesteron ti*, 1097b23), and we should expect only as much precision and clarity as the subject admits or requires, Aristotle has already warned his readers at 1094b12–22. For different assessments of the function argument, see: Clark 1975: 14–27, Wilkes 1978, Kraut 1979 and 1989: 312–19, Devereux 1981, Irwin 1980 and 1988: 363–5, Hutchinson 1986: chapter 3, Roche 1988, Whiting 1988, Gomez-Lobo 1989, Achtenburg 1991, Broadie 1991: 34–41, S. White 1992: 139–57, Bostock 2000: 15–29, Natali 2001: 138–51, Lawrence 2001 and 2006, and Cleemput 2006.

34 Although notably, not piety. Piety is also absent from the Platonic list of virtues in the *Republic* and later dialogues. Plato and Aristotle seem to think the domain of piety, once one has a proper appreciation of the divine and its relation to human affairs, is encompassed by the other virtues – hence the suggestion in Plato's *Euthyphro* that piety is a 'part of justice' (*Eu.* 12d). On Aristotelian piety, see Broadie 2003.

35 On the 'nameless virtues' see 1107b1–2, 7–8, 1108a16–19; cf. 1125b17–21, 26–9, 1126b19–20, 1127a6–7, 14.

36 '*Hexis*' is sometimes rendered 'habit', but this is a mistake. Virtue of intellect, no less than virtue of character, is a *hexis* (disposition), according to Aristotle (*EN* 1139b13).

37 'Slavish' renders '*aneleutheros*'. Rowe translates it 'avaricious', which obscures its connection to freedom (*eleutheria*).

38 On the stability of a *hexis*, see Hutchinson 1986: chapter 2.

39 The doctrine of the mean is articulated at *EN* 1104a11–27, 1106a26–b28, 1107a2–6; cf. 1108b11–13, 1109a20–4, 1138b18–20. For discussion, see: Urmson 1973, Clark 1975: 84–97, Hardie 1980: chapter VII, Hursthouse 1980 and 2006, Losin 1987, Kraut 1989: 327–41, Salkever 1990, Broadie 1991: 95–103, Leighton 1995, Welton and Polansky 1999, Curzer 1996, Young 1996, L. Brown 1997, Natali 2001: 35–7, Müller 2004, Rapp 2006, Gottlieb (unpublished), and the papers in Bosley *et al.* (eds) 1995.

40 Insensibility is one of the dispositions for which, Aristotle claims, there exists no term in ordinary Greek. He coins for it the term 'insensibility' – meaning a failure of appropriate sensuality (1107b6–8).

41 Although later in antiquity, members of Aristotle's school seem to have interpreted it in this way. See Dillon 1983 and Annas 1993: chapter 18.

42 Here I follow Lesley Brown's interpretation of the Milo example (Brown 1997).

43 Given that Oedipus was ignorant of this crucial fact his action was not voluntary (1110b33–1111a19). Aristotle devotes EN III 1–5 to the topic of voluntariness and related subjects, which we will discuss below. Here we are concerned only with the doctrine of the mean: Oedipus's action was patricide, even if his ignorance excuses him from being blamed for it.

44 EN 1106b21–3, 1115b15–19, 1118b25–7, 1119b16–18; cf. 1120b30–1, 1125b8–10, 19–20, 31–2, 1126a13–15, 26–8, 32–5, b5–6, 17–19.

45 See Tracy 1969 and Hutchinson 1988.

46 Plato, Stsm. 284e, 305d; cf. 286d, Aristotle, EN 1096a31–4, 1104a3–10, 1178a10–14.

47 While Plato's account of the doctrine of the mean (to metrion – also translated 'due measure') in the Statesman is admittedly obscure, one thing that is clear is that whether something is 'metrion' concerns its relation to the goal of the enterprise in question. In the context of the productive crafts, it is 'the necessary nature of what is coming into being' (Stsm. 283d8–9).

48 It is sometimes translated as 'choice' (Ross 1925), 'preferential choice' (Charles 1984), 'rational choice' (Crisp 2000) or 'decision' (Irwin 1985c and 1999, and Rowe, in Rowe and Broadie 2002). All these translations have the disadvantage of obscuring the fact that a person's prohairesis reveals her motivation or goal.

49 The example is from Herman 1996: 53.

50 For other discussions of Aristotle on prohairesis, see Anscombe 1965, Hardie 1980: chapter 9, Charles 1984: 148–55: Hutchinson 1986: chapter 5, Broadie 1991: 179–85, Reeve 1995: 87–91, and Natali 2001: 67–9. On the distinction between doing what the virtuous person would do and doing it as the virtuous person would do it, cf. EE 1248b38–1249a16, discussed by Kenny 1992: 11–15, 19–22, and Woods 1982 ad loc.: 44.

51 Praiseworthiness of dispositions depends on the quality of the actions, feelings and motivations to which they give rise: EN 1110a19–23, 1118b25–8, 1126a35–b9, 1127b9–12, 1138a32, 1144a26, 1148b5–6, 1169a30–1, 1175b28–9. On Aristotle's conception of praiseworthiness, see Meyer 1993: 44–50.

52 Aristotle's paramount concern in the discussion of voluntariness with actions that reflect the agent's character is further evident in a notorious oddity in his remarks about involuntariness. Even an action that fails to originate in the agent (and thus is not voluntary) still does not count as involuntary, according to Aristotle, unless it is painful to the agent (1110b18–24, 1111a19–21; cf. 1111a32). If I am jostled from behind and as a result push you into the path of a moving train, but am quite unmoved by this result, this indicates something ethically significant about my character. Only actions that 'go against the grain' of character will be classified as 'involuntary' (akousion) by Aristotle. Hence Rowe prefers to translate akousion by 'counter-voluntary'. For a defence of the usual rendering as 'involuntary', see Meyer 1993: 9–14. For discussion of the requirement of pain and regret, see Sauvé 1988.

53 Classifying such actions as voluntary in the EN also seems to be a change of mind from EE 1225a12–14. See Meyer 1993: 93–100.

54 For further discussion of Aristotle's account of voluntariness see the section 'Responsibility for character' later in this chapter. Alternative interpretations

are offered by Furley 1977, Hardie 1980: chapter VIII, Irwin 1980a, 1988: 340–4, Charles 1984: chapter 2, Curren 1989, Roberts 1989, Brickhouse 1991, Broadie 1991: chapter 3, Métivier 2000: 171–99.

55 On the voluntariness of states of character, which Aristotle discusses in EN III 5, see below.

56 Following Ross, I translate *phronêsis* as 'practical wisdom'. Other translations include 'intelligence' (Irwin 1985c), 'prudence' (Irwin 1999) and 'wisdom' (Rowe). See Appendix 2.

57 Aristotle is here using 'intelligence' (*nous* – 1144b8) to stand for practical wisdom (*phronêsis*) – in particular, practical wisdom's grasp of the 'particulars' of the situation (cf. 1143a35–b5).

58 For different interpretations of the 'naturally virtuous' person in EN VI 13, see Kraut 1989: 247–51, S. White 1992a, Reeve 1995: 84–7, Ramsay 1998, Natali 2001: 52–4, Müller 2004, Richardson Lear 2004: 117–19, Viano 2004.

59 Alternatively, we might say he values standing up for himself, but regulates his pursuit of this goal in the light of his higher commitment to the *kalon*.

60 Hence Rowe translates *epistêmê* as 'systematic knowledge'. Related theoretical excellences are *nous*: grasp of those first principles (*EN* VI 6) and *sophia*, the combination of *nous* and *episteme* (*EN* VI 7). The translations of these inter-related terms varies considerably from translation to translation. See Appendix 2: 'Aristotle's intellectual virtues' for a guide.

61 On Aristotle's theory of scientific knowledge in the *Posterior Analytics*, see Barnes 1969 and Burnyeat 1981.

62 On Aristotle's denial of universal principles in ethics, see Winter 1997, Natali 2001: 27–35. On the question of whether there is a demonstrative science of ethics, see also Upton 1981, Reeve 1995: chapter 1, and Richardson Lear 2004: chapter 5.

63 On the question of precision in ancient ethics and other disciplines, see Kurz 1970, Hutchinson 1988, Anagnostopolous 1994, and Irwin 2000.

64 Aristotle recognizes that there is an important place for generalizations in the expression of craft expertise (indeed, it is the possession of such principles that distinguish the expert from the amateur dabbler who operates simply by experience of a limited range of cases – 1180b13–23). Nonetheless he insists of the crafts in general that the content of their expertise cannot be expressed in universal principles: 1104a3–10; cf. 1137a10–17, 1112b2–8). In both claims, he follows Plato, *Statesman*, 294b–295b.

65 Knowing when and whether a rule applies requires an appreciation of the point of the enterprise – which in the ethical case is to abide above all by what is *kalon*, in the baker's case to produce a good loaf of bread.

66 See for example Herman 1996: 36–7, 54–5.

67 It is a common refrain in Aristotle's ethics that action has to do with 'particulars': *EN* 1110b6–7, 1141b16; cf. 1107a29–30. On grasping the particulars, see Cooper 1975a: 46–58, Devereux 1986, Broadie 1991: 242–60, Reeve 1995: 67–73, Lories 1998, Natali 2001: 52.

68 This is the use of *nous* at 1144b4–16, quoted above.

69 In some ways it is also like the trained ear of the expert musician, or the discriminatory capacity of the expert wine taster.

70 While the interpretation of Aristotle's own analysis of the acratic behaviour (*EN* 1146b31–1147b19) is controversial, his aim is clearly to identify either a kind of knowledge (universal or particular), or a way of possessing that knowledge (merely 'having' knowledge as opposed to 'using' that knowledge) that the acratic agent lacks. For discussions of Aristotle on *acrasia*, see Robinson 1969, Mele 1981, Charles 1984: chapters 3–4, Dahl 1984, Irwin 1988a, Lawrence

1988, Broadie 1991: chapter 5, McDowell 1996a, Bostock 2000: chapter 6, Natali 2001: 100–9, Destrée 2004, and Price 2006.

71 'Pathos' is often translated as 'emotion' or by the old fashioned term 'passion', of which it is the etymological antecedent.

72 For a fuller discussion, see the classic discussion in Burnyeat 1980.

73 Some interpreters take practical wisdom (phronêsis) to be knowledge of a general theory of happiness (Irwin 1988a, Cooper 1975a, Kraut 1989 and 1993), while others take it to involve simply the ability to apply the concepts of kalon and aischron (McDowell 1980, 1996, 1996a, Broadie 1991: chapter 4). On the dispute, see Meyer 1998, Bostock 2000: 84–8, and Whiting 2001. On McDowell's interpretation of Aristotle, see Wallace 1991. For further discussion of phronêsis, see Sorabji 1973/4, Wiggins 1980, Engberg-Pedersen 1983, Dahl 1984, Tuozzo 1991, Reeve 1995: chapter 2, Lories 1998, Natali 2001, and the papers in Chateau 1997.

74 'Habit' translates ethos, not êthos (character). At most, Aristotle says that ethical excellence 'arises from habit' (ex ethous, 1103a17) – not that it is a habit. And in this context it is clear that arising 'from habit' means resulting from habituation (ethismos), as Aristotle's repeated use of the verb 'ethizesthai' (to habituate) makes clear (1103a17–26).

75 Thanks to Robert Sauvé for the phrase. On the difficulty, if not impossibility, of changing the state of character one has acquired, see EN 1114a13–18 and Catg. 13a23–36.

76 The context (1113b30–1114a31) is his claim that some states of ignorance are also voluntary (bad character being a prime case of ethical ignorance). It is important to recognize that the issue of whether our character is up to us is not introduced, as it is often thought to be, at the beginning of EN III 5 (1113b3–14) where the claim about 'virtue and vice' being up to us must be read, on pain of attributing fallacious argument to Aristotle, as claims about virtuous and vicious action (see Meyer 1994, 2006).

77 On responsibility for character in Aristotle, see also Bondeson 1974, Irwin 1980a, Curren 1989, Roberts 1989, Brickhouse 1991, Broadie 1991: 159–78, Meyer 1994: chapter 5.

78 Aristotle identifies practical wisdom with the political craft (EN 1141b23–4), which Plato identifies as the 'using craft' of the Euthydemus (291c).

79 On the Peripatetics, see Sharples 1983 and 1999.

80 For a response to this objection, see Cooper 1985.

81 Aristotle emphasizes that happiness is the exercise, not merely the possession of the excellences (EN 1095b31–1096a1, 1098b32–1099a7). Natali 2001: 171–6 notes that this is a point on which Aristotle marks a significant disagreement with Plato and the Academy. On the accounts of happiness put forth by Plato's early successors, see Clement, Stromata II.22.133,4–7, quoted and discussed by Natali 2001: 117–18.

82 For discussion of this argument, see Irwin 1985a.

83 For further discussion of Aristotle's views on the role of external goods in happiness, see Kraut 1989: 253–5, Natali 2001: 161–171, Annas 1993: chapter 18, Reeve 1995: chapter 4, Kenny 1992: chapters 5–6, S. White 1992a: 68–87, 109–36, Johnson 1997, Everson 1998: 90–3, and E. Brown 2006a.

84 Indeed, Aristotle implies that such impediment is significant enough to undermine the excellence itself. When one loses happiness due to enormous and repeated external disaster (as happened in the case of Priam, who lost his kingship, his city, his son, even his personal dignity), recovery of happiness requires time and practice (1101a11–13), which suggests that it is the ethical disposition that must be built up again, not just a supply of external resources.

4

EPICURUS AND
THE LIFE OF PLEASURE

History, biography, and texts

The period after the death of Aristotle in 322/3 BCE is called the Hellenistic period because it coincided with the 'Hellenization' of much of the Mediterranean and Near Eastern world by the conquests of Alexander the Great.[1] After Alexander's death (coincidentally in the same year as Aristotle, who had been his boyhood tutor), the lands he had conquered were divided up into three 'empires' – that of the Ptolmaies in Egypt, the Seleucids in a vast area from Turkey to Afghanistan, and the Antigonids in Macedon. These empires introduced Greek language, culture, and political institutions to the lands they controlled and promoted them over the indigenous languages and cultures. Greek became the international language and the language of all educated persons. During this period Athens continued to be the philosophical centre to which intellectuals flocked from all corners of the now greatly enlarged Greek-speaking world.[2]

One of these was Epicurus (341–271 BCE), son of expatriate Athenian parents. Although born during Aristotle's lifetime, he first came to Athens more than a decade after the philosopher's death. Here he purchased a property that came to be known as 'the Garden', where he lived with a tightly knit community of friends and followers. The Garden was a centre of philosophical activity on a par with the Academy, founded by Plato, and the Lyceum founded by Aristotle. In contrast with these older schools, however, the Garden had a closed, cultish flavour, since Epicurus advocated withdrawal from much of the business and preoccupations of public life. Before arriving in Athens, Epicurus had founded similar communities elsewhere.

In addition to writing 'pastoral' letters to these far-flung communities (not unlike the letters of Paul of Tarsus to early Christian communities), Epicurus wrote many treatises. The inventory of titles preserved in Diogenes Laertius counts over 300 rolls in all, including the massive 37-roll treatise *On Nature*. Unfortunately, very little of these writings has survived. With the exception of a few letters preserved in their entirety by Diogenes Laertius, only fragments of the treatises survive. Most miraculous are the pieces of papyrus preserved in the ruins of a Roman villa overwhelmed by lava in the eruption of Mt Vesuvius in 79 CE. More often, our surviving evidence consists of quotations from or paraphrases of Epicurus's works by later writers who themselves had access to Epicurus's treatises but were not always sympathetic to his views or concerned to give a careful and fair exposition of them. The same is generally true of writings of later Epicureans, such as Philodemus of Gadara (first century BCE) and Diogenes of Oenoanda (second century CE). The one notable exception is Lucretius – a Roman poet of the first century BCE who wrote a massive poem, *De Rerum Natura* (On the Nature of Things), which articulates many of the themes and arguments of Epicurean philosophy, and has survived intact.[3]

The Roman statesman and intellectual Marcus Tullius Cicero (106–43 BCE) is also an extremely valuable source of Epicurean philosophy – indeed of all Hellenistic philosophy. As a youth, Cicero studied philosophy in Athens as a student in the Academy. Although an adherent of the Academic school, Cicero was learned in the philosophy of all the major schools in Athens at the time: the Academy, the Lyceum, the Garden, and the Stoa (the subject of the next chapter). While philosophy in his day was considered an essentially Greek intellectual enterprise, Cicero's mission was to make it accessible and intellectually respectable to a Roman audience (*Fin.* 1.1–10). To this end, he wrote many Latin treatises in which eminent Romans rehearse and defend the doctrines of the different Athenian philosophical schools.[4]

Cicero disclaims originality in these treatises, which he composed in some haste, mostly in the two years before his assassination in 43 BCE.[5] He appears to have drawn liberally from current Greek sourcebooks of philosophy, or from the works of Stoics, Epicureans, and Academics available in his day. He translated the Greek philosophy into Latin idiom (from which much of our current philosophical vocabulary in English derives), illustrated it with Roman examples, and interjected his own criticisms from an Academic standpoint. While his criticisms are sometimes uncharitable, his practice of putting long continuous exposition of the different philosophies into the mouths of their adherents has given us the most complete and balanced exposition of the state of the art of these philosophical schools in the first century BCE.

Our information about Epicurean ethics depends largely on two texts. Cicero's *De Finibus* (On Moral Ends) is an important source of the ethical philosophy of both Stoics and Epicureans. Book I gives a systematic exposition of Epicurean ethics, while Book II presents criticism of that theory from an Academic perspective. Our other main source is Epicurus's own *Letter to Menoeceus* (preserved in Diogenes Laertius X 121–35). In addition to these two continuous expositions, two collections of aphorisms have survived. One is the *Kuriai Doxai* (*KD*) (Principal Doctrines) a collection of sayings well known in antiquity, which Epicureans were supposed to memorize (*Fin.* 2.20, DL 10.36, 116). It too is preserved in Diogenes Laertius (10.139–54). Another set of Epicurean sayings was preserved in a Vatican library and is known as 'Vatican Sayings' (*VS*).[6]

Epicurean philosophy

In contrast with Plato and Aristotle, who considered philosophy to be an esoteric discipline requiring expertise in specialized disciplines such as logic or 'dialectic', Epicurus insists that philosophy is in principle quite simple and accessible.[7] The central truths one must grasp are about the natural world, and the point to learning them is quite practical. The goal of philosophy is, quite simply, to produce happiness (*eudaimonia*) (*Men.* 122).

Like all philosophers of his era, Epicurus understands the notion of *eudaimonia* according to Aristotle's clarification: it is the ultimate goal (*telos*) of life, that for the sake of which we do everything we do, and which we do not pursue for the sake of anything else. Epicurus calls this goal the 'starting point (*archê*) for every choice and avoidance' (*Men.* 128–9). Thus Epicurus and later philosophers agree on the central question in ethics:

> We are investigating . . . what is the final and ultimate good? This, in the opinion of every philosopher, is such that everything else is for the sake of it (*ad id omnia referri*), while it is not itself for the sake of anything.
>
> (*Fin.* 1.29; cf. 2.5)

According to Epicurus, the answer to this question is 'pleasure'.

Epicurus' reason for taking the *telos* to be pleasure is quite simple. It requires no argument, he claims, to see that pleasure is to be pursued and pain avoided (*Fin.* 1.30).[8] These facts are as evident to the senses as the fact that fire is hot or snow is white (*Fin.* 1.30; DL 10.32, 34). Pleasure is naturally 'congenial' (*oikeion*)[9] to us (*Men.* 129; *KD* 7). It is thus our natural goal (*KD* 25).

We can see that our natural inclination is to pursue pleasure and avoid pain, Epicurus and his followers maintain, because it is exhibited by all animals (including ourselves) right from birth:

> Every animal as soon as it is born seeks pleasure and rejoices in it, while shunning pain as the highest evil and avoiding it as much as possible. This is behaviour that has not yet been corrupted, when nature's judgment is pure and whole.
>
> (*Fin.* 1.30)

Birth is supposed to be the best time to see our natural inclinations in their uncorrupted form because they have not yet been influenced by learning or by any factors other than nature (*Fin.* 1.71). On this, both Epicureans and their opponents agree. Indeed, it was the practice of most philosophical schools in the Hellenistic period to 'visit the cradle' in support of their claims about the goal of life (*Fin.* 5.55), from which such arguments have come to be dubbed 'cradle arguments'.[10]

According to Epicurus, it is not only in infancy that we 'recognize [pleasure] as our first innate (*sungenikon*) good' (*Men.* 129). We continue to pursue pleasure as our ultimate goal throughout life, although we develop many mistaken views that impede our pursuit of it (*Fin.* 1.32). Thus the task of philosophy is to clear away those mistaken views and allow us to pursue our natural goal successfully and without impediment.

This is not to say, Epicurus and his followers hasten to add, that we never knowingly choose to do anything painful or burdensome, or that we indulge in every opportunity for pleasure that comes our way. Far from it, he claims. The intelligent pursuit of pleasure will often involve forgoing pleasures or enduring pains voluntarily (*VS* 73). Since it is the pleasant life we pursue, not just the pleasant moment (cf. *Fin.* 2.87), we must take both the long- and short-term consequences of our choices into consideration (*Men.* 129; KD 8). In illustration of this aspect of the Epicurean view, Cicero gives the following anecdote:

> Timotheus . . . after dining . . . with Plato and being much delighted with the entertainment said, when he saw him the next day: 'Your dinners are indeed delightful, not only at the time, but on the following day as well.'
> (Cicero, *Tusculan Disputations* 5.100, translated by King)

The wise person's choices will thus follow the principle that 'pleasures are to be rejected when this results in other greater pleasures; pains are selected when this avoids worse pains' (*Fin.* 1.33; *TD* 5.95). In taking long-term pleasure and pain into consideration, the Epicureans distinguish themselves from their hedonist rivals the Cyrenaics, who advocated pursuit of the present pleasure.[11]

A further feature that distinguishes the Epicureans from other hedonists is a distinction they make between types of pleasures. On the one hand, they claim, there is the familiar sort of pleasure 'which stirs our nature with its sweetness and produces agreeable sensations in us' (*Fin.* 1.37). It 'arouses the senses[12] when experienced and floods them with a delightful feeling' (*Fin.* 2.6). Epicurus classifies this type of pleasure as 'kinetic' (*kinêtikê*). It is to be contrasted with a very different kind of pleasure, which he calls 'static' (*katastêmatikê*). The latter pleasure is 'what one feels when all pain is removed' (*Fin.* 1.37, 2.16). Although our sources sometimes abbreviate the definition of *katastematic* pleasure to 'the absence of pain', the full and proper account is that it is the feeling or awareness of that absence of pain. Otherwise, it would entail that inanimate things and the dead would be having pleasures. Pleasure is a feature of experience, as both the Epicureans and their critics are well aware.[13]

Although this is not how the term 'pleasure' (*hedonê* in Greek, Latin *voluptas*) is ordinarily used,[14] the Epicureans argue that experiencing the absence of pain is no less a pleasure than is feeling a delightful sensation:

> [W]hen we are freed from pain, we take delight in that very libera-
> tion and release from all that is distressing. Now everything in
> which one takes delight is a pleasure (just as everything that dis-
> tresses one is a pain). And so every release from pain is rightly
> termed a pleasure.
>
> (*Fin.* 1.37)

For example, being thirsty is a pain or discomfort. Drinking when thirsty is a kinetic pleasure. The condition of not being thirsty – that is, of not experiencing the pain of thirst, is a static pleasure. In every case in which a pain is removed, a static pleasure results. (*Fin.* 1.37–39; DL 10.136). Thus there is no intermediate condition between feeling pain and feeling pleasure: 'whoever is to any degree conscious of how he is feeling must to that extent be feeling either pleasure or pain' (*Fin.* 1.38).[15]

According to the Epicureans, experiencing the absence of pain is not only a pleasure, it is indeed a greater pleasure than kinetic pleasures: 'the absence of all pain [Epicurus] held to be not only true pleasure, but the highest (*summam*) pleasure' (*Fin.* I 38). This is not to say that static pleasure is more pleasant than kinetic pleasure when measured on the same scale. Rather, he thinks, the two types of pleasure cannot be compared on the same scale at all. This is because kinetic pleasure admits of both increase and diminution, while static pleasure does not. (*Fin.* 1.38, 2.10; *TD* 3.47, *KD* 18, DL 10.121).

We can appreciate this point as follows. When one is feeling pained or distressed, this distress will be lessened as each pain is eliminated, but once all pain has been removed, one has achieved the upper limit (*peras*) of 'freedom from pain'. The sorts of kinetic pleasures one experiences en route to this freedom from pain, or subsequent to achieving it, will only 'vary', but not increase the static pleasure (*KD* 18). For example, one can achieve freedom from the bodily distress of hunger and thirst by eating bread and water, or by consuming Champagne and caviar. But neither of these very different 'kinetic' routes to the condition of bodily satisfaction produces any greater freedom from the pains of hunger and thirst than the other. Similarly, once one is no longer hungry and thirsty, one might enjoy the further kinetic pleasures of listening to music, or smelling flowers, or engaging in philosophical discussion. But none of these very different pleasant experiences will make the person who experiences them any more free from hunger or thirst.[16] For these reasons, Epicurus claims that static pleasure constitutes the 'limit (*horos*) of the magnitude of pleasure' (*KD* 3).[17] Kinetic pleasure, by contrast, has no intrinsic limit (*KD* 15, 20).

Static rather than kinetic pleasure is the goal of life, Epicurus claims. He responds to those who mistakenly characterize his hedonism as advocating a voluptuous and self-indulgent lifestyle:

> When we say that pleasure is the goal we do not mean the pleasures of the profligate or the pleasures of consumption, as some believe, either from ignorance and disagreement or from deliberate misinterpretation, but rather the lack of pain in the body and disturbance in the soul.
>
> (*Men.* 131; cf. 128, *KD* 18)

Far from being a doctrine of sensual indulgence, Epicureanism is a 'serious, sober, and severe' philosophy of life (*Fin.* 1.37).

The fact that the Epicureans identify static rather than kinetic pleasure as the goal of life allows them to defend their view from familiar and powerful objections to hedonism. But, while Epicureans do give reasons to defend their claim that the feeling between kinetic pleasure and pain is a pleasure (*Fin.* 1.37, quoted above), we do not have any record of arguments specifically in support of the claim that static, rather than kinetic pleasure is the *goal* of life. Presumably, they must take the cradle argument to establish this result.

It is commonly objected that the cradle argument fails to establish that freedom from pain is our natural goal. Critics regularly claim that the evidence adduced in the cradle argument, if it shows that we have a natural orientation to pursue pleasure, shows that kinetic pleasure is our goal. So the Cyrenaics assume in their version of the cradle argument (DL 2.88). Cicero criticizes the Epicurean cradle argument in just these terms:

> Epicurus could hardly have obtained proof of this equation [sc. static pleasure = the goal of life] by looking at young children or even at animals, though he regards them as mirrors of nature. He could hardly have claimed that natural instinct leads them to seek the pleasure of feeling no pain. This is not the sort of thing that can arouse appetitive desire. The static condition of freedom from pain produces no motive force to impel the mind to act. . . . Only the caress of sensual pleasure has this effect. So it is the fact that kinetic pleasure is attractive to young children and animals that Epicurus relies on to demonstrate that pleasure is what we naturally seek.
>
> (*Fin.* 2.32)

So too Clement of Alexandria, centuries later, articulates what seems to have become a standard criticism of the Epicureans.[18]

The criticism, however, is not a fair one. Let us consider the evidence of the 'cradle' more carefully. To be sure, the Epicureans allow that we have a natural inclination to pursue kinetic pleasures. And newborn animals do clearly enjoy the kinetic pleasures of eating, drinking and warmth. These kinetic pleasures, however, are also the means of attaining the static pleasure of freedom from the distress of hunger, thirst, and cold. The crucial question for us is, What impels the infant to seek out food, drink, and warmth in the first place? Is it a natural inclination to pursue kinetic pleasures (of which they have no experience), or a natural inclination to recoil from the distress of hunger, thirst, and cold?

Newborn behaviour, especially in humans, displays plenty of distress at hunger, thirst, and discomfort. A crying baby needs to be fed, changed, or cuddled. It is entirely reasonable for the Epicureans to claim that what impels the newborn to seek or demand nourishment and comfort is the pain it feels from being hungry, thirsty, cold, or wet: that the primary impulse manifested by newborns is not an orientation to pursue delightful sensations, but a strong impulse away from bodily pain. A crying infant expresses his hunger, thirst, or other bodily discomfort, and seeks relief from these distressing sensations. Indeed the early weeks of infancy are a cycle of alternating periods of distress and content – long before the baby expresses anything like delight or enjoyment of the kinetic variety.

Indeed, if we consider the formulation of the Epicurean cradle argument preserved in Diogenes Laertius, we can see that his language favours interpreting the pleasure sought by the newborn as freedom from pain, rather than kinetic enjoyment:

> [Epicurus] uses as proof that the goal is pleasure the fact that animals, as soon as they are born are satisfied with it (*euartesthai*) but are in conflict with suffering (*ponos*) by nature and apart from reason. Left to our own feelings, then, we shun pain.
>
> (DL 10.137; translation adapted from IG and Hicks 1931)

The natural impulse in the cradle is here summed up as an inclination to avoid pain. The pleasures aimed at in the cradle are ones of satisfaction rather than lively sensation. If we grant that a natural impulse away from pain is exhibited in the cradle, Epicurus is correct to conclude that animals display a natural impulse to pursue static pleasure.[19]

Although the pains experienced in the cradle are all bodily sensations, the Epicureans are well aware that many pains are not bodily. Pain is a kind of disturbance or distress (*tarachê*), and such distress, they recognize, can occur both in the body and in the mind (or 'soul' – *psuchê*). The goal of life is to achieve 'lack of pain in the body and disturbance (*tarachê*) in the soul' (*Men.* 131). Hence the condition of the person who has achieved Epicurean happiness is described as *ataraxia* (freedom from distress – Latin, *quietas*), sometimes rendered as 'tranquility'.[20]

The fourfold remedy

Epicurus identifies the four principle sources of mental distress to which human beings are susceptible as: fear of the gods, fear of death, fear that we won't be able to achieve happiness, and fear that terrible things will befall us. Accordingly, the central piece of his ethical teaching, known as the 'Fourfold remedy' (*tetrapharmakon*), is designed to eliminate these fears:

> THE FOURFOLD REMEDY
> God presents no fears, death no worries. And while the good is readily attainable, what is terrible (*deinon*) is readily endurable.
> (Philodemus, *Against the Sophists*, fragment)[21]

In our surviving texts, these fears are typically addressed in the same order.[22] The *Letter to Menoeceus* is roughly organized as a presentation of the fourfold remedy: taking first the fear of the gods (123–4), second the fear of death (124–7), and finally the worries about achieving happiness and avoiding evil (127–132).[23] Note that the fears addressed in the *tetrapharmakon* do not assume the Epicurean analysis of good and evil – or any other Epicurean doctrine. These are fears that arise for those who are ignorant of Epicurean philosophy. Learning the tenets of that philosophy are the antidote or remedy (*pharmakon*) for those fears.

Epicurus begins his *Letter to Menoeceus* by urging him (as presumably he did all members of Epicurean communities) to rehearse the philosophical arguments that treat those fears. 'Do and rehearse (*meletan*) what I have been continually declaring to you, believing these to be the elements of living well' (*Men.* 123). In the *Letter to Herodotus*, he stresses the importance, for Epicurean practice, of committing to memory certain key doctrines (*DL* 10.36). The recommended philosophical 'exercise' is like a meditative or spiritual practice, to be performed individually or in pairs: 'Practise (*meletan*) these and the related precepts day and night, by yourself (*pros seauton*) and with (*pros*) a like-minded friend, and you will never be disturbed either awake or in sleep, and you will live as a god among Men' (*Men.* 135).

Fear of the gods

The first step of the fourfold remedy addresses the fear of the gods. Popular conceptions of the gods at the time portray them as supernatural beings responsible for natural phenomena – especially impressive or frightening ones such as earthquakes, thunderstorms, and astronomical phenomena. They also take a great interest in human affairs, and visit disaster upon the wicked or the overweening – as well as those who have failed to honour them properly or have incurred their dislike for some other reason (see DL 10.81). Lucretius describes the sort of fear such views engender:

> Whose mind does not contract in panic fear
> of gods? Whose knees don't shake and knock together
> When the earth shudders at a lightning blast
> And thunder's rumble rolls along the sky?
> Don't peoples tremble, haughty monarchs cower
> Supposing that the hour of doom has come
> For some base action, for some arrogant word?
> (Lucretius 5.1218–25 /LS 23A6; translated by Humphries)

It is not easy to predict what will satisfy these gods, who according to tradition can sometimes be angered at persons through no fault of their own. To believe in such gods is to consider oneself a relatively small and powerless being in a world where large, powerful and capricious beings demand service and visit calamity upon those with whom they are displeased or against whom they are otherwise motivated to do ill. It is a perspective of extreme vulnerability.

Such a set of beliefs about the gods is the source of great fears (Lucr. 6.68–79 /LS 23D; cf. LS 23I; *KD* 10–13; *DL* 10.81), but it is quite false, according to Epicurus. While he insists that there are in fact gods (*Men.* 123) and that it is pious to worship them,[24] the gods 'are not such as the many believe them to be'. Indeed, he goes so far as to claim that the popular conception of the gods is impious (*Men.* 123).

We can see what Epicurus thinks is wrong with the popular stories about the gods by focusing on what he calls our 'preconception' (*prolêpsis*) of the gods.[25] This is something like an innate idea or conception of the gods – shared by all human beings, according to Epicurus. While different peoples tell different stories about the gods, the universal conception of the gods on which all agree is that the gods are 'blessed' (*makarios*; a superlative of 'eudaimon') and immortal or imperishable (*aphthartos*) (*KD* 1, *Men.* 123, *ND* 1.45). This core conception of divinity which, according to Epicurus, is our *prolêpsis*, is due neither to human customs, laws, or institutions, and is therefore a deliverance of nature, to be trusted as true in the same way as the other deliverances of nature – such as those that tell us that pleasure is to be pursued and pain avoided. If we keep this core conception of divinity in mind, we can evaluate the other sorts of claims that are attributed to the gods, rejecting as false all those that are inconsistent with the core conception. As Epicurus writes to Menoeceus: 'do not attribute to god anything foreign to his indestructibility or repugnant to his blessedness' (*Men.* 123).

As completely happy beings, the gods, on the Epicurean conception of happiness, are without trouble or disturbance (*KD* 1). As such, they will be without anger (which is a disturbance in the soul), and hence without motive to visit retribution on human beings (*KD* 1). Indeed, even considering them to be grateful towards or pleased with human beings is inconsistent with their *ataraxia* – presumably because this implies a prior state of need or pain which human beings fulfilled with their sacrifices, as well as dependence on humans (either to give them good things or refrain from doing bad things to them). Anger and gratitude are signs of weakness (*KD* 1) and 'imply dependence (*prosdêsis*) on neighbours' (DL 10.77); hence they imply lack of self-sufficiency (*autarkeia*), which (we will see) is integral with the Epicurean conception of happiness. The gods have so little need of us, the later Epicurean Lucretius says, that they have no incentive to even think of us, let alone create us (Lucr. 5.156 /LS 13F1–4).

Also inconsistent with divine blessedness is the popular view that natural phenomena (meteorological or astronomical) are controlled by the gods. While Epicureans invoke many reasons to be sceptical that the gods are in control of the natural world,[26] the point central to the fourfold remedy is that conceiving of the gods at work in nature is inconsistent with their *ataraxia* (DL 10.76–7).[27] As the Epicurean speaker in Cicero's *On the Nature of the Gods* explains:

> What can be less tranquil than rotating about an axis without a moment's break at the heaven's amazing speed? And yet nothing is blessed if it is not tranquil (*quietum*). . . . Or if god is some being within the world, there to rule, to control, to maintain the orbits of the heavenly bodies, the succession of seasons, and the variations and regularities of things, to watch over land and sea and guard Men's well-being and lives, he is surely involved in a troublesome and laborious job.
>
> (*ND* 1.52; translation by Long and Sedley 13H1)

Thus Epicurean philosophy teaches that a major source of fear in life is unfounded. If we properly understand our natural conception of the gods, we will see that we have no reason to fear them. We need simply to remind ourselves of the relevant facts at regular intervals by rehearsing the epitome of the Epicurean argument captured in the first of the Principal Doctrines: 'what is blessed and indestructible has no troubles itself, nor does it give trouble to anyone else, so that it is not affected by feelings of anger or gratitude' (*KD* 1; cf. *Fin.* 1.43).

Fear of death

The second major source of anxiety addressed by the fourfold remedy is the fear of death. Unlike the fear of the gods, which we can overcome by realizing that the stories about divine interference in nature and in human lives are quite untrue, this fear requires a different strategy for its removal. While we are wrong to think our well-being is contingent on the whims of supernatural deities, we are not mistaken in believing that we are vulnerable to death. 'One can attain security against other things, but when it comes to death all Men live in a city without walls' (VS 31). We overcome the fear of death, according to Epicurus, not by learning that we will never die, but by coming to see that death itself is not a bad thing. In the memorable (and to be memorized) dictum, 'Death is nothing to us' (KD 2, Men. 124).[28]

The argument against this fear in the Letter to Menoeceus (124–127) is simple and straightforward. In a nutshell:

> Get used to believing that death is nothing to us. For all good and bad consists in sense experience, and death is the privation of sense experience.
>
> (Men. 124; cf. Fin. 2.100–1)

The argument consists of two premises from which the famous conclusion follows:

P1 Anything good or bad to us consists in sense experience.
P2 Death is the privation of sense experience.
C3 Therefore, death is nothing [good or bad] to us.

The first premise P1 relies on Epicurean hedonism, according to which even though freedom from distress in the mind as well as the body is the goal of life, the only proper objects of mental distress have ultimate reference to bodily pain.[29]

The second premise also depends on Epicurean natural philosophy, according to which death occurs when the soul (a collection of especially fine atoms distributed throughout the body) is separated from the body and disperses (DL 10.63–6). It is the soul that gives the body the power of sensation (10.63–4). When the soul is separated from the body, neither it nor the body retains this power. Thus, as P2 claims, when we die we no longer have any sensations or experiences.[30] Since being dead is a condition in which we experience nothing, nothing bad (or for that matter, good) can happen to us when we are dead. So being dead is nothing we have any reason to dread.

Although the argument, as it is initially stated here in the *Letter to Menoeceus* (124), depends on some distinctively Epicurean premises, it has force even against those who reject hedonism and the details of the Epicurean physical theory. As long as you believe that nothing good or bad can happen to a person unless it is something he or she experiences (= P1 modified), and that when we die, we simply cease to exist (= P2 modified) – from which we can infer that we have no experiences when dead – it follows that C3: being dead cannot be bad for us. Epicurus himself summarizes the argument in this more general form a little later in the letter: 'Death . . . is nothing to us; since when we exist, death is not yet present, and when death is present, then we do not exist' (*Men.* 125). Lucretius articulates such a generalized form of the argument:

> If there lies ahead
> Misery and suffering for any man, he must be there
> Himself to feel its evil, but since death
> Removes this chance, and by injunction stops
> All rioting of woes against our state,
> We may be reassured that in our death
> We have no cause for fear. We cannot be
> Wretched in non-existence.
>
> (Lucretius, 3.861–6 /LS24E5)

The passage in Lucretius goes on to offer the additional consideration: 'when immortal death snatches away a mortal life, it is no different from never having been born' (3.867–9, translation by Long and Sedley 24E). This epitomizes an additional line of argument developed over 3.830–869, which makes a different use of the claim (P2) that death is simply non-existence, and does not depend on any version of P1. The argument aims to show that the non-existence constituted by death is nothing bad to us by inviting us to consider the period of non-existence that precedes a person's existence. We do not think that it is a bad thing for us not to exist during this long period before our lives begin, so why should we think that the non-existence following our lives is any worse?[31] This set of considerations, known as the 'symmetry argument' is alluded to briefly in passing in the exposition of Epicurean ethics in Cicero's *On Moral Ends*. A person whose courage is based on Epicurean principles 'disparages death, in which one is simply in the same state as before one was born' (*Fin.* 1.49).[32]

There is no evidence in any of the texts attributed to Epicurus himself that he gave such an argument. The symmetry argument is most likely a response by later Epicureans to critics of the Epicurean position on death. The canonical argument given by Epicurus shows that it is a confusion to suppose that death is bad on the grounds that being dead is a bad thing. It invites the objection, however, that this is not why death is to be feared.

The challenge to the objector is to explain what is bad about death. One attempt at such an explanation, anticipated and responded to by Epicurus in *Men.* 125, attempts to locate the badness of death during one's life: death is painful in anticipation (*Men.* 125). Epicurus replies that this is foolish: such painful anticipation (that is, fear) is groundless unless death, when it comes, is something bad, which is precisely what Epicurus contests: 'that which while present causes no distress causes unnecessary pain when merely anticipated' (*Men.* 125).

A better attempt to motivate the objection points out that death deprives a person of good things that she otherwise would have had. Lucretius provides a compelling illustration of the sort of loss invoked in this objection:

> 'No longer will you happily come home
> To a devoted wife, or children dear
> Running for your first kisses, while your heart
> Is filled with sweet unspoken gratitude.
> You will no longer dwell in happy state,
> Their sword and shield. Poor wretch,' men tell themselves,
> 'One fatal day has stolen all your gains.'
>
> (Lucr. 3.894–9)

To such worries, the symmetry argument provides a response: If you do not think it is bad to have missed out on the good things you could have had by being born earlier, it is inconsistent to claim that death is bad because it deprives you of goods you could have had by living longer.

Epicurus's own response to such worries, by contrast, is to deny that the experiences of which death deprives us would have made our lives any happier. Unlike kinetic pleasures, which have no inherent limit, and of which one can always have more, the pleasure of *ataraxia* is a limit: the complete absence of pain. Once this has been achieved, it cannot be increased. In particular, it cannot be increased by duration.[33] Thus, just as the Epicurean does not 'choose the largest amount of food but the most pleasant' – that is, he chooses simply enough food to satisfy the basic natural appetites,[34] so too 'he savours not the longest time but the most pleasant' (*Men.* 126). Thus:

> Unlimited time and limited time contain equal pleasure, if one measures its limits by reasoning.
>
> (*KD* 19; cf. 20)

The pleasure that consists in the absence of pain cannot be increased, but only varied (*KD* 18). Given that this type of pleasure is the goal of life, it follows that our life would not be better (that is, more pleasant) if it was longer. Once one has reached painlessness, it cannot be made better by increased duration (*Fin.* 2.87). Prolonging life may increase our quantity of kinetic pleasures, and it may increase the length of time for which we are free from pain, but it does not make us any more free from pain. Thus death, whether it comes early or late, is nothing to us.

This response by Epicurus is deeply rooted in the controversial details of his hedonism – in particular the view that absence of pain is the greatest pleasure. It will therefore not be convincing to those who do fail to subscribe to his view of pleasure. By contrast, the symmetry argument employed by his later followers does not rely on any such controversial premises, and thus will be an effective remedy for a wider group of those who suffer from the fear of death.[35]

Good is easy to obtain

Having ruled out supernatural sources of evil, and the prospects of evil after death, the third and fourth remedies in the *tetrapharmakon* address worries a person might have about her prospects for achieving happiness in the natural world and within a human life. The third remedy, captured in the slogan 'good is easy to obtain', assures us that happiness is within our reach. We are mistaken to worry that it depends on factors beyond our control. Since the Epicurean considers happiness to consist in freedom from pain in the body, along with 'reliable expectation concerning this',[36] the remedy provides us with a simple strategy for freeing the body from pain. Once provided with this foolproof strategy, we lose our grounds for fearing that happiness may elude our grasp.

Central to this strategy is a distinction that Epicurus makes between types of desires, the careful observance of which furnishes us with a 'guide for good living' (*Fin.* 1.45).[37] The distinction invokes two criteria for classifying desires. First of all, desires are either natural or not (*Men.* 127, *Fin.* 1.53). Our sources devote little attention to explaining this criterion, which indicates that it was well understood or at any rate not controversial. Natural desires are all species of appetites for food, drink, and warmth.[38] Even if our environment, experience, or culture trains and shapes these appetites, so that we desire particular types of food or drink rather than others, it is a function of our nature to desire food and drink in the first place. All species of these desires are based at least in part on our nature, which distinguishes them from desires for things that satisfy no natural need – e.g. a desire to live by the ocean or to marry a millionaire. Non-natural desires are not contrary to nature; they simply do not aim at satisfying a natural need (*endeia*).[39]

Within natural desires, the Epicureans make the further distinction between the necessary and the non-necessary (*Men.* 127, *KD* 26, 29, cf. *KD* 30, *Fin.* 1.45, *TD* 5.93). More precisely, these are desires for necessary and unnecessary objects. Necessary desires are for objects such that, if they are not obtained, the body will be in distress (*KD* 26, 30; scholion on *KD* 29).[40] That is, they are desires for objects that the body needs. Fulfilling a natural and necessary desire 'removes the feeling of pain owing to want (*endeia* – *KD* 21; cf. 18). Examples of such desires are the desire for food when one is hungry or the desire for drink when one is thirsty. If you are hungry but get nothing to eat, or thirsty and get nothing to drink, then your body is in distress. In fact, that is just what the feelings of hunger and thirst are – feelings of distress or discomfort. The natural and necessary desires thus turn out to coincide with the 'natural impulses' invoked in the cradle argument.

A natural but unnecessary desire, by contrast, is for a particular kind of food, drink or shelter – for example, the desire to eat an apple, or to drink spring water. While eating an apple will suffice to alleviate the feeling of hunger, and while drinking spring water will slake one's thirst, this particular type of food or drink is not necessary to relieve the bodily distress. The apple relieves hunger because it is food, not because it is the particular kind of food that it is. Thus in desiring to eat an apple, and not just any food, one is desiring something that is not necessary for alleviating one's hunger. A banana or a potato, or a gourmet treat would do the job just as well. Similarly the desire to drink spring water, as opposed to any type of water or drink, aims at something that is unnecessary to satisfy the natural appetite of thirst.

These examples show that what makes a natural desire unnecessary is not that it is for an extravagant or expensive way of satisfying a bodily appetite, but rather that it is for a specific way of satisfying it. Natural and necessary desires are generic: a desire to eat (any food will do), or to drink (any drink will do), or to be warm (any clothing or shelter will do). The desire to drink Perrier and the desire to drink tap water are equally unnecessary.

Once one understands these distinctions between desires, the Epicurean recipe for living a happy life is 'simple and direct' (*Fin.* 1.57): restrict your desires to those that are natural and necessary (*Fin.* 1.43–44, 51, 62; cf. *TD* 5.93). Indeed it is a mark of an unnecessary desire that it can be eliminated (*KD* 26, 30). The therapy may be through argument – since unfounded opinions are in Epicurus's view the source of both non-natural desires (*Men.* 127) as well as unnecessary natural ones (*KD* 30). The remedy may also involve habituation and practice. For example, 'If you take away the chance to see and talk and spend time with [the beloved], then the passion of sexual love is dissolved' (*VS* 18).[41] Whatever the method of therapy, the Epicurean agent is instructed to ask, of each of his or her desires: 'What will happen to me if what is sought by [this] desire is achieved, and what will happen if it is not?' (*VS* 71). This is to ask, of each desire, whether it is necessary. If bodily pain will result unless the desire is satisfied, then the desire can be kept. Otherwise, it is to be eliminated.[42]

Nature is abundant with the resources to satisfy our natural and necessary desires, Epicurus insists (*Men.* 130–132, *KD* 15, 18–21, *VS* 25; *Fin.* 1.45, 2.90–1). Thus we can be confident that we will be able to live lives free from hunger, thirst, and cold. To understand that the freedom from bodily pain required by *ataraxia* is so easily achieved is to grasp the third remedy in the tetrapharmakon: 'the good is easily achieved'. By restricting one's desires to those objects for which nature supplies abundant resources, Epicurus teaches, one secures for oneself a life free not only from bodily pain, but also, and more importantly, from any need to worry (or fear) that one might experience such pain:

> The cry of the flesh, not to be hungry, not to be thirsty, not to be cold. For if someone has these things and is confident of having them in the future, he might contend even with [Zeus] for happiness.
>
> (*VS* 33)

By following the strategy of pruning away all desires beyond the necessary and natural, and understanding the rationale behind this, one will have secured the goal of life, which is to be free of bodily and mental distress: 'the stable condition (*katastêma*) of the flesh, and the reliable expectation concerning this'.[43]

If on the other hand, you cultivate unnecessary desires – such as a preference for gourmet coffee or a vegetarian diet[44] or an Ivy League education – then you will be desiring things that you cannot be confident of securing. You will likely have to go to some trouble and bother (*tarachê* or *ponos*) to try to secure these objectives, you will be subject to worries about whether you will succeed, and you will suffer the pain of disappointment if you fail. Such pain, however, has no bodily basis. It is not the sign of any unfulfilled natural need (*endeia*). The only way to remove the pain involved in natural needs is to satisfy them. But there are two ways to remove or ward off the mental pain that comes from unfulfilled unnecessary desires. You can fulfil the desire, which is not always easy or within your power, or you can remove it. From an Epicurean perspective, the latter is by far the better strategy to adopt for someone wishing to live a happy life. As an Epicurean quips: 'If you wish to make Pythocles wealthy, do not give him more money; rather, reduce his desires'.[45]

It is important to recognize that the Epicurean strategy here is about which desires to cultivate, rather than which activities to engage in. Epicurus does not advise us to abstain from luxuries and delicacies, for example. He says simply to make sure that we do not desire them, which is not the same as desiring not to have them. There are many things that afford considerable kinetic pleasure even if one does not desire them. The point is not, he says, to 'make do with few things under all circumstances', but rather to be able, if circumstances provide only limited opportunities, to make do with these without disappointment, dissatisfaction, or regret (*Men.* 130). Indeed, he claims, the person who does not desire a particular extravagance (e.g. a gourmet meal) gets more kinetic enjoyment from it than someone who does – presumably because the former lacks the latter's anxiety and concern about whether he will get what he desires. The Epicurean strategy is a matter of cultivating the proper desires by habituation. One should accustom oneself (*sunethizein*) to simple fare because of the bodily health (and resulting lack of pain) that this will produce, and more importantly because this eliminates the desire for special foods that exposes one to the possibility of disappointment if such fare is not available. It is not with a goal of turning one's nose up at such opportunities for fine dining that come along. (*Men.* 131)

By restricting our desires to the natural and necessary we achieve what Epicurus calls *autarkeia*, or self-sufficiency (*Men.* 130, VS 44, 45, 65, 67, 77). To be self-sufficient, as the Epicureans understand it, is to have it entirely in one's control whether one is happy or not, to have security (*asphaleia*) against any evil that might befall one (*KD* 7, 13, 14, 39–40; VS 31).[46] It is to have the dignity associated with the status of a free (*eleutheros*) person who controls her own destiny (*VS* 67, 77) as opposed to being vulnerable or dependent on the whims of fortune (*Fin.* 1.63) or on other forces beyond her control (*Men.* 133–5; *KD* 16, *VS* 14, 17, 81).

This Epicurean promise of invulnerability to disaster is, however, open to the objection that there is a significant class of bodily pains that cannot be eliminated simply by limiting the scope of our desires. These include, for example, the pains of injury and disease, which can befall us regardless of how carefully we prune our desires, and which cannot be alleviated by the simple measures that can relieve the pains involved in our natural impulses. To be sure, Epicurus can claim, and implicitly does claim at *Men.* 131, that limiting one's desires and 'accustoming oneself to simple fare' will have considerable health benefits, thus reducing the range of painful bodily ailments to which one is susceptible. But he cannot and does not claim that such pains are easily eliminated or avoided. Instead he offers, in the final remedy of the *tetrapharmakon*, a strategy for enduring them.

Enduring unavoidable pain

Even the wise man will feel pain, the Epicureans claim (DL 10.120; *Fin.* 2.88) – and not only in circumstances in which enduring pain now will result in future greater pleasures. Sometimes bodily pain is unavoidable; but nonetheless it is to be endured, and can be dealt with in such a way that it does not diminish a person's happiness. Enduring unavoidable pain is a large part of Epicurean practice, and is the focus of the last item

111

in the fourfold remedy: 'what is terrible (*deinon*) is readily endurable (*eukartereton*)' (Philodemus, *Against the Sophists* /LS 25J).

To understand the strategies Epicurus identifies for enduring pain, we must appreciate two further points about pleasures on which the Epicureans insist. The first is that, despite their insistence that static pleasure (freedom from distress) is greater than kinetic pleasure and is the ultimate goal of life, the Epicureans insist that the life they recommend is in fact replete with kinetic pleasures. The happy life is 'filled with pleasure from every source' (*KD* 10). The happy person 'experiences a large and continuous variety of pleasures, both of mind and of body' (*Fin.* 1.40). These include the pleasures of 'eating, drinking, hearing sweet sounds, and indulging in the more indecent pleasures' (*Fin.* 2.7):

> For I at least do not even know what I should conceive the good to be, if I eliminate the pleasures of taste, and eliminate the pleasures of sex, and eliminate the pleasures of listening, 'and eliminate the pleasant motions caused in our vision by a sensible form'.
>
> (Epicurus, *On the Goal*)[47]

As we have seen, the Epicurean practice of restricting desires is not a recommendation to eschew such pleasures (*Men.* 130), but rather paves the way to getting the maximum enjoyment from them. For these are activities or experiences from which one can get pleasure even without having an antecedent desire for them. As Epicurus says, 'those who least need extravagance enjoy it the most' (*Men.* 130).

The Epicureans claim that a sufficient array of such kinetic pleasures can outweigh various kinds of bodily distress that a person inevitably experiences. The quest for pleasure involves seeking not only a greater long-term balance of pleasure over pain (as we have seen), but also seeking the preponderance of kinetic pleasure over pain at a given time. By properly following Epicurean practice, 'the wise will be in a constant state of pleasure, since there is no time in which they do not have more pleasure than pain' (*Fin.* 1.62). Thus the Epicureans recognize two ways in which to deal with an experience of pain. One is to remove the pain itself, in accordance with the third remedy, either by satisfying or removing the desire that is its source. The other, employed in the fourth remedy, is to neutralize the pain, by arraying against it a greater quantity of kinetic pleasures (cf. *TD* 3.43–6). Such pleasures are plentiful in life, especially a life unencumbered by the pains of unnecessary desires.

For example, even the wise person will experience feelings of hunger and thirst on a regular basis. The Epicurean is well equipped to satisfy these desires, and will do so, but he is not concerned to keep them from arising in the first place, or to stifle them as soon as they appear. The Epicurean pursuing static pleasure does not shrink from these feelings of bodily discomfort or try to avoid them entirely. This does not frustrate his ultimate goal of achieving freedom from pain, because such discomforts are typically outweighed, especially in their earlier less intense stages, by feelings of pleasure. It is possible to ignore feelings of hunger and thirst, or to have little consciousness of them, if one is engaged in other absorbing or otherwise pleasant activities. On balance, one's experience can be pleasant even if one is feeling some discomfort.

The pleasant life sought by the Epicureans is therefore not free from pain in the sense that would make Epicureanism a doctrine of softness and squeamishness in the face of pain, one that advocates avoiding all kinds of discomfort. It teaches instead that many pains are endurable because they are outweighed by the multitude of pleasant experiences with which a well-ordered life is replete. Still, one might object, not all unavoidable pains are endurable by this route, especially those of serious illness or injury. Here a second Epicurean claim about pleasure is relevant.

Epicurus and his followers maintain that every bodily pain or pleasure has a mental corollary or component. When a person experiences the pleasure of a cool drink on a hot day, there are two feelings of pleasure: the bodily sensation, and the mind's enjoyment. Without the appropriate mental attitude, the pleasure will be significantly diminished. For example, the pleasure you experience in eating a delicious food can be significantly diminished by the expectation that it will make you violently ill the next morning. Similarly with the experience of pain. Having a hearty appetite (that is, being very hungry) when you anticipate having a good meal is bearable, even enjoyable, whereas experiencing the same craving for food without any expectation (or worse, with doubt) that one will get anything to eat in the near future is quite another matter – a serious discomfort. The mental attitude one takes towards the pain has a large effect on whether it is bearable, and can make even intense discomfort bearable (*Fin.* I 55–7; cf. Diogenes of Oenoanda (Chilton 1967) 38.1.8–3.14 /LS 21V).

According to the Epicureans, the mental aspect of pleasure and pain is so much more significant for our total experience than our bodily or sensory experience, that we can, by focusing our thoughts appropriately, achieve a state of pleasure even while experiencing the worst bodily pains. They offer two mental strategies for achieving this result.

The first strategy exploits the fact that the mental component of pleasure is not limited to the duration of its bodily counterpart. 'In the case of the body, all we can feel is what is actually now present. With the mind, both the past and the future can affect us' (*Fin.* 1.55). That is,

> We are cheered by the prospect of future goods, and we enjoy the memory of past ones. But only fools are troubled by recol-lected evils; the wise are pleased to welcome back past goods with renewed remembrance. We have within us the capacity to bury

past misfortune in a kind of permanent oblivion, no less than to maintain sweet and pleasant memories of our successes.

(*Fin.* 1.57; cf. 2.104–5)

The body is pleased for only so long as it perceives a present pleasure, while the mind perceives a present pleasure just as much as the body does, but also foresees a pleasure which is coming in the future and does not let a past pleasure slip from its grasp. So the wise man will always have a continuous and interconnected [set of] pleasures, since the expectation of hoped-for pleasures is linked to the memory of pleasures already perceived.

(*TD* 5.96; cf. 5.73–4)

The Epicureans teach that it is possible, simply by the disciplined use of memory, to marshal kinetic mental pleasures sufficient to counterbalance even intense bodily pain. We might call this feature of Epicurean practice a 'discipline of gratitude'. 'Misfortunes must be cured by a sense of gratitude (*charin echein*) for what has been' (*VS* 55).[48] Such is the strategy Epicurus himself claims to have employed on his deathbed:

I write this to you while experiencing a blessedly happy day (*makarian hemeran*), and at the same time the last day of my life. Urinary blockages and dyserteric discomforts afflict me which could not be surpassed for their intensity. But against all these things are ranged the joy in my soul produced by the recollection of the discussions we have had. Please take care of the children of Metrodorus.

(Epicurus, *Letter to Idomeneus*, DL 10.22)

While one might be sceptical that summoning the memories of past pleasures is sufficient to outweigh excruciating physical torment,[49] this discipline of memory and gratitude may be supplemented by an additional mental exercise that exploits the superiority of mental over physical pain.

If in addition to a stabbing pain in the stomach one also has thoughts like 'this is terrible, I can't stand another minute of it, it will never end', the thoughts make the experience of pain much worse. The fourth remedy teaches us that such thoughts are false: 'Pain is generally long lasting but slight, or serious but brief' (*Fin.* 1.40, 2.22, 93; *TD* 2.44–5). In Epicurus' own succinct expression, 'the limit of bad things either has a short duration or causes little trouble' (*Men.* 133). Unpacked in the fourth Principal Doctrine (cf. *Fin.* 1.40; *KD* 28), the more elaborated version of the claim is that:

The feeling of pain does not linger continuously in the flesh; rather, the sharpest is present for the shortest time, while what merely

114

exceeds the feeling of pleasure in the flesh lasts only a few days. And diseases which last a long time involve feelings of pleasure which exceed feelings of pain.

(KD 4)

Unavoidable bodily pains are here divided into two basic types: those in which the feeling of pain outweighs the feelings of pleasure, and those in which the feelings of bodily pleasure predominate. Pains in the latter category, once recognized as such, give no grounds for mental anxiety – since even at the bodily level pleasure outweighs the pains.

For pains in the latter category, even if the discipline of memory and gratitude cannot marshal sufficient kinetic mental pleasures to tip the balance, one can still avoid mental anxiety by focusing on the thought that they are of limited duration. Epicurus teaches that pains in the most severe category are of extremely brief duration and that those in the second category are also relatively short. Thus, he claims, it is possible to endure even these pains with equanimity. During an episode of the most intense pains, keeping in mind the message of the *tetrapharmakon* – e.g., 'this won't last long'[50] – can eliminate the mental anxiety that will compound the distressing physical experience. For the second category of pains, less intense but still strong enough to make one's on-balance bodily experience unpleasant, one can modify this strategy to achieve the same equanimity by keeping in mind the thought that, e.g., 'it will all be over by next Wednesday'. This is an attitude well designed to get through an endurance event without succumbing to despair or giving up. For pains of the last category, one reminds oneself that 'it's not so bad after all: I can still. . . .' Thus even in cases where the body's pain does outweigh its experience of kinetic pleasure, it will never be accompanied by mental distress.

While it is not in our power to avoid suffering bodily distress, even distress of significant intensity or duration, it is in our power to control the mental component that, according to the Epicureans, is much more significant for determining just how pleased or pained we are as a result. This is not to say that the afflicted person will not cry out in pain or exhibit other signs of physical distress. On his deathbed, Epicurus acknowledges the intensity of his physical pains. And while they insist, contrary to Plato and Aristotle, that the wise person will be happy even while he is tortured on the rack, they do not deny that he will moan and groan (DL 10.118).[51]

One may object that this overstretches the limits of hedonism or of empirical credulity. Surely one of the most terrible features of torture is that it is not guaranteed to be of brief duration.[52] Nonetheless, there is much that is attractive about the doctrine – not least its promise of *autarkeia*: even in the face of the worst things that can happen to us ('the limit of bad things', *Men.* 133) it is still entirely in our power to achieve happiness.

Pleasure and the virtues

So far we have seen how Epicurean philosophy lives up to its promise of securing happiness (*Men.* 122). It uses the cradle argument to identify pleasure as the goal of life, and deploys the fourfold remedy to show us how easy it is to reach that goal. We have not yet seen any role for the virtues[53] in the happy life – something that looms large in Plato's and Aristotle's ethics. Indeed, Cicero quips that Epicurus hardly ever uses 'words like wisdom, courage, justice, and temperance' (*Fin.* 2.51). Epicurus and his followers, however, deny that they have neglected the virtues. In their view, a life aimed at the pleasure of *ataraxia* and guided by the fourfold remedy is the same as the virtuous life. It is impossible to live pleasantly, they claim, without living wisely, nobly, and justly (*Men.* 132, *KD* 5; *Fin.* 1.57, 2.51, 70) – that is, without exercising the recognized virtues of character.[54] The Epicurean spokesman explains this interdependence at length in Cicero's *On Moral Ends* 1.42–53 (cf. 1.57–9), where he takes up in order the four cardinal virtues, wisdom, temperance, courage, and justice.[55]

It is easy to see why Epicurus thinks one cannot live pleasantly without living wisely. On his view, the requisite 'knowledge of good and bad' (*Fin.* 1.43) is expressed in the *tetrapharmakon* – which provides all one needs to eliminate pain and anxiety from one's life. Following the third remedy will also quite naturally yield temperate and just behaviour. A person who has pruned away all desires beyond the natural and necessary will have desires that are regulated by reason and will not be plagued by desires that oppose her rational judgment (*Fin.* 1.45–8). Since satisfying her desires will require only those resources of which there are ample supplies for everyone, such a person will be without the motive for the overreaching characteristic of injustice (1.53). And having taken to heart the lessons of the first remedy (that death is nothing to us) and of the fourth (that pain is endurable), she will be without the motives to cowardly behaviour (1.49). Thus, one can argue, the recognized virtues of character are 'inseparable' from the pursuit of Epicurean pleasure.

Their critics are not convinced, citing examples in which, they allege, the pursuit of pleasure is at odds with the demands of virtue. For example, Cicero charges, 'money brings many pleasures in its wake' (*Fin.* 2.55) and so the Epicurean has a motive to steal when he can get away with it. Furthermore, many courageous actions bring pain rather than pleasure to the agent:

> When [Publius Decius] charged at the massed Latin ranks, entrusting himself to death and setting his horse at a gallop, did he have any thought of his own pleasure? Where and when would he enjoy it? He knew he was to die at any moment.
>
> (*Fin.* 2.61)

Such objections as these, however, do not measure pleasure in Epicurean terms. The only desires we must satisfy in order to achieve *ataraxia* require resources which are in ample supply. Amassing great wealth does not increase one's ability to satisfy these desires, and so is not necessary to achieve happiness. Only someone with unnecessary or non-natural desires would have any incentive to secure wealth unjustly. Similarly in the example of courage. According to the Epicurean, nothing bad happens to Decius as a result of his courageous charge. Any bodily pains he encounters in his death wounds are bearable (via the fourth remedy), and the prospect of their ending in death is of no consequence either, since being dead is not painful. Nor is the fact that the charge will shorten his life an incentive to hold back, since Epicurean *ataraxia*, once attained, is a good that cannot be increased by duration.

Still, a critic might persist, even if an Epicurean agent has no disincentive to acting courageously, he also has no incentive. What incentive does the pursuit of pleasure provide for going to the considerable trouble involved in efforts such as those of Decius? (Recall the Epicurean's own claim that toil is incompatible with the blessedly happy nature of the gods – *ND* 1.52). The problem is that many courageous acts seem to require an altruistic motivation. For example, Decius risks his life in battle for the sake of defending his country. If the Epicureans are to defend their claim that 'living pleasantly' is inseparable from acting courageously, they need to explain how such other-regarding actions are required by the pursuit of *ataraxia*.

The Epicureans meet this challenge by invoking the benefits that we gain from the social institutions that are supported and defended by such other-regarding actions. A solitary life without the benefit of protection and support by friends and community who will defend us against enemies and wild animals is fraught with anxiety, Epicureans point out. Thus human beings have banded together in societies based on a pledge of mutual self-defence and non-aggression – an implicit social contract not to harm others on condition that they refrain from harming you (*KD* 31–3, 40; Lucr. 5.1019–27). Allegiance to this beneficial contract provides a motive for acting courageously in its defence. Indeed, Epicurus points out, fear of the social sanctions one will incur from breaking the terms of the contract provides good reason to abide by its terms – even in circumstances in which one might be better off by breaking them (*KD* 34–5, *VS* 70, *Fin.* 1.50).[56]

One might object, as Cicero does at *Fin.* 2.71–2, that someone who performs a courageous or just action from fear of punishment or other social sanctions does not have a properly virtuous motivation. We will consider that objection shortly. At present, however, our concern is whether someone living according to Epicurean principles will even perform the actions required by the virtues. Cicero offers two reasons to doubt that the fear of social sanctions will deliver this result. First of all, a person may be in a position to commit injustice with well-founded confidence that he will not be found out or punished (*Fin.* 2.53–5). Second, a consistent Epicurean, who has learned from the fourfold remedy that death is not an evil and that pain is endurable, should view with equanimity the prospect of any punishment (2.57). In neither case, Cicero concludes, will fear of punishment provide an incentive to abide by the social contract.

Cicero is probably right on these points. The fear of reprisals invoked by the Epicureans functions better in an explanation of why life under the social contract is preferable to the alternative than as a reliable motivation for the performance of virtuous actions.[57] Nonetheless, these points do not disprove the Epicurean claim that living pleasantly is inseparable from acting virtuously (*Men.* 132). Even if a non-Epicurean might be inclined to consider seriously the option of robbing widows and orphans when he could do so without fear of social repercussions, this does not show that someone with a consistently Epicurean motivation (and who thus has no desire to rob orphans) will commit injustice in those circumstances. And even if Cicero is right that the assurances of the fourfold remedy give the Epicurean agent no reason to fear punishment, such a person will not have any incentive to commit injustice in the first place. Cicero has not found a counter-example to the claim that living according to Epicurean principles will entail acting justly.

Even if the Epicureans can mount a reasonable defence of the thesis that living pleasantly requires that one act as virtue requires, they are still open to the objection (mentioned above) that acting virtuously is not simply a matter of performing the right actions. A point brought home forcefully by Aristotle is that ethical excellence requires having the proper motivation – not just doing the right action, but doing it for the right reasons (*EN* 1105a28–33). Critics object that on the Epicurean view of human motivation even people whose actions conform with the demands of virtue have inappropriate motivation. Thus, they charge, the Epicurean ethical philosophy 'does away with' genuine virtue (*Fin.* 2.59, 2.71).

To appreciate this objection, recall that the Epicureans' central thesis is that pleasure is our ultimate goal (*telos*) in life. By this they mean that it is for the sake of pleasure (understood as *ataraxia*) that we do everything we do, while we do not pursue it for the sake of anything else (*Fin.* 1.29, 1.42, 2.5).[58] This thesis applies to our pursuit of the virtues no less than to any other endeavour. Thus, the Epicureans claim that we pursue the virtues (and are right to pursue them), only because of their contribution to living pleasantly (*Fin.* 1.42). If (contrary to fact) the virtues did not remove pain and fear, they would not be worth pursuing (*KD* 10, *Fin.* 2.21, *TD* 3.42 /LS 21L2). In deliberately provocative language, the Epicurean asks:

> Those exquisitely beautiful virtues of yours – who would deem them praiseworthy or desirable if they did not result in pleasure?
> (*Fin.* 1.42; cf. *TD* 2.28)

In a similar vein, Epicurus is quoted as saying:

> We should honour rectitude (*to kalon*) and the virtues and such-
> like things if they bring us pleasure: but if not, we should say
> goodbye to them.
>   (Athenaeus 546F (Kaibel ed. 1887); translation by LS 21M)

In making such claims the Epicureans are explicitly rejecting their critics'
thesis that the virtues are to be pursued for their own sakes (*Fin.* 1.25,
1.35, 2.45). As the later Epicurean Diogenes of Onoeanda writes in
response to the Stoics, 'the virtues are not the *telos*, but productive
(*poiêtikas*) of the *telos*'.[59] If the virtues did not rid us of pain and anxiety,
we would have no reason to pursue them; thus they are desirable not in
themselves, but only insofar as they have this desirable effect.

Their critics claim that such a view is antithetical to a proper account of
virtuous motivation. A virtuous person must do the right thing for its own
sake (*propter se*), without regard to the good consequences it might bring
about for herself (*Fin.* 2.45). The mark of a virtuous person is to do her
duty even if it is painful or otherwise not in her interest to do so. Hence
paradigmatic examples of virtuous action are cases where a person acts for
the sake of his country or family, or more generally for the sake of duty
(*officium*) or the fine (*honestum*)[60] (*Fin.* 1.24, 2.45, 58, 60–1).

This criticism is so prominent in the debate over Epicureanism that
Cicero introduces it as a general challenge to the whole of Epicurean
ethics, even before the Epicurean speaker has a chance to expound the
Epicurean doctrine. Of the original Titus Torquatus, a fourth-century
Roman consul who received the name 'Torquatus' for the metal neckband
(torque) he wrested from a Gaul whom he killed in single combat and who
was also famous for having his son beheaded for conspiracy to commit
mutiny, Cicero says:

> [He] did not tear that famous chain from his enemy's neck with
> the aim of experiencing bodily pleasure. Nor did he fight against
> the Latins at Veseris in his third consulship for the sake of pleasure.
> Indeed, in having his son beheaded, he even appears to have
> deprived himself of many pleasures. For he placed the authority of
> the state and of his rank above nature herself and a father's love.
>   (*Fin.* 1.23)

Lucius Torquatus responds by reaffirming that, Cicero's observations notwithstanding, his ancestor's actions were in fact directed, ultimately, at his
own pleasure (*Fin.* 1.34–35). The pursuit of Epicurean pleasure, he reminds
Cicero, does not require a person always to pursue the present pleasure,
and always to avoid actions that are painful (1.36). The intelligent pursuit

of pleasure will require one to forgo the present pleasure on many occasions, and to incur or withstand certain pains. This will be on those occasions in which doing so will result in greater pleasure in the long run (*Fin.* 1.32–33; cf. *Men.* 129–30). Thus even though the illustrious deeds of the first Torquatus were not pleasant to perform, they secured greater pleasure for him in the long run. In wresting the chain from his enemy's neck, Titus Manlius defended his own life, and secured glory and esteem for himself (as evident in the epithet Torquatus), 'which are the firmest safeguards of a secure life' (*Fin.* 1.35). Similarly, in sentencing his son to death:

> If he did so without a reason, I would not wish to be descended from someone so harsh and cruel; but if he was bringing pain upon himself as a consequence of the need to preserve the authority of his military command, and to maintain army discipline at a critical time of war by spreading fear of punishment, then he was providing for the security of his fellow-citizens, and thereby – as he was well aware – for his own.
>
> (*Fin.* 1.35)

Note that it is the Epicurean static pleasure involving security, not kinetic pleasures, that Lucius Torquatus cites as the ultimate goal of his ancestor's actions.

Cicero's rejoinder in Book II gets to the heart of the issue. Attributing such a motivation to the original Torquatus is an insult (*Fin.* 2.60, 66–7). To say that he acted with a view to his own pleasure is to imply that he was not in fact courageous (2.73). For the same reasons, the person who refrains from acting unjustly or intemperately due to fear is not just or temperate (2.71; cf. 2.53–8, 2.60). Someone who openly avowed that his actions were ultimately for the sake of his own interest (whether this consists in pleasure or in something else) would reveal himself as untrustworthy (2.74–6). Thus, the critics conclude, Epicureans cannot allow for genuine virtue. To the extent that the rank of avowed Epicureans includes many persons of indubitable virtue, like Lucius Torquatus and even Epicurus himself, their lives are inconsistent with their philosophy (*Fin.* 2.70, 80–81, 96, 99).

Can the Epicureans defend themselves against this criticism? The core assumption behind the charge is that the virtuous person's commitment to doing the right action is not conditional on its serving his own interest:

> THE CORE ASSUMPTION: The good person will do what virtue requires even in circumstances where his own interest would be better served by acting otherwise.
>
> (*Fin.* 2.45)

The problematic feature of the Epicurean position is their view that the value of virtue is purely instrumental to our pursuit of pleasure:

THE EPICUREAN THESIS ABOUT VIRTUE: We pursue the virtues only because of the pleasure they produce.

(*Fin.* 1.42; *TD* 2.28)

The critics charge that the Epicurean Thesis about Virtue is inconsistent with the Core Assumption. But it is far from obvious that this is the case. The Epicurean Thesis in fact admits of two different interpretations, on only one of which it is incompatible with the Core Assumption.

When Epicurus and his followers say that our only reason for valuing or pursuing the virtues is their role in producing pleasure, they might be talking about our motivation for performing individual actions. That is, when we decide whether to act as virtue requires in a particular situation, we consider the long-term consequences on our prospects for achieving *ataraxia* of, for example, risking life and limb in this battle, or forgoing this particular opportunity for illicit gain. If acting as virtue requires in these circumstances better promotes our quest for *ataraxia*, we choose it, but otherwise not. On this interpretation of the Epicurean Thesis about Virtue, which is clearly the way Cicero understands it (*Fin.* 2.60), the Epicurean agent's commitment to the virtuous action is indeed contingent on its serving his own interest, and this does contradict the Core Assumption. I shall call this interpretation the 'action interpretation'.

A different interpretation of the Epicurean Thesis about Virtue is what I shall call the 'disposition interpretation'. On this reading, considerations about our *ataraxia* are brought to bear not when considering whether to perform a virtuous action, but rather when evaluating the reasons to cultivate a virtuous disposition. The question addressed by the thesis is whether being disposed to perform virtuous actions for their own sake is a good idea. Having decided that it is, because it conduces to our goal of *ataraxia*, the Epicurean agent then sets out to cultivate the sort of unconditional attachment to virtue described in the Core Assumption.[61] Once she has formed such a disposition, she will perform virtuous actions for their own sake – that is, without further regard to whether the particular virtuous action she performs promotes her *ataraxia*. As a result, she will do what virtue requires even in circumstances where her own pleasure might appear to be better served by acting otherwise.

While it may seem paradoxical to claim that we best serve our own pleasure by developing dispositions to disregard (in certain circumstances) considerations of our own pleasure, there is no inconsistency in such a view. Indeed, the Epicurean Thesis about Virtue, on this 'disposition interpretation' would be a version of the well-known paradox of hedonism – that the best way to secure your own pleasure is to stop thinking about yourself and put the pleasure of others first. Utilitarians in the modern era have shown that it is one thing to be committed to a set of principles, and quite another to have a view about the advantages of being so committed. Our reasons for holding a principle need not necessarily 'bleed through' to colour the motivation on which we act when following that principle. For example, the general happiness pursued by the utilitarian may best be served by adhering strictly to principles that forbid us, in certain circumstances, from acting with a view to promoting the general happiness.[62]

Given the ultimate goal of any enterprise, it is an empirical question whether that goal is better served by keeping it constantly in mind in all of our decisions to act, or by adopting a set of policies which can then be applied without further invoking that ultimate goal. Many successful strategies are of the latter sort – for example the 'buy and hold' strategy for maximizing return on investments. On the 'disposition interpretation', the Epicurean Thesis about Virtue is also a strategy of this sort. So interpreted, it does not entail that the virtuous person is always 'acting with a view to his own pleasure'. Only when addressing philosophical questions about the good life (when asking, for example, what is valuable about the recognized virtues) should a person invoke the Epicurean Thesis about Virtue. Far from contradicting the Core Assumption, the Epicurean Thesis about Virtue, so interpreted, would provide a basis and justification for it.

If the Epicureans' own understanding of their Thesis about Virtue is captured by the 'disposition interpretation', then they are in a position to refute the charge that it 'does away with virtue'. But is there reason to suppose that they do so understand it? It is quite implausible to suppose there would be uniformity on this issue (much less explicit recognition of the question) across the many centuries of Epicureanism. But there are several pieces of evidence in favour of attributing the view to at least some Epicureans.

First of all, Cicero himself reports that 'the masses' who are attracted to the Epicurean philosophy are under the mistaken impression that Epicurus advocates performing virtuous actions for their own sakes:

> As to the question of why so many people are followers of Epicurus, well, there are many reasons, but what is most alluring to the masses is their perception that Epicurus said that happiness – that is pleasure – consists in performing right and moral actions for their own sake (*recta et honesta . . . facere ipsa per se*).
>
> (*Fin.* 1.25)

Cicero immediately claims that the masses are mistaken, on the grounds that the view they attributed to Epicurus is inconsistent with the Epicurean Thesis about Virtue. But the charge of inconsistency is unfounded, we have seen, on the 'dispositional interpretation' of that thesis, so it cannot be used as a reason to reject that interpretation. In any case, there must be some explanation of the widespread impression reported here that Epicurus advocates performing moral actions for their own sakes – the most likely of which is that this is what he or his followers say. If this is correct, then the 'action interpretation' of the Epicurean thesis must be false.

There is, in any case, abundant evidence that the Epicureans took their Thesis about Virtue to address a general question about the virtues (rather than to supply a decision procedure for actions). In all of the texts in which the Epicurean Thesis is reported or quoted the question at issue concerns the value of such things as: virtues and the *kalon* (*honestum*);[63] particular virtues or character traits (*Fin.* 1.49); or certain kinds of pleasures (*KD* 10, *Fin.* 2.21). This is not surprising, since the context in which the Epicureans (as opposed to their critics) insist on the instrumental value of virtue is in their defence of the claim that pleasure rather than virtue is the *telos* of life. It is a theoretical or philosophical context, not a context in which one engages in practical deliberations about what action to perform in determinate circumstances.

To be sure, Epicurus does claim his philosophy helps us 'refer (*epanagein*) every choice and avoidance to the health of the body and the freedom of the soul from disturbance' (*Men.* 128 /LS 21B). But this does not mean that we are supposed to invoke considerations of our ultimate pleasure in every decision to act. The criterion Epicurus offers to assist us in this endeavour is the 'unwavering contemplation' of his distinction between natural, unnatural, necessary and unnecessary desires (*Men.* 127). The strategy of pruning away all desires beyond the natural and necessary (identified by Cicero as the Epicurean 'guide to good living' – *Fin.* 1.45) applies to the problem of deliberating about what sorts of desires to cultivate. The 'sober calculation that searches out the reasons for every choice and avoidance and drives out the opinions which are the source of the greatest turmoil for men's souls' (*Men.* 132) is a global or 'policy' decision that identifies the sorts of motivation that it is good for us to have, rather than a feature of every action's motivation.[64]

Finally, the Epicureans take their Thesis about Virtue to explain the behaviour not only of people who are avowed Epicureans, but of all those who perform virtuous actions – including those who are innocent of or disavow Epicurean philosophy. Even though the original Torquatus was not an Epicurean, Lucius Torquatus claims that his actions are directed towards the ultimate goal of Epicurean pleasure. Given the controversial nature of Epicurean philosophy, it is highly implausible to claim that such persons were 'thinking like Epicureans' in their deliberations about how to act, or that they would assent to the ascription to them of such a motivation. Hence it is highly unlikely that the Epicureans were attributing such a conscious motivation to them in their Thesis about Virtue.

Having seen that the Epicureans can successfully rebut the charge that their philosophy 'does away with virtue', let us now turn to consider their account of friendship, which their critics charged was open to the same objections as their account of virtue (*Fin.* 2.48).

Friendship

Friendship has an honoured status in Epicurean philosophy. Epicurus himself was renowned for his circle of friends and Epicurean communities typically styled themselves as communities of friends (*Fin.* 1.65, 2.80–1). According to Epicureanism, friendship is a great good (*VS* 52, 78) and is valuable for exactly the same reasons as the virtues (*Fin.* 1.66, 68, 2.82, 85).[65] Just as one cannot live pleasantly without exercising the virtues of character, so too is friendship inseparable from the pleasant life.[66]

The pleasures they see originating from friendship include many kinetic ones that arise from the activities that friends share. Philosophical discussion between friends is one of the greatest joys of life.[67] Eating without a friend is 'to feed like a lion or a wolf' (Seneca, *Epistle* 10.10). Even helping our friends is a source of pleasure.[68] More importantly, however, Epicureans see friendship as a source of static pleasure: the freedom from anxiety and the confidence that constitutes *ataraxia* (*KD* 28, *VS* 34). The isolated, friendless life is fraught with worry and anxiety, while friendship brings one confidence and security (*Fin.* 1.67–8). Thus the pursuit of pleasure as the *telos* requires us to be good friends no less than it requires us to be temperate, courageous, and just. In a nutshell, Epicurus teaches:

> Friendship cannot be divided from pleasure and should be cultivated for the very reason that no life can be pleasant without it, since without it no life can be secure and free from fear.
>
> (*Fin.* 2.82)

Critics charged that this fundamental orientation to our own pleasure is inconsistent with a central feature of genuine friendship: that one care about the friend for the friend's own sake (*Fin.* 2.78–83; cf. 1.65, 69). To be interested in the welfare of another because it promotes your own pleasure, they claim, is inconsistent with valuing that other person for his own sake; thus it is not an attitude of genuine friendship. How could you be valuing a friend for her own sake when you care about her as a means to your own happiness? The Epicurean who has her own pleasure in mind when she makes efforts on behalf of her friend, is not a true friend to the other (*Fin.* 2.78–9). At best their relation is what Aristotle disparages as 'friendship of utility' (*EN* 1156a10–12).

Nonetheless, the Epicureans insist that the friendship they value is the genuine variety in which you care for your friend for her own sake (*Fin.* 1.67–8, 2.78). We are pleased at the pleasures of friends, but also pained at their pains, they insist. More significantly, an Epicurean friend will undertake risks, undergo dangers, in extreme circumstances even undergo torture, for the sake of a friend; he will never betray a friend.[69] Nonetheless, their critics insist, these attitudes are inconsistent with the Epicurean thesis that friendship is valuable only as a means to our own pleasure. Although Epicurus and many of his followers may have been great friends, ready to die on behalf of their friends, this is not consistent with their philosophical commitment to pleasure as the *telos* (*Fin.* 2.79–81, 84). In Cicero's words, 'these people are a living refutation of their doctrines' (*Fin.* 2.81).

In response to this criticism, Epicureans distinguish between the reasons we have for forming friendships (which does depend on the advantage we get from having friends), and the motivations we have once we have become friends. While the former reasons are self-interested, they claim, the latter are not. The latter are attitudes internal to friendship, and are unaffected by the reasons we have for becoming friends. Three different versions of this response are sketched at *Fin.* 1.66–70.[70] I set out here the common features of the response.

The 'calculation of advantage' with which Cicero charges the Epicurean 'friend' (*Fin.* 2.78–9) applies only to the initial stage in the process whereby a person sets out to make friends.[71] At such a stage in the process of making friends one can quite reasonably be motivated by the thought that life would be much better and more enjoyable with friends. Here one can acknowledge the truth of Epicurus' dictum that friendship is one of the greatest goods in life (*Fin.* 1.65, 2.80, *KD* 27). One need not be an Epicurean to see the point here. This is a self-interested motivation to be sure, but it is not a reprehensible one.

To fail to bring into friendship a sense of the enjoyment and benefit one gets from being friends is also a sign of deficiency in friendship, Epicurus insists. Friendship is not a joyless exercise in dutiful self-sacrificing altruism, nor a mere commercial exchange, but a marvellous relationship with much mutual benefit and enjoyment to be had by both parties (*VS* 39, *Fin.* 1.62). Thus once friendship has been formed, the Epicurean friend will still be alive to the pleasures and benefits that come from friendship. Nonetheless, the friend at this stage will no longer be motivated by thoughts of his own pleasure in his dealings with or on behalf of his friend. This is the stage at which he will gladly sacrifice his own pleasure for the sake of his friend. His concern for the friend is not contingent on its yielding pleasure for himself in the long run. It is unconditional, even if the fact that he has such an unconditional attachment can be explained in self-interested terms.[72]

Thus it is still true, in a sense, to say that the person's genuinely friendly behaviour is for the sake of his own pleasure or benefit – since he adopted that attitude in the first place with that goal in mind. As Cicero imagines the Epicurean saying, It is to my advantage to love the friend as myself – and that is why I do so love her (*Fin.* 2.78). As a friend, I do not have my own pleasure in mind in acting on behalf of my friend; I am even prepared to sacrifice my own interest for her sake. I am not prepared to sacrifice or drop my friend when the relationship no longer yields pleasure. My ultimate orientation to pleasure motivates my strategy of seeking out and cultivating friends, but it does not 'bleed through' to contaminate the attitudes internal to the friendship that I form. Within friendship, there is none of the 'calculation of advantage' that Cicero alleges (*Fin.* 2.78–9).

Cicero is unimpressed with the Epicurean response. If we accept at face value the Epicurean claims that once friendship is established, one cares about the friend for the friend's own sake, he claims, then this is to make a concession fatal to the Epicurean philosophy: that 'there can be a right action (*posse recte fieri*) where pleasure is neither expected nor sought' (*Fin.* 2.82). But Cicero is wrong about Epicurean virtues no less than about Epicurean friendship. The Epicureans can consistently maintain that pleasure is our ultimate goal in life, even though, when we act on behalf of our friends or engage in certain virtuous actions, we are not explicitly 'expecting or seeking' pleasure.[73]

Hedonism and eudaimonism

In order to maintain the proper perspective on these criticisms of the Epicureans, we should keep in mind that the question the Epicureans address with their Thesis about Virtue is not significantly different from the one raised by Glaucan and Adeimantus in Book II of Plato's *Republic*. The brothers demand that Socrates show them the benefits of acting justly. In response, Socrates, like Epicurus, points to the significant psychological benefits of such behaviour. The brothers' demand is in keeping with the background assumption that guides Plato's ethical thinking – that the pursuit of excellence aims at a life that is in every way worthwhile, both good and admirable for a human being. Any kind of life that is presented as an excellent one has to live up to the demand that it be good for the person who lives it.

Justice, in Plato's day, appears problematic in light of this assumption, since it involves refraining from opportunities to acquire the things that are popularly recognized as goods: wealth, power, and the like. Plato's Socrates addresses this issue by invoking the significant psychological benefit a person gets from having the virtues, which is far more valuable than any external advantages one could gain by being vicious. Aristotle follows Plato in this respect. Although addressing an audience that does not ask to be convinced of the benefits of cultivating the virtues, Aristotle follows Plato in conceiving of the ethical virtues as psychological dispositions in which reason, the distinctively human faculty, rules the impulses that we share with the lower animals. Thus he too honours the assumption that we pursue the virtues, no less than the external advantages, in order to achieve happiness (EN 1097b2–5).

In insisting that the virtues must be good for us, Epicurus, then, is in agreement with Plato and Aristotle. It is tempting to suppose that the criticisms we find articulated in Cicero – to the effect that the virtuous act must be performed for its own sake, regardless of any advantage that might accrue to the agent – mark a fundamental change in the assumptions guiding ethical philosophy, and an abandonment of the 'eudaimonist' paradigm common to Plato, Aristotle, and Epicurus. But such an impression is deeply mistaken.

First of all, we have seen that Aristotle himself insists that the virtuous action is to be performed for its own sake (EN 1105a32). Plato's Socrates, no less than Cicero, says that one must perform the right action regardless of its cost to us in the external advantages (Ap. 28b–d). And even those philosophers in the Hellenistic period who criticize the Epicureans for saying that virtues are to be pursued for the sake of pleasure share with them the assumption that there is an ultimate telos in life for the sake of which we do everything we do (Fin. 1.11). Their disagreement with the Epicureans is not about whether we should pursue such a goal, but about what the correct specification of that goal is.

We find in Plato, Aristotle, and (we will see in the next chapter) the Stoics the same constellation of views that critics find problematic in Epicurean ethics: that the virtues are good for us, that we pursue them for the sake of our own happiness, and that virtuous actions are to be performed for their own sake. Yet, we have no evidence that critics in the ancient tradition charged any of these philosophers with inconsistency on these points.[74] In ancient ethics, the view that a virtuous person acts 'tou kalou heneka' is not eo ipso viewed as inconsistent with the eudaimonist assumption that her ultimate goal in acting is her own happiness. The fact that virtue is good for the agent does not 'contaminate' the content of the virtuous person's motivation (such that she is thinking about herself in acting). By parity of reasoning, then, the Epicurean agent's ultimate commitment to the pursuit of ataraxia is perfectly consistent with her acting, like the Aristotelian agent, tou kalou heneka.

Why then are the Epicureans singled out for this criticism? The explanation must lie with Epicurus's answer to the telos question, rather than with his insistence that it be answered. Both Plato and Aristotle recognize that pleasure appears to many to be the ultimate good in life. Indeed, Plato in the Protagoras (351c–354e) has Socrates appeal to a version of hedonism.[75] But both philosophers, although they acknowledge that pleasure is an important and indeed inextricable part of the happy life, reject the view that it is the ultimate good or (telos) in life.[76] No doubt part of the motivation for this is their conception of virtue as the 'using craft', with pleasure being one of the many objectives whose pursuit is to be regulated by the virtuous person's ultimate commitment to the kalon.

The problem with identifying pleasure as the *telos* is that it appears to reverse the relation of subordination essential to the practice of virtue. Instead of our pursuit of pleasure being subordinated to our pursuit of the *kalon*, such an answer to the *telos* question gives the impression that our pursuit of the *kalon* is subordinated to the pursuit of pleasure. This impression, however, is highly misleading. First of all, the Epicurean will concede to his opponents that the sort of pleasure they think must be regulated by the pursuit of virtue is indeed to be so regulated, for such kinetic pleasures are not what he identifies as the *telos*. More importantly, the Epicurean is no less entitled than the Aristotelian to insist his reason for cultivating the virtues (their conduciveness to happiness) is not something he has in mind as his conscious motivation when he acts virtuously.

Clearly many thorny questions arise for the eudaimonist tradition about the implications, of its teleological account of human behaviour, for our understanding of the motivations of individual agents. In the course of our discussion of both Aristotle and Epicurus, we have seen that the 'for the sake of' relation encompasses a surprisingly rich and varied range of goal-directed behaviour, whose precise boundaries are open to dispute even within the eudaimonist tradition. Such disputes concern issues that are extremely difficult to formulate and address precisely, and that cannot be solved simply by invoking what the expression 'for the sake of' (*heneka tinos*) means in ordinary Greek usage of the time. In adopting 'goal directedness' as the central notion in their ethical philosophy, the eudaimonists make it a philosophical notion, whose content will develop along with the theories it serves, even if it stretches beyond the bounds of the ordinary use of the term.

Notes

1 'Hellenization' (roughly 'Greek-making') derives from the Greek term '*Hellas*' (Greece).
2 Historians date the end of the Hellenistic period with the fall of the Roman Republic and beginning of the Roman empire in 31 BCE. But the philosophical schools that originate in this period still survive and are active during the Roman empire; hence Hellenistic philosophy continues in the post-Hellenistic period. For a succinct history of the Hellenistic period, see Boardman *et al.* 1986: chapter 13. For a brief account of the different Hellenistic schools of philosophy, see Sharples 1996. For fuller discussion, see Algra *et al.* 1999.
3 On the spread of Epicurean philosophy in the Greco-Roman world, see H. Jones 1989.
4 Cicero's philosophical works include the *Academica, On Moral Ends (De Finibus), Tusculan Disputations, On the Nature of the Gods, On Divination, On Fate,* and *On Duties (de Officiis).*
5 Cicero's disclaimer of originality: *Att.* 12.52; *Off.* 1.6; cf. MacKendrick 1989: 3–7. For details of the rapid composition of the philosophical works in which he immersed himself (*Att.* 12.20) between March 45 and November 44 BCE, see Powell (ed.) 1995: xv–xvi.

6 Epicurus's letters, the *Principal Doctrines* (*KD*), and the *Vatican Sayings* (*VS*) are translated into English along with much other Epicurean material in Inwood and Gerson 1994 and 1997. Cicero's *On Moral Ends* is translated into English by Raphael Woolf in Annas (ed.) 2001. Much of the same material is collected and translated with helpful commentary in LS volume 1. The translations of Cicero's *On Moral Ends* used in this chapter are those of Woolf; translations of Lucretius are by Humphries. All other translations are by Inwood and Gerson, unless otherwise indicated. Occasionally I adapt these translations to fit my own terminology.

7 Epicurus rejects dialectic: *Fin.* 1.71–2, 2.4, 12, 18, 30; DL 10.31.

8 Unlike Epicurus, some later Epicureans offered arguments in support of the *telos* claim (*Fin.* 1.30, 40–41).

9 The term '*oikeion*' (akin, or proper to) and its opposite, '*allotrion*' (alien) are prominent terms in Stoic ethics. This has no doubt influenced some of our later sources for Epicureanism, e.g. DL who at 10.137 reports the Epicurean view as that pleasure is *oikeion* and pain *allotrion*.

10 On cradle arguments, see Brunschwig 1986, Sedley 1995, and Brunschwig 2001.

11 Cyrenics were followers of Aristippus (435–350 BCE), who was a contemporary of Plato and a follower of Socrates. They reject the long-term consideration of a whole life, because they reject the importance of pursuing happiness. See Classen, 1958, Gosling and Taylor 1982: 394–6, Annas 1993: 21–2, 227–36, Irwin 1991a, Long 1992 and 1999: 632–9, Sedley 2002, Fine 2003, N. White 2006: 26–7. Socrates in Plato's *Protagoras* articulates a version of hedonism that, like Epicureanism, pursues the greatest balance of pleasure over pain measured over the long term (*Pr.* 351c–354e). On the hedonism of the *Protagoras*, see Irwin 1995: chapter 6, Kahn 1996: chapter 8, and Rudebusch 1999. On the hedonic calculus in Epicureanism, see Mitsis 1988: 23–32.

12 This quote is misleading, since Epicureans allow that there are kinetic mental pleasures: DL 10.136.

13 On kinetic vs. static pleasures, see Gosling and Taylor 1982: chapter 19, Mitsis 1988: 45–51, and Erler and Schofield 1999: 653–4. On the relation between kinetic pleasures and 'feelings' (*pathê*), see Konstan 2006.

14 A fact made much of by their critics – see *Fin.* 2.6–8, 77. The Cyrenaics acknowledge only kinetic pleasure (DL 2.88–9, 10.136; *Fin.* 1.39, 2.41).

15 On the Epicurean denial of a neutral state between pleasure and pain, see Mitsis 1988: 32–6, Purrington 1993: 283–7.

16 On the other hand, the Epicureans argue in a different context (*Fin.* 1.55), the enjoyment one gets from a kinetic pleasure can be increased by the addition of static pleasure. When feeling very distressed, the pleasure you get, e.g., from eating a delicious meal or listening to lovely music is considerably diminished.

17 Compare Aristotle's claim that the final good is not one that can be summed along with goods (*mê sunarithmoumenê*, *EN* 1097b16–20). The interpretation of this passage is controversial. See S. White 1992 and Irwin 1999 ad loc for differing interpretations.

18 Clement, *Stromates* 2.21,127.2 (Stählin *et al.* 1985) /IG I–11 p. 45.

19 Cicero's criticisms in *Fin.* 2.31–32 concede that static pleasures of the cradle variety are the ones involved in what the Stoics call *oikeiôsis*.

20 On the Epicurean goal of *ataraxia*, see Mitsis 1988: 51–8, Striker 1990. On the roots of *ataraxia* in the philosophy of the Presocratic atomist Democritus, see Warren 2002.

21 Herculaneum Papyrus 4.9–14; translation adapted from LS 25J.

22 The first four of the *Principal Doctrines* also present the fourfold remedy in the canonical order; cf. *KD* 11. Other statements of the *tetrapharmakon* include

KD 11, *Men.* 133; *Fin.* 1.40–1. Texts that include some but not all of the four 'remedies' include *Fin.* 1.49; *KD* 10, 18, 20.

23 It might appear that *Men.* 127–32 discusses only the third fear and not the fourth. But the fourth is included in the summary at 133. The appearance that it is missing is due to the fact that the third and fourth are two sides of the same coin: the worry is the same in each (that we won't be able to achieve happiness), while the remedy addresses it in two pieces: it is easy to satisfy our desires (third) and no evil can befall us that we are not able to master (fourth).

24 Philodemus, *On Piety* 30.841–70, 31.877–98 (Obbink 1996) /IG I-55, 56, p. 79; cf. Cicero, *ND* 1.45). On Epicurean attitudes to traditional Greek religion, see Obbink 1996: 1–23.

25 Cicero, *ND* 1.45 gives an account of the general notion of *prolêpsis*, and its particular application to the conception of gods. For discussion, see Sandbach 1971, Schofield 1980, and Glidden 1985.

26 Typically, in our texts, the Epicureans are responding to a providential view of nature defended by the Stoics (with roots in Plato's *Timaeus* – cf. *ND* 1.18). The reasons offered in support of this view are insufficient, the Epicureans argue (*ND* 1.18–23). They counter that phenomena invoked in support of the providential thesis can be equally well accounted for by their own hypothesis that there are an infinite number of worlds (*ND* 1.53; cf. LS 13D3, 13E, 13I-J), and there is in any case significant counter-evidence to the thesis of divine providence (Lucr. 5.196–227 /LS 13F 5–7). Epicurus' *Letter to Herodotus* (DL X.34–83) contains a detailed explanation of the natural world without invoking divine causation.

27 The Epicureans' positive account of the nature of the gods is that they are kinds of dream images or mental constructs (*ND* 1.46–9 /LS 23E6–7; cf. LS 23F–G; 23L). This view attracted much criticism in antiquity, and incurred the charge that Epicureans were covert atheists (see Long and Sedley's commentary on 23F) but there is no evidence that this theoretical account of the gods played any role in the argument to dispel fear of the gods.

28 On Epicurean arguments against the fear of death, see Miller 1976, Wallach 1976, Furley 1986, Rosenbaum 1989, Mitsis 1989, 1993 and 2002, Grey 1999, Lesses 2002, O'Keefe 2003, Draper 2004, and Warren 2004.

29 On the bodily focus of all Epicurean pleasure and pain see *Fin.* 1.25, 2.7, 89, 98, 106–107; *TD* 3.37, 41–2, 46, 51; DL 2.89).

30 On Epicurus' conception of the soul, see Kerferd 1971.

31 The argument is interspersed with yet a third set of considerations aimed at someone who rejects the Epicurean physical analysis of death, and supposes that sensation can continue after death, if the material constituents of the body are re-aggregated. Appealing to very modern-sounding considerations about the importance of memory and psychological continuity for personal identity, the argument is that in such conditions, even though a person will exist, it will not be the same person as the one who dies (Lucr. 3.843–61).

32 On the symmetry argument, see Rosenbaum 1989a, Belshaw 1993, Kaufman 1995, Warren 2001 and 2004: chapter 3.

33 Regarding Epicurus's claims about the duration of pleasure, see Gosling and Taylor 1982: 355–9, Mitsis 1988: 24–6 and 1989.

34 See below on the third and fourth elements of the fourfold remedy.

35 We find in Lucretius 3.966–1023 /LS 24F yet another argument against the fear of death. This one relies on the results of the first remedy: one should not fear torments in the afterlife because there are no gods to torment you.

36 Epicurus, *On the Goal*, quoted in Plutarch, *A Pleasant Life* 1089d /IG I-36, p. 75.

37 The distinction (between natural and unnatural, necessary and unnecessary desires) is given in whole or in part in *Men.* 127, *KD* 26, 29, 30; *TD* 5.93; *Fin.* 1.45, 53; and criticized at *Fin.* 2.26).

38 Sexual appetite (Lucr. 4.1084-120) does not appear on the Epicurean lists of natural desires – presumably because it is not manifested in the cradle. Compare Aristotle on the natural desires (*EN* 1118b15-19). On Epicurean attitudes to sex, see Brennan 1996 and Sorabji 2000: 283-4.

39 Natural desires and need (*endeia*): *KD* 18, 21; *Men.* 127-8; cf. *Fin.* 1.39.

40 Thus it is imprecise to say that a natural desire is one that is painful if not satisfied, for many of the desires that Epicureans classify as unnecessary can certainly be so intense that failure to satisfy them would result in significant psychological distress. The pain that results from not satisfying a necessary desire must be bodily; psychological distress such as disappointment or anger does not count.

41 *VS* 18 does not establish that Epicurus advocates doing away with the (arguably natural) desire for sexual satisfaction. It gives a method for eliminating an unnecessary version of such a natural desire: one that craves sexual gratification with a particular person. There is some disagreement in the sources about Epicurus's attitude to sexual desire. Some texts may attribute advocacy of sexual abstinence to Epicurus himself (DL 10.118, but see 10.19l and *TD* 4.70) and some Epicureans classify sexual pleasure as unnecessary (Porphyry: *On Abstinence* 1.51.6-52,1 /LS 21J), while others clearly took sexual activity to be within the scope of natural and necessary desires (*TD* 5.94; Athenaeus, *Deip.* 12, 546ef /IG I-37, p. 75) or at any rate among the kinetic pleasures of a happy life (*Fin.* 2.7). For discussion of this issue, see Brennan 1996.

42 On natural and necessary desires in Epicureanism, see Gosling and Taylor 1982: 408-11, Mitsis 1988: 29-36, Annas 1993: 190-7.

43 Plutarch, *A Pleasant life* 1089d / Usener 68 /IG I-36, p. 75.

44 Even though the desire to eat meat is an unnecessary desire (Philodemus *On Abstinence* 1.51.6-52.1 /Usener 464/ LS 21J) the desire to have a meat-free diet is equally unnecessary.

45 Stobaeus, 3.495 (Wachsmuth 1884) /IG I-45 p. 77.

46 Compare Aristotle, where *autarkeia* is a feature of happiness (*EN* 1097b7-16, 1177a27-b1) and happiness is within the reach of anyone 'not handicapped in relation to excellence' (1099b18-20).

47 Epicurus, *On the Goal*, quoted in Athenaeus, *Deip.* 12, 546ef /IG I-37, p. 75. The passage is also quoted by Cicero at *TD* 3.41-2 /LS 21L.

48 On the importance of gratitude for human happiness, see also *VS* 17, 19; *Men.* 122; cf. *VS* 69, 75; *DL* 10.118. A companion strategy is to dwell on the present in the face of pleasant experiences: *Fin.* 1.62; *VS* 14.

49 Cicero expresses such scepticism at *Fin.* 2.104; cf. *TD* 5.75, 2.44-5; *Fin.* 5.80. For discussion of the strategy of summoning memories of past pleasures, see Görler 1997.

50 The pain will either stop, or end in death. The second remedy ('death is nothing to us') is supposed to make the latter a matter for equanimity.

51 Other Epicurean texts about the wise man on the rack: *Fin.* 2.88-9, 5.80; *TD* 2.17, 5.73-4; *DL* 10.118.

52 Cicero articulates such criticisms at *Fin.* 2.88-9, 93-95.

53 Since 'virtue' derives from the term *virtus*, which Cicero uses to translate the Greek *arête*, I will use 'virtue' instead of 'excellence' in this chapter (and the next).

54 On Epicurus's treatment of the virtues, see Long 1986, Mitsis 1988: chapter 2, Annas 1993: chapter 16, and Ehrler and Schofield 1999.

55 The explanation in *Fin.* 1.42–53 of how living virtuously and living pleasantly are necessarily correlated is interwoven with a further argument, which we will consider shortly, that the virtues are desirable only because they result in pleasure. Our concern here is only with the former argument.

56 While the fear of social repercussions is particularly linked to the Epicurean defence of justice (*Fin.* 1.50–3), Epicurus is reported to have claimed that fear of social opprobrium is an incentive to comply with all the virtues (*Fin.* 2.48–9). On the Epicurean social contract, see Mitsis 1988: 79–92.

57 In contrast with Epicurus, his successor Hermarchus taught that the benefit of the social contract is itself sufficient incentive to right action on the part of those who are aware of it, and that the fear of punishment is a necessary incentive only for those who do not understand the intrinsic benefit of maintaining the contract (Porphyry, *On Abstinence* 1.7.1–9.4 (Bouffartigue and Patillon 1977–79) /LS 22M).

58 That is, Epicurean hedonism is a descriptive thesis (sometimes called 'psychological hedonism'), not just a normative thesis. Here I follow Woolf 2004 against Cooper 1999.

59 Diogenes of Oenoanda, *Fragmenta* (Chilton 1967) 26.3.8 /LS 21P.

60 *Honestum* is the Latin translation of the Greek *kalon.*

61 More realistically, agents do not deliberate about whether to cultivate virtuous dispositions in advance of beginning the process of acquiring them. Nonetheless, the Epicurean Thesis about Virtue addresses a question that can arise in reflection at any stage of moral development: granted that I care about virtue for its own sake, what good (if any) is there in having such an attachment?

62 For example, the general happiness is better served if we take special care of the needs and interests of those near and dear to us, rather than trying to act with impartial concern for the general happiness.

63 *Fin* 1.42, *TD* 3.42, Athenaeus, *Deip.* 12 546ef /IG I–37 p. 75.

64 It is reasonable to interpret in a similar vein *KD* 25: 'If you do not, on every occasion, refer (*epanapherein*) each of your actions to the goal of nature, but instead turn prematurely to some other [goal], your actions will not be consistent with your reasoning.' The verb '*epanapherein*' is close in meaning to '*epanagein*' in *Men.* 128 and is presumably the one translated '*referre*' in Cicero's rendering of the *telos* formula: '*quod tale debet esse ut ad id omnia referri oporteat*' (*Fin.* 1.29). Epicurus here is concerned with the direction or nisus of the action, rather than the content of one's motivation. For the contrary interpretation of *KD* 25 and *Men.* 128, 132, see Mitsis 1988: 29–30; cf. Annas 1993: 241n30.

65 Indeed, in one text, he even calls friendship an excellence (*aretê*) *VS* 23, where the manuscript reads 'all friendship is a virtue in its own right (*di'heautên aretê*)'. The reading is emended by Uesner to 'every friendship is choiceworthy in its own right' (*di'heautên hairetê*)', but is accepted by Long and Sedley Vol 2: 22F. See Rist 1972: 131, Long 1986: 305, Mitsis 1988: 100n6, Erler and Schofield 1999: 668n62, E. Brown 2002.

66 Friendship is inseparable from the pleasant life: *KD* 27, *VS* 23, *Fin.* 1.65, 2.82; cf. Plutarch, *Against Epicurean Happiness* 1097a (Pohlenz and Westman 1959) /LS 22G.

67 The pleasures of discussing philosophy with friends: (Diogenes of Oenoanda, *Fragmenta* 21.1.4–14 (Chilton 1967) /LS 22S; *Men.* 135; DL 10.22).

68 Plutarch, *Against Epicurean Happiness* 1097a (Pohlenz and Westman 1959) /LS 22G.

69 We are pleased at friends' pleasures and pained at their pains: *VS* 66, *Fin.* I 68; undergoing torture for a friend: *VS* 56–7; cf. *VS* 28, Plutarch, *Against Colotes* 1111b /LS 22H; never betray a friend: DL 10.120.

70 Cicero's Epicurean speaker indicates that these arguments are the work of Epicureans later than Epicurus.

71 Even if making friends comes naturally without any effort, the question can still arise as a philosophical or justificatory question. Someone who cherishes her friends for their own sake might ask, or be asked: is there any good in having such attachments?

72 Here I disagree with Annas 1993: 240–1, who reads *KD* 25 (discussed in note 64 above) as precluding such a 'two-level' theory of motivation.

73 For other discussions of Epicurus on friendship, see Rist 1972: chapter 7, and 1980, Long 1986, Mitsis 1987 and 1988: chapter 3, O'Connor 1989, Konstan 1993, Annas 1993: 236–44, E. Brown 2002, Evans 2004.

74 By contrast, this has been a general criticism of eudaimonist ethics in the modern period, at least since the time of Kant, according to whom the pursuit of one's own happiness is antithetical to a properly moral motivation. The only Ancient philosophical school that rejected eudaimonism are the Cyrenaics, but their reasons for doing so have nothing to do with the sort of criticism we are here considering. See Irwin 1991a.

75 On the hedonism in the *Protagoras*, see Irwin 1977: chapter 4, 1995a: chapter 6, Zeyl 1980, Gosling and Taylor 1982: chapter 3, Kahn 1996: chapter 8, and Rudebusch 1999.

76 Pleasure as an important part of the happy life: Plato, *Rep.* 582e–583a; *Phlb.* 22a–c; Aristotle, *EN* 1099a7–21; cf. 1097b2. Pleasure is not the ultimate good: Plato, *Rep.* 505c, *Phlb.* 11b–c, 22c; Aristotle, *EN* 1095b19–22, 1152b 1–1154b31.

5

THE STOICS:
FOLLOWING NATURE

The Stoics were followers of Zeno of Citium (*c*.333–262 BCE).[1] Zeno arrived in Athens at the age of twenty-two, where he attended lectures in the Academy and studied as well with the logician Diodorus Cronus, Stilpo the Megarian, and the Cynic Philosopher Crates.[2] He began teaching philosophy himself in a public hall in Athens known as the *stoa poikilê* (painted colonnade), as a result of which his followers were known as the men of the *Stoa*. Upon his death, he was succeeded as head of the school by his disciple Cleanthes (d. *c*.232). The third head of the school was Chrysippus of Soli (*c*.281–206), the intellectual giant of early Stoicism whose voluminous writings worked out the details of and arguments for Stoic theses, and defended them against attack from the Academy, which had undergone its 'sceptical turn' under the direction of Arcesilaus in the mid-third century. The enormous impact of Chrysippus on the development of Stoicism is reflected in the saying, 'Had there been no Chrysippus, there would have been no Stoa' (DL 7.183). Later Greek Stoics included Diogenes of Babylon (*c*.240–152 BCE), Panaetius of Rhodes (*c*.185–109) and his pupil Posidonius (b. *c*.135), who was one of Cicero's teachers. Stoicism continued to attract adherents well into the Roman Empire. Notable Stoics in the Roman era included Seneca (4 BCE–65 CE), Epictetus (55–135) and the Emperor Marcus Aurelius (d. 180).

None of the writings of the Greek Stoics, including the 705 volumes of Chrysippus mentioned by Diogenes Laertius (7.180), have survived. As in the case of Epicureanism, we must rely on quotations, paraphrases and attributions in later authors, most notably Cicero (106–43 BCE), Plutarch (d. *c*.120 CE), the second-century physician Sextus Empiricus, the third-century biographer and doxographer Diogenes Laertius, and the fifth-century anthologist John Stobaeus. Our earliest continuous accounts of Stoic ethics are from the first century BCE – Book Three of Cicero's *On Moral Ends*, and a summary of Stoic ethics by the doxographer Arius Didymus, which is preserved in the *Eclolgai* ('Selections') of the fifth-century CE anthologist John Stobaeus.[3] Later, but also very important, is the long summary of Stoic ethics that Diogenes Laertius includes in his biography of Zeno (DL 7.83–131).[4]

The goal of life

The Stoics agree with the Epicureans that the 'cradle' is the proper place to start when trying to identify the goal of life (*Fin* 3.16, DL 7.85–6). However, they do not think that infancy is the only time of life at which our natural inclinations are evident, and they disagree with the Epicurean analysis of the behaviour exhibited 'in the cradle'. In the Stoic view, the newborn's natural impulse to seek food, drink and warmth, although it may be impelled by feelings of pain and may result in pleasure, has as its goal self-preservation. The proper analysis of such behaviour, they claim, is that nature endows every animal with an awareness of itself, and the impulse to do what is beneficial to itself (what preserves its '*sustasis*' or constitution – *Fin.* 3.16–20; DL 7.85–86; Seneca *Ep*. 121.5–24). This includes not only seeking after food, drink, and shelter, but also avoiding predators and other dangers. For example, the chicken naturally fears the hawk. While the Epicureans would say that its behaviour is impelled by pain (fear being a species of pain), the Stoic responds that the chicken does not fear the goose or the peacock, even though they are larger than the hawk. Why not? Because the hawk, unlike the goose or the peacock, is a danger to it (Seneca *Ep*. 121.18–19). Thus the chicken naturally fears what is a danger to it. The incentive provided by pain is in service to the larger natural goal of self-preservation. Self-love, they conclude, rather than an aversion to pain, is the primary natural impulse of animals (121.7–9).[5]

In further support of their disagreement with the Epicureans, the Stoics point out that such self-preserving behaviour is part of a wider pattern of activity in the natural world. Activity conducive to self-preservation is natural to plants as well as animals, even though plants have no experience of pleasure or pain (DL 7.86, Seneca *Ep*. 121.15). And the natural impulses of animals include some that move them despite pain and resistance:

> Far from it being fear of pain that drives them . . . they even strive for their natural motions when pain discourages them. Consider a baby who is practising standing up and learning to walk. As soon as he begins to try his strength he falls and, in tears, gets up again and again until, despite the pain, he trains himself to the [function] demanded by his nature.
>
> (Seneca *Ep*. 121.7–8)

Not only do some natural impulses impel animals to push past pain and discomfort, others move them even in the absence of feelings of pain.

Seneca (*Ep.* 121.8) cites the example of a turtle on its back, in which position, he claims, it feels no pain or discomfort but still struggles to return to its normal position.

Even if Seneca is wrong that the turtle feels no discomfort when on its back, the Stoics make the general and more plausible claim that animals have a natural (that is, unlearned or untaught) facility with the handling of their own bodies. Like a skilled artist's facility with the care and handling of his own tools, nature endows us with innate knowledge of how to operate and maintain the equipment with which it endows us, along with the impulse to do so (Seneca *Ep.* 121.5–6, 9, 22–3; Hierocles 1.34–9, 51–7, 2.1–9 (von Arnim 1906) /LS 57C). The Stoics label this set of natural tendencies *oikeiôsis*: a natural inclination to pursue what is appropriate or proper (*oikeion*)[6] to oneself (DL 7.85, Seneca *Ep.* 121.17 Hierocles 9.3–10, 11.14–18 /LS 57D). As a living creature, it is *oikeion* to preserve oneself and one's parts (Plurach, *St. Rep.* 1038b). Given the particular sort of living creature one is, it is *oikeion* to use one's limbs and faculties in the species-typical manner. Thus the newborn colt struggles to its feet, the sunflower turns to the sun, and all animals care for their offspring.[7]

For human beings, the natural objects of pursuit include not only self-preservation, but also exercising our senses to acquire knowledge (*Fin.* 3.17). Nor do the Stoics think that our natural concern is limited to ourselves and our offspring. Nature inclines us to care not only for our offspring but also for other people – indeed for all people – thus furnishing the natural basis for justice, in their view.[8] In addition, the Stoics claim that it is natural for us to pursue health, property or wealth, strength, beauty, good birth and friendship as well as freedom from pain[9] – and to pursue these things in a community (*polis*). Like Aristotle and Plato, the Stoics agree that human beings are 'political animals' (*Fin.* 3.63–66; Stob. 2,6 /W 2.75,7–10).

Not all of these natural inclinations are revealed in the cradle, of course, but the Stoics claim, reasonably enough, that in creatures with complex natures the fullness of one's natural inclination will not be revealed there (DL 7.86; cf. *Fin.* 3.21–2, 4.41). What is *oikeion* to a living thing will change over the course of its natural development (Seneca *Ep.* 121.14–16). We have in us plant-like tendencies (e.g., growth and nutrition), as well as animal ones (sensation and impulse), and at a certain point in our natural development, we reach the age of reason (DL 7.86; *Fin.* 3.23). As these different faculties emerge in the course of natural development, the behaviour that is *oikeion* to us also changes.

When the faculty of reason emerges, it then becomes natural (and hence *oikeion*) for us to 'live according to reason' (*kata logon zen*, DL 7.86). By this, the Stoics understand that reason shapes or controls the impulses to pursue the things to which we are otherwise naturally inclined to pursue. To do so is not simply (or primarily) to use reason in the service of our pursuit of these ends, (e.g., to calculate how to pursue health and wealth most efficiently). Rather, when using reason properly, one selects among the available natural objects of pursuit according to whether, in the circumstances, it would be *kalon* to pursue them (DL 7.88). Reason may tell us, on occasion, that it would be *kalon* to risk life and limb by standing courageously in battle, or to commit suicide (*Fin.* 3.60–1; cf. DL 7.108–9). According to the Stoics, reason furnishes us with a principle for selecting among the natural objects of impulse, not simply a tool for pursuing whichever of them we happen to desire.[10] This priority of reason to impulse is captured in the enigmatic characterization of reason as the 'craftsman (*technitês*) of impulse' (DL 7.86).

Thus, as Cicero reports the Stoic view, the characteristic activity of a human being is to exercise the capacity for choice or selection (*selectio*, *Fin.* 3.20; DL 7.88), that is, to select among the various opportunities to pursue the natural objects of pursuit. When one selects properly (that is, rationally) among these natural objects of pursuit, one does the 'appropriate thing' (in Greek, *kathêkon* – rendered into Cicero's Latin as *officium*, 'duty').[11] The 'appropriate acts' (*kathêkonta*) are the actions required by the ethical virtues, since the standard by which reason judges actions is that of the *kalon* (Latin: *honestum*) (cf. *Fin.* 3.22).[12]

A person reaches the summit of moral development when 'such selection becomes continuous and finally consistent[13] (*constans*) and in agreement with nature' (*Fin.* 3.20). At this point, one's actions are not merely 'appropriate' (*kathêkonta*), but also 'completely correct' (*katorthômata*).[14] The person not only performs the actions required by virtue, but does them from a virtuous disposition (*Fin.* 3.59, Sextus, M 11.200–1; cf. Aristotle, *EN* 1105a27-b1, b5–11). Virtue, according to the Stoics, is the knowledge of how to choose properly among the natural objects of impulse (health, wealth, etc.). Hence they refer to the virtuous person as the 'wise man', and they call his knowledge the 'art of living' – the Stoic version of Plato's 'using craft.'[15] They typically frame normative questions as 'Will the wise man do X ?'[16]

To achieve and exercise wisdom, the art of living, is to be 'following nature', or 'living in agreement with nature' and this, the Stoics claim, is the *telos* of life:[17]

A human being's earliest concern is for what is in accordance with nature. But as soon as one has gained some understanding . . . and sees an order and as it were concordance in the things which one ought to do, one then values that concordance much more highly than those first objects of affection. . . . [O]ne concludes that this is the place to find the supreme human good, that good which is to be praised and sought on its own account. This good is what the Stoics call *homologia*. . . . Herein lies that good, namely

moral action and morality itself, at which everything else ought to
be directed.

(*Fin.* 3.21)

In calling it 'that good . . . at which everything else ought to be directed'
the Stoics claim that 'living in agreement with nature' satisfies the formal
conditions for happiness (*eudaimonia*) articulated by Aristotle in EN I 7.
As Arius reports, 'They say that the *telos* is to be happy (*eudaimonein*), for
the sake of which everything is done, but it is not done for the sake of anything else' (Stob. 2,6e /W 2.77,16–17).

Following nature

There are a number of different ways in which the Stoics understand such
a person to be 'following nature' or 'living in agreement with nature'. At
the simplest level, such a person is acting according to his own nature as
a rational animal – using reason rather than just following impulse. But
it is not just her individual nature that she follows, Chrysippus claims, but
also 'the nature of the whole' (DL 7.88).[18] To appreciate this point we
need to attend to some Stoic physics and theology.

According to the Stoics, the world is a compound of two principles: an
active principle, called reason (*logos*) and identified with God, and a passive
principle called matter (*hule*) (DL 7.134, 139, Sextus M 9.11).[19] The active
principle permeates the passive principle to produce and constitute the cosmos (DL 7.134–138). It does this at two levels. First of all, it holds together
each individual thing, and gives it its characteristic properties and causal
powers. The Stoics recognize three different grades of this cohesiveness or
unity of individual things. The lowest level they call *hexis* ('tenor' in the
translation of LS; literally 'holding together'). This is the unity of inorganic
substances such as rocks and earth. At the next level, there is organic
unity, which they call *phusis* (nature): this is the principle that unifies and
animates plants, and the plant-like part of each person (it corresponds to
what Aristotle calls the nutritive soul – *DA* 415a23–25). Third is the degree
of unity characteristic of animals, called soul (*psuchê*). At the highest level
of unity, the last principle is called *logos* (reason) or *nous* (mind).[20] This is
what makes human beings what they are, since we are rational creatures.

In addition to holding together and giving qualities to the individual
inorganic, organic, and animate constituents of the world, the active principle unifies these disparate items into a unified, organic, rational whole.
Reason, the active principle, imbues the universe as a whole, making it a
'cosmos' (order). Indeed, the Stoics go so far as to claim that the cosmos
has the unity characteristic of a rational animal (DL 7.139).

In the Stoic view, reason is manifested in the universe in two different
ways. First of all, it is manifested in the natural activity of any existing

thing: whether it be the simple 'tensile' power that holds together inorganic substances, the organic forces manifested in living things, the psychological and locomotive capacities of animals, or, in its highest grade, in the rationality exhibited by human beings. Second, and more importantly, all existing things are related to each other and organized into a universe that is itself administered by reason in its full, unadulterated sense – the same sort of reason that is natural for human beings to possess:

> The cosmos is administered by mind (*nous*) and providence (*pronoia*) ... since mind penetrates every part of it just as soul does us. But it penetrates some things more than others. For it penetrates some as *hexis* – for example, bones and sinews, and others as mind, for example, the leading part (*hegemonikon*) of the soul. In this way, the entire cosmos too, [is] an animal and alive and rational.
>
> (DL 7.138–9)

Therefore, in using reason properly to select among the natural objects of pursuit, a person is not simply following her own nature as a rational creature, but is attuned to and following the rational cosmic nature that governs the universe (DL 7.88).

This conception of the goal of life does not amount to the view that 'living naturally' is the goal.[21] For plants and animals, in doing what is *oikeion* to themselves, are also acting 'naturally' (*kata phusin*).[22] Humans who pursue the natural objects of affection (life, health, etc.) are also following natural impulses; thus the coward who flees from battle to save his life may be described as 'acting naturally'. Nonetheless, the pursuit of these objects, however natural it may be for humans, does not count as 'following nature' in the sense identified as the *telos* by the Stoics. To 'follow nature' in this special sense is to regulate these otherwise 'natural' pursuits by reason. It is to exercise one's rational faculties in selecting among the natural objects of pursuit (sometimes even abstaining from their pursuit if the standards of morality (*honestum*) require it). In acting thus, one is following the rational nature that imbues the cosmos, since an individual human being's reason is an 'offshoot' of the divine reason (Epictetus, *Diss.* 1.1.12).

The Stoics take the rational structure of the universe to be the work of God, but they do not conceive of God as a supernatural being distinct from the natural world. Rather, they think God, as the reason that imbues and governs all things, is immanent in the natural world. Thus in 'following nature', one is following the will of Zeus. In a person who has perfected the art of living, 'all things are done according to the harmony of the divinity (*daimôn*) in each of us with the will of the administrator of the universe' (DL 7.88).

Natural law

The 'will of god' with which the virtuous person's life is in agreement is often described by the Stoics as law (nomos). As a result, the Stoics are often credited with being the first exponents of a theory of 'natural law'. According to Chrysippus in his lost work On Ends:

> Our natures are part of the nature of the universe. Therefore, the goal becomes 'to live following nature', that is, according to one's own nature and that of the universe, doing nothing which is forbidden by the common law (nomos ho koinos), which is right reason [orthos logos], penetrating all things, being the same as Zeus who is the leader of the administration of things.
>
> (DL 7.88)

This passage refers to the divine reason pervading the universe as 'common law' – a phrase that appears more often in the context of Stoic political theory[23] – where the modifier 'common' highlights the fact that the rational nature followed by any particular person is the same rational nature to be found in any other human being. The label 'law' (nomos) indicates the prescriptive force of the divine reason that all human beings must follow if they are to achieve excellence and happiness.[24] Thus Chrysippus's lost work, On Law, begins:

> Law is king of all things human and divine. Law must preside over what is honourable (kalon) and base (aischron), as ruler and as a guide, and thus be the standard of what is right (dikaion) and wrong (adikon), prescribing to animals whose nature is political what they should do, and prohibiting them from what they should not do.
>
> (Marcian, Corpus iurus civilis I; SVF 3.314;
> translation by LS 67R)

Against an enduring tradition according to which the laws or customs (nomoi) that dictate the standards of morality (to kalon) or justice (dikaion) are merely conventional human creations,[25] the Stoics insist that standards of living well are based in nature, and are binding on all human beings.[26] Thus they invoke the notion of a 'natural law', binding on all rational creatures:[27]

> The world is like a city consisting of gods and men, with the gods serving as rulers and men as their subjects. They are members of a community because of their participation in reason, which is a natural law (phusei nomos).
>
> (Arius Didymus apud Eusebius, Preparatio Evangelica
> 15.15.4–5 (Mras 1954–6); translation by LS 67L)

In saying that what is right and wrong, or fine and shameful, is a matter of natural law, the Stoics do not thereby commit themselves to a position on the form that such law must take. They are not committed to the view that right and wrong can be codified in a set of moral rules that give absolute prohibitions against certain kinds of behaviour (such as taking up arms in the service of a tyrant, or endangering one's health), nor indeed absolute requirements to perform certain types of actions.[28] Indeed the early Stoics, particularly Zeno, were notorious in later antiquity for rejecting some prevailing social taboos (e.g. those prohibiting incest and cannibalism, or promoting traditional gender roles).[29] Furthermore, a prominent theme in Stoic ethics is what we may call the 'situational flexibility' of moral rules. While many Stoics advocated the importance of using simple rules in moral teaching (Seneca, *Ep.* 94,1–16) they, like Plato and Aristotle before them, recognized that there are some situations in which it would be wrong to follow these rules (such as 'return what you have borrowed'), and claimed that the wise person, who has perfected the art of living, will be able to recognize such exceptions.[30]

In this context it is useful to keep in mind that the Stoics typically speak of natural *law* in the singular – not of natural *laws*. The natural law is the rational standard (*kanôn*) that grounds the rightness or wrongness of any particular action – whether it falls under a simple moral rule or not. It is in 'agreement' (*homologia*) with this rational standard that they claim one must exercise one's own faculty of choice if one is to live well. This is what it is to follow nature, on their view.

Only the admirable is good

To return to the bigger picture, we have seen that the Stoics identify the goal of life as 'following nature'. They further specify that following nature in this way is to live virtuously,[31] that is, to aim in all one's actions at doing what is fine (*kalon*) and avoiding what is shameful. The Greek term '*kalon*' is rendered into Latin as '*honestum*', so Cicero gives an alternative characterization of the good of 'agreement' as 'fine action (*honeste facta*) and the fine itself (*ipsumque honestum*)' (*Fin.* 3.21).[32] Thus while the Stoics' canonical thesis about the *telos* of life is that it is 'agreement with nature' or 'following nature', they claim that the *summum bonum* (highest good, *to ariston* in Greek) is the *kalon* (3.12).[33]

In claiming that the *kalon* is the highest good, the Stoics are not in genuine disagreement with Aristotle. Where they do diverge significantly from Aristotle is in their further claim that the *kalon* is the only good. In the banner slogan of ancient Stoicism, 'only the admirable (*honestum, kalon*) is good'.[34] Aristotle and the Peripatetics consider such things as health, wealth, and family success to be goods; that is, these are choiceworthy in themselves, although also pursued for the sake of the ultimate good

141

(*EN* 1097b2–4). The Stoics disagree. The only thing that is good is the virtuous activity itself. Only at the point when one achieves the consistency and agreement with nature that is the hallmark of virtue, does one achieve anything truly good (*Fin.* 3.20).[35] Achieving the summit of moral development, for the Stoics, involves a transfer of allegiance away from the initial objects of pursuit (health, wealth, etc.), and towards the newly discovered good of 'agreement':

> A human being's earliest concern is for what is in accordance with nature. But as soon as one has gained some understanding, or . . . what the Stoics call *ennoia*, and sees an order and as it were concordance in the things which one ought to do, one then values that concordance much more highly than those first objects of affection. . . . This good is what the Stoics call *homologia*. . . . Herein lies that good . . . at which everything else ought to be directed. Though it is a later development, it is nonetheless the only thing to be sought (*expetendum*) in virtue of its own power and worth, whereas none of the primary objects of nature is to be sought on its own account.
>
> (*Fin.* 3.21)

Not only is living in agreement (*homologia*) the greatest good, it is the *only* good according to the Stoics.

The implications of this claim are startling. If virtue[36] is the only good (and vice the only evil), then the life of illness and poverty is no worse than the life of health and wealth – as long as one acts virtuously:

> [Our ancestors] thought that the life of a morally good person (*eius qui honeste viveret*) which also had health, reputation and wealth would thereby be preferable, better and more desirable than the life of a person who was equally moral but . . . was 'beset on all sides by illness, exile and poverty.' . . . The Stoics, on the other hand, consider that [the former] life is merely to be preferred in one's choices, not because it is a happier life but because it is more suited to nature.
>
> (*Fin.* 4.62–3)

In explanation of this extraordinary claim, the Stoics invoke an analogy with archery (*Fin.* 3.22; cf. 54). Archery is the art of shooting an arrow at a target. The archer displays maximum skill when taking appropriate aim at the target by making the appropriate adjustments and choices in the light of the prevailing conditions. Such perfection of skill does not consist in actually hitting the target; this depends on luck in addition to skill. Similarly, living well (happiness), which consists in exercising the 'art of living', depends entirely upon making the appropriate choices and adjustments in one's aiming at the natural objects of pursuit (health, wealth, etc.).

For example, in making (and following through on) all the right decisions about when and how to promote his health, the virtuous person has done the best he can, and indeed as well as anyone should care about. That is, he eats properly, gets regular exercise, and visits the doctor. Whether he keeps his health, or, despite his best efforts, is stricken with a painful and debilitating disease, *makes no difference* to how well he is living, since the 'art of living' consists in selecting properly, not in actually securing what one has selected. Thus the Stoics claim that the natural objects of pursuit, as well as their opposites, are 'indifferent' – that is, neither good nor bad. Securing them makes no difference to whether we are living well (happy) or not.

In calling health, wealth and the like 'indifferent', the Stoics are not saying that we should neglect them. This would be characteristic of the Cynics. For example, the Cynic philosopher Crates, teacher of Zeno, is reported to have sold all his possessions and given the money away and Diogenes the Cynic reportedly lived in a barrel and regularly exposed himself to unhealthy conditions (DL 6.23, 87). By contrast, the Stoics insist that virtue requires us to make the appropriate choices, and perform the appropriate actions, concerning our health, wealth, etc. The Stoic wise person, no less than the Aristotelian, will take care of her health. She will eat well, exercise regularly, visit the doctor, and stay out of danger – except in circumstances when it would be *kalon* to do otherwise. Similarly with wealth, family, and the other natural objects of pursuit. The actions and choices of the Stoic will be indistinguishable from those of the Aristotelian. The disagreement on this point between the Stoics and Aristotelians concerns the philosophical question of whether the virtuous person is better off securing the natural objectives than she would be if her attempts to secure them fail.[37] The Peripatetic view is that she is of course better off, while the Stoic answer is that she is not.

We might summarize the disagreement between the Stoics and Peripatetics according to the significance they attach to two questions one might ask about the natural objects of pursuit (health, wealth, family, etc.):

a. Did I choose correctly in my pursuit of them?

b. Did I succeed in getting what I pursued correctly?

The first question asks whether I pursued health, wealth, and the like only when it was *kalon* to do so, and did nothing shameful (*aischron*) in the pursuit of these ends. The Stoics and the Peripatetics agree that the answer to this question concerns the most important thing in life: rational or virtuous activity. Unless one has properly regulated one's pursuit of these natural objects by the art of living, then one has gained nothing worthwhile in life.

It is in their attitudes to the second question that the Stoics and Peripatetics disagree. According to Aristotle's school, even if I have consistently acted virtuously and honorably in my pursuit of health, wealth, and the like, it still makes a difference to the quality of my life whether I have succeeded in securing these objectives. For the Stoics, by contrast, I am no better off in health and wealth than I would be in disease and poverty, provided I have conducted myself properly in my pursuit of these ends. This is what the Stoics mean by their oft repeated claim, 'Only the admirable (*kalon, honestum*) is good.'[38]

Virtue, happiness, and external goods

It is worth noting that Aristotle's own position on this issue is far less clear than that of his successors. As we saw in Chapter 3, Aristotle does say that a person cannot be happy if he suffers the misfortunes of Priam (1100a4–9), and that the virtuous person cannot be happy on the rack (*EN* 1153b18–21; cf. 1095b31–1096a2). Like his Peripatetic successors, Aristotle insists that happiness requires a certain level of success in achieving the natural objects of pursuit: wealth, power, friends, family, and the like (1099a31–b8, 1101a14–16, *Pol.* 1323a25–7). However, his reason is that such 'external goods' are necessary for the unimpeded exercise of virtue (1099a31–33, 1100b29–30, 1153b17–19).[39] Such a view falls short of claiming, and indeed does not even allow the possibility, that a person might successfully exercise the virtues of character and still lack health, wealth, and the other natural objects of pursuit. The Stoic and Peripatetic disagreement, however, concerns precisely this situation: that of a person who, in 'following nature', has achieved unimpeded exercise of the virtues, but still suffers pain, disease, poverty, etc. The Peripatetics, therefore, must not subscribe to Aristotle's own statements on the relation between virtuous activity and the 'external goods'.[40]

To modern readers, the Peripatetic answer may seem obviously correct, and the Stoic position perverse beyond belief. But the Stoics are responding to the pull of considerations that are arguably as strong as the ones to which Aristotle's followers respond, even if they are not as easily accessible to us today. The Stoic view respects the pull of the original pre-philosophical notion of *aretê* (virtue, excellence) as success in life, encompassing everything worth striving for and being admired for. On such a conception, as we saw in Chapter 1, the life of excellence and the life of happiness coincide.

Once Plato and Aristotle transform the notion of *aretê* into an internal psychological disposition that can be distinguished from a happy life, and once the notion of excellence is understood as the 'using craft', it becomes clear that one can have this *aretê* and exercise it without having all the 'external goods'. The original assumptions that *aretê* and *eudaimonia* coincide and that *eudaimonia* requires having the 'external goods' cannot both stand. Once this tension is recognized, the ethical philosopher is faced with a theoretical choice: either give up the close connection between virtue and happiness and retain the view that health and the like are good (the Peripatetic route), or give up the ordinary view that health, wealth, and the like are in fact good, and retain the inseparability of virtue and happiness (the Stoic route). Either choice has a cost, and the decision is a foundational one for the Stoics (*Fin.* 4.45–6).

The good and the admirable

The Stoics offer a number of arguments in support of their trademark thesis that only the admirable (*kalon*) is good.[41] One of them is summarized at *Fin.* 3.27:

> Whatever is good (*bonum*) is praiseworthy (*laudabile*); whatever is praiseworthy is fine (*honestum*); therefore, whatever is good is fine.

The argument (and its equivalent in Greek) may be set forth as follows:[42]

(1)   Whatever is good (*agathon*) is praiseworthy (*epaineton*).
(2)   Whatever is praiseworthy is admirable (*kalon*).
(3)   Therefore, whatever is good (*agathon*) is admirable (*kalon*).

The Stoics explicitly recognize that the first premise is controversial, and summarize their defence of it as follows:

(4)   Whatever is good is to be sought (*expetendum*).
(5)   Whatever is to be sought is pleasing (*placens*).
(6)   Whatever is pleasing is worthy of choice (*diligendum*).
(7)   Whatever is worthy of choice is commendable (*probandum*).
(8)   Whatever is commendable is praiseworthy (*laudabile*).
(9)   Therefore, whatever is good is praiseworthy [= (1), QED].

There is nothing the Peripatetic would disagree with in premises (4) through (6) or in (8).[43] Premise (7) may appear more objectionable, on the ground that it is external objects such as health and wealth that are worthy of choice, but choice itself, or the agent who is commendable. The Stoic, however, can easily respond that it is not external objects but actions that

145

are worthy of choice: one chooses to pursue the external object, and it is in virtue of this choice that one is commendable. However, once it is clarified that (4) through (6) concern not the external objects themselves but actions in pursuit of them, (4) becomes controversial. The Peripatetics, in particular, have no reason to accept it, since they do not think that every 'external good' is to be pursued in all circumstances.[44]

A second type of argument is presented at *Fin.* 3.28. It goes something[45] like this:

(a)   Unhappiness is something to be ashamed of.
(b)   Therefore, a life to be proud of must be happy.
(c)   A virtuous life (*honesta vita*) is one to be proud of.
(d)   Therefore, a virtuous life must be happy.

To resist the conclusion, the Peripatetics must reject either premise (a), or the inference to (b) – since premise (c) is clearly one they agree with. For modern readers, the obvious response would be to reject (a); unhappiness, if it depends on external factors rather than our own choices, is nothing to be ashamed of. But this is a much harder response to make in the ancient context, where the original conception of happiness is of a desirable and admirable life, and falling short of success is indeed taken to be a matter for shame.

According to Callicles in Plato's *Gorgias*, possessing a certain range of external goods and the power to protect them is a condition of self-respect. It is shameful to be weak or poor and defenceless (Plato, *Ap.* 28b; *Gorg.* 521b–d; cf. 508d–e, 511a). This sort of view has endured, in vestiges, to this day.

Given these presuppositions, it is hard to reject the Stoic premise (a), that unhappiness is something to be ashamed of. However, this is precisely what the Peripatetics must do in order to resist the Stoic conclusion. The price they must pay for rejecting the Stoic thesis (d) that virtuous activity on its own suffices for happiness is to reject a deeply entrenched view about happiness.

The final argument offered by Cicero's Stoic speaker (*Fin.* 3.29) appeals to a model of virtuous activity endorsed by Aristotle: that of the brave or magnanimous person who 'makes light of' the vicissitudes of fortune (cf. *EN* 1100b30–1101a6, 1124a12–16). On the basis of this model, they assert:

1.   The good person does not consider death or dishonour to be an evil.
2.   Therefore death and dishonour are not evil.

The argument can be generalized to apply to all the alleged external 'goods'. A suppressed premise is presumably that the virtuous person is wise, and therefore correct in her value judgments. The Peripatetics would not contest this assumption, or the validity of the argument. They would resist, however, the first premise, which goes beyond what the Aristotelian model of virtue implies. The courageous person does not think that death, in any circumstance, is not an evil. It is only in circumstances in which death would be *kalon* that he pays no heed to it (*EN* 1115a32–4). Even if Aristotle thinks that death in such circumstances is preferable to life, this in no way commits him to affirming that death itself is not a bad thing. Similarly, even if a magnanimous person bears the loss of external goods with equanimity, it need not be because such goods have no value; they might simply have less value than the virtue one would compromise by acting aggrieved at the loss.

Having surveyed the arguments offered in support of the Stoic claim that only what is admirable is good, and the responses available to their Peripatetic opponents, we may reasonably remain unconvinced of the Stoic position. Given the foundational nature of the Stoic thesis, however, one should not expect them to have a conclusive argument for it. We will get a better appreciation for what attracts the Stoics to this thesis if we examine in more detail the perspective of the person 'living in agreement with nature', for it is from this vantage point, Cicero reports, that all the natural objects of pursuit are evidently 'indifferent' (*Fin.* 3.21).

Goodness and value: the eclipse

Even though the Stoics deny that the natural objects of pursuit are good, they do allow that they have 'worth' (*axia*; Latin *aestimatio*)[46] (*Fin.* 3.20, 4.56; Stob. 7f /W 2.83,10–84,3; cf. *Fin.* 3.34). This means, roughly, that they are worth pursuing.[47] Nonetheless, the Stoics claim, the goodness of living in agreement completely 'eclipses' the worth of obtaining any of these natural objectives:

> It is like the light of a lamp eclipsed and obliterated by the rays of the sun; like a drop of honey lost in the vastness of the Aegean sea; a penny added to the riches of Croesus, or a single step on the road from here to India. Such is the worth of bodily goods[48] that is unavoidably eclipsed, overwhelmed and destroyed by the splendour and grandeur of virtue as the Stoic candidate for the highest good.
> (*Fin.* 3.45)

The worth, for example, of health in relation to that of virtue is so small that it does not make life any better, in the way that lighting a candle at noon does not make the day brighter, or adding a penny to the wealth of Croesus[49] does not make him wealthier. These additions (or subtractions) are matters of 'indifference' to the question of whether Croesus is wealthy or whether the day is bright, and so too the presence or absence of health in a virtuous life make no difference to its goodness.

The Peripatetics (and other opponents of the Stoics) will agree that certain kinds of external 'goods' are matters of indifference to the happiness of a life. For example, whether one has certain 'small pleasures' or possessions (in a notorious example, an oil flask – *Fin.* 4.30) makes no difference to the happiness of a life. But they deny that this is true of all the 'external goods': some, like an additional month of an enjoyable life, are not negligible, and others, like health and freedom from great pain or poverty are of great significance (4.29–30). It does not follow, Cicero points out, from the fact that some external goods may be 'eclipsed' by the value of virtue, that none of them, or that no quantity of them, makes a difference to the goodness of a life. Indeed, the examples in the Stoic analogy leave unchallenged the assumption that the worth of health and the value of virtue are measured on the same scale – in Cicero's terminology, that health and the like are 'parts of a happy life':

A penny is swamped by the riches of Croesus, but it is still a part of those riches. Hence, though what we refer to as 'things in accordance with nature' may be swallowed up in a happy life, they are still a part of the happy life.

(*Fin.* 4.31)

The objection is that the value of one thing may eclipse that of another even if they are both good.

This objection, however, makes the mistake of supposing that the eclipse analogies are intended to *establish* that health and wealth and the like do not make a difference to the happiness of a life. But these analogies are not part of the arguments the Stoics offer in support of this signature thesis (3.27–9). Rather, they are offered in illustration of the sort of gulf the Stoics claim there is between the worth of health and wealth, on the one hand, and the goodness of virtue or 'following nature', on the other. The point of the analogy is to *say* that just as the value of a penny is swallowed up in the riches of Croesus, so too the worth of health and freedom from poverty is 'eclipsed, overwhelmed and destroyed' by the value of living in agreement with nature. Rather than offering reasons to accept the Stoic claim that health and disease make no difference to the goodness of a life, the eclipse analogies put constraints on how we should understand the goodness they attribute to the virtuous life.

No degrees of goodness

Of course, the wealth of Croesus consists of a certain quantity of pennies. If he gains (or loses) a sufficient quantity of them, it will make a difference to his wealth. According to the Stoics, however, goodness does not stand to mere worth as enormous wealth stands to a penny. Virtue eclipses the worth (*axia*) of health not by having much more of the worth that health has, but by having value of an entirely different kind. No matter how much health or wealth you accumulate, its worth will never add up to anything good, the Stoics claim (*Fin.* 3.34). This is because, on their view, goodness does not admit of degree.[50]

If goodness does not admit of degree then a life cannot be made better by the addition of health or wealth, or made worse by their loss. But why deny that there are degrees of goodness? The denial is a fundamental thesis within Stoicism, on a par with the claim that virtue is the only good (*Fin.* 4.54; cf. 3.48). Thus, as in the case of the former thesis, we should not expect arguments establishing it, but rather explanations, analogies, and defences of its controversial implications. (The most notorious of the defences is the thesis that all wrong doing is equal and no person is wiser or more virtuous than another.[51])

A general motivation for the claim that there are no degrees of goodness is provided by the Stoic definition of 'good' and 'beneficial'. As Cicero's Stoic spokesperson explains:

> The term 'good', used so much in this discussion, may also be clarified by a definition. The Stoics define it in a number of slightly different ways, which none the less point in the same direction. I side with Diogenes [of Babylon] in defining the good as what is complete (*absolutum*) by nature. Following from that, he also stated that the 'beneficial' . . . is movement or rest which originates from what is complete by nature.
> (*Fin.* 3.33; cf. DL 7.94; Stob. 2,5d /W 2.69,11–70,7)

To be 'complete by nature' (*absolutum*: Greek *teleion*)[52] is to have reached the goal (*telos*) of one's natural development. In the case of human beings, this is to be exercising rationality in perfect harmony with the divine reason that governs the universe.

Completeness, or perfection, is an all-or-nothing condition. While we might talk loosely about 'degrees' of completeness or perfection, these are not, strictly speaking, degrees of being complete or perfect. Rather, they are conditions that approach completeness or perfection more or less closely. The Stoics grant the obvious fact that different people can approach the moral ideal of virtue more or less closely, and that the same person can make significant progress towards that ideal.[53] They insist, however, that such progress towards virtue is not an increase in virtue (and hence not an increase in goodness). Virtue is the status one reaches at the end of that process of development, and not at any point before.

They offer a number of famous analogies in illustration of this point:

> When submerged below the water one can no more breathe if one
> is just below the surface and on the verge of getting out, than one
> can in the depths. A puppy that has almost reached the point of
> opening its eyes can no more see than one newly born. In the same
> way one who has made some progress towards the acquisition of
> virtue is just as unhappy as one who has made no progress at all.
>
> (*Fin.* 3.48; cf. 4.64)

Their critics reply that different analogies are better for the process of
acquiring virtue:

> One person has blurred eyesight, another a weak body. By apply-
> ing a remedy they improve day by day. Every day one gets stronger,
> the other sees better. It is like this for every keen seeker after
> virtue.
>
> (ibid. 4.65)

On the rival analogies, a person can become more and more virtuous.
Becoming completely virtuous is simply to have reached the end of the
process. On the Stoic analogies, by contrast, becoming virtuous involves
what we might call a 'break-through point': a change that happens all at
once at the end of the process of moral development.

We must take the Stoic analogies, rather than their rivals', to put a
constraint on how we interpret their account of virtue and moral development. The analogies imply that becoming virtuous involves a break-through
point, not just a gradual development of what one has at the end of the
process. Just as the swimmer under water can no more breathe when he is
one foot below the surface than when he is five feet below, the person who
reaches the summit of moral development, and is in the status of 'living in
agreement with nature', has achieved something that he had not even
partially achieved earlier in the development. The person who is becoming
progressively better at practical reasoning (selecting among the natural
objects of pursuit) is getting closer to the goal, but has not achieved any
more than she had at the beginning of what she will have once she reaches
that goal.

The Stoics are not making the simple logical point that no matter how
far one is from achieving 100% 'agreement with nature', it is equally true
that one falls short of 100% (for example, that it is no less true of 98%
than of 30% that it falls short of 100%).[54] Such a logical point would be
consistent with the view, which they reject, that at 98% agreement a
person has achieved more of what she will have at 100% than she had at
30%. They must be claiming instead that, having traversed the whole
series and reached the limit, a transformation or breakthrough occurs (like
the swimmer being able to breath).

Consider another version of the metaphor reported by Diogenes Laertius (7.120). A person who is one stade away from the town of Canopus is no more *in Canopus* than one who is 100 stades away.[55] Here we can distinguish two different things: traversing the distance between one's starting point and Canopus, on the one hand, and being in Canopus on the other. While the former admits of degree, the latter does not. Suppose being in Canopus will change you in some way, the way being in the Emerald City makes everything look green to you. Getting closer to Canopus does not bring about any part of that change, any more than getting closer to the Emerald City makes one's field of vision progressively greener.

The Stoics must therefore make a similar distinction between the thing one gets better at during moral progress, on the one hand, and the thing one achieves once one has achieved virtue, on the other. What one sees or grasps upon reaching the *telos* is something one has not seen before, Cicero reports: 'At this point that which can truly be said to be good first appears and is recognized as such' (*Fin.* 3.20). The 'consistency' that the Stoics identify with this goal is like the consistency of a mathematical system, which does not admit of degree. Making the final step to becoming virtuous is not like acquiring the last dollar that makes you a millionaire, but more like positioning the final tumbler that opens the lock to the door. The door is no more open before that final tumbler is in place than it was when the first tumbler fell into place. So too for the Stoics, reaching the limit of moral development is a breakthrough to a vision or grasp of something which one has not glimpsed, even dimly, until reaching that point.

The Stoic version of this 'beatific vision' is knowledge of the universe. It is to grasp the goodness of the world order and experience oneself as being in complete intellectual harmony with the rationality that structures the cosmos. Like Plato's philosophers grasping the forms, the person who achieves this complete agreement with the rationality that imbues the world is 'assimilated to God' (*Fin.* 3.73; cf. DL 7.119).[56] The Stoics teach that achieving and recognizing this perfect assimilation to the rational principle that governs the cosmos is a 'breakthrough' akin to emerging from the water and drawing a breath, or opening your eyes to the light.

Nature and moral development

Having considered the arguments and analogies the Stoics offer in support and elucidation of their view that the only good is the condition of living in agreement with nature, let us now consider the two main criticisms that were levelled against the trademark Stoic claim by their contemporaries. The first concerns their conception of moral development, the second their explanation of rational action.

According to the Stoic view of moral development sketched by Cato in *Fin.* 3.16–21, there is a radical discontinuity in one's orientation to the 'natural objects of pursuit' (which include, in addition to life, health and bodily integrity, such things as wealth, honour, and the well-being of family members, friends, and fellow citizens). On the Stoic view, a human being's initial natural impulse is towards preserving its physical constitution (feeding, seeking warmth, avoiding predators) and exercising its faculties in their natural way (locomotion, sensation). At the next stage of development, one's natural impulse is to 'take what is in accordance with nature and reject its opposite' (3.20). At the next level, one exercises reason in selecting among these natural objects of pursuit. Finally, one's rational selection among these objects is always correct and 'consistent and in agreement with nature' (*Fin.* 3.20). Here, at the summit of moral development, a person recognizes that this 'agreement' itself is the only good (3.20–21), and transfers her allegiance away from 'those first objects of affection' (3.21) and to this 'agreement'. Our natural inclination to pursue those natural objects has served to 'introduce' us to this agreement but, once introduced, we value the agreement immeasurably more than our initial objects of pursuit. We cease to find it desirable to actually secure those objectives.

Cicero's criticisms in *Fin.* 4.25–8 accept the general account of moral development up until the final point at which one abandons the natural goals other than those of reason itself:

> Now I ask the Stoics . . . How and where did you suddenly abandon the body and all those things that are in accordance with nature but not in our power . . . ? How is it that so many of the things originally commended by nature are suddenly forsaken by wisdom?
>
> (*Fin.* 4.26)

The charge is not that the Stoic agent will fail to take appropriate care of his health, family and property (it is the Cynic, rather than the Stoic who fails to do so). The 'forsaking' of the natural objectives by wisdom complained of by Cicero is the Stoic claim that the fully rational agent will care only about aiming properly at health and the like, not about actually achieving these natural objectives. Cicero's criticism is that if our natural orientations underwrite our good, then it is illicit to identify our good with the goal of only one of these natural orientations.

Even if reason is the best part of our nature and the pinnacle of human development, Cicero complains, it is not the only part (4.28). It completes nature, so its task must be to complete the work that nature leaves unfinished. If nature was aiming at preserving life and bodily integrity, then reason is not successful unless its activity too secures these ends (4.34–6). Cicero invokes the analogy of a sculptor to make this point:

A great sculptor like Phidias can start a work from scratch and carry it through to completion, or can take over an unfinished work from someone else and perfect it. Wisdom corresponds to the latter case. It did not itself generate the human race; it took it over, unfinished, from nature. So it ought to watch nature closely, and perfect her work as if it were a statue.

(*Fin.* 4.34)

The metaphor of the unfinished work of art is not inapt. The Stoic Cleanthes is reported as saying that until a human being achieves virtue he is as incomplete as an unfinished line of iambic poetry (Stob. 2,5b8 /W 2.65, 7–8 /LS 61L).

Reason, on this picture, need not be subordinate to the other natural impulses, as in the case of the apprentice in the great master's studio who fills in the details in the way intended by the master – 'polishing and perfecting the details', as Cicero puts it at *Fin.* 4.35. Reason, as the Stoics conceive it is more like a great master who completes the incomplete work of another, where the incompleteness is that of an unfinished symphony, or of a statue only partly emerged from the rock without a blueprint. On this version of the analogy, reason has an important and independently significant job to do, but what counts as its success is still constrained by the aims and accomplishments of the original artist's work. It can shape and regulate the pursuit of those original aims, but not pervert or subvert them. If it undermines those aims it does not count as completing or perfecting the original work, but rather as producing a new work in its own right. Thus reason, if it is to complete the work of nature, must succeed in achieving (not just in aiming at) nature's original goals. Or so the objection goes.

Some Stoics seem to have responded to such objections by denying that natural development is always cumulative. What nature aims at earlier in development may simply be a necessary precursor to, rather than a part of, the successful outcome. As Cicero paraphrases the response: 'in the case of corn, nature guides it through from blade to ear and then discards the blade as of no value' (*Fin.* 4.37). Seneca invokes a similar example:

There is something good in a stalk of wheat, but it is not yet present in the sappy sprout nor when the tender ear [first] emerges from the husk, but when it ripens with the heat of summer and its proper maturity.

(Seneca, *Ep.* 124.11)

On this rival model of reason completing the work of nature, virtue is not the crowning touch to nature's masterpiece, but the masterpiece itself.

Pursuit of those other objectives along the way (the stalk, the blade) is indispensable and necessary for securing this ultimate goal, but they are in no way parts of that result.

It is easy to object to the Stoics (as an Aristotelian would) that the good of the corn plant consists in the set of its life activities (growing, maintaining, and reproducing itself) which include, but are not limited to, producing the fruit. Once the stalk has withered, its peak has passed, even though the ripe corn is still upon it. It is then on the downhill path after reaching the zenith of its natural flourishing. The ripe corn is a part of the plant's proper functioning, but it is not the totality of it. Only from the anthropocentric perspective of those who take corn plant to be essentially a source of food does it seem plausible it achieves its natural goal only when the ear is ripe.

This objection, however, has no purchase on the Stoics, whose teleology is unabashedly anthropocentric. More precisely, they claim that the cosmos is organized 'for the sake of humans and gods' (Fin. 3.67, ND 2.133 /LS 54N). That is, plants are for the sake of animals, and animals and plants are for the sake of humans. Human beings, in turn, are for the sake of each other and for the gods.[57] Humans are not, strictly speaking, the ultimate reference points of this cosmic teleology, since they too are for the sake of 'contemplating and imitating the world' (cf. ND 2.38 /LS 54H; Diss. 4.1.104). That is, they are for the sake of 'becoming like the god' by living in agreement with nature.[58] Nonetheless, they are the central reference point for everything else in the cosmos – including the corn and wheat of the examples in question. The Stoics are quite consistent with their own teleology in claiming that the corn is for the sake of humans. So it makes perfect sense that the mature ear is, after all, the telos of the corn.

The corn stalk, prior to producing the ear, or if it failed to produce an ear, would be incomplete in a very different way than the partly finished statue or painting is incomplete. In the latter cases we can say truly that the goal has been partly achieved once the intermediate objectives are achieved (the original artist's achievements). But in the case of the corn, whose goal is to produce food for humans (and for other animals), it has achieved no part of this goal until it has produced the fruit.

Similarly in the case of human beings, when a person has perfected her exercise of reason so as to achieve perfect agreement with the divine reason that structures the cosmos, she has reached a goal that goes beyond, and does not include the achievements of the earlier goals of her nature – just as the cornstalk has left behind much of its own nature when it succeeds in producing a mature fruit (and even more so especially when it is eaten by an animal for whose sake it has grown!). It is a general feature of the nested teleologies that make up the world, on the Stoic picture, that a creature may reach its telos beyond and outside its own individual nature.[59]

A simpler answer to the objection available to the Stoics, but not reported in any of our ancient sources, does not presuppose the peculiarities of Stoic teleology. The objector who complains that the Stoic sage has abandoned the objectives of his pre-rational nature is conflating the Stoic theory of the good with their view about appropriate actions. The Stoic agrees with the Peripatetic about what are the appropriate actions to perform in pursuit of such natural objectives as life, health, and family prosperity. Thus she will take the same measures to secure the natural objectives as the Aristotelian would.

On the Stoic view, the activity of reason, even when perfected, *does* involve the pursuit of the same natural objectives that one pursued before achieving the summit of moral development. The Stoic sage will pursue his own health, life, and the other natural objectives as faithfully as anyone at a less advanced stage of moral development – indeed, no less reliably than the Peripatetic. The 'redirection' of concern involved in thinking that health is indifferent rather than good is not a decision to abandon health as an object of pursuit, and similarly for the other natural objectives.

But the objector will surely ask, why will the Stoic take care of his health, if health is not good but indifferent? To invoke the analogy of the archer: if hitting the target is not important, why should the archer aim at it? This brings us to the second major challenge to the Stoic view of the good.

Aristo and the standard of choice

Since the Stoics conceive of virtue as the 'art of living', their view that only virtue is good invites the challenge:

> How [will it] be possible to live a life if we think it makes no difference whether we are well or ill, free from pain or in agony, able to stave off cold or hunger or not?
>
> (*Fin.* 4.69; cf. 3.14)

Let us call this challenge the 'inaction objection'. The general idea is that virtue, as the Stoics conceive it, is a kind of practical knowledge that is displayed in choosing one's actions well. But what counts as choosing well? The critic challenges the Stoics to identify the standards of what is choiceworthy if all the possible objects of pursuit are, as they claim, 'indifferent'.

The orthodox Stoic response is that nature herself supplies the standards (*Fin.* 3.31). Nature inclines us to pursue health, wealth, and so on, and to shun illness, poverty, and the like. Thus the former are worthy of pursuit, and the latter worthy of rejection (*Fin.* 3.20; Stob. 2,7a, f /W 2.79,18–80,13, 83,10–84,3). This gives rise to the classification of health, wealth, etc. as 'preferred indifferents' and their opposites as 'dispreferred indifferents'.[60] It is by invoking this classification that the Stoics claim to have a principle on which to act, while at the same time resisting the Peripatetic claim that the natural objects of pursuit are good.

Their critics make fun of this position, claiming that it amounts to mere verbal quibbling (*Fin.* 4.60, 69–72; cf. 3.10). As Cicero sums up the charge:

> What difference does it make whether you say that wealth, power and health are 'good' or 'preferred', given that those who call them good rate them no more highly than you who call them preferred?
>
> (*Fin.* 4.23; cf. 4.57)

This criticism is so central to their contemporaries' understanding of Stoicism that Cicero uses it to motivate the whole exposition of Stoic doctrine in the first place (*Fin.* 3.10).

Interestingly enough, the criticism was in fact first raised from within Stoicism. Aristo of Chios (*fl.* 250 BCE), a younger contemporary and pupil of Zeno (DL 7.160–4), disagreed with his master's distinction between 'preferred' and 'dispreferred' indifferents:

> Aristo of Chios said that health and everything similar to it are not preferred indifferents. For to say that it is a preferred indifferent is tantamount to claiming that it is good, since they practically differ only in name.
>
> (Sextus, *M* 11.64; cf. *Fin.* 2.43)

Aristo denies that health, for example, is to be preferred on the grounds that it is not always appropriate to pursue it:

> If it were necessary for healthy men to serve a tyrant and for this reason to be executed, while sick men were released from service and so also freed from destruction, the wise man would choose sickness over health on such an occasion. And in this way health is not unconditionally (*pantôs*) a preferred thing (*proegmenon*), nor is disease rejected (*apoproegmenon*).
>
> (Sextus, *M* 11.66 /IG 256)

It depends on circumstances, Aristo claims, whether it is appropriate to prefer health over disease, and thus health itself is no more to be preferred than rejected (Sextus, *M* 11.65).

The orthodox Stoics, who followed Zeno in his dispute with Aristo, do not deny that in certain circumstances it is appropriate (*kathêkon*) to neglect one's health or even – as in Aristo's example – to pursue disease. They recognize that certain appropriate actions (*kathêkonta*) 'depend on circumstances':

> Some [actions] are appropriate (*kathêkonta*) without regard to circumstances, while some are conditioned by circumstances. Without regard to circumstances are these: looking out for one's health and sense organs, and similar things. Those with regard to circumstances [include] maiming oneself and throwing away one's possessions. The analogous [point] applies too for the things which are contrary to what is appropriate.
>
> (DL 7.109; cf. Stob. 2,7f /W 2.83,13–84,1)

But this passage makes it equally clear that, for these Stoics, some kathêkonta are '*without* regard to circumstances'. These are actions in pursuit of the natural objectives (health, bodily integrity, etc.). These are the *kathêkonta* for which they claim nature provides the 'principles' of action (*Fin*. 3.22, 23, 4.46–8; cf. Plutarch, *Comm. Not*. 1069e /LS 59A). It is on this last point that Aristo dissents. To say that health, in itself, is something we have reason to pursue, a reason which can be overridden only in special circumstances, does seem only verbally different from telling us that health is good. As a critic of the orthodox Stoic puts it, 'the sum total of goods must include everything worth adopting, choosing, or wishing for' (*Fin*. 4.46).

But if Aristo denies that nature gives us reason to prefer health to disease, how can he answer the 'inaction argument'? Indeed, the orthodox Stoics insisted that it was against Aristo, not themselves, that the 'inaction argument' is effective (*Fin*. 3.50, 4.70; cf. 2.43).

But it is far from clear that the followers of Zeno are correct in this criticism of Aristo. To see this, let us distinguish a weaker and a stronger version of the challenge posed by the 'inaction argument'.[61] On the one hand the challenge might ask a normative question:

THE NORMATIVE QUESTION: What reason will the wise person have to pursue anything?

On the other hand, it might ask an explanatory question:

THE EXPLANATORY QUESTION: By what is the wise person moved to pursue anything?

Zeno and his followers, in making the distinction between preferred and dispreferred indifferents, are clearly trying to answer the normative question. In calling health 'preferred' they are not simply making a psychological observation that people *do* in general prefer it and will pursue it except in extraordinary circumstances. Rather, they take this psychological fact as the basis for a normative claim: that we *should* prefer health to disease, and wealth to poverty, and the like. These objectives are not simply pursued, but 'to be pursued' (*adsumenda* – *Fin.* 4.43; cf. 3.20). As Cicero's Cato reports the Stoic view:

> For some, though not all,[62] of the items which have worth, there is good reason (*satis esse causae*) to prefer them to other things (*quam ob rem quibusdam anteponerentur*), as is the case with health, well-functioning senses, freedom from pain, honour, wealth, and so on. Likewise, with the items which are not deserving of value, some offer good reason to reject them – for example pain, illness, loss of a sense, poverty, ignominy, and so forth – while others do not. This is the source of Zeno's term *proêgmenon*, and its contrary *apoproêgmenon*.
>
> (*Fin.* 3.51)

While the orthodox Stoics answer the normative question by claiming that we have reason to pursue health, wealth, and the like, Aristo rejects all such claims as false. It is not that he thinks that the wise person will have no reason for deciding whether or not to pursue health on a particular occasion.[63] He simply declines to articulate that reason, on the grounds that there are no general principles of appropriate action (Seneca, *Ep.* 94.1, 5–8). The wise person will decide whether or not to pursue health in particular circumstances, and will decide rationally (94.2–3), but there is no general characterization we can give of his reasons.[64]

Thus Aristo refuses to answer the normative question. What he offers instead is an answer to the explanatory question. According to Cicero, Aristo responds to the opponent who asks, 'By what is the wise person moved to pursue anything?'[65] by saying that it is whatever comes into the wise person's mind (*quodcumque in mentem incideret, quodcumque tamquan occurret, Fin.* 4.43). Cicero's uncharitable report makes Aristo appear to claim that the sage will act arbitrarily, without any reason. But we know that in fact Aristo insists that the sage will act wisely, taking into account all the relevant features of the circumstances (Seneca, *Ep.* 94.2–3). Nor is Aristo's answer vulnerable to scepticism about how reason on its own could provide an impetus to action. Like any other Stoic, Aristo no doubt allows that nature provides us with impulses to pursue health and the like and shun their opposites, and that reason's role is to regulate these impulses.[66] These two factors are sufficient to explain 'how we come to pursue [things]'. In order to explain where the impulse to action comes from, Aristo need not agree with Zeno that it is *rational* to pursue health over disease, and the like. All he needs to grant is that it is *natural*. The real import of Aristo's answer is better captured by Cicero's next comment. He concedes that Aristo's account does allow for 'some kind of striving (or pursuit)' (*aliquod genus appetendi*, *Fin.* 4.43) – that is, it solves the problem of inaction. Aristo can in fact escape the charge that he is vulnerable to the 'inaction objection'.

Once we distinguish the explanatory version of the inaction objection from the normative version, it is not at all obvious that the Stoics need to answer the normative question. Moreover, we have seen, the orthodox Stoics' answer to this question leaves them open to the criticism that they have only a verbal difference with their Peripatetic rivals. In order to escape this indictment, the orthodox Stoics need to point to a substantial difference between their own doctrine and that of the Peripatetics. In the next section we will see that their doctrine of the passions allows them to do just that.

The passions

While the Stoic insistence that health and the like are 'preferred indifferents' as opposed to goods, makes no difference to the actions the wise person will perform, it does make a big difference, they claim, to the way he will perform them. They make a distinction between 'seeking' the natural objectives, on the one hand, and merely 'selecting' or 'adopting' them, on the other. Only virtue is to be 'sought' (*expetenda*) or desired (*optanda*), they claim. Any other objectives, such as health, are to be 'selected' (*seligenda*) or 'adopted' (*sumenda*) rather than 'sought' (*expetenda*) (*Fin.* 3.10, 22, 38, 44; 4.39, 62, 72; cf. 4.43). As Cicero paraphrases Zeno's position:

> In the case of [a preferred indifferent] I speak not of 'seeking' (*expetere*) but of 'selecting' (*legere*), not of 'desiring' (*optare*) but of 'adopting' (*sumere*); while its opposite [a dispreferred indifferent] one does not 'flee' (*fugere*) but as it were 'sets aside' (*secerne*).
>
> (*Fin* 4.72)

This is not mere verbal hair-splitting. We can see this if we understand the distinction in the context of the Stoic doctrine of the 'passions'.

Although treated extremely briefly in Cicero's exposition of Stoic ethics (*Fin* 3.35), the passions (*pathê*) are a central topic in Stoic ethical philosophy (DL 7.84; cf. Epictetus, *Diss.* 3.2.3). Their account is expounded at length in several texts: DL 7.110–116; Stob. 2,9b–10e /W 2.88–93), Seneca's *On Anger* (*Ir.*) and Cicero's *Tusculan Disputations* (*TD*) 3.22–5, 4.8–11.[67]

Passion (*pathos*), sometimes translated as 'affection' (Latin, *adfectus*, *adfectio*, *perturbatio*), is a general term used in antiquity to refer to emotions, desires, and aversions. Typical examples include: desire (*epithumia*), anger, fear, malice, spite, friendliness, hatred, envy, pity, shame, jealousy, and indignation.[68] All schools generally agree that the passions are types of pleasure or pain either at what has happened or at what one expects or anticipates will happen.[69] For example, anger is a painful desire for revenge for an apparent injustice (Seneca, *Ir.* 1.2.3; Aristotle, *Rhet.* 1378a30–32), and malice involves taking pleasure in another's misfortunes (Plato, *Phlb.* 48b).

According to the Stoics, virtue requires the elimination of all passions. In their characteristic locution, 'the wise man will be free from passions' (*Fin.* 3.35; DL 7.117; cf. *TD* 4.14). In this they dissent strongly from the views of Plato and Aristotle, who held that the passions are capable of being trained to follow reason, and that this 'concord' of reasons and the passions is the goal of moral education.[70] The Stoics, by contrast, claim that the passions are essentially antithetical to reason. In Zeno's definition, endorsed by Chrysippus,[71] a passion is 'an irrational (*alogon*) and unnatural (*para phusin*) movement of the soul, or an excessive impulse' (DL 7.110; cf. Stob. 2,10 /W 2.88,8–10; *TD* 3.24, 4.11). As such, virtue requires the extirpation, not simply the proper cultivation, of the passions.

In further contrast with Plato and Aristotle, who maintain that the passions issue from a non-rational part or faculty of the soul,[72] the Stoics claim the seat of passion is the faculty of reason itself. As Arius reports, 'All passions belong to the leading (*hêgemonikon*) part of the soul' (Stob. 2,10 /W 2.88,10).[73] According to Seneca:

> It is not the case that [reason and passion] dwell apart, in isolation from one another. Reason and passion are the mind's transformations for better or for worse.
>
> (Seneca *Ir.* 1.8.3)

A passion, in their view, is a judgment or belief.[74] It is irrational in virtue of being false (Plutarch *Vir. Mor.* 447a, DL 7.110, *Fin.* 3.35).

In classifying them as judgments of the rational faculty (typically called the '*hêgemonikon*' or 'leading part' of the soul (Aetius 4.21.1 /LS 53H1), the Stoics are not denying that passions are feelings and desires, for they also claim that a passion is an impulse (*hormê*) – as on Zeno's definition (quoted above). While it may seem odd to modern readers to claim that an impulse is also a belief or judgment, the view is perfectly intelligible in the context of Stoic philosophy of action and mind. According to the Stoics, both belief and action result from a causal process in which something external makes an 'impression' (*phantasia*) on an animal. The impression is how things 'appear' to the animal. For an example, an apple might give me the impression that that there is an apple in front of me, or it might give me the impression that I should eat it. The latter is an 'impulsive impression'.[75]

Non-human animals simply follow their impressions, but humans, being rational, have the faculty of assent (*sunkatathesis*, Latin adsensio).[76] Only if I assent to the impression that there is an apple in front of me will I believe this to be the case. Similarly, only if I assent to the impression that I should eat the apple will I have the impulse to eat it. Thus for a human being to have an impulse, she must have assented to some claim, and thus formed a judgment. In Seneca's phrase, 'Do you really think, then, that anything can be sought or shunned without the mind's assent?' (Seneca, *Ir.* 2.3.5).[77]

Zeno and his followers divide the passions into four main categories, which they label Desire, Pleasure, Fear, and Distress, distinguished according to the direction and content of the impressions.[78] A desire, on the Stoic view, is an impulse (*hormê*) towards something that appears to be good, while pleasure is an expansion (*eparsis*) or elation upon achieving such an objective. Fear, in all its forms, is an aversion to and reaching away (*ekklisis, declinatio*) from what one believes to be bad, while distress is a contraction (*sustolê*) upon incurring such an apparent evil.[79]

In all these cases, the Stoics claim, a passion involves a false judgment about the good. The person acting on 'desire' believes falsely that it is good for him to secure what he aims at; his 'pleasure' upon securing that apparent good rests on the same false judgment. The person acting on 'fear' believes falsely that it will be bad if the outcome he seeks to avoid befalls him; the 'distress' he feels when it befalls him involves the same misjudgment.

The falsity of the passion's normative judgment is easiest to see in the case of emotions such as spite and envy. The spiteful person, for example,

Table 5.1 The four types of passions

Passion type	Greek	Latin	Examples
Desire	*epithumia*	*libido*	erotic love, hatred, anger
Pleasure	*hêdonê*	*Voluptas, laetitio*	spite, self-satisfaction
Fear	*phobos*	*metus, formido*	shame, terror
Distress	*lupê*	*aegritudo*	grief, pity, envy

Table 5.2 The objects of the passions

	Apparent goods	Apparent evils
Expected	Desire (*epithumia*)	Fear (phobos)
Present	Pleasure (*hedonê*)	Distress (lupe)

mistakenly thinks that it is good when misfortune befalls those he dislikes, and the envious person feels pain at the good fortune of another. But we should not be misled into thinking that it is only disreputable passions such as these (which tend to dominate the Stoic lists) that involve mistaken value judgments. The pitying person, in contrast with the spiteful person, thinks it bad when misfortune befalls another, but the Stoics think his judgment is just as mistaken as the other's. They claim that spite and envy, on the one hand, and pity, on the other, make a common mistake. It is the mistake of supposing that anything other than virtue is good, or anything other than vice is bad.

To be sure, the spiteful and envious persons make the additional mistake of having impulses towards inappropriate objects, such as the pain and misfortune of others. The person who feels pity, by contrast, has an impulse towards an appropriate objective, the well-being of others (cf. *Fin.* 3.62–70). Nonetheless, the pitying person has a defective understanding about *why* aiding others is appropriate. To feel pity is to judge it bad, rather than simply dispreferred, for misfortune to befall a human being. To grieve for a dead child is to think it is bad, rather than simply dispreferred, that one's children should die young. The same false judgment is involved in having a desire that one's child live a full life, or a fear that she will die. Similarly (to take a passion in the genus of pleasure), to rejoice at winning the lottery is to judge that wealth is good, rather than simply preferred.

Thus, even the person who selects appropriately among the natural objects of pursuit (and hence performs the *kathêkonta*) must be careful to avoid the passions. If you act on the supposition that it is good to secure a preferred indifferent, or bad to incur its opposite, you are acting on a false judgment. In believing that it is good to get the preferred indifferent one aims at, or bad to incur the dispreferred indifferent one aims to avoid, a person overstates the value of his objective. It is only to be preferred, after all, not good. This overvaluation of the objective's value generates an excessive impulse towards it – excessive in that its strength is out of proportion to the value.

By contrast, the impulses of the Stoic sage will be measured and proportionate to the value of the indifferents they target for pursuit or avoidance. His impulses are the so-called 'good feelings' (*eupatheiai*; Latin, *constantiae*), which the Stoics identify as the proper alternatives to the passions (DL 7.116, TD 4.12–14).[80] Instead of acting on desire (*epithumia*), the wise person will aim at health, wealth, etc. with a more restrained impulse, which they label 'wish' (*boulêsis*). Wish reaches towards its objective rationally and perfectly in proportion to its value. Thus the sage will 'have a measured and controlled reaching (*orexis*) for things insofar as they are admirable (*kalon*) and within his reach' (Epictetus, *Diss.* 4.1.84; cf. 170). If he succeeds in obtaining his objectives he will not be elated (which is

Table 5.3 The 'good feelings' and their corresponding passions

	Nature and object of impulse			
	Aims at X	*Reaction to securing X*	*Aims to avoid Y*	*Reaction to failing to avoid Y*
Passion	*epithumia* (desire)	*hêdonê* (pleasure)	*phobos* (fear)	*lupê* (distress)
Good feeling	*boulêsis* (wish)	*chara* (enjoyment)	*eulabeia* (caution)	–
	Examples: goodwill, kindliness, welcoming, affection	*Examples:* joy, good spirits, cheerfulness	*Examples:* modesty, reverence	(the wise person shrinks from nothing that happens)

to experience an irrational expansion). Rather he will experience a more restrained, modest expansion, which the Stoics call 'enjoyment' (*chara*; Latin, *gaudium*).

In aiming to avoid illness and poverty, the sage will be moved not by fear but by a more restrained impulse, 'caution' (*eulabeia*). Unlike fear, the impulse of 'caution' will not be so vehement that it will carry him into distress if, for example, he becomes ill despite all his efforts to live a healthy life. Upon losing the preferred indifferents or incurring the dispreferred, the Stoic sage will react with no distress at all (DL 7.118). Thus it is especially in circumstances of loss or misfortune that the wise person displays the stereotypically 'Stoic' attitude to life: failure to be distressed when misfortune or disaster strikes.[81] In general, to have the 'good feelings' is to be moved by impulses whose strength is consistent with the value of their objectives – hence the Latin term for them, '*constantiae*' ('consistencies' *TD* 4.14).

Given the range of affective attitudes that the Stoics classify as 'good feelings' (see Table 5.3), one might quibble with their denial that the 'good feelings' are passions. For example, the good feeling 'enjoyment' *chara* turns up on Aristotle's list of the passions (*EN* 1105b21–23). One might charge that the Stoics do not really advocate the extirpation of the passions, but only of those passions that they deem inappropriate, and for these they (perversely) reserve the term 'passion'. Even if this criticism is apt, the Stoics are still making a substantial, and controversial, point in advocating the extirpation of the feelings that they classify as passions.

Chrysippus offers an analogy to explain the difference between the excessive impulse of the 'passions' and the more measured, appropriate impulse of the 'good feelings'. In Book I of his lost work, *On the Passions*, he writes:

> When someone walks in accordance with his impulse, the move-
> ment of his legs is not excessive but commensurate with the
> impulse, so that he can stop or change whenever he wants to. But
> when people run in accordance with their impulse, this sort of
> thing no longer happens. The movement of their legs exceeds their
> impulse, so that they are carried away and unable to change
> obediently, as soon as they have started to do so. Something
> similar, I think, takes place with impulses, owing to their going
> beyond the rational proportion.
>
> (Chrysippus apud Galen, *Plac.* 4.2 /translated by LS 65J6–8)

The person whose impulse towards the preferred indifferents is measured
and proportionate to their value is like the walker. He can stop as soon as
he gets to his destination, or even sooner if he decides against going there,
or it proves impossible to get there. The excessive impulse of the passionate person, by contrast, is like that of the runner. Passionate impulse
overshoots its mark, by going too vehemently towards it. The runner will
overshoot his mark (if he reaches it) and display motion beyond what is
reasonable: the excess energy of the impulse will be expressed in the
expansive pleasure, if he achieves it, or the recoil of disappointment, if he
misses it. If he changes his mind about whether it is appropriate to pursue
that objective, the impulse will persist.[82] If he encounters obstacles he will
trip and feel pain: he will recoil against the world that did not yield the
outcome towards which he launched himself.

The Stoic doctrine of the passions shows that there are genuine practical
implications of the Stoic insistence that health, wealth, etc. are not good
but merely preferred. The impulse of the person who thinks such things
are good will be like that of the runner in Chrysippus's example. That of
the Stoic sage, who thinks they are 'to be preferred' rather than good, will
be like that of the walker – more restrained, always under the control of
the agent, proportionate to the value of its objective. This difference will
be evident in the respective reactions of the Stoic and the Peripatetic sage
to getting what they pursue (the Peripatetic will be more pleased) and
especially when disaster strikes (the Peripatetic will grieve, while the Stoic
will not).

In developing the disposition not only to pursue the right objectives, but
also to pursue them with the right intensity, a person reaches the summit
of Stoic moral development. As Cicero reports, the person whose proper
selection among the natural objects of pursuit becomes 'consistent (*constans*)
and in agreement with nature' (Cic. *Fin.* 3.20) has only then and for the
first time achieved the good. Cicero's Latin term for the 'good feelings'
(*eupatheiai*) is *constantiae* ('consistencies' – *TD* 4.14; cf. 12–13). Thus the
person who pursues appropriate actions 'consistently' is pursuing them
with the 'good feelings' (*constantiae*). As Cato the Stoic speaker mentions

in his peroration, the wise person is of 'consistent' (*constans*) character (*Fin.* 3.75). Hence virtue is called '*constantia*' (3.50) and wrongdoing '*inconstantia*' (4.77).

Objections to Stoics on the passions

The Stoic doctrine of the passions attracted much criticism in antiquity, and on many fronts. Perhaps most controversial of all was their insistence that the passions are an activity of reason. By contrast, Plato and Aristotle each identified one or more 'non-rational' parts of the human soul involved in action, in addition to reason, and took the passions to be activities of these parts. Their later followers therefore objected strongly to the Stoic claim that we have only one faculty, the 'leading faculty' (*hegêmonikon*) that issues in all the impulses. The later Stoic Poseidonius (b. *c*.135 BCE) dissented from orthodoxy on this point, endorsing instead a division of the practical soul along Platonic lines – which the Platonist physician Galen (second century CE) reports approvingly and at length in his work *On Hippocrates and Plato's Doctrines (Plac.).*[83]

That reason and the passions are different sources of motivation, Plato and Aristotle took to be evident from the familiar phenomenon of psychological conflict. A person feels like doing one thing, but also wants very much not to do it, as when a desperately thirsty shipwreck survivor struggles against his desire to drink seawater, which he knows may kill him.[84] The Stoics do not deny that, in such cases, the passion involved is opposed by an impulse of reason. But they resist their opponents' contention that the passion issues from a source other than the faculty of reason.

All passion, for the Stoics, is 'disobedient to reason' (Stob. 2,10 /W 2.88,9; *TD* 4.11). Nonetheless, they classify it is an impulse of reason on the ground that it originates in assent and 'all impulses are assents' (Stob. 2,9b /W 2.88,1 /LS 33I; cf. Plutarch *Vir. Mor.* 447a). Although no longer in the control of the rational part once it has been assented to and 'unleashed' (as on Chrysippus's running example) it is still an expression of the rational part. Moreover, they claim, the passionate impulse is not simultaneous with the rational impulse that opposes it. What Plato and Aristotle interpret as an impulse from reason struggling against a simultaneous impulse from a non-rational faculty is, in the Stoic view, the single faculty of reason alternating back and forth between the two impulses at such a speed that they appear to be simultaneous (Plutarch, *Vir. Mor.* 446f–447a /LS 65G).

Other criticisms of the Stoics concern their insistence that the passions be eradicated from our lives. Those sympathetic to the Peripatetic view object that passions are sometimes helpful or even necessary for the performance of appropriate actions. The Stoic Seneca considers this objection in his essay *On Anger*:

165

[Anger] rouses and spurs on the mind. Without it, courage can achieve nothing magnificent in war – without the flame of anger beneath, to goad men on to meet danger with boldness.

(Seneca, *Ir*. 1.7.1)

Seneca's reply (1.7–8, 9–11) is that the rational impulse alone is sufficient to get the deed done. Reason 'rises to action aroused and relaxed to the extent that it thinks necessary, in just the same way that the range of a missile shot from a catapult is under the control of the operator' (1.9.1). Anger, by contrast, since it is an impulse excessive to what right reason mandates and no longer under reason's control is less rather than more effective at achieving its goals. What is required against the enemy in battle, Seneca notes, 'is not impulses to be poured out, but to remain well tuned and responsive'. He asks, rhetorically, 'Do you suppose the hunter to be angry with his prey?' (1.11.1–2).

A related objection is that a passion is sometimes the appropriate response to a situation. Anger, one might object, is often an appropriate reaction to a wrong done. To the Peripatetic who objects, 'Is the good man not angry if he sees his father slain and his mother ravished?' (*Ir*. 1.12.1), Seneca replies that he is not. The man will of course take revenge on the perpetrator and protect his other family members, but his filial devotion is sufficient impetus for this. The proper thinking of a good person in such a situation is:

My father is about to be killed – I will defend him; he has been killed – I will avenge him; not because I am pained, but because I should

(*Ir*. 1.12.2)

More expansively:

What is fine and honourable is to go forth in defence of parents, children, friends and fellow citizens, under the guidance of duty (*officium*) itself, in the exercise of will, judgment, and foresight – and not through some raving impulse.

(*Ir*. 1.12.5)

One might concede the point about anger, but still insist that other passions are appropriate and even intrinsic to the most valuable relations with those 'parents, children, friends, and fellow citizens'. For example, friends have special concern and affection for each other, as do parents and children, and family members more generally. To live up to the demands of friendship and family love, it is not sufficient to coldly 'do one's duty'.

The Stoics, however, do not require that we should be cold and devoid of affect. A look at the list of the various 'good feelings' classified under

166

the three headings of 'wish', 'joy', and 'caution' is sufficient to establish that the sage will have feelings, for example friendliness (*eumeneia*) and affection (*agapêsin* – DL 7.116).[85] He is affable (*homilêtikon*) and accommodating (*euarmoston*) and will seek out friendly relations with other people (Stob. 2,11m /W 2.108,5–11). His lack of 'passion' is something the Stoics explicitly distinguish from the coldness and lack of affect characteristic of vice (DL 7.117). One Stoic writes that a person is not fulfilling his duties (*kathêkonta*) 'as a son, a brother, a father, and a citizen' if he is 'impassive like a statue' (Epictetus, *Diss.* 3.2.4 /LS 56C6). The good person actively seeks out friendship (Stob. 2,11m /W 2.108,6–7), which, in the Stoic view, also requires that one hold the other as dear, or almost as dear, as oneself (*Fin.* 3.70; cf. DL 7.124). Concern and affection for family, friends, and other people is, furthermore, natural, according to the Stoics:

> Now the Stoics consider it important to realize that parents' love for their children arises naturally.... Our impulse to love what we have generated is given by nature herself as manifestly as our aversion to pain. This is also the source of the mutual and natural sympathy between humans.
>
> (*Fin.* 3.62–3; cf. DL 7.120; Epictetus, *Diss.* 4.1.126)

As such, it cannot be a passion, since passions are 'unnatural' (*para phusin*).

The Stoic Epictetus devotes an entire chapter of his *Discourses* to *philostorgia* (family affection) (*Diss.* 1.11). He here castigates a father who abandoned his daughter in her illness. He points out that the mother has affection for the child, and rightly did not abandon her (1.11.22), and that the father, who claims to love the child, should have done likewise. Duty requires that even a dying child be supported by those who 'love and care for her' (1.11.23).

The goodwill, friendliness and affection essential to proper relations with friends and dear ones are completely acceptable attitudes for the Stoic sage to have. It is only when a person's attachment to others is stronger than these impulses that it is classified as a passion, and denounced as unacceptable. The father castigated in Epictetus's story in *Discourse* 1.11 does have an excessive impulse regarding the daughter he loves. His excess, however, is not in loving his daughter, but feeling so much pain at her suffering that he cannot bear to be with her (1.11.4).

One might agree with Epictetus that a love so strong as to drive you away from your beloved at the very time your presence is most needed is indeed defective and inappropriate. However, one could still object that feeling pain at your beloved's pain is part of what it is to love, and that the Stoics, who allow the existence of no 'good feelings' involving pain, cannot accommodate this. In the classic example used by Epictetus, the wise person will feel no grief at the death of his wife or child:

> If you kiss your child or your wife, say that you are kissing a
> human being; for when it dies you will not be upset.
>   (*Ench.* 3; translation by N. White 1983; cf. 14, 16, 26)

While it may be admirable of a person without distress when poverty or
illness strikes him, the opposite would seem to be true of someone who is
unmoved by the death of a loved one. Grief and sorrow, on this objection,
are appropriate consequences of love and attachment. To love is to expose
yourself to the risk of grief.

Passions and 'pre-passions'

To assess the strength of this objection, which is arguably the most powerful criticism of Stoic ethics, we must consider carefully what the Stoics can
and do say about the pain of bereavement. To be sure, they deny that the
wise person will experience any feeling in the general category they label
'distress' (*lupê*). But this does not imply that the sage will experience no
pain of other sorts – the ordinary physical pain from illness and disease,
for example, and also, perhaps, some kinds of psychological distress. The
orthodox Stoic doctrine that humans naturally have affection for their
children and sympathy with each other (*Fin.* 3.62–3, quoted above cf. DL
7.120), would arguably imply that it is natural to feel at least some degree
of pain at the loss or pain of a loved one. Any such natural reaction would
not be a passion (*pathos*), since passions are, on the Stoic view 'contrary to
nature' (DL 7.110, Stob. 2,10 /W 2.88,9–10).

Chrysippus in fact explicitly allows that the sage will experience psychological pain:

> The wise man will be pained (*algein*) but not wracked with
> torment (*basanizesthai*), for he will not give in to his soul. He
> will experience dread (*deisthai*) but not welcome or accept it
> (*prosdechesthai*).
>   (Stobaeus, *Florilegium* 7,21 /SVF 3.574; my translation)[86]

Later Stoics reported by Aulus Gellius, distinguish a kind of natural and
necessary 'fear' that even the wise man may experience, from the passion
of fear that he will not. As Epictetus explains,

> When some terrifying (*formidabilis*) sound . . . or anything else of
> that kind occurs, even a [Stoic] wise man's mind must be slightly
> moved and contracted and frightened – not by a preconceived
> opinion of anything bad but by certain rapid and involuntary
> movements which forestall (*praeverentibus*) the proper function of

mind and reason. Soon, however, the wise man does not ... assent to such impressions nor does he add an opinion to them.

(Epictetus fragment 9, quoted in Aulus Gellius 19.17–18; translation by LS 65Y)

Seneca, in his essay *On Anger* gives an extended discussion of such 'involuntary movements', and explicitly distinguishes them from passions. Such movements are as involuntary as our reactions when 'we shiver when cold water is sprinkled on us or recoil at the touch of some things' or when 'bad news makes our hair stand on end ... indecent language brings on a blush [or] ... vertigo ... follows the sight of a precipice' (*Ir* 2.2.1). Equally involuntary is 'the first mental jolt that affects us when we think ourselves wronged', which happens even to the 'wisest of men' (2.2.2).

> That is why we join in laughing with those who laugh, why a crowd of mourners depresses us, why we boil over at conflicts which have nothing to do with us. But these are not cases of anger, any more than it is grief which makes us frown at a shipwreck on stage. ... No, all these are motions of mind with no positive wish to be in motion. They are not passions (*adfectus*), but the preliminaries, the prelude to passions.
>
> (*Ir.* 2.2.5)

Such reactions are not passions, Seneca explains, because they do not involve assent. So too Epictetus says of the 'natural and necessary fear' that it is a contraction (*sustolê*) that arises without assent (fr. 9, quoted above); thus it does not count as the '*sustolê*' (contraction) of the genuine passion, fear. This involuntary movement is caused by the impression itself, without any intervening assent. If assented to, the impression will generate an impulse (the passion) much stronger than the involuntary movement brought about by the impression itself. Such movements are simply involuntary feelings, to be contrasted with genuine passions, which involve the judgment that it is appropriate to be moved in this way.[87]

Thus the extirpation of the passions advocated by the Stoics is perfectly consistent with a person's experiencing these natural 'preliminaries' to the passions.[88] To return to the case of bereavement, we might note that Seneca's examples of such preliminaries include tears and sighing (*Ir.* 2.3.3), which are reasonably construed as 'preliminaries' to the passions of grief and sorrow. Would it be implausible for the Stoics to claim that the former alone suffice to show the depth of the bereaved person's attachment to the beloved? As a natural phenomena beyond the range of choice, might not a significant degree of the wrenching pain one experiences upon losing a loved one itself be classified as a 'preliminary'? Recall that on the Stoic account, the passion grief involves the judgment that losing the beloved is a bad thing. 'Alas! Poor Me!', in Epictetus's phrase, is the judgment constitutive of grief (*Ench.* 26).

The falsity of this judgment is the Stoics' reason for insisting that the passion must be extirpated from the soul. If we concentrate on this reason when we reflect on the Stoic claim that the wise person will not grieve at the loss of her child, we need not understand them as claiming that the bereaved must go about her daily business as if nothing had happened, and not take time to heal her wounds.

On such a reading, Epictetus's advice to the bereaved is less callous that it may appear, when he counsels them to think about how they react to the deaths of strangers:

> Someone else's child is dead or his wife. There is no one would not say, 'It's the lot of a human being'. But when one's own dies, immediately it is 'Alas! Poor me!' But we should have remembered how we feel when we hear of the same thing about others.
> (Epictetus, *Ench.* 26; translation by N. White 1983)

The mental exercise Epictetus recommends here is intended to help the bereaved resist assenting to the impression 'Alas, poor me', rather to extirpate the pain a person naturally experiences upon losing a beloved. That natural feeling is the 'preliminary' movement that accompanies the impression 'Alas, poor me!', but itself involves no assent to that judgment, and hence is not a passion.

Indeed, the mental exercise recommended by Epictetus has elements in common with many mourning rituals. For example, Jewish mourners traditionally recite the *Kaddish Yatom* (Mourner's Kaddish) – a prayer that is recited on behalf of the dead, but that celebrates the goodness of the world we live in. The goal of reciting the Kaddish is not to suppress the pain of loss. On the contrary, the practice often facilitates the experience of that pain in those who are numbed by the shock of the loss. Instead, the practice serves to orient the bereaved to a different perspective (functionally similar to Epictetus's recommendation to take the point of view of nature) on which it is easier to resist the judgment that the loss, however painful, is an evil that has befallen one.

Epicureans vs. Stoics on the life without distress

It is useful to compare the life free from passion advocated by the Stoics with the life free from fear and distress advocated by the Epicureans. Both lives will be free of mental distress and the pain of unfulfilled desires, but they will be achieved by very different strategies. The Epicurean avoids frustration and distress by restricting his objectives to those that are easily attainable. The Epicurean is unafraid of hunger and homelessness because he is confident that he will not be hungry and homeless. The natural abundance of the world provides him, he thinks, with an insurance policy against this risk.

The Stoic, by contrast, knows he has no such insurance policy. He knows he runs the risk of hunger and homelessness but is unafraid because he thinks that such things, even if they happen to him, are not bad. In contrast with the Epicurean, he has no objection to pursuing a wider array of worldly objectives. This is because – again, unlike the Epicurean, who is in this respect like the Peripatetic – the Stoic will not care whether he succeeds in achieving these worldly objectives. The Epicurean still cares about whether he goes hungry; his equanimity comes from his confidence that he will not go hungry. The Stoic's equanimity, by contrast, rests on his conviction that being hungry is not bad for him. He omits no effort that the Epicurean or the Aristotelian would make in pursuit of food and shelter. Unlike them, however, his sole concern is whether he chooses rightly in selecting these actions. As a result, he will pursue his objectives with more restrained impulses than his Epicurean or Peripatetic counter-parts, impulses that are calibrated to bring him just to his objective, but no further, and will not rebound into pain and distress if his best efforts fail.

We might summarize the contrast between Epicurean and the Stoic equanimity as follows. The Epicurean restricts the objectives he pursues to those he is confident of achieving. The Stoic, by contrast, restricts not his objectives but the intensity of the impulse with which he pursues them. The Epicurean is confident that he will attain these objectives. The Stoic is content with the confidence that in aiming properly at these objectives, he has achieved the only thing that matters.

Only the wise are free

While the Epicureans stress the security and invulnerability of the wise person's life, the Stoics stress his freedom and power:

> He is ... uniquely free, the servant of no master, the slave of no appetite, truly unconquerable (*invictus*). The wise may have their body put in chains, but you will never chain their soul.
> (*Fin.* 3.75; cf. Stob. 2,11g /W 2.99,19–22)

This view is summarized in the familiar Stoic slogan, 'only the wise are free' – one of the famous self-styled paradoxes for which the Stoics were notorious in antiquity.[89]

It is important not to mistake the freedom (*eleutheria*) that the Stoics attribute to the wise for the kind of 'freedom' which, in modern discus-sions, is often spoken of in contrast with determinism (on the latter issue, see Appendix 1). Rather, the freedom the Stoics have in mind is to be contrasted with slavery – hence the flip side of the slogan 'only the wise person is free' is 'everyone else is a slave' (*Ac.* 2.136; DL 7.32–3, 121; *PS* 35). This ideal of freedom is deeply rooted in Greek and Roman society, where slavery was commonplace. In contrast with the lot of the slave who does not get to live his life as he sees fit, but must live at the behest of another, a free person is in charge of his own life. As Callicles articulates the ideal in Plato's *Gorgias*, 'How could a man prove to be happy (*eudaimôn*) if he's enslaved to anyone at all?' (491e).[90]

One of Plato's concerns in the *Gorgias* is to criticize Callicles' understanding of this ideal, according to which freedom amounts to complete licence and the disregard of all standards of decency and justice in the pursuit of one's own desired satisfaction:

> [W]hat in truth could be more shameful and worse than self-control and justice for [those] people who, although they are free to enjoy good things without any interference, should bring as master upon themselves the law of the many, their talk, and their criticism? . . . Rather, the truth of it, Socrates . . . is like this: wantonness, lack of discipline and freedom (*eleutheria*) if available in good supply, are excellence and happiness.
>
> (Plato, *Gorg.* 492b–c)

Plato's Socrates criticizes this conception of the good life, arguing that knowledge and self-control are necessary for living well and that happiness requires one to have the virtues of justice and moderation. However, he does not abandon the ideal of freedom (*eleutheria*), for he regularly calls 'free' (*eleutheros*) the person in whom these virtues have been inculcated, in contrast with the 'slavish' person who is in thrall to his appetites.[91] Aristotle too uses 'freedom' in a similar sense (*EN* 1118b4–6). *Eleutheria* is in fact the name he gives to the virtue involved in giving and taking money (*EN* IV 1). The 'liberal' person (from '*liber*', the Latin version of *eleutheros*) is not so fond of money that he will fail to give it to those in need, or stoop to earn it from ignoble means.[92] This contrast between freedom and slavishness, although clearly related to the original political sense, concerns a person's state of character, rather than his political or legal status. Thus Plato and Aristotle internalize the notion of freedom, just as they do the notion of excellence.

The Stoics agree with Plato and Aristotle that the ideal of freedom requires cultivating appropriate desires, not just avoiding the legal status of a slave (Epictetus, *Diss.* 4.1,6–10, 57; cf. 144–150). However, their definition of freedom appears, at least on the face of it, to have little in common with Plato and Aristotle's concern with the character of a free person. Epictetus gives the standard definition[93] in his essay 'On Freedom':

> He is free who lives as he wishes, neither compelled nor impeded
> nor forced, whose impulses are unhindered, whose strivings (*orexeis*)
> hit their mark, and whose aversions succeed in avoiding what they
> would avert.
>
> (*Diss.* 4.1,1; cf. 46, 56–7)

'Living as one wishes', in the first part of the definition, amounts to the success in one's strivings and aversions mentioned at the end. The middle part of the definition identifies the two ways in which one's strivings and aversions would be unsuccessful. These are (a) impediment or hindrance (in which one's impulses are prevented from achieving their objectives) and (b) force or compulsion (in which one is forced to choose that to which one is averse). Thus the core of the Stoic conception of freedom is the claim that the free person is neither hindered (*koluesthai*) nor compelled (*anankasthai*).[94] As Epictetus boasts: 'I have never been impeded in getting what I wanted or compelled to do what I did not want' (*Diss.* 4.1.89).

Hindrance and compulsion are here understood in their ordinary senses. For example, I may be hindered in my pursuit of an education by having insufficient money, or prevented from catching the train by being caught in traffic or by breaking my ankle on the platform. I am compelled to do something if it is something I do not want to do but circumstances (or another person) force me to choose between doing it and losing something else I hold dear. Such is the case of the ship's captain who is compelled to throw his cargo overboard in a storm in order to avoid capsizing, or the parent who must pay a ransom to kidnappers in order to save the life of her child (cf. Aristotle EN 1110a4–11). In cases of compulsion, the Stoics remark, circumstance, or another person, is our master (*Diss.* 4.1,59–60). The mark of compelled actions is pain, grief, or reluctance, since one is forced to do something that one does not want to do.[95]

Hindrance and constraint are clearly the lot of the chattel slave, who is compelled to serve his master, and prevented from escaping or spending his time as he wishes (Epictetus, *Diss.* 4.1.11). However, while they dominate the life of the slave, hindrance and constraint are not unique to his status in life. Even a person who is legally free may be hindered or compelled. Indeed, it would seem to be a common feature of human experience to have to choose between things we value, or to be prevented from achieving what we set out to do. Thus the Stoics are making an extremely strong statement (and on the face of it, an implausible one) with their claim that the wise person's life is free from hindrance and constraint.

Plato's portrait of Callicles in the *Gorgias* offers one conception of a life without hindrance and constraint. For Callicles, the person living as he wishes is he whose superior strength and resources enable him to overcome every obstacle in his pursuit of wealth, power, and the other good things in life, and who is never subject to the will of another. The Stoics, of course, have something very different in mind when they claim that the life of the wise person is unhindered and unconstrained. They do not mean that such a person always achieves the health, wealth, or other 'preferred indifferent' that he pursues. They mean rather that the person living in agreement with nature, whose impulses are proportional to the value of their objectives, always succeeds in achieving the only thing he values: to be choosing appropriately. External factors may prevent his choices and efforts from achieving their objectives, but the Stoic does not count this as a bad thing. What he really cares about is keeping his choices in line with nature. Only this is good, in his view, and it is out of the reach of external hindrance. As Epictetus boasts 'you can fetter my limbs, but not even Zeus has the power to overpower my decision (*prohairesis*)' (*Diss.* 1.1,23–4; cf. *Fin.* 3.75).

In claiming that the sage will not be compelled, the Stoics are not saying that he will drown with his ship rather than throw the cargo overboard. Nor do they mean that he will leave his children to the kidnappers' mercy rather than pay the ransom. The sage will perform all appropriate actions. Thus, he will jettison the cargo and pay the ransom in circumstances in which it is appropriate to do so.[96] Such actions will not count as 'compelled', however, because the sage has no attachment to his money, or his cargo, beyond the commitment to make appropriate choices in pursuit and protection of it. Losing his cargo or his money are not things to which he is averse; he is averse only to making bad choices about them. In most circumstances he will aim at preserving the cargo (or money), but his impulse to do so will not be excessive, and will stop short of the attachment that would make it painful to hand over his fortune to kidnappers or to lose his investment.

The Aristotelian sage, by contrast, will be motivated by what the Stoics classify as 'passions'. He will be attached to his money and his cargo with stronger impulses than those of the Stoic – impulses borne of the judgment that having them is good, rather than just to be preferred. Thus if he is forced to choose between them and something he values more highly, as in the case of the sea captain or the kidnapping, his action will count as compelled. He will be forced to do something he thinks is bad, even if it is the lesser of two evils. For similar reasons, the Aristotelian sage can be hindered. Unlike his Stoic counterpart, he cares about staying healthy and avoiding poverty, not just about choosing properly in his pursuit of them. As a result, he is susceptible to hindrance and frustration.

At the root of the Stoic contention that only the sage is free is their equally notorious doctrine that the sage will be free from the passions. The latter doctrine allows them to add a twist to the conception of slavishness emphasized by Plato and Aristotle. The earlier two philosophers stress the slavishness involved in caring more for the wealth, health, and so on than for the standards of justice and decency. In their view, freedom requires that our desires be for appropriate objectives. On this point the Stoics agree, but they also add the further point that even desires for appropriate objects can be slavish. If these desires are 'passions' rather than 'good feelings' they open one up to the impediment, compulsion and frustration that are characteristic features of the slave's life.

For anyone other than the Stoic sage, life is a rough and bumpy road in which one often stumbles, encounters obstacles and impediment, and is forced to go where one wants not to. Epictetus characterizes this aspect of the slavish and unhappy life as its 'difficult flow' (*dusrhoiein*' – *Diss.* 4.1,34, 52) – an explicit contrast with the 'good flow' (*eurhoia* 4.1.46) of the life in agreement with nature:

> Therefore, the goal becomes 'to live consistently with nature' ... And this itself is the virtue of the happy man and a smooth flow of life (*eurhoia biou*), whenever all things are done according to the harmony of the daimon in each of us with the will of the administrator of the universe.
>
> (DL 7.88/ LS 63C4; cf. *Diss.* 4.1.38)

Achieving the Stoic *telos* involves having not only one's choices, but also the intensity of one's impulses, in harmony with the reason that imbues nature. If, on occasion, nature does not deliver a result that he has wisely chosen to pursue, the Stoic is not disappointed: she acquiesces in the course of nature and is not distressed.

As the Stoics see it, this is an not attitude of resignation but empowerment. They do not advise us to be meek and submissive to the forces of a world whose workings we cannot fathom and control. On the contrary, they hold that the person who is living in agreement with nature 'sees eye to eye' with the universe.[97] With his choices and impulses completely in line with the rationality imbued in nature, he is at one with the splendour and majesty of the universe, with the very constellation of forces that may keep him, on occasion, from achieving the natural objectives he elects to pursue. He gives up concern for achieving these objectives not because (like Epicurus) he cannot be sure of achieving them, but rather because from the vantage point of his 'god's eye view' he sees that he has achieved what is valuable beyond measure. In comparison with what he has achieved in reaching this *telos*, his failure to get what he aimed at along the way is of no consequence to him.

Notes

1 Not to be confused with the Presocractic philosopher Zeno of Elea, famous for his paradoxes about motion.
2 The Megarians (or 'Dialectical school'), specialists in logic, were followers of Diodorus Cronus (d. 284; see Sedley 1977). The Cynics, severe moralists who

preached asceticism and repudiated most social conventions, were followers of Antisthenes, a companion of Socrates. Later Stoics acknowledge their debt to Cynicism: the second-century Stoic Apollodorus writes that Cynicism is a short cut (*suntomon . . . hodon*) to virtue (DL 7.121); Epictetus cites Antisthenes in illustration of Stoic claims about freedom (*Diss.* 3.24.67, 4.1.114). On the Cynic movement, see Dudley 1937, the essays in Branham and Goulet-Cazé 1996, Long 1999: 623–32, and Prince 2006.

3 Stobaeus, *Anthology* Volume 2, chapters 5–12 (Wachsmuth 1884: 57–116). There is some dispute about whether Arius is the author of the 'Epitome' preserved in Stobaeus; see Göransson 1995, reviewed by Inwood 1996, and the papers in Fortenbaugh 1983. The *Epitome* is translated into English in Inwood and Gerson 1997 (=IG), 203–32, as well as in Pomeroy 1999 (with Greek text and notes). When citing the *Epitome*, I will give both the chapter headings (used in IG – e.g. '2,5a-b'), and the volume, page and line references in Wachsmuth (e.g. 'W 2.87,5–12').

4 These texts, along with many additional sources on Stoicism, are translated in IG. Shorter extracts from these texts, arranged topically, are translated with commentary in LS. Unless otherwise indicated, translations quoted in this chapter are by Inwood and Gerson, except those from Cicero's *On Moral Ends*, which are by Woolf (in Annas (ed.) 2001) and those from Seneca's *De Ira* (On Anger) which are from Cooper and Procopé 1995. Occasionally I adapt these translations to fit my own choice of terminology.

5 While the Stoics ascribe self-consciousness to the infant as the explanation of such behaviour (*Fin.* 3.16), the important point for their cradle argument is not this explanation but the direction of the behaviour, as stressed in Seneca's account (*Ep.* 121.19).

6 Annas 1993 renders '*oikeion*' as 'familiar' (vs. 'alien' for its opposite, *allotrion*). Long and Sedley 1987 render it as 'appropriate'; Inwood and Gerson 1997 and Cherniss 1976 use 'congenial'.

7 On Stoic *oikeiôsis*, see Pembroke 1971, Ioppolo 1980: chapter 5, Striker 1983 and 1991, Engberg-Pedersen 1986 and 1990, Long 1993, Lories 1998: chapter 5, Inwood and Donini 1999: 677–82, and Schofield 2003: 243–6.

8 So-called 'social *oikeiôsis*': *Fin.* 3.62–71; DL 7.120; Hierocles 9.3–10, 11.14–18 (LS 57D); Stobaeus, 4.671,7–673,11 (LS 57G); Epictetus, *Diss.* 4.1.126. See Blundell 1990 and McCabe 2005.

9 The natural objects of pursuit: DL 7.107; Stob. 2,7f /W 2.83,16–84,1 (LS 58D); Stob. 2,7a (W 2.79,20–80,3); *Fin.* 3.16–22, 59–61, 62–3; 5.18. These are what the Stoics classify as 'preferred indifferents' or as having 'worth' (*axia*): Fin 3.51; 4.20, 23, 62, 69, 71–2; DL 7.102–7; Sextus, M 11.63; Stob. 2,7b (W 2.80,14–21).

10 It is not a straightforward matter to determine what action is appropriate (*kathêkon*) in particular circumstances. In fact, a large body of Stoic literature (now lost) gave practical advice on this question. Cicero's *de Officiis* ('On Duties') is in this genre.

11 *Kathêkonta* (*officia*): *Fin.* 3.20–2; 3.56–61; 4.14–15; DL 7.107–109; Stob. 2,8 (W 2,85,12–86,4 /LS 59B); cf. DL 7.88. LS translate *kathêkon* as 'proper function'.

12 This is not to say that every person acts for the sake of the *kalon*. Rather, the *kalon/honestum* is reason's appropriate standard of action – the one proper to it. It is the standard of practical rationality.

13 I differ from Woolf, in rendering Cicero's '*constans*' by 'consistent' in *Fin.* 3.20. I do so in order to preserve the connection with the doctrine of '*constantia*' ('*eupatheiai*') in *TD* 4.14. See below on the Stoic doctrine of the passions.

14 Completely correct actions (*katorthômata*): Stob. 8–8a, 11a, 11e (W 2.85,18–86,9 /LS 59B; 2.93,14–18 /LS 65S; 2.96,20–97,14 /LS 59M; 5.906–7 /IG II–97, p. 232; cf. Sextus, *M* 11.200–201 /IG II–96, p. 232; Plutarch, *St. Rep.* 1037c, 1038a–c /IG II–114, p. 254). On the distinction between *kathêkonta* and *katorthômata*, see Bonhöffer 1996 [1894]: 244–89.

15 Virtue as the 'art of living' (*technê peri ton bion*; Latin, *ars vivendi*) *Fin.* 4.16, Sextus, *M* 11.170, 181, 184, 201; cf. *Fin.* 3.24–5, 5.16. Virtue as the using craft: 'The wise man knows how to use all things' *Fin.* 3.75; cf. Stob. 2,5m (W 2.74,17–20), 2,11q (W 2.114,4–6).

16 For example, will the wise man take part in politics, marry, or have children? (DL 7.120–4); cf. Stob. 2,11b (W 2.94,8–20), 2,11d (W 2.95,24–96,9).

17 According to the Stoic Diogenes of Babylon, the goal of life is 'reasoning well in the selection (*eklogê*) of things that are according to nature (*kata phusin*)' (DL 7.88). However, the standard Stoic definition of the *telos* – reflected in Cicero's locution, 'consistent and in agreement with nature' (*Fin.* 3.20 quoted above) – is that it is 'living in agreement with nature' or 'following nature'. Following nature = '*akolouthôs tei phusei zên*' (DL 7.88, 89). Agreement with nature = '*homologoumenôs tei phusei zên*' (DL 7.87; Stob. 2,6e /W 2.77,18–19 /LS 63A; cf, Stob. 2,6a /W 2.75,11–76,15 /LS 63B). Cicero translates '*homologia*' (agreement) by '*convenentia*' (*Fin.* 3.21, 4.14). Another version of the *telos* formula is 'concord (*sumphônia*) between one's own reason and that of the cosmos' (DL 7.88). On the different versions of the Stoic *telos* formula, see Bonhöffer 1996 [1894]: 209–38, Kidd 1955, Soreth 1968, Striker 1986, 1991: 14–35.

18 According to Cleanthes, the only relevant nature is that of the whole (DL 7.89). On individual vs. cosmic nature in the Stoic *telos* formula, see Inwood and Donini 1999: 682–4.

19 The Stoics use the term '*hulê*' (matter) very differently than Aristotle. For them, matter is 'a substance without quality' (DL 7.134).

20 Three levels of unity: DL 7.138–9, Galen *Medical Introduction* (Kühn 1821–33) 14.726,7–11 (LS 47N); Philo, *Allegories of the Laws* (Cohn and Wendland 1896–1930) 2.22–3 (LS 47P); cf. LS 47C5–6, 47M, 53A.

21 'Naturally' would be rendered by '*kata phusin*', whereas the goal is to live 'in agreement with' (*homologoumenôs*) nature. Hence Arius's equation of the two locutions at Stob. 2,6e (W 2.77,18–19 /LS 63A1) muddies the waters.

22 Indeed, the notion of *kathêkon* (appropriate act) belongs to animals and plants as well as to humans (DL 7.107 /LS 59C).

23 Plutarch, paraphrasing Zeno's *Republic*: 'there should be one way of life (*bios*) and order (*kosmos*), like that of a herd grazing together and nurtured by a common law' (Plutarch, *On the Fortune of Alexander* 329a-b (LS 67A); translation by LS). For more on law and justice: Stob. 2,11d (W 2.96,10–17), 2,11i (W 2.102,4–10) and note 25 below.

24 Here I follow Inwood 1999.

25 The fifth-century distinction between *nomos* (law, convention) and *physis* (natura) is depicted in Antiphon, fr. 44 (Diels-Kranz). Plato depicts Callicles as the proponent of such a view (*Gorg.* 482e–484c; cf. *Rep.* 339c).

26 Justice is natural not conventional: DL 7.128; Stob. 2,11b (W 2.94,7); Cicero, *De Republica* 3.33 (LS 67S).

27 For the same reason, the Stoics deny that our relations with non-rational animals are governed by such a law (DL 7.129; *Fin.* 3.67).

28 By 'absolute' I mean, 'not admitting of exceptions'. Thus an absolute prohibition on infanticide would make it wrong to kill a newborn under any circumstances, and an absolute requirement to tell the truth would make it wrong to

deceive another person, no matter what the circumstances. I follow Inwood 1999 in claiming that the Stoics are not committed to the existence of absolute rules. For discussion and controversy on this point, see also Watson 1971, Sedley 1999a, Striker 1984, Kidd 1987, Mitsis 1993a and 1994, and Vander Waerdt 1994.

29 Zeno's *Republic* advocates a 'community of wives' and similar attire for men and women (DL 7.32–3 /LS 67B). Chrysippus, in his *Republic*, is reported to have condoned cannibalism in special circumstances (Sextus, *PH* 3.247–8 /LS 67G).

30 Plato's ethical dialogues are replete with refutations of simple moral rules such as 'return what you've borrowed' (*Rep.* 331c-e) or 'stand your ground in battle' (*La.* 190e–191c). Aristotle explicitly claims that ethical precepts defy precise generalization (*EN* 1094b14–22). Similarly, the Stoics recognize a class of 'situation-dependent appropriate actions' (*peristatika kathêkonta*), actions that are ordinarily wrong to perform, but appropriate in certain circumstances (DL 7.109; Sextus, *M* 11.66 /IG II–116, p. 256; see also Philo *de Cherubim* 14 (SVF 3.513) and Seneca *Ep.* 71.1, cited by Inwood 1999: 102n26, 116n62. On such actions, see N. White 1978.

31 *Fin.* 3.10, 4.40–43, 45–47, 54–55; DL 7.87.

32 My translation. Woolf translates the phrase 'acting morally and morality itself' in keeping with his practice of rendering '*honestum*' and its cognates by 'moral-ity' and its cognates. While this rendering communicates the right general idea, and makes for better English than my preferred translation, it obscures the connection between the *kalon* invoked by the Greek philosophers and the *honestum* which is its counterpart in Latin translation.

33 Alternatively, the *sumum bonum* is 'to live admirably (*honeste*)', that is, vir-tuously, or simply 'virtue' (*Fin.* 4.43, 54). This imprecision in the Stoic designa-tion of the *summum bonum* replicates a similar imprecision in Aristotle. While he never explicitly states that the *kalon* is the highest good, Aristotle's account of the virtuous person's motivation in *EN* II–V makes it clear that the *kalon* is the ultimate goal in such a person's practical deliberations. But according to Aristotle's account of happiness in *EN* I, it is not the *kalon* itself but the life organized around its pursuit – i.e., the life of excellent activity – that is identi-fied as the human *telos*. (I here ignore complications from the role of *theôria* in the happy life.)

34 The Greek phrase, 'only the *kalon* is *agathon*' (DL 7.101) translated into Latin as 'only *honestum* is *bonum*', is ubiquitous in Cicero's report of Stoicism: *Fin.* 3.11, 27–29, 39, 58; 4.43, 45, 78). Woolf translates this as 'only morality is good'.

35 Thus the Stoic Seneca writes that our natural impulse is not directed towards the good until we have developed the reason (*Ep.* 124.11).

36 In these contexts 'virtue' has to be understood as 'virtuous activity'. Unlike Aristotle, the Stoics almost never use 'virtue' for the psychological state, as opposed to its activity, in ethical contexts.

37 Sometimes this is misleadingly put as the question of which life is more choiceworthy (*Fin.* 4.62–3, quoted above). But the choice between lives here is purely theoretical. There is no practical option of virtue without health that the Aristotelian would choose but the Stoic would not, since the Stoic no less than the Aristotelian pursues health unless it is *kalon* to do otherwise.

38 On the Stoic attitude to the so-called 'goods of fortune', see Lesses 1989.

39 For instance, one cannot exercise the virtue of generosity without having money, or various other of the civic excellences without having friends and fellow citizens. See Cooper 1985 for an elaboration and defence of this interpretation.

For alternative views, see Irwin 1985a, Annas 1993: chapter 18, Reeve 1995: 159–73, Kenny 1992: chapters 5–6, White 1992.

40 On the Peripatetic position, see Sharples 1983, Annas 1993: chapter 20, and S. White 2002. On the differences between Aristotle's and the Stoics' position, see Irwin 1986.

41 They are reported in DL 7. 100–101; *Fin.* 3.27–29; criticized at 4.48–51; cf. Stob. 2,5i (W 2.72,19–25).

42 See Schofield 1983.

43 Premise (5) might appear controversial if interpreted as a hedonist claim, but it is not. '*Placeo*' in this context has to do with approval, or seeming right.

44 At *Fin.* 4.50 Cicero criticizes a simpler version of this argument and charges that it commits the fallacy of a *sorîtes* argument. This is an argument that proceeds by small steps (like adding grains of rice to a heap – *soros*), each of which introduces a true premise, and appears to make a valid inference, but the inference from the initial premise to the conclusion is invalid.

45 Cicero is careless in Cato's formulation of the argument at *Fin.* 3.28 and does not give the same formulation when criticizing it at 4.50, but I take the general strategy to be as I have reconstructed it.

46 Thanks to Jason Rheins for suggesting this translation of *axia /aestimatio*. The more common translation is 'value' (Woolf, LS, IG, and Pomeroy 1999).

47 This is the orthodox Stoic position. We will see below that Aristo of Chios dissents from this point.

48 The Stoic claim applies not only to 'bodily goods', but health is the example at issue in the wider context of this passage (*Fin.* 3.45).

49 Croesus was the Bill Gates of Ancient Greece and Persia. King of Lydia in the sixth century, he was legendary for his enormous wealth. See Herodotus, *History* 1.6.1–94.

50 Goodness does not admit of degree: DL 7.101, 7.127; *Fin.* 3.45, 48, 4.67–8.

51 All wrongdoing is equal: DL 7.127, Stob. 2/11L (W 2.106,21); 2,11o (W 2.113,18–23); *Fin.* 3.48, 4.21, 55, 63, 67–8.

52 Cicero's use of '*absolutum*' here (*Fin.* 3.33) to render the Greek '*teleion*' is unusual, but intelligible. As in its English descendant, 'absolve', Cicero's term connotes completeness in the performance of an obligation. Hence what is '*absolutum*' in terms of its nature has fulfilled completely the goals of its natural development. Thanks to Josiah Davis for helpful discussion of this point.

53 Moral progress: *Fin.* 3.48, 4.21, 4.64, 4.67; Stobaeus, *Anthology* 5.906–7 /SVF 3.510 /IG II–97, p. 232).

54 As may be suggested by the arguments reported at DL 7.120, Stob. 2,11L (W 2.107,2–7), and *Fin.* 4.75. According to the analogies at *Fin.* 4.75, it is equally true of any lyres that are out of tune that they are out of tune, and of any two crooked sticks that they are not straight.

55 A 'stade' (*stadion*) is roughly 180 metres.

56 'Those ancient precepts of the wise that bid us to [among other things]' . . . 'follow god' . . . cannot be grasped in their full force without a knowledge of physics (*Fin.* 3.73). For more on 'assimilation to god', see Sedley 1997 and 1999.

57 The world is for the sake of gods and humans: Cicero *ND* 2.133 (LS 54N) 2.37–8 (LS 54H); *Fin* 3.67; Plutarch, *St Rep* 1044d (LS 540); Porphyry, *On Abstinence* 3.20.1 (LS 54P); Gellius 7.1.1 (LS 54Q).

58 On 'becoming like god' in Stoicism, see Russell 2004.

59 I have benefited from the discussion of Stoic teleology in Chapter 5 'Providentialism' of Goggins 2005.

60 Preferred indifferents: Sextus, *M* 11.62–3; *Fin.* 3.50–1; cf. 4.20, 23, 71–3; Stob. 2,7b (W 2.80,14–81,18); DL 7.102–7.

61 The normative version of the challenge is expressed or responded to in *Fin.* 3.14 and 31. The challenge as expressed at 4.43 and 4.69 is clearly the explanatory version.

62 The qualification 'but not all' in *Fin.* 3.51 acknowledges the 'circumstantial *kathêkonta*' – cases where circumstances make it appropriate to disregard, or even positively undermine, one's health (DL 7.109; cf. Stob. 2,7f /W 2.83, 13–84,1; Sextus, *M* 11.66).

63 As Cicero implies in his report at *Fin.* 4.43, aptly characterized as a 'patently . . . disingenuous misunderstanding' (Annas 1993: 101).

64 For fuller discussion of Aristo's disagreement with mainstream Stoicism on the question of indifferents, see Ioppolo 1980, N. White 1985, Annas 1993: 99–105, Inwood and Donini 1999: 690–99, and Sedley 1999a: 128–33. For an additional disagreement about the unity of virtue, see Schofield 1984 and Inwood and Donini 1999: 707–14.

65 *Fin.* 4.43. My translation. Woolf renders the phrase, 'the motive force of the wise person's desire'.

66 Indeed, even Stoics who disagreed with Aristo's doctrines admire him for having 'followed nature herself' (*Fin.* 3.11).

67 Selections from these and other texts on the passions are collected and translated into English with commentary in LS Section 65. A continuous translation of Cicero's account in *Tusculan Disputations* is in Graver 2002. For discussions of the Stoic views on the passions, see Lloyd 1978, Gill 1983 and 1997, Fillion-Lahille 1984, Inwood 1985: chapter 5: M. Frede 1986, Couloubaritsis 1986, Nussbaum 1994: chapter 10, Lories 1998: chapter 5, Long 1999a: 580–4, Inwood and Donini 1999: 699–709, Sorabji 2000, Brennan 2003 and 2005: chapter 7, Becker 2004, Gill 2005 and Price 2005, as well as the papers in Braund and Gill 1997 and Sihvola and Engberg-Pedersen 1998.

68 Plato, *Phlb.* 47e; 50 b–c; Aristotle, *EN* 1105b21–23, 1107a10–11; *Rhet.* II 2–11. Standard Stoic lists tend to discriminate the passions more finely, (DL 7.111–12; Stob. 2,10b /W 2.91,1–9 /LS 65E). Although Plato does not use the generic term '*pathos*', his lists in the *Philebus* overlap with Aristotle's and the Stoics' list of *pathê*.

69 Passions as pleasures and pains: Plato, *Laws* 644c; cf. 631e–632a; Aristotle, *EN* 1105b23; *Rhet.* 1378a19–22; cf. 1382a21–2 (fear), 1383b12–14 (shame), 1385b13–14 (pity).

70 Passions are capable of following reason: Plato, *Rep.* 431c, *Laws* 653a–c; Aristotle, *EN* 1102b13–28; cf. *Rep.* 429c–d.

71 Chrysippus apud Galen, *Plac* 4.2.10 /LS 65J3).

72 Passions issue from a non-rational faculty: Plato, *Laws* 653a–c; Aristotle, *EN* 1102b13–28.

73 On passions as arising from the rational faculty of the soul, see also Plutarch, *Vir. Mor.* 441c (LS 61B8–9), 446f (LS 65G1); Galen, *Plac.* 5.6.37 /LS 65I).

74 While some later reports of the Stoics say that the passions are due to or arise from judgments or opinions (e.g. Cicero, *TD* 3.24–5), the canonical view is that passions *are* judgments (DL 7.111; Chrysippus apud Galen, *Plac.* 4.2.1 /LS 65D1) issuing from the rational part of the soul (Stob. 2,10 /W 2.88,10). On this point Posidonius dissented from orthodoxy (Galen, *Plac.* 4.7.24–41 /LS 65P).

75 Impulsive impressions: Stob. 2,9 (W 2.86,18); Seneca *Ep.* 113.18; Cicero, *On Fate* 40 (see Bobzien 1998: 246–7 ad loc.). See also the texts collected in LS section 53 (esp. A4–5, H1, J, P, Q, R, S). For a general discussion, see Annas 1992a: 89–102.

76 The faculty of assent: Origen, *On Principles* (Koetschau ed. 1913) 3.1.3 (LS 53A5); Aetius 4.21.1 (LS 53H1); cf. Plurarch, *St. Rep.* 1057a (LS 53S). On the

issue of whether animals have assent, see Inwood 1985: 72–91 and Long 1999a.

77 Thus the Stoics deny that non-human animals have passions (Galen *Plac.* 5.6.37 (LS 65I4); cf. Seneca, *Ir.* 1.3.4–8).

78 Four Stoic genera of passions: *Fin.* 3.35; DL 7.110–11; Stob. 2,10 (W 2.88,14–15 /LS 65A). Specific passions: DL 7.111–12, Stob. 2,10b (W 2.90,19–91,9 /LS 65E).

79 The objects of the passions: DL 7.111–14, *Stob.* 2,10b (W2.90,7–18); Andronicus *On Passions* 1 (LS 65B); cf. Epictetus, *Diss* 3.2.3 (LS 56C5).

80 On the Stoic 'good feelings': Stob. 2,5k (W 2.73,2–4), 2,9a (W 2.87,14–22), 2,5b (W 2.58,8–9), discussed by Inwood 1985: 173–5.

81 Plato's Socrates also endorses such an attitude to misfortune (*Rep.* 387d–e).

82 Lack of control is emphasized in Seneca, *Ir.* I.7,3–4, and Cicero, *TD* 4.22; cf. Plutarch, *Vir. Mor.* 441d (LS 61B11); Stob. 10a (W 2.89,6–9).

83 On Poseidonius's view of the passions, see Cooper 1998, Sorabji 2000: chapter 6. On Galen's account, see Tieleman 1996.

84 Conflict between reason and the passions: Aristotle, *EN* 1102b13–21; Plato, *Rep.* 439a–440d; cf. *Laws* 644c–645a.

85 Inwood and Gerson's translation of the list of 'good feelings' at DL 7.116 tends to obscure their affective aspect. What I have rendered 'affection' they translate as 'contentment'.

86 Cited by LS vol. 2: 417.

87 Stoic passions involve the judgment that the impulse is appropriate (*kathêkon*): Stob. 2,10b (W 2.90,17–18); Andronicus *On Passions* 1 (LS 65B1); Cicero, *TD* 3.25.

88 On the 'pre-passions', see Abel 1983, Fillion-Lahille 1984: 167, Inwood 1985: 175–81, Long and Sedley 1987 Vol. 2: 417, Cooper 1998 [1999]: 453–7, Rist 1989: 2003, Graver 1999, and Sorabji 2000: chapter 4.

89 Only the wise are free, and other Stoic paradoxes: *Fin.* 3.75, *Ac.* 2.136; DL 7.32–3, 121; cf. Stob. 2,11g (W 2.99,3–2.100,14).

90 On the original, political sense of 'eleutheria' (freedom), see Nestle 1972 and Raaflaub 2004. On the Stoic conception of freedom, see Bobzien 1998: 338–43 and Inwood 2005a.

91 Plato on freedom (*eleutheria*) and 'slavishness' (*aneleutheria*): *Gorg.* 485c (see Dodds 1959 ad loc.); 518a; *Pr.* 312b; *Rep.* 402c (where '*eleutheriotês*' is translated 'frankness' by Grube and Reeve 1992); *Laws* 741e, 919d–e.

92 There is no good English term to translate *eleutheria* in *EN* IV 1, where it is sometimes translated as 'generosity' (Irwin 1999, Crisp 2000), 'liberality' (Ross 1925) or even 'open handedness' (Rowe and Broadie 2002). These renderings capture the aspect of *eleutheria* relevant to giving; but they fail to capture the restraints on earning that are equally important to the Aristotelian virtue (*EN* 1120a31-b2). The latter aspect of '*eleutheros*' is captured rather well by the antiquated term 'gentleman'. This sense of 'freedom' is at the root of our conception of a 'liberal' education: an education befitting a free person. In this vein, Zeyl's translation of the *Gorgias* (in Cooper (ed.) 1997) renders the cognate adjectives nicely as 'well-bred' and 'ill-bred' (e.g. 485c, 518a). Rowe's translation of the contrary term '*aneleutheria*' as 'avariciousness' obscures the term's connection to freedom.

93 This definition of freedom is also used by Cicero in *PS* 34 (*potestas vivendi ut velis*). Cicero's discussion of the paradox 'only the wise man is free' in *PS* 33–41 is strikingly parallel in structure and content to Epictetus's *Diss.* VI. 1 'On Freedom'.

94 Indeed, in many contexts the slogan that only the wise are free is expressed as the claim that only they are free from hindrance and compulsion (*Fin.* 3.26, Stob. 11g /W 2.99,19–22).

95 This conception of compulsion has a long history in the Greek tradition. Aristotle has a rich discussion of force (*bia*) and compulsion (*ananke*) in *EE* II 8 and *EN* III 1; for discussion, see Sauvé 1988 and Meyer 1994: 93–100.

96 These would be cases that the Stoics classify as 'circumstantial *kathêkonta*' (DL 7.109; cf. Stob. 2,7f /W 2.83,13–84,1).

97 Hence the claim that virtue requires knowledge of physics – *Fin.* 3.73. See Menn 1995.

APPENDIX 1
FREEDOM AND WHAT IS
'UP TO US' IN STOICISM

It is important not to mistake the freedom (*eleutheria*) that the Stoics contrast with slavery for another kind of 'freedom' which, in modern discussions, is often spoken of in contrast with determinism. To be sure, the Stoics were embroiled in a lively dispute with their contemporaries about whether their thesis of fate (a determinist thesis) had the unwelcome consequence that our actions are not 'up to us' (*eph' hêmin*).[1] However, the disputed notion in these contexts, 'what is up to us' (*to eph' hêmin*), is quite different from the 'freedom' (*eleutheria*) that the Stoics attribute to the wise person.[2] On their view, the actions of both the sage and the fool are equally 'up to them', but it is only the wise who are free.

For the earlier Stoics, the question of whether our actions are up to us is arguably not even an ethical issue. What is 'up to us' does not appear on any of the lists of Stoic ethical topics, or in the reports of early Stoic ethical views. The question of whether our actions can be up to us if they are fated is an issue in their metaphysics and philosophy of nature – which is why we do not discuss that question in this volume.[3] In the ethical teaching of the Roman Stoic Epictetus, by contrast, the notion of what is 'up to us' does figure prominently, and is closely linked to the freedom of the sage. But even here, the issue of determinism is not at stake.[4]

Epictetus, like Socrates, wrote nothing. In the *Discourses*, an extensive catalogue of his teachings written down by his pupil Arrian, the topic of what is 'up to us' (*eph' hêmin*) is the subject of the opening chapter (*Diss.* I.1). It also is a dominant notion in the *Handbook* (*Encheiridion*) – a short collection of Epictetus's sayings compiled by Arrian as a practical resource for people trying to live their lives according to Stoic principles:

> Whoever wants to be free . . . let him not want or avoid anything
> that is up to others. Otherwise he will necessarily be a slave.
> (*Ench.* 14; translated by N. White; cf. 1, 12, 19, 31)

Epictetus says that we are free only if we restrict our concern to what is 'up to us' (*Diss.* 4.1.64–7). And the only thing that is 'up to us', he argues, is 'the correct use of impressions' (*Diss.* 1.1.7; 4.1.68–76, 83). To use impressions correctly, on his view, is to assent only to the true and correct ones, and withhold assent from the false and wrong ones. It is to exercise the art of living (4.1.63–4) and thereby be without passions (4.1.4–5, 23, 57, 84, 86; cf. 52). A free person will assent only to those impulsive impressions that are proportional to the value of their objectives and will refuse assent to any impression that these objectives are good, as opposed to indifferent. Thus Epictetus's recipe for freedom amounts to the classic Stoic doctrine that restricting our concern to the correctness of our choices and impulses is the path to freedom. Only the person who in fact succeeds in assenting correctly, thereby eliminating all passions from her psyche, will have achieved this freedom – hence the claim that only the wise are free.

In claiming that the only thing that is up to us is the correct use of impressions, Epictetus diverges from the earlier Stoic notion of 'what is up to us'. According to the earlier Stoics, an action is 'up to me' (roughly) if the impulse that causes it depends on my assent (Alexander, *On Fate* 181.13 /LS 62G1; cf. Cicero, *On Fate* 43). For example, it is up to me to eat the apple in front of me, if whether I eat it depends on whether I assent to the impulsive impression that I should. On such a view, the actions of both the wise and the foolish can be, and generally are, up to them, since they are equally due to assent. This is why, in the debate about fate, the earlier Stoics agree with their opponents that praise and blame are appropriate only for what is up to us (Gellius, 7.2.6–13 /LS 62G). For Epictetus, by contrast, it is not actions but only impulses and assents that are 'up to us', and of these only those that amount to 'the correct use of impressions' – so the vicious person's impulses are not up to him.

The reason Epictetus gives for denying that anything other than the correct use of impressions is 'up to us' is that only this cannot be hindered or compelled (*Diss.* 4.1.64–78; cf. 1.1.7–12). That is, his criteria for being 'up to us' simply replicate the conditions for freedom ('He is free who lives as he wishes, neither compelled nor impeded nor forced' – *Diss.* 4.1,1; quoted in full in Chapter 5).

Thus Epictetus's conception of freedom, even though it invokes the notion of what is 'up to us', does not invoke the same notion of 'up to us' as the earlier Stoics, about which the worries about determinism were raised in antiquity.

Notes

1 The criticism is articulated, along with the Stoic reply, at Cicero, *On Fate* 39–43 /LS 62C and Gellius 7.2.6–13 /LS 62D. For a discussion of the issue, and the merits of the Stoic response, see Meyer 1994 and 1999, Bobzien 1998 and Salles 2001.

2 In these contexts even '*eph hêmin*' falls short of the 'freedom to do otherwise' that is typically at stake in modern worries about the compatibility of freedom

with determinism. The ancient dispute about 'eph hêmin' concerns whether our actions are due to internal causes (in which case they are up to us) or to external ones (in which case they are not). On the difference between the ancient and the modern issue of compatibilitism, see Bobzien 1998a and b, Salles 2001, and Meyer 2003.

3 By contrast, Epicurus does say, in his summary of ethical teaching in the *Letter to Menoecus*, that the wise person will reject fate (*Men.* 133). Even so, Epicurus is not worried about the modern question of whether the 'ability to do otherwise' is compatible with determinism. He is worried that the thesis of fate introduces a 'mistress' (*despotin*) to which we are 'slaves'. The rejection of fate does not make it on to the 'big four' of the *Tetrapharmakon* – presumably because it is not an ordinary fear, but only likely to worry those who read non-Epicurean philosophy.

4 So Bobzien 1998: chapter 7 and Long 2002: 229–30. For a dissenting opinion, see Dobbins 1991: 121.

APPENDIX 2

INTELLECTUAL EXCELLENCES IN ARISTOTLE'S NICOMACHEAN ETHICS

In *Nicomachean Ethics* Book VI, Aristotle distinguishes nine different intellectual excellences. Unfortunately, there is considerable inconsistency among translators' renderings of Aristotle's terminology (see Bostock 2000: 76–7). Here is a key to the most widely available English translations.

Table A2.1 Aristotle's intellectual excellences translated

	Aristotle's term	This volume	Translation into English				
			Rowe 2002	Crisp 2000	Irwin 1999	Thomson 1955	Ross 1925
VI.3	*epistēmē*	scientific knowledge	systematic knowledge	scientific knowledge	scientific knowledge	science	knowledge
VI.4	*technē*	craft	technical expertise	skill	craft knowledge	art	art
VI.5	*phronēsis*	practical wisdom	wisdom	practical wisdom	prudence intelligence (First edition)	practical wisdom	practical wisdom
VI.6	*nous*		intelligence	intellect	understanding	intelligence	comprehension
VI.7	*sophia*	wisdom	intellectual accomplishment	wisdom	wisdom	wisdom	wisdom
VI.8	*politikē*	politics	political expertise	political science	political science	political science	political wisdom
VI.9	*euboulia*	good deliberation	excellence of deliberation	good deliberation	good deliberation	wise deliberation	excellence in deliberation
VI.10	*sunesis*		comprehension	judgement	comprehension	understanding	understanding
VI.11	*gnōmē*		sense	discernment	consideration	fellow-feeling	judgement

BIBLIOGRAPHY

Abel, K. (1983) 'Das Propatheia-Theorem: Ein Beitrag zur stoischen Affectenlehre', *Hermes* 111: 78–97.

Achtenberg, D. (1991) 'The Role of the *Ergon* Argument in Aristotle's Nicomachean Ethics', *Essays in Ancient Greek Philosophy*, Vol. 4: *Aristotle's Ethics*, J. Anton and A. Preus (eds) Albany, NY: State University of New York Press: 59–72.

Ackrill, J. L. (1972) 'Aristotle On "Good" and the Categories', in S. M. Stern, A. Hourani and V. Brown (eds) *Islamic Philosophy and the Classical Tradition*, Oxford: Oxford University Press: 17–25.

—— (1973) *Aristotle's Ethics*, London: Humanities Press International.

—— (1974; reprinted 1980) 'Aristotle on Eudaimonia', *Proceedings of the British Academy* 60: 339–59. Reprinted in A. O. Rorty (ed.) *Essays on Aristotle's Ethics*, Berkeley: University of California Press: 15–33.

Adkins, A. W. H. (1960) *Merit and Responsibility*, Oxford: Clarendon Press.

—— (1971) 'Homeric Values and Homeric Society', *Journal of Hellenic Studies* 91: 1–14.

—— (1973) '*Arete, Techne*, Democracy and Sophists', *Journal of Hellenic Studies* 93: 3–12.

Ahbel-Rappe, S. and R. M. Kamtekar (eds) (2006) *A Companion to Socrates*, Oxford: Basil Blackwell.

Alberti, A. (1995) 'The Epicurean Theory of Law and Justice', in A. Laks and M. Schofield (eds) *Justice and Generosity*, Cambridge: Cambridge University Press: 161–90.

Algra, K., J. Barnes, J. Mansfeld and M. Schofield (eds) (1999) *The Cambridge History of Hellenistic Philosophy*, New York: Cambridge University Press.

Allan, D. J. (1953) 'Aristotle's Account of the Origin of Moral Principles', *Actes du XIe Congrès Internationale de Philosophie* XI: 120–7.

—— (1955) 'The Practical Syllogism', in J. Moreau (ed.) *Autour D'aristote, Recueil D'études De Philosophie Ancienne et Médiévale Offert à Monseigneur A. Mansion*, Louvain: Publications Universitaires: 325–40.

Anagnostopolous, G. (1994) *Aristotle on the Goals and Exactness of Ethics*, Berkeley: University of California Press.

Ando, T. (1971) *Aristotle's Theory of Practical Cognition*, The Hague: Martinus Nijhoff.

Annas, J. (1980) 'Aristotle on Pleasure and Goodness', in A. O. Rorty (ed.) *Essays on Aristotle's Ethics*, Berkeley: University of California Press: 285–99.

—— (1981) *An Introduction to Plato's Republic*, Oxford: Oxford University Press.

—— (1987) 'Epicurus on Pleasure and Happiness', *Philosophical Topics* 15: 5–21.

—— (1988) 'The Heirs of Socrates', *Phronesis* 33: 100–12.

—— (1989) 'Epicurean Emotions', *Greek, Roman and Byzantine Studies* 30(2): 145–64.

—— (1990) 'The Hellenistic Version of Aristotle's Ethics', *The Monist* 73: 80–96.

—— (1992) 'Ancient Ethics and Modern Morality', *Philosophical Perspectives* 6: 119–36.

—— (1992a) *Hellenistic Philosophy of Mind*, Berkeley: University of California Press.

—— (1993) *The Morality of Happiness*, Oxford: Oxford University Press.

—— (1993a) 'Virtue as the Use of Other Goods', *Apeiron* 26: 53–66.

—— (1995) 'Prudence and Morality in Ancient and Modern Ethics', *Ethics* 105: 241–57.

—— (1996) 'Aristotle and Kant on Morality and Practical Reasoning', in S. Engstrom and J. Whiting (eds) *Aristotle, Kant, and the Stoics*, Cambridge: Cambridge University Press: 237–58.

—— (1999) *Platonic Ethics Old and New*, Ithaca, NY: Cornell University Press.

—— (ed.) (2001) *Cicero: On Moral Ends*, edited by Julia Annas and translated by Raphael Woolf (Cambridge Texts in the History of Philosophy), Cambridge: Cambridge University Press.

Annas, J. and C. Rowe (eds) (2002) *New Perspectives on Plato Modern and Ancient*, Washington DC: Center for Hellenic Studies.

Anscombe, G. E. M. (1965) 'Thought and Action in Aristotle', in R. Bambrough (ed.) *New Essays on Plato and Aristotle*, New York: Humanities Press: 143–58.

Anton, J. P. and A. Preus (eds) (1991) *Essays in Ancient Greek Philosophy*, Vol. 4: *Aristotle's Ethics*, Albany, NY: State University of New York Press.

Arrighetti, G. (1960) *Epicuro Opere*, Turin: Einaudi.

Asmis, E. (1989) 'The Stoicism of Marcus Aurelius', *Aufstieg und Niedergang der römischen Welt II* 36(3): 2228–52.

Austin, J. L. (1967) '*Agathon* and *Eudaimonia* in the Ethics of Aristotle', in J. M. E. Moravcsik (ed.) *Aristotle, a Collection of Critical Essays*, New York: Doubleday Anchor: 261–96.

Ax, W. (ed.) (1933) *Cicero: De Natura Deorum*. Leipzig: Teubner.

Bailey, C. (1926) *Epicurus*, Oxford: Clarendon Press.

—— (1928) *The Greek Atomists and Epicurus*, Oxford: Clarendon Press.

—— (ed.) (1947) *Lucretii De Rerum Natura Libri Sex* (Oxford Classical Texts), Oxford: Clarendon Press.

Barnes, J. (1969) 'Aristotle's Theory of Demonstration', *Phronesis* 14: 123–52.

—— (1981) 'Aristotle and the Methods of Ethics', *Revue Internationale de la Philosophie* 34: 490–511.

—— (ed.) (1984) *The Complete Works of Aristotle*, The Revised Oxford Translation, Princeton, NJ: Princeton University Press.

—— (1997) 'Roman Aristotle', in J. Barnes and M. Griffin (eds) *Philosophia Togata* Vol. 2: *Plato and Aristotle in Rome*, Oxford: Clarendon Press: 1–69.

Barnes, J. and M. Griffin (eds) (1989) *Philosophia Togata I: Essays on Philosophy and Roman Society*, Oxford: Clarendon Press.

—— (1997) *Philosophia Togata II: Plato and Aristotle in Rome*, Oxford: Clarendon Press.

Barnes, J., M. Schofield and R. Sorabji (eds) (1977) *Articles on Aristotle* Vol. 2 *Ethics and Politics*, London: Duckworth.

Barney, R. (2003) 'A Puzzle in Stoic Ethics', *Oxford Studies in Ancient Philosophy* 24: 303–40.

Bastiannini, G. and A. A. Long (1992) *Hierocles, Elementa Ethica*, Part I. Vol. 1, Florence: L. Olschki.

Becker, L. (1992) *A History of Western Ethics*, New York: Garland.

—— (2004) 'Stoic Emotion', in S. Strange and J. Zupko (eds) *Stoicism: Traditions and Transformations*, Cambridge: Cambridge University Press: 250–75.

Bekker, I. (ed.) (1831) *Aristotelis Opera*, Berlin: Reimer.

Belshaw, C. (1993) 'Asymmetry and Non-Existence', *Philosophical Studies* 70: 103–16.

Benson, H. (ed.) (1992) *Essays on the Philosophy of Socrates*, New York: Oxford University Press.

—— (2000) *Socratic Wisdom: The Model of Knowledge in Plato's Early Dialogues*, Oxford: Oxford University Press.

—— (2006) 'Plato's Method of Dialectic', in H. Benson (ed.) *A Companion to Plato*, Oxford: Blackwell: 85–100.

Betegh, G. (2003) 'Cosmological Ethics in the *Timaeus* and Early Stoicism', *Oxford Studies in Ancient Philosophy* 24: 273–302.

Bett, R. (1989) 'The Sophists and Relativism', *Phronesis* 34: 139–69.

—— (2002) 'Is there a Sophistic Ethics?' *Ancient Philosophy* 22(2): 235–62.

—— (1997) *Sextus Empiricus: Against the Ethicists* [*Adversus Mathematicos* XI], Translation, Commentary, and Introduction, Oxford: Clarendon Press.

Billerbeck, M. (1991) 'Greek Cynicism in Imperial Rome', in M. Billerbeck (ed.) *Die Kyniker in Der Modernen Forschung*, Amsterdam: John Benjamins: 147–66.

Blank, D. (1998) *Sextus Empiricus against the Grammarians*, (*Adversus Mathematicos* I), translated with an introduction and commentary, Oxford: Oxford University Press.

Blecher, I. (2006) 'The Stoic Method of Happiness', *Apeiron* 39(2): 157–76.

Bluck, R. S. (ed.) (1961) *Plato's Meno: Greek Text and Commentary*, Cambridge: Cambridge University Press.

Blundell, M. W. (1989) *Helping Friends and Harming Enemies*, Cambridge: Cambridge University Press.

—— (1990) 'Parental Nature and Stoic *Oikeiosis*', *Ancient Philosophy* 10: 221–42.

Boardman, J., J. Griffin, and O. Murray (eds) (1986) *The Oxford History of the Classical World*, New York: Oxford University Press.

Bobonich, C. (1994) Review of C. D. C. Reeve, *Practices of Reason*, *The Philosophical Review* 103: 567–9.

—— (2002) *Plato's Utopia Recast*, Oxford: Oxford University Press.

—— (2006) 'Aristotle's Ethical Treatises', in R. Kraut (ed.) *The Blackwell Guide to Aristotle's* Nicomachean Ethics, Oxford: Blackwell: 12–36.

Bobzien, S. (1998) *Determinism and Freedom in Stoic Philosophy*, Oxford: Oxford University Press.

—— (1998a) 'The Inadvertent Conception and the Late Birth of the Free-Will Problem', *Phronesis* 43: 133–75.

Bolton, R. (1991) 'Aristotle on the Objectivity of Ethics', in J. P. Anton and A. Preus (eds) *Essays in Ancient Greek Philosophy*, Vol. 4: *Aristotle's Ethics*, Albany: State University of New York Press: 7–28.

Bondeson, W. (1974) 'Aristotle on Responsibility for One's Character and the Possibility of Character Change', *Phronesis* 19: 59–65.

Bonhöffer, A. (1890) *Epictet Und Die Stoa*, Stuttgart: Teubner.

—— (1996 [1894]) *The Ethics of the Stoic Epictetus (Die Ethik Des Stoikers Epictet*, translated into English by W. O. Stephens). New York: Peter Lang. Original publication Stuttgart: Teubner.

Bosley, R., R. A. Shiner and J. D. Sisson (eds) (1995) *Aristotle, Virtue, and the Mean, Apeiron* Special volume 25(4), Edmonton: Academic Publishing.

Bostock, D. (1988) 'Pleasure and Activity in Aristotle's Ethics', *Phronesis* 33: 251–72.

—— (2000) *Aristotle's Ethics*, Oxford: Oxford University Press.

Bouffartigue, J. and M. Patillon (eds) (1977–79) *Porphyre: De L'abstinence*, (*De Abstinentia*), Introduction Par Jean Bouffartigue et Michel Patillon, texte êtabli et traduit par Jean Bouffartigue, Paris: Belles Lettres.

Branham, R. B. and M. O. Goulet-Cazé (eds) (1996) *The Cynics: The Cynic Movement in Antiquity and its Legacy*, Berkeley: University of California Press.

Braund, S. and C. Gill, (eds) (1997) *The Passions in Roman Thought and Literature*, Cambridge: Cambridge University Press.

Brennan, T. (1996) 'Epicurus on Sex, Marriage, and Child-Rearing', *Classical Philology* 91: 346–52.

—— (1998) 'The Old Stoic Theory of Emotions', in J. Sihvola and T. Engberg-Pedersen (eds) *The Emotions in Hellenistic Philosophy*, Dordrecht: Kluwer: 21–70.

—— (2000) 'Reservation in Stoic Ethics', *Archiv für Geschichte der Philosophie* 82(2): 149–77.

—— (2001) 'Fate and Free Will in Stoicism: A Discussion of Susanne Bobzien, *Determinism and Freedom in Stoic Philosophy*', *Oxford Studies in Ancient Philosophy* 21: 259–86.

—— (2003) 'Stoic Moral Psychology', in B. Inwood (ed.) *The Cambridge Companion to the Stoics*, Cambridge: Cambridge University Press: 257–94.

—— (2005) *The Stoic Life: Emotions, Duties, and Fate*, Oxford: Oxford University Press.

Brickhouse, T. (1991) 'Roberts on Responsibility for Character in the *Nicomachean Ethics*', *Ancient Philosophy* 11: 137–48.

Brickhouse, T. and N. Smith (1984) 'Socrates on Goods, Virtue, and Happiness', *Oxford Studies in Ancient Philosophy* 5: 1–27.

Brickhouse, T. and N. Smith (eds) (1994) *Plato's Socrates*, Oxford: Oxford University Press.

Brickhouse, T. and N. Smith (2006) 'The Socratic Paradoxes', in H. Benson (ed.) *A Companion to Plato*, Oxford: Blackwell: 263–77.

Broadie, S. (1987) 'Nature, Craft and *Phronesis* in Aristotle', *Philosophical Topics* 15: 35–50.

—— (1987a) 'The Problem of Practical Intellect in Aristotle's Ethics', *Proceedings of the Boston Area Colloquium in Ancient Philosophy* 3: 29–52.

—— (1991) *Ethics with Aristotle*, Oxford: Oxford University Press.

—— (1999) 'Aristotle's Elusive *Summum Bonum*', *Social Philosophy and Policy* 16: 233–51.

—— (2003) 'Aristotelian Piety', *Phronesis* 48(1): 54–70.

—— (2005) 'Virtue and Beyond in Plato and Aristotle', *Southern Journal of Philosophy* 43 Supplement: 97–114.

—— (2006) 'Aristotle and Contemporary Ethics', in R. Kraut (ed.) *The Blackwell Guide to Aristotle's Nicomachean Ethics*, Oxford: Blackwell: 342–61.

Brown, E. (2002) 'Epicurus on the Value of Friendship (*Sententia Vaticana* XXIII)', *Classical Philology* 97: 68–80.

—— (2006) 'Socrates in the Stoa', *A Companion to Socrates*, S. Ahbel-Rappe and R. M. Kamtekar (eds) Oxford: Basil Blackwell: 275–84.

—— (2006a) 'Wishing for Fortune, Choosing Activity: Aristotle on External Goods and Happiness', *Proceedings of the Boston Area Colloquium in Ancient Philosophy* 21.

Brown, L. (1997) 'What is "the Mean Relative to Us" in Aristotle's Ethics?', *Phronesis* 42: 77–93.

Brown, P. M. (1997) *Lucretius. De Rerum Natura III*, edition, translation, and commentary, Warminster: Aris & Phillips.

Brunschwig, J. (1986) 'The Cradle Argument in Epicureanism and Stoicism', in M. Schofield and G. Striker (eds) *The Norms of Nature: Studies in Hellenistic Ethics*, Cambridge: Cambridge University Press: 113–44.

—— (2001) 'Cradle Arguments', in L. Becker (ed.), *Encyclopedia of Ethics: I*, Second edn, New York: Routledge: 355–7.

Brunschwig, J. and M. Nussbaum (eds) (1993) *Passions and Perceptions: Studies in Hellenistic Philosophy of Mind*, Cambridge: Cambridge University Press.

Bryant, J. M. (1996) *Moral Codes and Social Structure in Ancient Greece: A Sociology of Greek Ethics from Homer to Epicureans and Stoics*, Albany NY: State University of New York Press.

Burger, R. (1995) 'Aristotle's "Exclusive" Account of Happiness: Contemplative Wisdom as a Guise of the Political Philosopher', in M. Sim (ed.) *The Crossroads of Norm and Nature: Essays on Aristotle's Ethics and Metaphysics*, Lanham, MD: Rowman & Littlefield: 79–98.

Burnet, J. (ed.) (1900) *The Ethics of Aristotle*, London: Methuen.

—— (ed.) (1900–1907) *Platonis Opera* (Oxford Classical Texts), Oxford: Clarendon Press.

Burnyeat, M. F. (1980) 'Aristotle on Learning to be Good', *Essays on Aristotle's Ethics*, A. O. Rorty (ed.) Berkeley: University of California Press: 69–92.

—— (1981) 'Aristotle on Understanding Knowledge', in E. Berti (ed.) *Aristotle on Science: Proceedings of the Eighth Symposium Aristotelicum*, Padua: Editrice Antenore.

—— (2000) 'Plato on why Mathematics is Good for the Soul', in T. Smiley (ed.) *Mathematics and Necessity: Essays in the History of Philosophy*, Oxford: Oxford University Press: 1–81.

Bywater, I. (ed.) (1894) *Aristotelis Ethica Nicomachea* (Oxford Classical Texts), Oxford: Clarendon Press.

Carone, G. R. (2005) 'Plato's Stoic View of Motivation', in R. Salles (ed.) *Metaphysics, Soul, and Ethics in Ancient Thought: Themes from the Work of Richard Sorabji*, Oxford: Oxford University Press: 365–81.

—— (2005a) *Plato's Cosmology and its Ethical Dimensions*, Cambridge: Cambridge University Press.

Carratelli, G. (ed.) (1983) *Syzhthsis: Studi Sull' Epicureismo Greco e Latino Offerti a Marcello Gigante*, Naples: G. Machiaroli.

Carter, L. B. (1986) *The Quiet Athenian*, Oxford: Clarendon Press.

Castner, C. J. (1988) *Prosopography of Roman Epicureans*, Frankfurt-am-Main: Peter Lang.

Charles, D. (1984) *Aristotle's Philosophy of Action*, London: Duckworth.

—— (1986) 'Aristotle: Ontology and Moral Reasoning', *Oxford Studies in Ancient Philosophy* 4: 119–44.

—— (1999) 'Aristotle on Wellbeing and Intellectual Contemplation: Primary and Secondary Eudaimonia', *Proceedings of the Aristotelian Society* 73 Supplement: 205–23.

Chateau, J.-Y. (ed.) (1997) *La Vérité Pratique: Aristote, Ethique à Nicomaque, Livre VI*. Paris: Vrin.

Cherniss, H. (ed.) (1976) *Plutarch: Moralia*, Vol. XIII.2, edited and translated, Loeb Classical Library, Cambridge, MA: Harvard University Press.

Chilton, C. W. (ed.) (1967) *Diogensis Oenoandensis Fragmenta*, Leipzig: Teubner.

Chilton, C. W. (1971) *Diogenes of Oenoanda, the Fragments*, a translation and commentary, London and New York: Published for the University of Hull by Oxford University Press.

Clark, S. (1975) *Aristotle's Man: Speculations upon Aristotelian Anthropology*, Oxford: Clarendon Press.

Classen C. J. (1958) 'Aristippus', *Hermes* 86:182–92.

Clay, D. (1983) *Lucretius and Epicurus*, Ithaca, NY: Cornell University Press.

Cleemput, G.-V. (2006) 'Aristotle on *Eudaimonia* in *Nicomachean Ethics* 1', *Oxford Studies in Ancient Philosophy* 30: 127–57.

Cohn, L. and P. Wendland (eds) (1896–1930) *Philonis Alexandrini Opera*, Berlin: Reimer.

Cooper, J. (1975) 'The *Magna Moralia* and Aristotle's Moral Philosophy', *American Journal of Philology* 94: 327–49.

—— (1975a; reprinted 1986) *Reason and Human Good in Aristotle*, Cambridge, MA: Harvard University Press. Reprinted 1986, Indianapolis: Hackett.

—— (1977; reprinted 1999) 'Plato's Theory of Human Good in *Philebus*', *Journal of Philosophy* 74: 714–30; Reprinted in G. Fine (ed.) *Plato* II: *Ethics, Politics, Religion, and the Soul*, Oxford: Oxford University Press, 1999: 329–44.

—— (1977a) 'The Psychology of Justice in Plato', *American Philosophical Quarterly* 14: 151–7.

—— (1984) 'Plato's Theory of Human Motivation', *History of Philosophy Quarterly* 1: 3–21.

—— (1985) 'Aristotle on the Goods of Fortune' *Philosophical Review* 94: 173–96.

—— (1987) 'Contemplation and Happiness: A Reconsideration', *Synthese* 72: 187–216.

—— (1988) 'Some Remarks on Aristotle's Moral Psychology', *Southern Journal of Philosophy* 27: 25–42.

—— (1989) 'Greek Philosophers on Suicide and Euthanasia', in B. A. Brody (ed.) *Suicide and Euthanasia*, Dordrecht: Kluwer: 9–38.

—— (1995) 'Eudaimonism and the Appeal to Nature', *Philosophy and Phenomenological Research* 55: 587–98.

—— (1996) 'Reason, Moral Virtue, and Moral Value', in *Reason and Emotion*, Princeton, NJ: Princeton University Press: 253–80.

—— (ed.) (1997) *Plato: Complete Works*, Indianapolis: Hackett.

—— (1998) 'Poseidonius on the Emotions', in J. Sihvola and T. Engberg-Pedersen (eds) *The Emotions in Hellenistic Philosophy*, Dordrecht: Kluwer Academic Publishers: 71–112. Reprinted in his *Reason and Emotion: Essays on Ancient Moral Psychology and Ethical Theory*. Princeton, NJ: Princeton University Press, 1999.

—— (1999) 'Pleasure and Desire in Epicurus' in *Reason and Emotion: Essays on Ancient Moral Psychology and Ethical Theory*, Princeton, NJ: Princeton University Press: 485–514.

—— (2003) 'Moral Theory and Moral Improvement: Seneca', *Proceedings of the Boston Area Colloquium in Ancient Philosophy* 19: 57–83.

—— (2003a) 'Plato and Aristotle on 'Finality' and 'Self-Sufficiency'', in R. Heinaman (ed.) *Plato and Aristotle's Ethics*, Aldershot: Ashgate: 117–47.

Cooper, J. and J. Procopé (eds) (1995) *Seneca: Moral and Political Essays*, Cambridge: Cambridge University Press.

Cordner, C. (1994) 'Aristotelian Virtue and its Limitations', *Philosophy* 69: 269, 291–316.

Couloubaritsis, L. (1986) 'La Psychologie chez Chrysippe', *Entretiens Hardt* 32 (Aspects de la philosophie Hellenistique): 99–146.

Creed, J. L. (1973) 'Moral Virtues in Thucydides' Time', *Classical Quarterly* 23: 213–31.

Crisp, R. (1994) 'Aristotle's Inclusivism', *Oxford Studies in Ancient Philosophy* 12: 111–36.

—— (trans.) (2000) *Aristotle's Nicomachean Ethics*, Cambridge: Cambridge University Press.

Crombie, I. M. (1962/3) *An Examination of Plato's Doctrines*, London: Prometheus.

Cross, R. C. and A. D. Woozley (1964) *Plato's Republic: A Philosophical Commentary*, London: Macmillan.

Curren, R. (1989) 'The Contribution of *Nicomachean Ethics* III,5 to Aristotle's Theory of Responsibility', *History of Philosophy Quarterly* 6: 261–77.

Curzer, H. (1991) 'The Supremely Happy Life in Aristotle's *Nicomachean Ethics*', *Apeiron* 24(1): 47–69.

—— (1996) 'A Defense of Aristotle's Doctrine That Virtue is a Mean', *Ancient Philosophy* 16: 129–38.

Dahl, N. (1984) *Practical Reason, Aristotle, and Weakness of Will*, Minneapolis: University of Minnesota Press.

—— (1991) 'Plato's Defence of Justice', *Philosophy and Phenomenological Research* 51: 809–34.

Dancy, R. M. (2004) *Plato's Introduction of Forms*, Cambridge: Cambridge University Press.

—— (2006) 'Platonic Definitions and Forms', in H. Benson (ed.) *A Companion to Plato*, Oxford: Blackwell: 70–84.

De Lacy, P. (ed.) (1978–84) *Galen: On the Doctrines of Hippocrates and Plato*, Edited and translated with commentary, Corpus Medicorum Graecorum, Berlin: Akademie-Verlag.

Defourney, P. (1977) 'Contemplation in Aristotle's Ethics', in J. Barnes, M. Schofield and R. Sorabji (eds) *Articles on Aristotle's Ethics* Vol. 2: *Ethics and Politics*, London: Duckworth: 104–12.

den Boer, W. (1979) *Private Morality in Greece and Rome*, Leiden: Brill.

Dent, N. (1984) *The Moral Psychology of the Virtues*, Cambridge: Cambridge University Press.

Deslauriers, M. (2002) 'How to Distinguish Aristotle's Virtues', *Phronesis* 47(2): 101–26.

Destrée, P. (2004) 'Acrasia entre Aristoteles e Socrates', *Analytica* 8(2): 135–64.

Devereux, D. (1981) 'Aristotle on the Essence of Happiness', in D. J. O'Meara (ed.) *Studies in Aristotle*, Washington, DC: Catholic University Press: 247–60.

—— (1986) 'Particular and Universal in Aristotle's Conception of Practical Knowledge', *Review of Metaphysics* 39: 483–504.

—— (1992) 'The Unity of the Virtues in Plato's *Protagoras* and *Laches*', *Philosophical Review* 101(4): 765–89.

Diels, H. (ed.) (1879) *Doxographi Graeci*. Berlin: Reimer.

Diels, H. and W. Kranz (eds) (1952) *Fragmente Der Vorsokratiker*, Sixth edition, Berlin: Weidmann.

Dillon, J. (1983) '*Metriopatheia* and *Apatheia*: Some Reflections on a Controversy in Later Greek Ethics', in J. P. Anton and A. Preus (eds) *Essays in Ancient Greek Philosophy*, Vol. 2, Albany: State University of New York Press: 508–17.

—— (1996) *The Middle Platonists: A Study of Platonism 80 BC To AD 220*, Ithaca, NY: Cornell University Press.

Dirlmeier, F. (1956) *Aristoteles: Nikomachische Ethik*, translation and commentary, Berlin: Akademie-Verlag.

Dobbin, R. (1991) '*Prohairesis* in Epictetus', *Ancient Philosophy* 11: 111–35.

—— (1998) *Epictetus: Discourses Book I*, translated with an introduction and commentary, Oxford: Oxford University Press.

Dodds, E. R. (ed.) (1959) *Plato: Gorgias*, Greek text with commentary, Oxford: Clarendon Press.

Dorandi, T. (1999) 'Chronology', in K. Algra, J. Barnes, J. Mansfeld and M. Schofield (eds) *The Cambridge History of Hellenistic Philosophy*, Cambridge: Cambridge University Press.

Dougan, T. W. and R. M. Henry, (eds) (1905–1934) *M. Tulli Ciceronis Tusculanarum Disputationum Libri Quinque*: A revised text with introduction and commentary, Cambridge: Cambridge University Press.

Dover, K. J. (1974) *Greek Popular Morality in the Time of Plato and Aristotle*, Oxford: Clarendon Press.

Draper, K. (2004) 'Epicurean Equanimity Towards Death', *Philosophy and Phenomenological Research* 69(1): 92–114.

Dudley, D. R. (1937) *A History of Cynicism from Diogenes to the 6th Century AD*, Cambridge: Cambridge University Press.

Dufour, R. (2004) *Chrysippe: Oeuvre Philosophique*, Paris: Belles Lettres.

Earl, D. (1967) *The Moral and Political Tradition of Rome*, Ithaca, NY: Cornell University Press.

Einarson, B. and P. de Lacy (eds) (1967) *Plutarch: Moralia* Vol. XIV, edited and translated, Loeb Classical Library, Cambridge, MA: Harvard University Press.

Engberg-Pedersen, T. (1981) 'For Goodness' Sake: More on *Nicomachean Ethics* I VII 5' *Archiv für Geschichte der Philosophie* 63: 17–40.

—— (1983) *Aristotle's Theory of Moral Insight*, Oxford: Clarendon Press.

—— (1986) 'Discovering the Good: *Oikeiôsis* and *Kathêkonta* in Stoic Ethics', in M. Schofield and G. Striker (eds) *The Norms of Nature*, Cambridge: Cambridge University Press: 145–83.

—— (1990) *The Stoic Theory of oikeiôsis: Moral Development and Social Interaction in Early Stoic Philosophy*, Aarhus: Aarhus University Press.

—— (1998) 'The Hellenistic Offentlichkeit: Philosophy as a Social Force in the Greco-Roman World' in P. Borgen, V. K. Robbins and D. B. Gowler (eds) *Recruitment, Conquest, and Conflict: Strategies in Judaism, Early Christianity, and the Greco-Roman World*, Atlanta, GA: Scholars Press: 15–38.

Englert, W. (1994) 'Stoics and Epicureans on the Nature of Suicide', *Proceedings of the Boston Area Colloquium in Ancient Philosophy* 10: 67–98.

Engstrom, S. and J. Whiting (eds) (1996) *Aristotle, Kant, and the Stoics: Rethinking Happiness and Duty*, Cambridge: Cambridge University Press.

Erler, M. and M. Schofield (1999) 'Epicurean Ethics', in K. Algra, J. Barnes, J. Mansfeld and M. Schofield (eds) *The Cambridge History of Hellenistic Philosophy*, New York: Cambridge University Press: 642–74.

Evans, M. (2004) 'Can Epicureans Be Friends?' *Ancient Philosophy* 24(2): 407–24.

Everson, S. (1990) 'Aristotle's Compatibilism in the *Nicomachean Ethics*', *Ancient Philosophy* 10: 81–99.

—— (1998) 'Aristotle on Nature and Value', in S. Everson (ed.) *Companions to Ancient Thought* Vol. 4: *Ethics*, Cambridge: Cambridge University Press: 77–106.

Farwell, P. (1995) 'Aristotle and the Complete Life', *History of Philosophy Quarterly* 12: 247–63.

Ferguson, J. (1958) *Moral Virtues in the Ancient World*, London: Methuen.

—— (trans.) (1991) Clement of Alexandria: *Stromateis*, Books 1–3, Washington, DC: Catholic University of America Press.

Fillion-Lahille, J. (1984) *Le De Ira De Sénèque et la Philosophie Stoïcienne Des Passions*, Paris: Klincksieck.

Fine, G. (1990) 'Knowledge and Belief in *Republic* V–VII', in S. Everson (ed.) *Companions to Ancient Thought*, Vol. 1: *Epistemology*, Cambridge: Cambridge University Press: 85–115.

—— (1993) *On Ideas: Aristotle's Criticisms of Plato's Theory of Forms*, Oxford: Clarendon Press.

—— (ed.) (1999) *Plato 2: Ethics, Politics, Religion, and the Soul*, Oxford: Oxford University Press.

—— (2003) 'Subjectivity Ancient and Modern: The Cyrenaics, Sextus, and Descartes', in B. Inwood and J. Miller (eds) *Hellenistic and Early Modern Philosophy*, Cambridge: Cambridge University Press.

Flaschar, H. and O. Gigon (eds) (1986) *Aspects de la Philosophie Hellénistique*, Fondation Hardt, Entretiens sur l'antiquité Classique, Geneva: Vandoeuvres.

Forschner, M. (1981) *Die Stoische Ethik*, Stuttgart: Klett-Cotta.

Fortenbaugh, W. (1975) *Aristotle on Emotion*, London: Duckworth.

—— (ed.) (1983) *On Stoic and Peripatetic Ethics: The Work of Arius Didymus*, (Rutgers University Studies in Classical Humanities), New Brunswisk NJ: Transaction.

Frankfurt, H. (1992) 'The Usefulness of Final Ends', *Iyyun* (41): 3–19.

Frede, D. (2006) 'Pleasure and Pain in Aristotle's Ethics', in R. Kraut (ed.) *The Blackwell Guide to Aristotle's Nicomachean Ethics*, Oxford: Basil Blackwell: 255–75.

Frede, M. (1986) 'The Stoic Doctrine of the Affections of the Soul', in M. Schofield and G. Striker (eds) *The Norms of Nature*, Cambridge: Cambridge University Press: 93–110.

—— (1999) 'On the Stoic Conception of the Good', in K. Ierodiakonou (ed.) *Topics in Stoic Philosophy*, Oxford: Clarendon Press: 71–94.

Freeman, K. (1948) *Ancilla to the Pre-Socratic Philosophers*, Cambridge: Harvard University Press.

Freeman, K. I. (1907) *Schools of Hellas*, London: Macmillan.

Friedlander, L. (1908–13) *Roman Life and Manners under the Early Empire*, 4 vols, London: Routledge.

Furley, D. J. (1967) *Two Studies in the Greek Atomists*, Princeton, NJ: Princeton University Press.

—— (1977) 'Aristotle on the Voluntary', in J. Barnes, M. Schofield and R. Sorabji (eds) *Articles on Aristotle*, Vol. 2, London: Duckworth: 47–60.

—— (1978) 'Self-Movers', in G. E. R. Lloyd and G. E. L. Owen (eds) *Aristotle on the Mind and the Senses*: Proceedings of the Seventh Symposium Aristotelicum, Cambridge: Cambridge University Press: 165–79.

—— (1986) 'Nothing to Us?' in M. Schofield and G. Striker (eds) *The Norms of Nature*, Cambridge: Cambridge University Press: 75–91.

Garver, E. (2006) *Confronting Aristotle's Ethics: Ancient and Modern Morality*, Chicago: University of Chicago Press.

Gauthier, R. A. and J. Y. Jolif (eds) (1970) *L'Éthique à Nicomaque*, translation with introduction and commentary, Louvain: Publications Universitaires.

Gentzler, J. (2005) 'How to Know the Good: The Moral Epistemology of Plato's *Republic*', *The Philosophical Review* 114 (4): 469–96.

Gerson, L. (2004) 'The Neoplatonic Interpretation of Platonic Ethics', in M. Migliori (ed.) *Plato Ethicus Philosophy Is Life (Lecturae Platonis 4)*, Sankt Augustin: Academia-Verlag: 150–64.

Giannantoni, G. (1990) *Socratis et Socraticorum Reliquiae*, Naples: Bibliopolis.

Gibert, J. (2003) 'The Sophists', in C. Shields (ed.) *The Blackwell Guide to Ancient Philosophy*, Malden, MA: Basil Blackwell: 27–50.

Gigante, M. (1995) *Philodemus in Italy: The Books from Herculaneum*, Ann Arbor: University of Michigan Press.

Gilbert-Thirry, A. (ed.) (1977) *Pseudo-Andronicus De Rhodes: Peri Pathôn*. Leiden: Brill.

Gill, C. (1983) 'Did Chrysippus Understand Medea?' *Phronesis* 28: 136–49.

—— (ed.) (1995) *Epictetus: The Discourses, Handbook, Fragments*, edited by Christopher Gill; translation revised by Robin Hard, London: Dent.

—— (1997) 'The Emotions in Greco-Roman Philosophy', in S. Braund and C. Gill (eds) *The Passions in Roman Thought and Literature*, Cambridge: Cambridge University Press: 5–15.

—— (2004) 'The Stoic Theory of Ethical Development: In What Sense is Nature a Norm?' in J. Szaif (ed.) *Was Ist Das Fur Den Menschen Gute? Menschliche Natur Und Guterlehre*, Berlin: De Gruyter: 101–25.

—— (2005) 'Competing Readings of Stoic Emotions', in R. Salles (ed.) *Metaphysics, Soul, and Ethics in Ancient Thought*, Oxford: Oxford University Press: 445–70.

Glidden, D. (1985) 'Epicurean Prolêpsis', *Oxford Studies in Ancient Philosophy* 3:175–217.

Glucker, J. (1988) 'Cicero's Philosophical Affiliations', in J. Dillon and A. A. Long (eds) *The Question of Eclecticism: Studies in Later Greek Philosophy*, Berkeley: University of California Press: 34–69.

Goggins, R. (2005) 'Divine Benevolence, Human Suffering, Providence and the Problem of Evil in Early Stoicism' (unpublished dissertation), Philadelphia: University of Pennsylvania.

Gomez-Lobo, A. (1989) 'The *Ergon* Inference', *Phronesis* 34: 170–84.

—— (1995) 'Aristotle's Right Reason', *Apeiron* 28(4): 15–34.

Göransson, T. (1995) *Albinus, Alcinous, Arius Didymus*, Göteborg: Ekblad & Co.

Görler, P. W. (1997) 'Storing up Past Pleasures', in K. Algra, M. H. Koenen and Schrijvers (eds) *Lucretius and his Intellectual Background*, Amsterdam: Koninklijke Nederlandse Adademie van Wetenschappen: 193–207.

Gosling, J. C. B. (1973) *Plato*, London: Routledge & Kegan Paul.

—— (1987) 'The Stoics and Akrasia', *Apeiron* 20(2): 179–202.

—— (1990) *Weakness of Will*, London: Routledge.

—— (1993) 'Mad, Drunk, or Asleep? – Aristotle's Acratic', *Phronesis* 38: 98–104.

Gosling, J. C. B. and C. C. W. Taylor (1982) *The Greeks on Pleasure*, Oxford: Oxford University Press.

Gottlieb, P. (1991) 'Aristotle and Protagoras: The Good Human Being as the Measure of Goods', *Apeiron* 24(1): 25–45.

—— (1993) 'Aristotle's Measure Doctrine and Pleasure', *Archiv für Geschichte der Philosophie* 75: 31–46.

—— (1994) 'Aristotle on Dividing the Soul and Uniting the Virtues', *Phronesis* 39: 275–90.

—— (1996) 'Aristotle's Ethical Egoism', *Pacific Philosophical Quarterly* 77(1): 1–18.

—— (2006) 'The Practical Syllogism', in R. Kraut (ed.) *The Blackwell Guide to Aristotle's Nicomachean Ethics*, Oxford: Blackwell: 218–33.

—— (unpublished) The Virtue of Aristotle's Ethics.

Gottschalk, H. (1990) 'Aristotelian Philosophy in the Roman World from the Time of Cicero to the End of the Second Century AD', *Aufstieg und Niedergang der römischen Welt* II 36: 1079–174.

Graver, M. (1999) 'Philo of Alexandria and the Origins of the Stoic *Propatheia*', *Phronesis* 44: 300–25.

—— (ed.) (2002) *Cicero on the Emotions: Tusculan Disputations 3 and 4*, Chicago: University of Chicago Press.

Greenwood, L. H. G. (ed.) (1909) *Aristotle: Nicomachean Ethics Book Six*, Cambridge: Cambridge University Press.

Grey, W. (1999) 'Epicurus and the Harm of Death', *American Journal of Philology* 77: 358–64.

Grgic, F. (2002) 'Aristotle on the Akratic's Knowledge', *Phronesis* 47(4): 336–58.

Griffin, M. (1976) *Seneca: A Philosopher in Politics*, Oxford: Oxford University Press.

Griffin, M. and E. Atkins (eds) (1991) *Cicero: On Duties*, edited and translated, Cambridge: Cambridge University Press.

Griffin, M. and J. Barnes (eds) (1989) *Philosophia Togata: Essays on Philosophy and Roman Society*, Oxford: Clarendon Press.

Grimal, P. (1989) 'Sénèque et Le Stoïcisme Romain', *Aufstieg und Niedergang der römischen Welt* II 36.3: 1962–92.

Grote, G. (1885) *Plato and the Other Companions of Sokrates*, Revised edition, London: John Murray.

Grube, G. M. A. and C. D. C. Reeve (1992) *Plato: The Republic*, translated by G. M. A. Grube and revised by C. D. C. Reeve, Indianapolis: Hackett.

Guthrie, W. K. C. (1971) *The Sophists*, Cambridge: Cambridge University Press.

Hahm, D. (1990) 'The Ethical Doxography of Arius Didymus', *Aufstieg und Niedergang der römischen Welt* II 36.4: 2935–3055.

Hardie, W. F. R. (1980) *Aristotle's Ethical Theory*, Oxford: Clarendon Press.

Heinaman, R. (1988) '*Eudaimonia* and Self Sufficiency in the *Nicomachean Ethics*', *Phronesis* 33: 31–53.

—— (2003) 'The Improvability of *Eudaimonia* in the *Nicomachean Ethics*', *Oxford Studies in Ancient Philosophy* 23(Winter): 99–145.

Hense, O. (ed.) (1884–1912) *Ioannis Stobaei Anthologium*, Vols. III–V, Berlin: Weidman.

Herman, B. (1993) *The Practice of Moral Judgment*, Cambridge, MA: Harvard University Press.

—— (1996) 'Making Room for Character', in S. Engstrom and J. Whiting (eds) *Aristotle, Kant, and the Stoics*, Cambridge: Cambridge University Press: 36–60.

Hershbell, J. (1986) 'The Stoicism of Epictetus', *Aufstieg und Niedergang der Romischen Welt* II 36(3): 2148–63.

Hicks, R. D. (ed.) (1931) *Diogenes Laertius: Lives of Eminent Philosophers*, Loeb Classical Library, Cambridge: Harvard University Press.

Hill, S. (1995) 'Two Perspectives on the Ultimate End', in M. Sim (ed.) *The Crossroads of Norm and Nature: Essays on Aristotle's Ethics and Metaphysics*, Lanham, MD: Rowman & Littlefield: 99–114.

Hobbs, A. (2000) *Plato and the Hero: Courage, Manliness, and Impersonal Good*, Cambridge: Cambridge University Press.

Hossenfelder, M. (1986) 'Epicurus, Hedonist malgré lui', in M. Schofield and G. Striker (eds) *The Norms of Nature*, Cambridge: Cambridge University Press: 245–63.

Hubert, C., W. Nachstädt, *et al.* (eds) (1929; reprinted 1972) *Plutarchi Moralia* Vol. III, Leipzig: Teubner.

Hughes, G. J. (2001) *Aristotle on Ethics*, London: Routledge.

Humphries, R. (trans.) (1968) *Lucretius: The Way Things Are*, Bloomington: Indiana University Press.

Hursthouse, R. (1980) 'A False Doctrine of the Mean', *Proceedings of the Aristotelian Society* 81: 57–92.

—— (1984) 'Acting and Feeling in Character: *Nicomachean Ethics* III,1', *Phronesis* 29: 252–66.

—— (1988) 'Moral Habituation', *Oxford Studies in Ancient Philosophy* 6: 201–19.

—— (2006) 'The Central Doctrine of the Mean', in R. Kraut (ed.) *The Blackwell Companion to Aristotle's Nicomachean Ethics*, Oxford: Blackwell: 96–115.

Hutchinson, D. S. (1986) *The Virtues of Aristotle*, London: Routledge & Kegan Paul.

—— (1988) 'Doctrines of the Mean and the Debate Concerning Skills in Fourth-Century Medicine, Rhetoric, and Ethics', *Apeiron* 21: 17–52.

Ierodiakonou, K. (ed.) (1999) *Topics in Stoic Philosophy*, Oxford: Clarendon Press.

Inwood, B. (1985) *Ethics and Human Action in Early Stoicism*, Oxford: Oxford University Press.

—— (1986) 'Commentary on Striker's "Origins of the Concept of Natural Law"', *Proceedings of the Boston Area Colloquium in Ancient Philosophy* 2: 95–101.

—— (1986a) 'Goal and Target in Stoicism', *Journal of Philosophy* 83(10): 547–56.

—— (1996) 'Review of T. Göransson, *Albinus, Alcinous, Arius Didymus*', *Bryn Mawr Classical Review* 7: 25–30.

—— (1999) 'Rules and Reasoning in Stoic Ethics', in K. Ierodiakonou (ed.) *Topics in Stoic Philosophy*, Oxford: Clarendon Press: 95–127.

—— (ed.) (2003) *The Cambridge Companion to the Stoics*, Cambridge: Cambridge University Press.

—— (2004) 'Moral Judgment in Seneca', in S. Strange and J. Zupko (eds) *Traditions and Transformations*, Cambridge: Cambridge University Press: 76–94.

—— (2005) *Reading Seneca: Stoic Philosophy at Rome*, Oxford: Clarendon Press.

—— (2005a) 'Seneca on Freedom and Autonomy', in R. Salles (ed.) *Metaphysics, Soul, and Ethics in Ancient Thought*, Oxford: Clarendon Press: 489–505.

Inwood, B. and P. Donini (1999) 'Stoic Ethics', in K. Algra, J. Barnes, J. Mansfeld and M. Schofield (eds) *The Cambridge History of Hellenistic Philosophy*, New York: Cambridge University Press: 675–738.

Inwood, B. and L. Gerson (eds) (1994) *The Epicurus Reader: Selected Writings and Testimonia*, Indianapolis: Hackett.

—— (1997) *Hellenistic Philosophy: Introductory Readings*, Second edition, Indianapolis: Hackett.

Ioppolo, A.-M. (1980) *Aristone De Chio e lo Stoicism Antico*, Naples: Bibliopolis.

—— (1990) 'Virtue and Happiness in the First Book of the *Nicomachean Ethics*', in A. Alberti (ed.) *Logica, Mente e Persona: Studi Sulla Filosofia Antica*, Firenze: Olschki: 119–48.

Irwin, T. H. (1977) *Plato's Moral Theory: The Early and Middle Dialogues*, Oxford: Clarendon Press.

—— (1980) 'The Metaphysical and Psychological Basis of Aristotle's Ethics', in A. O. Rorty (ed.) *Essays on Aristotle's Ethics*, Berkeley: University of California Press: 35–54.

—— (1980a) 'Reason and Responsibility in Aristotle', in A. O. Rorty (ed.) *Essays on Aristotle's Ethics*, Berkeley: University of California Press: 117–56.

—— (1981) 'Aristotle's Method of Ethics', in D. J. O'Meara (ed.) *Studies in Aristotle*, Washington, DC: Catholic University of America Press: 193–223.

—— (1985a) 'Permanent Happiness: Aristotle and Solon', *Oxford Studies in Ancient Philosophy* 3: 89–124.

—— (1985b) 'Aristotle's Concept of Morality', *Proceedings of the Boston Area Colloquium in Ancient Philosophy* 1: 115–43.

—— (1985c) trans. *Aristotle: Nicomachean Ethics*, Indianapolis: Hackett.

—— (1986) 'Stoic and Aristotelian Conceptions of Happiness', in M. Schofield and G. Striker (eds) *The Norms of Nature: Studies in Hellenistic Ethics*, Cambridge: Cambridge University Press: 205–44.

—— (1988) *Aristotle's First Principles*, Oxford: Clarendon Press.

—— (1988a) 'Some Rational Aspects of Incontinence', *Southern Journal of Philosophy* Supplement 27: 49–88.

—— (1991) 'The Structure of Aristotelian Happiness', *Ethics* 101: 382–91.

—— (1991a) 'Aristippus against Happiness', *Monist* 74: 55–82.

—— (1992) 'Plato: The Intellectual Background', in R. Kraut (ed.) *The Cambridge Companion to Plato*. Cambridge: Cambridge University Press: 51–89.

—— (1995) *Plato's Ethics*, Oxford: Oxford University Press.

—— (1995a) 'Prudence and Morality in Greek Ethics', *Ethics* 105: 284–95.

—— (1998) 'Socratic Paradox and Stoic Theory', in S. Everson (ed.) *Companions to Ancient Thought*, Vol. 4: *Ethics*, Cambridge: Cambridge University Press: 151–92.

—— (1999 [1985]) *Aristotle: Nicomachean Ethics*, Second edition, translated with introduction, notes, and glossary, Indianapolis: Hackett.

—— (2000) 'Ethics as an Inexact Science: Aristotle's Ambitions for Moral Theory', in B. Hooker and M. Little (eds) *Moral Particularism*, Oxford: Oxford University Press: 100–29.

—— (2003) 'Stoic Naturalism and Its Critics', in B. Inwood (ed.) *The Cambridge Companion to the Stoics*, Cambridge: Cambridge University Press: 345–64.

—— (2004) 'Aristoteles e seus interpretes sobre kalon e honestum', *Analytica* 8(2): 31–47.

Jackson-McCabe, M. (2004) 'The Stoic Theory of Implanted Preconceptions', *Phronesis* 49(4): 323–47.

Johnson, K. (1997) 'Luck and Good Fortune in the *Eudemian Ethics*', *Ancient Philosophy* 17: 85–102.

Jones, H. (1989) *The Epicurean Tradition*, London: Routledge.

Jones, H. S. and J. E. Powell (eds) (1958–60) *Thucydidis Historiae* (Oxford Classical Texts). Oxford: Clarendon Press.

Jones, M.-H. (1997) 'Moral Education and Moral Degeneration in Plato's Republic' (unpublished dissertation), University of Pennsylvania.

Joseph, H. W. B. (1935) *Essays in Ancient and Modern Philosophy*, Oxford: Oxford University Press.

Jost, L. J. (ed.) (2002) *Eudaimonia and Well-Being: Ancient and Modern Conceptions*, Edmonton: Academic Printing and Publishing.

Kaibel, G. (ed.) (1887) *Athenaei Naucratitae Dipnosophistarum Libri XV* [*Deipnosophistae*] Leipzig: Teubner.

Kahn, C. H. (1981) 'Did Plato Write Socratic Dialogues?' *Classical Quarterly* 31: 305–20.

—— (1983) 'Arius as Doxographer', in W. Fortenbaugh (ed.) *On Stoic and Peripatetic Ethics: The Work of Arius Didymus*, New Brunswick, NJ: Transaction Books: 3–13.

—— (1983a) 'Drama and Dialectic in Plato's *Gorgias*', *Oxford Studies in Ancient Philosophy* 1: 175–221.

—— (1992) 'Vlastos' Socrates: A Review of Gregory Vlastos, *Socrates: Ironist and Moral Philosopher*', *Phronesis* 37: 233–58.

—— (1996) *Plato and the Socratic Dialogue*, Cambridge: Cambridge University Press.

—— (1998) 'Pre-Platonic Ethics', in S. Everson (ed.) *Companions to Ancient Thought, Vol. 4: Ethics*, Cambridge: Cambridge University Press: 27–48.

Kaster, R. (2005) *Emotion, Restraint, and Community in Ancient Rome*, New York: Oxford University Press.

Kaufman, F. (1995) 'An Answer to Lucretius' Symmetry Argument against Fear of Death', *Journal of Value Inquiry* 29: 57–64.

Kenny, A. (1978) *The Aristotelian Ethics: A Study of the Relationship between the Eudemian and Nicomachean Ethics of Aristotle*, Oxford: Clarendon Press.

—— (1979) *Aristotle's Theory of the Will*, London: Duckworth.

—— (1988) 'Aristotle on Moral Luck:', in J. Dancy, J. M. E. Moravcsik and C. C. W. Taylor (eds) *Human Agency: Language, Duty, and Value*, Stanford, CA: Stanford University Press: 105–19.

—— (1991) 'The Nicomachean Conception of Happiness', *Oxford Studies in Ancient Philosophy* Supplement: 67–80.

—— (1992) *Aristotle on the Perfect Life*, Oxford: Clarendon Press.

Kerferd, G. B. (1971) 'Epicurus' Doctrine of the Soul', *Phronesis* 16: 80–96.

—— (1981) *The Sophistic Movement*, Cambridge: Cambridge University Press.

—— (1997) 'The Sophists', in C. C. W. Taylor (ed.) *From the Beginning to Plato*, London: Routledge: 244–70.

Keyser, P. (1991) 'Review of *Recounting Plato* by G. Ledger', *Bryn Mawr Classical Review* 2(7): 402–27.

—— (1992) 'Review of *The Chronology of Plato's Dialogues* by L. Brandwood', *Bryn Mawr Classical Review* 3(1): 58–74.

Keyt, D. (1983) 'Intellectualism in Aristotle', in J. P. Anton and A. Preus (eds) *Essays in Ancient Greek Philosophy*, Vol. 2, Albany, NY: State University of New York Press: 364–87.

—— (1989) 'The Meaning of *bios* in Aristotle's Ethics and Politics', *Ancient Philosophy* 9: 15–21.

—— (2006) 'Plato on Justice', in H. Benson (ed.) *The Blackwell Companion to Plato*, Oxford: Basil Blackwell: 341–55.

Kidd, I. G. (1955) 'Stoic Intermediates and the End for Man', *Classical Quarterly* 5: 181–94. Reprinted in A. A. Long, (1971, reprinted 1996) *Problems in Stoicism*, London: 1971: 150–72.

—— (1987) 'Moral Action and Rules in Stoicism', in J. Rist (ed.) *The Stoics*, Berkeley: University of California Press.

King, J. E. (1971) *Cicero: Tusculan Disputations*, with an English translation, Cambridge, MA: Harvard University Press.

Kirwan, C. A. (1963) 'Glaucon's Challenge', *Phronesis* 10: 162–73.

—— (1990) 'Two Aristotelian Theses About Eudaimonia', in A. Alberti (ed.) *Studi sull' Etica di Aristotele*, Naples: Bibliopolis: 149–92.

Klein, J. (1965) *A Commentary on Plato's Meno*, Chapel Hill: University of North Carolina Press.

Klosko, G. (1981) 'The Technical Conception of Virtue', *Journal of the History of Philosophy* 19: 95–102.

—— (1987) 'Socrates on Goods and Happiness', *History of Philosophy Quarterly* 4: 251–64.

Koetschau, P. (ed.) (1913) *Origen, De Principiis*. Leipzig: Hinrichs.

Konstan, D. (1993) 'Friendship from Epicurus to Philodemus', in G. Giannantoni and M. Gigante (eds) *Epicureismo Greco e Romano*, Naples: Bibliopolis, I: 387–96.

—— (2006) 'Epicurean "Passions" and the Good Life', in B. Reis and S. Haffmans (eds) *The Virtuous Life in Greek Ethics*, Cambridge: Cambridge University Press: 194–205.

Kosman, L. A. (1980) 'Being Properly Affected: Virtues and Feelings in Aristotle's Ethics', in A. O. Rorty (ed.) *Essays on Aristotle's Ethics*, Berkeley: University of California Press: 103–16.

Kraut, R. (1973) 'Reason and Justice in Plato's Republic', in E. N. Lee, A. P. D. Mourelatos and R. M. Rorty (eds) *Exegesis and Argument: Studies in Greek Philosophy Presented to Gregory Vlastos, Phronesis* Suppl. Vol. 1, Assen: Van Gorcum: 207–24.

—— (1979) 'The Peculiar Function of Human Beings', *Canadian Journal of Philosophy* 9: 467–78.

—— (1979a) 'Two Conceptions of Happiness', *The Philosophical Review* 88: 167–97.

—— (1989) *Aristotle on the Human Good*, Princeton, NJ: Princeton University Press.

—— (1992) 'The Defense of Justice in the Republic', in R. Kraut (ed.) *The Cambridge Companion to Plato*, Cambridge: Cambridge University Press: 311–37.

—— (1993) 'In Defense of the Grand End: Review of Sarah Broadie, *Ethics with Aristotle*' *Ethics* 103: 361–74.

—— (1998) 'Aristotle on Method and Moral Education', in J. Gentzler (ed.) *Method in Ancient Philosophy*, Oxford: Clarendon Press: 271–90.

—— (2006) 'How to Justify Ethical Propositions: Aristotle's Method', in R. Kraut (ed.) *The Blackwell Guide to Aristotle's Nicomachean Ethics*, Oxford: Basil Blackwell: 76–95.

—— (2006a) 'Doing without Morality: Reflections on the Meaning of "*dein*" in Aristotle's *Nicomachean Ethics*', *Oxford Studies in Ancient Philosophy* 30: 169–200.

Kühn, K. G. (1821–33) *Claudii Galeni Opera omnia*, Leipzig: Teubner (reprint 1965 Hildesheim: G. Olms).

Kurz, D. (1970) *Akribeia: Das Ideal Der Exaktheit bei den Griechen bis Aristoteles*, Göppingen: Kmmerle.

Laks, A. and M. Schofield (eds) (1997) *Justice and Generosity: Studies in Hellenistic Social and Political Philosophy*, Proceedings of the Sixth Symposium Hellenisticum, Cambridge: Cambridge University Press.

Lane, M. S. (1998) *Method and Politics in Plato's Statesman*, Cambridge: Cambridge University Press.

Lännström, A. (2006) *Loving the Fine: Virtue and Happiness in Aristotle's Ethics*, Notre Dame, IN: University of Notre Dame Press.

Lawrence, G. (1988) 'Akrasia and Clear-Eyed Akrasia in *Nicomachean Ethics* 7', *Revue de Philosophie Ancienne* 6: 77–106.

—— (1993) 'Aristotle and the Ideal Life', *Philosophical Review* 102: 1–34.

—— (1997) 'Nonaggregatability, Inclusiveness, and the Theory of Focal Value: *Nicomachean Ethics* I,7.1097b16–20', *Phronesis* 42: 32–76.

—— (2001) 'The Function of the Function Argument', *Ancient Philosophy* 21: 445–75.

—— (2003) 'Snakes in Paradise: Problems in the Ideal Life', *Southern Journal of Philosophy* 43: 126–65.

—— (2006) 'Human Good and Human Function', in R. Kraut (ed.) *The Blackwell Guide to Aristotle's Nicomachean Ethics*, Oxford: Basil Blackwell: 37–75.

Ledbetter, G. (1994) 'The Propositional Content of Stoic Emotions', in K. Boudouris (ed.) *Hellenistic Philosophy*, Athens: International Center for Greek Philosophy and Culture: 107–13.

Lee, E. N., A. P. D. Mourelatos and R. M. Rorty (eds) (1973) *Exegesis and Argument: Studies in Greek Philosophy Presented to Gregory Vlastos, Phronesis* Suppl. Vol. 1, Assen: Van Gorcum.

Leighton, S. R. (1995) 'The Mean Relative to Us', in R. Bosely, R. A. Shiner and J. D. Sisson (eds) *Aristotle, Virtue and the Mean*, Edmonton: Academic Publishing, and *Apeiron* 25(4): 67–78.

Lennox, J. (1999) 'Aristotle on the Biological Roots of Virtue: The Natural History of Natural Virtue', in J. Maienschein and M. Ruse (eds) *Biology and the Foundations of Ethics*, Cambridge: Cambridge University Press: 10–31.

Lesses, G. (1989) 'Virtue and the Goods of Fortune in Stoic Moral Theory', *Oxford Studies in Ancient Philosophy* 7: 95–127.

—— (2002) 'Happiness, Completeness, and Indifference to Death in Epicurean Ethical Theory', in L. J. Jost (ed.) *Eudaimonia and Well-Being: Ancient and Modern Conceptions*, Edmonton: Academic Printing and Publishing: 57–68.

Lippitt, J. (2005) 'Is a Sense of Humour a Virtue?' *Monist* 88(1): 72–92.

Lloyd, A. C. (1978) 'Emotions and Decision in Stoic Psychology', in J. Rist (ed.) *The Stoics*, Berkeley: University of California Press: 233–46.

Lloyd, G. E. R. (1968) 'The Role of Medical and Biological Analogies in Aristotle's Ethics', *Phronesis* 13: 68–83.

Lockwood, T. (2005) 'A Topical Bibliography of Scholarship on Aristotle's Nicomachean Ethics: 1880 to 2004', *Journal of Philosophical Research* 30(1): 1–116.

Long, A. A. (ed.) (1971) *Problems in Stoicism*, London: Athlone Press.

—— (1983) 'Arius Didymus and the Exposition of Stoic Ethics', in W. Fortenbaugh (ed.) *On Stoic and Peripatetic Ethics: The Work of Arius Didymus*, New Brunswick, NJ: Transaction Books: 41–66.

—— (1986) 'Pleasure and Social Utility – the Virtues of Being Epicurean', *Aspects de la Philosophie Hellénistique, Entretiens Hardt* 32: 283–324.

—— (1986a) *Hellenistic Philosophy: Stoics, Epicureans, Sceptics*, Berkeley: University of California Press.

—— (1988) 'Socrates in Hellenistic Philosophy', *Classical Quarterly* 38: 150–71.

—— (1988a) 'Stoic Eudaimonism', *Boston Area Colloquium in Ancient Philosophy* 4: 77–101.

—— (1991) 'The Harmonics of Stoic Virtue', *Oxford Studies in Ancient Philosophy* Supplement: 97–116.

—— (1992) 'Cyrenaics', *Encyclopedia of Ethics*, 1, L. Becker (ed.) New York: Garland: 370–2.

—— (1993) 'Hierocles on *Oikeiôsis* and Self-Perception', in K. Boudouris (ed.) *Hellenistic Philosophy*, Athens: International Center for Greek Philosophy and Culture.

—— (1996) *Stoic Studies*, Cambridge: Cambridge University Press.

—— (1999) 'The Socratic Legacy', in K. Algra, J. Barnes, J. Mansfeld and M. Schofield (eds) *The Cambridge History of Hellenistic Philosophy*, New York: Cambridge University Press: 617–41.

—— (1999a) 'Stoic Psychology', in K. Algra, J. Barnes, J. Mansfeld and M. Schofield (eds) *The Cambridge History of Hellenistic Philosophy*, New York: Cambridge University Press: 560–84.

—— (2002) *Epictetus: A Stoic and Socratic Guide to Life*, Oxford: Clarendon Press.

Long, A. A. and D. N. Sedley (1987) *The Hellenistic Philosophers*, 2 vols, Cambridge: Cambridge University Press.

Long, H. S. (ed.) (1964) *Diogenes Laertius: Vitae Philosophorum*, Oxford Classical Texts. Oxford: Clarendon Press.

Lorenz, H. (2004) 'Desire and Reason in Plato's Republic', *Oxford Studies in Ancient Philosophy* 27(Winter): 83–116.

Lories, D. (1998) *Le Sens Commun et Le Jugement du Phronimos: Aristote et Les Stoïciens*, Louvain: Peeters.

Losin, P. (1987) 'Aristotle's Doctrine of the Mean', *History of Philosophy Quarterly* 4(3): 329–41.

Louden, R. B. (1991) 'Aristotle's Practical Particularism', *Essays in Ancient Greek Philosophy*, Vol. 4: *Aristotle's Ethics*, A. J. and A. Preus (eds) Albany, NY: State University of New York Press: 159–78.

Lovibond, S. (1991) 'Plato's Theory of Mind', in S. Everson (ed.) *Companions to Ancient Thought*, Vol. 2: *Psychology*, Cambridge: Cambridge University Press: 35–55.

Lynch, J. P. (1972) *Aristotle's School: A Study of a Greek Educational Institution*, Berkeley: University of California Press.

MacIntyre, A. (1981; Second edition 1984) *After Virtue: A Study in Moral Theory* London: Duckworth.

MacKendrick, P. (1989) *The Philosophical Books of Cicero*, London: Duckworth.

Marrou, H. I. (1956) *A History of Education in Antiquity*, New York: Sheed & Ward.

Marshall, P. K. (ed.) (1968) *A. Gellii Noctes Atticae*, Oxford Classical Texts. Oxford: Clarendon Press.

Matthews, G. (2006) 'Socratic Ignorance', in H. Benson (ed.) *The Blackwell Companion to Plato*, Oxford: Basil Blackwell: 103–18.

McCabe, M. M. (2005) 'Extend or Identify: Two Stoic Accounts of Altruism', in R. Salles (ed.) *Metaphysics, Soul, and Ethics in Ancient Thought*, Oxford: Oxford University Press: 413–43.

McDowell, J. (1979) 'Virtue and Reason', *Monist* 62: 330–50.

—— (1980) 'The Role of Eudaimonia in Aristotle's Ethics', in A. O. Rorty (ed.) *Essays on Aristotle's Ethics*, Berkeley: University of California Press: 359–76.

—— (1996) 'Deliberation and Moral Development in Aristotle's Ethics', in S. Engstrom and J. Whiting (eds) *Aristotle, Kant and the Stoics: Rethinking Happiness and Duty*, Cambridge: Cambridge University Press.

—— (1996a) 'Incontinence and Practical Wisdom in Aristotle', in S. Lovibond and S. G. Williams (eds) *Identity, Truth and Value: Essays for David Wiggins*, Oxford: Basil Blackwell: 95–112.

—— (1998) 'Some Issues in Aristotle's Moral Psychology', in S. Everson (ed.) *Companions to Ancient Thought*, Vol. 4: *Ethics*, Cambridge: Cambridge University Press: 107–28.

McKirahan, V. T. (1994) 'The Socratic Origins of the Cynics and Cyrenaics', in P. Vander Waerdt (ed.) *The Socratic Movement*, Ithaca, NY and London: Cornell University Press: 367–91.

—— (1996) 'Epicurean Attitudes to Management and Finance', in G. Giannantoni and M. Gigante (eds) *Epicureismo Greco E Romano* Naples: Bibliopolis, II: 701–14.

McPherran, M. (2005) ' "What Even a Child Would Know": Socrates, Luck, and Providence at Euthydemus 277d–282e', *Ancient Philosophy* 25(1): 49–63.

McTighe, K. (1984) 'Socrates on the Desire for Good and the Involuntariness of Wrongdoing', *Phronesis* 29: 193–236.

Mele, A. R. (1981) 'Aristotle on Akrasia and Knowledge', *The Modern Schoolman* 58: 137–59.

—— (1981a) 'The Practical Syllogism and Deliberation in Aristotle's Causal Theory of Action', *The New Scholasticism* 55: 281–316.

—— (1984) 'Aristotle on the Roles of Reason in Motivation and Justification', *Archiv für Geschichte der Philosophie* 66: 124–47.

—— (1984a) 'Aristotle's Wish', *Journal of the History of Philosophy* 22: 139–56.

Menn, S. (1995) 'Physics as a Virtue', *Proceedings of the Boston Area Colloquium in Ancient Philosophy* 11: 1–34.

—— (2005) 'On Plato's *Politeia*', *Proceedings of the Boston Area Colloquium in Ancient Philosophy* 21: 1–55.

Merlan, P. (1960) *Studies in Epicurus and Aristotle*, Wiesbaden: O. Harrassowitz.

Métivier, P. (2000) *L'Éthique dans le Project Moral d'Aristote: Une Philosophie du Bien sur le Modèle des Arts et Techniques*, Paris: Cerf.

Meyer, S. S. (1993) *Aristotle on Moral Responsibility: Character and Cause*, Oxford: Basil Blackwell.

—— (1994) 'Moral Responsibility: Aristotle and After', in S. Everson (ed.) *Companions to Ancient Thought*, Vol. 4: *Ethics*, Cambridge: Cambridge University Press: 221–40.

—— (1998) 'Ethics and the History of Philosophy: A Critical Discussion of Jennifer Whiting and Stephen Engstrom (eds) *Aristotle, Kant, and the Stoics: Rethinking Happiness and Duty*', *Apeiron* 31(1): 75–98.

—— (1999) 'Fate, Fatalism, and Agency in Stoicism', *Social Philosophy and Policy* 16(2): 250–73.

—— (2003) 'Review of Susanne Bobzien, Determinism and Freedom in Stoic Philosophy', *The Philosophical Review* 112: 117–20.

—— (2005) 'Class Assignment and the Principle of Specialization in Plato's Republic', *Proceedings of the Boston Area Colloquium in Ancient Philosophy* 20(Summer): 229–43.

—— (2006) 'Aristotle on the Voluntary', in R. Kraut (ed.) *The Blackwell Guide to Aristotle's Nicomachean Ethics*, Oxford: Basil Blackwell: 137–57.

Miller, F. D. (1976) 'Epicurus on the Art of Dying', *Southern Journal of Philosophy* 14: 169–77.

Mitsis, P. (1987) 'Epicurus on Friendship and Altruism', *Oxford Studies in Ancient Philosophy* 5: 127–53.

—— (1988) *Epicurus' Ethical Theory: The Pleasures of Invulnerability*, Ithaca, NY: Cornell University Press.

—— (1989) 'Epicurus on Death and the Duration of Life', *Proceedings of the Boston Area Colloquium in Ancient Philosophy* 4: 295–314.

—— (1993) 'Epicurus on Death and the Deprivations of Death', in G. Giannantoni and M. Gigante (eds) *Epicureismo Greco e Romano*, Naples: Bibliopolis, II: 805–112.

—— (1993a) 'Seneca on Reason, Rules and Moral Development', in J. Brunschwig and M. Nussbaum (eds) *Passions and Perceptions: Studies in Hellenistic Philosophy of Mind*, Cambridge: Cambridge University Press: 285–312.

—— (1994) 'Natural Law and Natural Right in Post-Aristotelian Philosophy: The Stoics and their Critics', *Aufstieg und Niedergang der Romischen Welt* II 36(7): 4812–50.

—— (1999) 'The Stoic Origin of Natural Rights', in K. Ierodiakonou (ed.) *Topics in Stoic Philosophy*, Oxford: Clarendon Press: 153–77.

—— (2002) 'Happiness and Death in Epicurean Ethics', in L. J. Jost and R. Shiner (eds) *Eudaimonia and Well-Being: Ancient and Modern Conceptions*, *Apeiron* 35 (Special Issue): 41–55.

Mitsis, P and J. DiFilippo (1994) 'Socrates and Stoic Natural Law', in P. Vander Waerdt (ed.) *The Socratic Tradition*, Ithaca, NY: Cornell University Press: 252–71.

Molager, L. (ed.) (1971) *Cicéron: Les Paradoxes Des Stoïciens*. Paris: Belles Lettres.

Moline, J. N. (1989) 'Aristotle on Praise and Blame', *Archiv für Geschichte der Philosophie* 71: 283–302.

Monan, J. D. (1968) *Moral Knowledge and Its Methodology in Aristotle*, Oxford: Clarendon Press.

Moravcsik, J. (ed.) (1967) *Aristotle: A Collection of Critical Essays*, Garden City, NY: Anchor Books.

Morford, M. (2002) *The Roman Philosophers: From the Time of Cato the Censor to the Death of Marcus Aurelius*, London: Routledge.

Morreschini, C. (ed.) (2005) *M Tullius Cicero de Finibus Bonorum et Malorum*, Leipzig and Munich: K. G. Saur Verlag.

Morrow, G. (1960) *Plato's Cretan City: A Historical Interpretation of the Laws*, Princeton, NJ: Princeton University Press.

Moss, J. (2005) 'Shame, Pleasure, and the Divided Soul', *Oxford Studies in Ancient Philosophy* 29(Winter): 137–170.

Mras, K. (ed.) (1954–56) *Eusebius, Die Praeparatio Evangelica*. Berlin: Akademie-Verlag.

Müller, A. W. (2004) 'Aristotle's Conception of Ethical and Natural Virtue: How the Unity Thesis Sheds Light on the Doctrine of the Mean', in J. Szaif and M. Lutz-Bachmann (eds) *What Is Good for a Human Being?* New York: Walter de Gruyter: 18–53.

Murphy, N. R. (1962) *The Interpretation of Plato's Republic*, Oxford: Oxford University Press.

Mutschmann, H. (ed.) (1912–54) *Sexti Empirici Opera*. Leipzig: Teubner.

Nails, D. (1995) *Agora, Academy, and the Conduct of Philosophy*, Dordrecht and Boston: Kluwer Academic Publishing.

—— (2002) *The People of Plato: A Prosopography of Plato and Other Socratics*, Indianapolis: Hackett.

Nannery, L. (1983) 'The Problem of the Two Lives in Aristotle's Ethics: The Human Good and the Best Life for a Man', *International Philosophical Quarterly* 21: 277–93.

Natali, C. (1987) '*Adoleschia, Leptologia* and the Philosophers in Athens', *Phronesis* 32: 232–41.

—— (2001) *The Wisdom of Aristotle*, trans. G. Parks, Albany: State University of New York Press (revised version with new afterword of *La saggezza di Aristotele*, Naples: Bibliopolis, 1989).

—— (2004) 'Por que Aristoteles escreveu o livro III da *EN*?' *Analytica* 8(2): 47–75.

Nehamas, A. (1975) 'Confusing Universals and Particulars in Plato's Early Dialogues', *Review of Metaphysics* 29: 287–306.

—— (1990) 'Eristic, Antilogic, Sophistic, Dialectic: Plato's Demarcation of Philosophy from Sophistry', *History of Philosophy Quarterly*, January 1990: 3–16. Reprinted in *The Virtues of Authenticity*, Princeton, NJ: Princeton University Press, 1999: 108–24.

—— (1986) 'Socratic Intellectualism', *Proceedings of the Boston Area Colloquium in Ancient Philosophy* 2: 275–316. Reprinted in *The Virtues of Authenticity*, Princeton, NJ: Princeton University Press, 1999: 24–58.

Nestle, D. (1972). 'Freiheit' *Reallexikon für Antike und Christentum*, T. Klauser *et al.* (eds), Stuttgart: A. Hiersemann: 269–306.

Nettleship, R. L. (1901) *Lectures on the Republic of Plato*, London: Macmillan.

Nightingale, A. (1995) *Genres in Dialogue: Plato and the Construct of Philosophy*, New York: Cambridge University Press.

Nussbaum, M. (1986) 'Therapeutic Arguments: Epicurus and Aristotle', in M. Schofield and G. Striker (eds) *The Norms of Nature: Studies in Hellenistic Ethics*, New York: Cambridge University Press: 31–74.

—— (1987) 'The Stoics on the Extirpation of the Passions', *Apeiron* 20(2): 129–78. Reprinted as Chapter 10 of *The Therapy of Desire: Theory and Practice in Hellenistic Ethics*, Princeton, NJ: Princeton University Press, 1994.

—— (1993) 'Non-Relative Virtues: An Aristotelian Approach', in M. C. Nussbaum and A. Sen (eds) *The Quality of Life*, Oxford: Clarendon Press.

—— (1994) *The Therapy of Desire: Theory and Practice in Hellenistic Ethics*, Princeton, NJ: Princeton University Press.

Obbink, D. (1996) *Philodemus, on Piety*, Part I, critical text with commentary, Oxford: Clarendon Press.

O'Connor, D. (1989) 'The Invulnerable Pleasure of Epicurean Friendship', *Greek, Roman, and Byzantine Studies* 30: 165–86.

O' Keefe, T. (2003) 'Lucretius on the Cycle of Life and the Fear of Death', *Apeiron* 36(1): 43–65.

Osborne, R. (1997) 'The Polis and its Culture', in C. C. W. Taylor (ed.) *From the Beginning to Plato*, London: Routledge.

Osler, M. J. (ed.) (1991) *Atoms, Pneuma, and Tranquility*, Cambridge: Cambridge University Press.

Ott, W. (2006) 'Aristotle and Plato on Character', *Ancient Philosophy* 26(1): 65–79.

Owens, J. (1981) 'The *Kalon* in Aristotelian Ethics', in D. J. O'Meara (ed.) *Studies in Aristotle*, Washington, DC: Catholic University of America Press: 261–78.

Pakaluk, M. (2005) *Aristotle's Nicomachean Ethics: An Introduction*, New York: Cambridge University Press.

Parry, R. (2001) 'Eudaimonia, Eudaimonism', in L. Becker (ed.) *Encyclopedia of Ethics*, New York: Routledge: 489–92.

Pembroke, S. G. (1971) 'Oikeiosis', in A. A. Long (ed.) *Problems in Stoicism*, London: Athlone Press: 114–49.

Penner, T. (1971) 'Thought and Desire in Plato', in G. Vlastos (ed.) *Plato* II, Garden City, NY: Anchor Books, 2: 96–118.

—— (1973) 'Socrates on Virtue and Motivation', in E. N. Lee, A. P. D. Mourelatos and R. M. Rorty (eds) *Exegesis and Argument: Studies in Greek Philosophy Presented to Gregory Vlastos. Phronesis* Suppl. Vol. 1, Assen: Van Gorcum: 133–51.

Plasberg, O. (ed.) (1908) *Cicero: Paradoxa Stoicorum*. Leipzig: Teubner.

—— (ed.) (1922) *Cicero, Academica*. Leipzig: Teubner.

Pohlenz, M. (1948) *Die Stoa*, Göttingen: Vandenhoeck & Ruprecht.

Pohlenz, M. and R. Westman (eds) (1959) *Plutarch: Moralia* Vol. VI.2, Leipzig: Teubner.

Pomeroy, A. J. (ed.) (1999) *Arius Didymus: Epitome of Stoic Ethics*, text and translation, Graeco-Roman Religion Series, Atlanta, GA: Society of Biblical Literature.

Powell, J. G. (ed.) (1995) *Cicero the Philosopher*, Oxford: Clarendon Press.

Price, A. W. (2005) 'Aristotelian Virtue and Practical Judgement', in C. Gill (ed.) *Virtue, Norms, and Objectivity: Issues in Ancient and Modern Ethics*, Oxford: Clarendon Press: 257–78.

—— (2005a) 'Were Zeno and Chrysippus at Odds in Analysing Emotion?', in R. Salles (ed.) *Metaphysics, Soul, and Ethics in Ancient Thought*, Oxford: Oxford University Press: 471–88.

—— (2006) 'Acrasia and Self-Control', in R. Kraut (ed.) *The Blackwell Guide to Aristotle's Nicomachean Ethics*, Oxford: Basil Blackwell: 234–54.

Prince, S. (2006) 'Socrates, Antisthenes, and the Cynics', in S. Ahbel-Rappe and R. M. Kamtekar (eds) *A Companion to Socrates*, Oxford: Basil Blackwell: 75–92.

Prior, W. J. (1991) *Virtue and Knowledge: An Introduction to Ancient Greek Ethics*, London: Routledge.

Purrington, J. S. (1993) 'Epicurus on the Telos', *Phronesis* 38: 281–320.

Raaflaub, K. (2004) *The Discovery of Freedom in Ancient Greece*, [*Die Entdeckung Der Freiheit* (Munich: Beck, 1985) revised and updated], trans. R. Franciscono, Chicago: University of Chicago Press.

Ramsay, H. (1998) 'Natural Virtue', *Dialogue* 37(2): 341–60.

Rapp, C. (2006) 'What Use Is Aristotle's Doctrine of the Mean?' in B. Reis and S. Haffmans (eds) *The Virtuous Life in Greek Ethics*, Cambridge: Cambridge University Press: 99–126.

Reeve, C. D. C. (1988) *Philosopher Kings: The Argument of Plato's Republic*, Princeton, NJ: Princeton University Press.

—— (1995) *Practices of Reason: Aristotle's Nicomachean Ethics*, Oxford: Oxford University Press.

—— (2006) 'Aristotle on the Virtues of Thought', in R. Kraut (ed.) *The Blackwell Guide to Aristotle's Nicomachean Ethics*, Oxford: Basil Blackwell: 198–217.

Reynolds, L. D. (ed.) (1965) *L. Annaei Senecae Ad Lucilium Epistulae Morales* (Oxford Classical Texts), Oxford: Clarendon Press.

—— (ed.) (1977) *L. Annaei Senecae Dialogi* (Oxford Classical Texts), Oxford: Clarendon Press.

—— (ed.) (1998) *M. Tullius Ciceronis de Finibus Bonorum et Malorum Libri Quinque*, Oxford: Oxford University Press.

Richardson Lear, G. (2004) *Happy Lives and the Highest Good: An Essay on Aristotle's Nicomachean Ethics*, Princeton, NJ: Princeton University Press.

—— (2006) 'Aristotle on Moral Virtue and the Fine', in R. Kraut (ed.) *The Blackwell Guide to Aristotle's Nicomachean Ethics*, Oxford: Basil Blackwell: 116–36.

—— (2006a) 'Plato on Learning to Love Beauty', in G. Santas (ed.) *The Blackwell Guide to Plato's Republic*, Oxford: Basil Blackwell: 104–24.

Rist, J. (1972) *Epicurus: An Introduction*, Cambridge: Cambridge University Press.

—— (ed.) (1978) *The Stoics*, Berkeley: University of California Press.

—— (1980) 'Epicurus on Friendship', *Classical Philology* 75: 121–9.

—— (1989) 'Seneca and Stoic Orthodoxy', *Aufstieg und Niedergang der römischen Welt* II 36(3): 1993–2012.

Roberts, J. (1987) 'Plato on the Causes of Wrongdoing in the Laws', *Ancient Philosophy* 7: 23–37.

—— (1989) 'Aristotle on Responsibility for Action and Character', *Ancient Philosophy* 9: 23–36.

—— (1989a) 'Political Animals in the *Nicomachean Ethics*', *Phronesis* 34(2): 185–204.

Roberts, R. C. (1989) 'Aristotle on Virtues and Emotions', *Philosophical Studies* 56: 293–306.

Robinson, R. (1969). 'Aristotle on Akrasia', in his *Essays in Greek Philosophy*, Oxford, Clarendon Press: 139–60. Reprinted in J. Barnes *et al.* (eds) (1977) *Articles on Aristotle*, Vol. 2: *Ethics and Politics*, London: Duckworth: 79–91.

Roche, T. (1988) '*Ergon* and *Eudaimonia* in *Nicomachean Ethics* I: Reconsidering the Intellectualist Interpretation', *Journal of the History of Philosophy* 26: 175–94.

—— (1988a) 'On the Alleged Metaphysical Foundations of Aristotle's Ethics', *Ancient Philosophy* 8: 49–62.

—— (1995) 'The Ultimate End of Action: A Critique of Richard Kraut's *Aristotle on the Human Good*', in M. Sim (ed.) *The Crossroads of Norm and Nature: Essays on Aristotle's Ethics and Metaphysics*, Lanham, MD: Rowman & Littlefield: 115–38; with reply by Richard Kraut: 139–48.

Rogers, K. (1993) 'Aristotle's Conception of *to kalon*', *Ancient Philosophy* 13: 355–71.

Roller, M. (2004) 'Exemplarity in Roman Culture', *Classical Philology* 99(1): 1–56.

Rorty, A. O. (ed.) (1980) *Essays on Aristotle's Ethics*, Berkeley: University of California Press.

Rosenbaum, S. (1986) 'How to Be Dead and Not Care: A Defense of Epicurus', *American Philosophical Quarterly* 23: 217–25.

—— (1989) 'Epicurus and Annihilation', *The Philosophical Quarterly* 37: 81–90.

—— (1989a) 'The Symmetry Argument: Lucretius against the Fear of Death', *Philosophy and Phenomenological Research* 50: 353–74.

—— (1990) 'Epicurus on Pleasure and the Complete Life', *The Monist* 73(1): 21–41.

Ross, W. D. (1925) *Aristotle: Nicomachean Ethics*, translated with introduction, Oxford: Oxford University Press.

Rowe, C. (1971) *The Eudemian and Nicomachean Ethics – a Study in the Development of Aristotle's Thought*, Cambridge: Cambridge University Press.

—— (1975) 'A Reply to John Cooper on the *Magna Moralia*', *American Journal of Philology* 96: 160–72.

—— (1984) *Plato*, New York: St. Martin's Press.

—— (1995) *Plato: Statesman*, text with translation and commentary, Warminster: Aris & Phillips.

—— (2005) 'What Difference Do Forms Make for Platonic Epistemology?', in C. Gill (ed.) *Virtue, Norms, and Objectivity: Issues in Ancient and Modern Ethics*, Oxford: Clarendon Press: 215–32.

Rowe, C. and S. Broadie (2002) *Aristotle: Nicomachean Ethics*, translation and introduction by Christopher Rowe and commentary by Sarah Broadie, Oxford: Oxford University Press.

Rowe, C. and M. Schofield (eds) (2000) *The Cambridge History of Greek and Roman Political Thought*, Cambridge: Cambridge University Press.

Rudebusch, G. (1999) *Socrates, Pleasure, and Value*, New York: Oxford University Press.

Russell, D. C. (2000) 'Epicurus and Lucretius on Saving Agency', *Phoenix* 54: 226–43.

—— (2004) 'Virtue As "Likeness to God" In Plato and Seneca', *Journal of the History of Philosophy* 42(3): 241–60.

Sachs, D. (1963) 'A Fallacy in Plato's Republic', *The Philosophical Review* 72: 141–58.

Salkever, S. (1990) *Finding the Mean: Theory and Practice in Aristotelian Philosophy*, Princeton, NJ: Princeton University Press.

Salles, R. (2001) 'Compatibilism: Stoic and Modern', *Archiv für Geschichte der Philosophie* 83: 1–23.

—— (2005) *The Stoics on Determinism and Compatibilism*, Burlington, VT: Ashgate.

Sandbach, F. (1971) 'Ennoia and Prolêpsis', in A. A. Long (ed.) *Problems in Stoicism*, London: Athlone Press: 22–37.

Sandbach, F. (1975) *The Stoics*, London: Chatto & Windus.

—— (1985) *Aristotle and the Stoics*, Cambridge: Cambridge Philological Society.

Santas, G. (1964) 'The Socratic Paradoxes', *The Philosophical Review* 73: 147–64.

—— (1969) 'Aristotle on Practical Inference, the Explanation of Action, and Akrasia', *Phronesis* 14: 162–89.

—— (2001) *Goodness and Justice: Plato, Aristotle, and the Moderns*, Oxford: Basil Blackwell.

—— (ed.) (2006) *The Blackwell Guide to Plato's Republic*, Oxford: Basil Blackwell.

Saunders, T. (1968) 'The Socratic Paradoxes in Plato's *Laws*', *Hermes* 96: 421–34.

Sauvé, S. (1988) 'Why Involuntary Actions Are Painful', *Southern Journal of Philosophy* 27 (Supplement): 127–58.

Sbordone, F. (ed.) (1947) *Philodemus: Adversus Sophistas*. Naples: Loffredo.

Schenkl, H. (ed.) (1916) *Epicteti Dissertationes ab Arriano Digestae, Fragmenta, Enchiridion*, Leipzig: Teubner.

210

Schofield, M. (1980) 'Preconception, Argument, and God', in M. Schofield, M. Burnyeat and J. Barnes (eds) *Doubt and Dogmatism: Studies in Hellenistic Epistemology*, Oxford: Clarendon Press: 283–308.

—— (1983) 'The Syllogisms of Zeno of Citium', *Phronesis* 28: 31–58.

—— (1984) 'Ariston of Chios and the Unity of Virtue', *Ancient Philosophy* 4: 83–96.

—— (1991) *The Stoic Idea of the City*, Cambridge: Cambridge University Press.

—— (2003) 'Stoic Ethics', in B. Inwood (ed.) *The Cambridge Companion to the Stoics*, Cambridge: Cambridge University Press: 233–56.

—— (2004) 'Epictetus: Socratic, Cynic, Stoic', *Philosophical Quarterly* 54(216): 448–56.

Schofield, M. and G. Striker (eds) (1986) *The Norms of Nature: Studies in Hellenistic Ethics*, Cambridge: Cambridge University Press.

Scott, D. (1999) 'Aristotle on Wellbeing and Intellectual Contemplation: Primary and Secondary *Eudaimonia*', *Proceedings of the Aristotelian Society* 73(supplement): 225–42.

—— (1999a) 'Platonic Pessimism and Moral Education', *Oxford Studies in Ancient Philosophy* 17(15–36).

—— (2000) 'Plato's Critique of the Democratic Character', *Phronesis* 45(1): 19–37.

—— (2000a) 'Aristotle and Thrasymachus', *Oxford Studies in Ancient Philosophy* 19: 225–52.

Sedley, D. N. (1977) 'Diodorus Cronus and Hellenistic Philosophy', *Proceedings of the Cambridge Philological Society* 23: 74–120.

—— (1995) 'The Inferential Foundations of Epicurean Ethics', in G. Giannantoni and M. Gigante (eds) *Epicureismo Greco e Romano*, Naples: Bibliopolis: 313–39.

—— (1997) ' "Becoming Like God" In the *Timaeus* and Aristotle', in T. Calvo and L. Brisson (eds) *Interpreting the Timaeus-Critias*, Sankt Augustin: Academia Verlag: 327–39.

—— (1999) 'The Ideal of Godlikeness', in G. Fine (ed.) *Plato* II (Oxford Readings in Philosophy), Oxford: Oxford University Press: 309–28.

—— (1999a) 'The Stoic–Platonist Debate on *Kathêkonta*', in K. Ierodiakonou (ed.) *Topics in Stoic Philosophy*, Oxford: Clarendon Press: 128–52.

—— (2002) 'Diogenes of Oenoanda on Cyrenaic Hedonism', *Proceedings of the Cambridge Philological Society* 48: 159–74.

—— (2003) 'The School, from Zeno to Arius Didymus', in B. Inwood (ed.) *The Cambridge Companion to the Stoics*, Cambridge: Cambridge University Press: 7–32.

Segvic, H. (2004) 'Aristotle on the Varieties of Goodness', *Apeiron* 37(2): 151–76.

—— (2006) 'No One Errs Willingly: The Meaning of Socratic Intellectualism', *A Companion to Socrates*, S. Ahbel-Rappe and R. M. Kamtekar (eds) Oxford: Basil Blackwell: 171–85.

Shackleton Bailey, D. R. (ed.) (1987) *Cicero: Epistulae Ad Atticum*. Stuttgart: Teubner.

—— (2000) *Valerius Maximus: Memorable Deeds and Sayings*, edited and translated, Cambridge, MA: Harvard University Press.

Sharples, R. W. (1983) 'The Peripatetic Classification of Goods', in W. Fortenbaugh (ed.) *On Stoic and Peripatetic Ethics: The Work of Arius Didymus*, New Brunswick, NJ: Transaction Books: 139–59.

—— (1983a) *Alexander of Aphrodisias: On Fate*, text, translation, and commentary, London: Duckworth.

—— (1985) *Plato: Meno*, edited with translation and notes, Warminster: Aris & Philips.

—— (1991) *Cicero: On Fate and Boethius: The Consolation of Philosophy IV. 5–7, V*, edited with translation and commentary, Warminster: Aris & Philips.

—— (1996) *Stoics, Epicureans, Sceptics: An Introduction to Hellenistic Philosophy*, London: Routledge.

—— (1999) 'The Peripatetic School, in D. Furley (ed.) *From Aristotle to Augustine*', New York: Routledge: 147–87.

Sherman, N. (1989) *Aristotle: The Fabric of Character*, Oxford: Oxford University Press.

—— (1997) *Making a Necessity of Virtue: Aristotle and Kant on Virtue*, Cambridge: Cambridge University Press.

Sherman, T. P. (2002) 'Human Happiness and the Role of Philosophical Wisdom in the Nicomachean Ethics', *International Philosophical Quarterly* 42(4): 467–92.

Sidgwick, H. (1905) 'The Sophists', *The Philosophy of Kant and Other Essays*, London: Macmillan: 323–71.

Sihvola, J. and T. Engberg-Pedersen (eds) (1998) *The Emotions in Hellenistic Philosophy*, Dordrecht: Kluwer Academic.

Skidmore, C. (1996) *Practical Ethics for Roman Gentlemen: The Work of Valerius Maximus*, Exeter: University of Exeter Press.

Smith, A. D. (1996) 'Character and Intellect in Aristotle's Ethics', *Phronesis* 41: 56–74.

Smith, M. F. (ed.) (1993) *Diogenes of Oinoanda: The Epicurean Inscription*, La Scuola De Epicureo. Naples: Bibliopolis.

Smith, R. (1999) 'Dialectic and Method in Aristotle', in M. Sim (ed.) *From Puzzles to Principles: Essays on Aristotle's Dialectic*. New York: Lexington Books: 39–55.

Solon (1925) *Anthologia lyrica graeca*, vol. 1 / ed E. Diehl. Leipzig: Teubner.

Sorabji, R. (1973/74) 'Aristotle on the Role of Intellect in Virtue', *Proceedings of the Aristotelian Society* 74: 107–29.

—— (2000) *Emotion and Peace of Mind: From Stoic Agitation to Christian Temptation*, Oxford: Oxford University Press.

Soreth (1968) 'Die Zweite Telosformel des Antipater von Tarsus', *Archiv für Geschichte der Philosophie* 50: 48–72.

Sparshott, F. (1994) *Taking Life Seriously: A Study of the Arguments of the Nicomachean Ethics*, Toronto: University of Toronto Press.

Sprague, R. (ed.) (1972) *The Older Sophists: a Complete Translation by Several Hands of the Fragments in Die Fragmente Der Vorsokratiker*, edited by Diels-Kranz, with a new edition of *Antiphon and Euthydemus*, Columbia, SC: University of South Carolina Press.

Stählin, O., L. Fruchtel and U. Treu (eds) (1985) *Clemens Alexandrinus Vol. Ii: Stromata Buch. I–IV*. Berlin: Akademie-Verlag.

Stalley, R. F. (1983) *An Introduction to Plato's Laws*, Indianapolis: Hackett.

Stewart, J. (1892) *Notes on the Nicomachean Ethics of Aristotle*, Oxford: Oxford University Press.

BIBLIOGRAPHY

Stokes, M. (1995) 'Cicero on Epicurean Pleasures', in J. G. Powell (ed.) *Cicero the Philosopher*, Oxford: Clarendon Press: 145–70.

Strange, S. and J. Zupko (eds) (2004) *Stoicism: Traditions and Transformations*, New York: Cambridge University Press.

Striker, G. (1983) 'The Role of *Oikeiosis* in Stoic Ethics', *Oxford Studies in Ancient Philosophy* 1: 145–67.

—— (1984) 'The Origins of the Concept of Natural Law', *Proceedings of the Boston Area Colloquium in Ancient Philosophy* 2: 79–94.

—— (1986) 'Antipater, or the Art of Living', in M. Schofield and G. Striker (eds) *The Norms of Nature*, Cambridge: Cambridge University Press: 185–204 (reprinted in her *Essays on Hellenistic Epistemology and Ethics*, Cambridge: Cambridge University Press, 1996: Chapter 14).

—— (1988) 'Greek Ethics and Moral Theory', *Tanner Lectures on Human Value* 9: 182–202.

—— (1990) '*Ataraxia*: Happiness as Tranquility', *The Monist* 73(1): 97–110.

—— (1991) 'Following Nature: An Essay in Stoic Ethics', *Oxford Studies in Ancient Philosophy* 9: 1–73.

—— (1993) 'Epicurean Hedonism', in J. Brunschwig and M. Nussbaum (eds) *Passions and Perceptions: Studies in Hellenistic Philosophy of Mind*, New York: Cambridge University Press: 3–17.

—— (1996) 'Plato's Socrates and the Stoics', *Essays on Hellenistic Epistemology and Ethics*, Cambridge: Cambridge University Press: 316–24.

Taylor, C. C. W. (1988) 'Platonic Ethics', in S. Everson (ed.) *Companions to Ancient Thought*, Vol. 4: *Ethics*, Cambridge: Cambridge University Press.

—— (1990) 'Popular Morality and Unpopular Philosophy', in E. M. Craik (ed.) *Owls to Athens: Essays on Classical Subjects Presented to Sir Kenneth Dover*, Oxford: Oxford University Press: 233–43.

—— (ed.) (1997) *From the Beginning to Plato*, London: Routledge.

—— (2006) *Aristotle: Nicomachean Ethics Books II–IV*, translated with commentary, Oxford: Clarendon Press.

Thomson, J. A. K. (1955) *The Ethics of Aristotle: The Nicomachean Ethics Translated*, New York: Penguin.

Tieleman, T. (1996) *Galen and Chrysippus on the Soul: Argument and Refutation in the De Placitis, Books II–III*, Leiden: Brill.

Tracy, T. (1969) *Physiological Theory and the Doctrine of the Mean in Plato and Aristotle*, Chicago: Loyola Press.

Tuozzo, T. (1991) 'Aristotelian Deliberation is not of Ends', in J. Anton and A. Preus (eds) *Essays in Ancient Greek Philosophy*, Vol. 4: *Aristotle's Ethics*, Albany, NY: State University of New York Press: 193–212.

—— (1995) 'Contemplation, the Noble, and the Mean: The Standard of Moral Virtue in Aristotle's Ethics' *Apeiron* 4: 129–54.

Upton, T. (1981) 'Aristotle's Moral Epistemology: The Possibility of Ethical Demonstration', *New Scholasticism* 56: 169–84.

Urmson, J. (1973) 'Aristotle's Doctrine of the Mean', *American Philosophical Quarterly* 10: 223–30.

—— (1988) *Aristotle's Ethics*, Oxford: Basil Blackwell.

Usener, H. (ed.) (1887) *Epicurea*, Leipzig: Teubner.

213

Vander Waerdt, P. (1987) 'The Justice of the Epicurean Wise Man', *Classical Quarterly* 37: 402–22.

—— (1988) 'Hermarchus and the Epicurean Genealogy of Morals', *Transactions of the American Philological Association* 118: 87–106.

—— (1991) 'Politics and Philosophy in Stoicism', *Oxford Studies in Ancient Philosophy* 9: 185–211.

—— (1994) 'Zeno's Republic and the Origins of Natural Law', in P. Vander Waerdt (ed.) *The Socratic Tradition*, Ithaca NY: Cornell University Press.

—— (ed.) (1994) *The Socratic Tradition*, Ithaca NY: Cornell University Press.

Viano, C. (2004) 'O que e a Virtude Natural? (*Eth. Nic.* VI, 13)', *Analytica* 8(2): 115–34.

Vlastos, G. (1969) 'Socrates on Acrasia', *Phoenix* 23: 71–88.

—— (1971) 'Justice and Happiness in the Republic', *Plato II*, Garden City, NY: Anchor Books.

—— (1985) 'Socrates' Disavowal of Knowledge', *Philosophical Quarterly* 35: 1–31.

—— (1991) *Socrates: Ironist and Moral Philosopher*, Ithaca, NY: Cornell University Press.

—— (1995) *Studies in Greek Philosophy* (edited by D. W. Graham), Princeton, NJ: Princeton University Press.

von Arnim, H. F. (ed.) (1906) *Hierocles: Ethische Elemertarlehre*. Berliner Klassikertexte, Berlin: Weidman.

von der Mühll, P. (ed.) (1922) *Epicuri Epistulae Tres et Ratae Sententiae a Laertio Diogene Servatae: Accedit Gnomologium Epicureum Vaticanum*. Leipzig: Teubner.

Vranas, P. (2005) 'Aristotle on the Best Good: Is Nicomachean Ethics 1094a18–22 Fallacious?' *Phronesis* 50(2): 116–28.

Wachsmuth, C. (ed.) (1884) *Ioannis Stobaei Anthologium*, Vols I–II, Berlin: Weidman.

Wallace, R. J. (1991) 'Virtue, Reason, and Principle', *The Canadian Journal of Philosophy* 21(December): 469–95.

Wallach, B. (1976) *Lucretius and the Diatribe against the Fear of Death: De Rerum Natura Iii, 830–1094*, Leiden: Brill.

Walsh, M. M. (1999) 'The Role of Universal Knowledge in Aristotelian Moral Virtue', *Ancient Philosophy* 19: 73–88.

Walsh, P. G. (1997) *Cicero: The Nature of the Gods*, translated with introduction and explanatory notes, Oxford: Clarendon Press.

Walzer, R. and J. Mingay (eds) (1991) *Aristotelis Ethica Eudemia*, Oxford: Oxford University Press.

Warren, J. (2001) 'Lucretius, Symmetry Arguments, and Fearing Death', *Phronesis* 46: 466–91.

—— (2002) *Epicurus and Democritean Ethics: An Archaeology of Ataraxia*, Cambridge: Cambridge University Press.

—— (2004) *Facing Death: Epicurus and His Critics*, Oxford: Clarendon Press.

Waterfield, R. (trans.) (1993) *Plato: Republic*, Oxford: Oxford University Press.

—— (2000) *The First Philosophers: The Presocratics and Sophists*, translated with commentary, Oxford: Oxford University Press.

Watson, G. (1971) 'Natural Law and Stoicism', in A. A. Long (ed.) *Problems in Stoicism*, London: Athlone Press: 216–38.

Wedin, M. (1981) 'Aristotle on the Good for Man', *Mind* 90: 243–62.

Welton, W. A. and R. Polansky (1999) 'The Viability of Virtue in the Mean', *Apeiron* 28: 79–102.

White, N. (1976) *Plato on Knowledge and Reality*, Indianapolis: Hackett.

—— (1978) 'The Basis of Stoic Ethics', *Harvard Studies in Classical Philology* 83: 143–78.

—— (1978a) 'Two Notes on Stoic Terminology', *American Journal of Philology* 99: 111–19.

—— (1979) *A Companion to Plato's Republic*, Indianapolis: Hackett.

—— (1983) *Epictetus: The Handbook*, translated with introduction, Indianapolis: Hackett.

—— (1985) 'Nature and Regularity in Stoic Ethics: A Review of Anna Maria Ioppolo, *Aristone De Chio e lo Stoicism Antico*', *Oxford Studies in Ancient Philosophy* 3: 289–305.

—— (1985) 'The Role of Physics in Stoic Ethics', *The Southern Journal of Philosophy* 23(suppl.): 57–74.

—— (1988) 'Good as Goal', *Southern Journal of Philosophy* 27(suppl.): 169–93.

—— (1990) 'Stoic Values', *The Monist* 73(1): 42–58.

—— (2002) *Individual and Conflict in Greek Ethics*, Oxford: Oxford University Press.

White, N. (2006) *A Brief History of Happiness*, Malden, MA: Blackwell.

White, S. (1990) 'Is Aristotelian Happiness a Good Life or the Best Life?' *Oxford Studies in Ancient Philosophy* 8: 103–44.

—— (1992) 'Natural Virtue and Perfect Virtue in Aristotle', *Proceedings of the Boston Area Colloquium in Ancient Philosophy* 8: 135–68.

—— (1992a) *Sovereign Virtue: Aristotle on the Relation between Happiness and Prosperity*, Stanford, CA: Stanford University Press.

—— (2002) 'Happiness in the Hellenistic Lyceum', in L. J. Jost (ed.) *Eudaimonia and Well-Being: Ancient and Modern Conceptions*, Edmonton: Academic Printing and Publishing: 69–93.

Whiting, J. (1986) 'Human Nature and Intellectualism in Aristotle', *Archiv für Geschichte der Philosophie* 68: 70–95.

—— (1988) 'Aristotle's Function Argument: A Defence', *Ancient Philosophy* 8: 33–48.

—— (2001) 'Strong Dialectic, Neurathian Reflection, and the Ascent of Desire: Irwin and McDowell on Aristotle's Methods of Ethics', *Proceedings of the Boston Area Colloquium in Ancient Philosophy* 17: 61–116.

—— (2002) 'Eudaimonia, External Results, and Choosing Virtuous Actions for Themselves', *Philosophy and Phenomenological Research* 65: 270–90.

Wiggins, D. (1980) 'Deliberation and Practical Reason', in A. O. Rorty (ed.) *Essays on Aristotle's Ethics*, Berkeley: University of California Press: 221–40.

Wielenberg, E. (2004) 'Egoism and *Eudaimonia*-Maximization in the *Nicomachean Ethics*', *Oxford Studies in Ancient Philosophy* 26: 277–95.

Williams, B. A. O. (1985) *Ethics and the Limits of Philosophy*, Cambridge, MA: Harvard University Press.

Wilkes, K. V. (1978) 'The Good Man and the Good for Man in Aristotle's Ethics', *Mind* 87: 553–71.

Winter, M. (1997) 'Aristotle, *hôs epi to polu* Relations, and a Demonstrative Science of Ethics', *Phronesis* 42(2): 163–89.

Winterbottom, M. (ed.) (1994) *M. Tulli Ciceronis De Officiis* (Oxford Classical Texts), Oxford: Clarendon Press.

Wolf, S. (1982) 'Moral Saints', *Journal of Philosophy* 79(8): 419–39.

Woodruff, P. (2006) 'Socrates among the Sophists', in S. Ahbel-Rappe and R. M. Kamtekar (eds) *A Companion to Socrates*, Oxford: Basil Blackwell: 36–45.

Woods, M. (1982) *Aristotle's Eudemian Ethics Books I, II, and VIII*, Oxford: Clarendon Press.

—— (1986) 'Intuition and Perception in Aristotle's Ethics', *Oxford Studies in Ancient Philosophy* 4: 145–66.

—— (1987) 'Plato's Division of the Soul', *Proceedings of the British Academy* 73: 23–47.

—— (1990) 'Aristotle on *Akrasia*', in A. Alberti (ed.) *Studi sull' Ethica di Aristotele*, Naples: Bibliopolis: 227–61.

Woolf, R. (2004) 'What Kind of Hedonist Was Epicurus?' *Phronesis* 49(4): 303–22.

Young, C. (1994) 'Aristotle on Liberality', *Proceedings of the Boston Area Colloquium in Ancient Philosophy* 10: 313–34.

—— (1996) 'The Doctrine of the Mean', *Topoi* 15: 89–99.

Zeller, E. (1870) *Stoics, Epicureans, and Skeptics*, trans. O. J. Reichel, London: Longmans, Green & Co.

Zeyl, D. (1980) 'Socrates and Hedonsim', *Phronesis* 25: 250–69.

—— (1982) 'Socratic Virtue and Happiness', *Archiv für Geschichte der Philosophie* 54: 225–38.

Ziegler, K. (ed.) (1960) *M. Tulli Ciceronis: De Re Publica*. Leipzig: Teubner.

INDEX LOCORUM

GENERAL INDEX

CPSIA information can be obtained at www.ICGtesting.com
Printed in the USA
LVOW10s2159150114

369640LV00004B/150/P